C000008584

Anonymous

Antiquarian Magazine and Bibliographer

7. Band

Anonymous

Antiquarian Magazine and Bibliographer
7. Band

ISBN/EAN: 9783337713065

Hergestellt in Europa, USA, Kanada, Australien, Japan

Cover: Foto ©ninafisch / pixelio.de

Weitere Bücher finden Sie auf **www.hansebooks.com**

The
Antiquarian Magazine
& Bibliographer.

EDITED BY

EDWARD WALFORD, M.A.,

Formerly Scholar of Balliol College, Oxford, and late Editor of " The Gentleman's Magazine," &c.

" Time doth consecrate,
And what is grey with age becomes religion."
SCHILLER.

VOLUME VII.

JANUARY—JUNE, 1885.

London:
GEORGE REDWAY, 15, YORK STREET,
COVENT GARDEN, W.C.

The Gresham Press.

UNWIN BROTHERS,
PRINTERS,
LONDON AND CHILWORTH.

List of Illustrations.

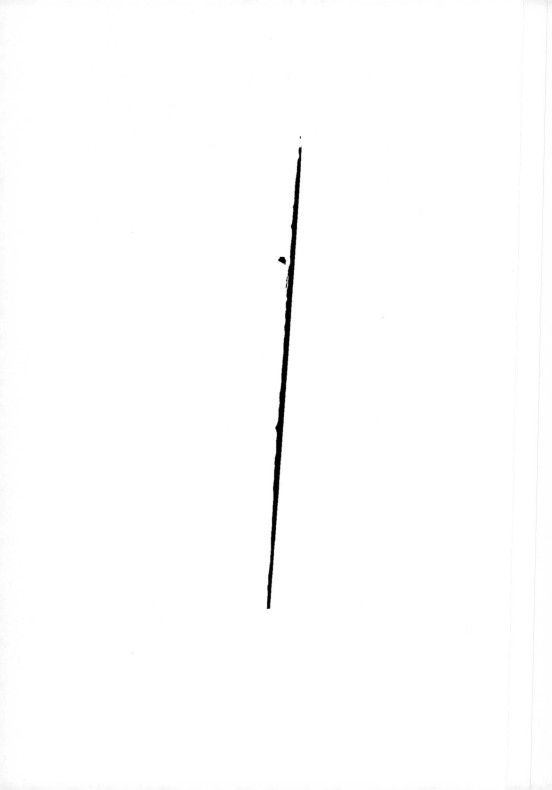

The

Antiquarian Magazine
& Bibliographer.

1885.

NOTHER year hath passed away—
  Another cometh in its place—
  We greet it with a smiling face,
Although the morn be late and grey.

Well, if the sky be dark, the day
  Be short, and even early come
  To close it in, yet still at home
We mark the dancing firelight play,

And, musing, dwell upon the time
  Of summer days, when we afield
  Learned how our English land can yield
Her store, as mellow as the chime

That sounds from out some tower old
  O'er sedge-bound mere, or rolling down
  Breaks gently on the good old town
Which ancient trees, like garment, fold.

Aye, merry days, when forth we went
  By ancient manor-house and mill,
  By many a lane, 'cross many a hill,
With our old England well content:

Or stood beside that castle * hoar,
   That stands upon its massive rock
   'Gainst which the wilder billows shock :
It seems we now can hear them roar.

Or by that vast cathedral † pile
   That looks forth where the waters flow
   Beneath the wooded banks below,
Where lingers long the day's last smile.

Or that time-honoured, goodly shrine ‡
   Which claims St. David's name ; and then
   We think upon those ancient men
Whose light through centuries still doth shine.

Or olden hall, or olden book,
   Or olden tombs of knights in sleep—
   Knights who their arms in death still keep—
And many a pleasant, quiet nook,

Where Time seems ever loth to press
   His ever-moving step, and leaves
   Old scenes—each one a memory weaves
A coronal of loveliness.

                          H. R. W.

Swift's Cadenus and Vanessa.

THERE is perhaps no more interesting chapter in the life of Jonathan Swift than that which describes his intercourse with Esther Van Homrigh, better known as Vanessa. The whole story, from its bright and happy commencement, in 1710, to its terribly sad termination, in 1723, when Vanessa died, has been so often discussed, and in many points so cruelly misrepresented, that it must ever retain a peculiar interest for all who value the memory of Swift—for those who admire his great talents, his splendid wit, and wonderful power of sarcasm—and also for all those who, without judging him too harshly under circumstances not fully understood, deeply regret his errors, and pity his misfortunes.

It was in 1710 that Mrs. Van Homrigh, having recently come to

---

* Bamborough Castle.   † Durham.   ‡ St. David's Cathedral.

London with her son and two daughters, made the acquaintance of Swift. Forster ("Life of Swift," p. 230) speaks of Bartholomew Van Homrigh as "a Dublin merchant, of Dutch extraction, to whom King William had given profitable employments in Ireland." This hardly places him in his right position, for Van Homrigh was Muster Master General and Lord Mayor of Dublin in 1697, when William the Third presented him with a gold collar of SS. He died in 1703, and his estates were important enough to require a special Act of Parliament to arrange their sale and division. Mrs. Van Homrigh, therefore, had moved in the highest society in Dublin, and when she came to settle in London as a wealthy widow—perhaps it might be fair to say an extravagant one, for she seems to have spent considerably more than her income—she at once took a good position in society, and received and visited people of rank and eminence. Hence, when Swift made the acquaintance of Hester, being introduced to the family by Sir Andrew Fountaine, she was a girl of seventeen, just entering the fashionable world under the most favourable and agreeable circumstances. It was at their house that Swift made the acquaintance of the beautiful and unfortunate Mrs. Anne Long, on which occasion the amusing little " Decree for Concluding the Treaty between Dr. Swift and Mrs. Long " was drawn up. Mr. Forster, by the way, states (p. 230) that this was first published in a little volume, 1719-20, but this is not the case ; it was first published by E. Curll in 1718, in a thin 8vo. volume of miscellanies, entitled " Letters, Poems, and Tales." Mrs. Van Homrigh died in 1714, leaving her property, a good deal involved, to her son Bartholomew, and her two daughters Hester and Mary. The son died in 1715, and the younger daughter in 1721, leaving Hester the general heir of the family. Finally she died, and it must be admitted, to use the common expression, of a broken heart, in May, 1723.

Swift was a man of very high conversational powers, and possessed of the most brilliant wit. That he was sought after by all the maids of honour, and courted by most of the toasts of the day, is evidence that he was a fascinating man. When he chose he could make himself very agreeable, and, even when he had no especial object in doing so, he would hardly fail to be attractive to a sprightly young girl like Hester Van Homrigh. It was pleasing to him to watch the rapid growth of her mental powers, to direct her studies, to see how all his suggestions were adopted, and his lessons remembered. The story runs on smoothly, naturally, and pleasantly ; at the time when he first saw her she was 17, and he was 41, but the days of girlhood were fast passing away ; and three years later, when he was 44, and she 21, the middle-aged clergyman, "the plump man just five feet eight inches and a half high, not very neatly dressed, in a black gown with pudding sleeves," as he then described himself, looked with pleasure and admiration on the handsome young woman whose mental attractions were all of his own creation : but alas! she had learned to look upon her teacher with very different eyes. A time of explanation came ; in a word, she made it clear to him that she loved him with a deep and true passion. The thing was a surprise and a shock to him, and it was then, in the year 1713, that he wrote and sent to her the poem, "Cadenus and Vanessa." He endeavoured to keep up the old relation of pupil and teacher, whilst he tried to convey to her the lesson that the thing was impossible, and had better be forgotten. It may fairly be taken for granted that Swift, when he wrote this poem, had no thought of its publication ; it was intended for Vanessa's eyes alone, and he no more contemplated that it would be printed than he did that the same fate would attend his most private letters and thoughts. Mr. Craik, in his recent and very valuable " Life of Swift," has pointed out that six years subsequently—that was, in 1719—Swift revised the poem (p. 318). It would appear that he desired Vanessa to send it to him for that purpose, and promised to return it to her shortly. If this was so, doubtless she first took a copy, to keep in case the original never came back to her. The question is a point of some interest, as suggesting, in the first instance, that Swift had possibly not himself kept a copy in 1713 ; and further, as showing that in 1719, when he revised it, there must at least then have been two MS. copies in existence.

Early in 1723 Swift had his last sad interview with Vanessa ; doubtless he afterwards bitterly regretted his sudden impulse of ungenerous passion, carried out in hot haste when all right feeling was overshadowed by morbid disease. A few weeks later poor Vanessa died, having within that period made a new will, in which the name of Swift did not appear, and leaving her property, which was of considerable value, about eight thousand pounds, to Dr. Berkeley and Mr. Marshall. It has been asserted that she desired that her correspondence with Swift might after her death be published, together with the poem of " Cadenus and Vanessa." Whether she really expressed any such desire seems very doubtful, but it is certain that the matter was not referred to in her will. Sheridan, in his " Life of

Swift" (p. 286), states that shortly before her death she laid a strong injunction on her executors to print and publish these papers, and that "accordingly they were put to the press, and some progress made in the letters, when Dr. Sheridan getting intelligence of it, and being greatly alarmed lest they might contain something injurious to his friend's character in his absence, applied so effectually to the executors that the printed copy was cancelled, but the originals still remained in their hands. The poem of 'Cadenus and Vanessa' was, however, sent abroad into the world, as being supposed to contain nothing prejudicial to either of their characters."

This fairly brings us to the question of publication, and here I will quote Mr. Craik (p. 323) :—

"The poem was published soon after Vanessa's death, which took place at the close of May, 1723. The best proof that Swift saw and dreaded the interpretation which the world might place upon the verses, is to be found in the shock the publication caused him. Angry with himself, tortured at once by remorse and by indignation at the tangle of circumstances that had woven itself round him, he withdrew for a time to the South of Ireland."

There are several points here raised which I think are very questionable, and, of course, the first turns upon the true date when the poem was published. There are, I think, plenty of statements that it came out in 1723, but I can find no evidence worth mentioning that it really was before the public till 1726. Whenever it came out, such a poem would attract attention, and make some noise in the literary world; and, whilst no copy bearing date 1723 appears to be known, the fact that at least six editions were printed in 1726, renders it more than probable that in that year, and not earlier, was the poem published. That the death of Vanessa was a terrible shock to Swift it is easy to believe, and that he left home and wandered about in the wilds of the south for some time is very credible, but his doing so had no connection with the publication of this poem.

In a recent article, Mr. S. Lane-Poole has given a useful list of Swift's publications now to be found in the Bodleian, British Museum, and several other national libraries; in this list the earliest date given to "Cadenus and Vanessa" is a copy at Trinity College Library, described as "Dublin, 8vo., 1726." Without a more minute description than this it is difficult to identify it. From what has already been said, it is evident that there must have been more than one MS. copy in existence at the time when Vanessa died, and it is probable that they were not identical. I believe that the poem came out in an unauthorised form in 1726, from the original poem in 1713, and not from the revised MS. of 1719. It is to be observed that there is towards the end of the poem a paragraph of ten lines, which is as follows :—

" But what success Vanessa met
Is to the world a secret yet.
Whether the nymph, to please her swain,
Talks in a high romantic strain ;
Or whether he at last descends
To act with less seraphic ends ;
Or to compound the business, whether
They temper love and books together,
Must never to mankind be told,
Nor shall the conscious muse unfold."

These lines are a great blot on the beauty of the poem ; they are vague, suggestive, flippant, and offensive, and are clearly written in a very different spirit and temper from all the rest of the poem ; and they have accordingly been dealt with in the most severe manner by all the critics who have written on the poem, from the caustic and venomous Orrery downwards. I will now describe what, till I am better advised, I shall regard as the true first edition :—

" Cadenus | and | Vanessa | a | Poem | from the original Copy | Dublin | Printed in the year 2726." 8vo. p. 32.

It is to be observed that in this issue the ten lines above given are not to be found. The error in the date is remarkable, and seems intentional ; it reminds one of the surreptitious edition of Swift's " Miscellanies " printed and published by Fairbrother of Dublin, " at his shop in Skinner Row over against the Thosel 2721."

2. The next edition which I have is entitled :—

" Cadenus and Vanessa a Poem—By Dr. S——t. London. Printed for N. Blandford, at the *London Gazette*, Charing Cross ; and sold by J. Peele at Locke's Head in Paternoster Row 1726 (Price 6d.) " 8vo. pp. 31.

This, though not said to be a reprint of the Dublin edition, appears to be one, and like it does not contain the ten lines " But what success," &c. It might be asked why the Dublin should be deemed the first, and why not the London ? But it is plain that as the poem stole into the world without authority, and probably from a Dublin MS., so the one with no printer or publisher's name was probably earlier than the London edition.

3. As soon as these two editions were before the public, a third was brought out, evidently not copied from them, but from another

independent manuscript. This did not give the author's name ; the title is :—

"Cadenus and Vanessa, a Poem. London Printed and sold by J. Roberts at the Oxford Arms in Warwick Lane. 1726. Price 6d." 8vo. pp. 37.

In this there were a good many small variations. Thus the line " Less modest than the speech of *Prudes*," is changed into *Druids*. "Yet *lik'd* three Footmen to her Chair" is printed *lock'd*. " To *manage* thy abortive scheme" is printed *Marriage*. " Of Foreign Customs, *Rites*, and Laws" is printed *Rights*. " From round the *Purlieus* of St. James" is printed *Parlours*. " Pointed *with* Col'nels, Lords, and Beaus" is printed *at*. " That when Platonick *Heights* were over" is printed *Flights*, &c. But especially is to be noted the addition of the objectionable ten lines.

4. " Cadenus and Vanessa, a Law Case. By Dean Swift, London. Printed for T. Warner, in Paternoster Row, MDCCXXVI." 12mo. pp. 36 ; to which is appended " Clavis," setting forth that " Vanessa means Mrs. Hester Van Homrigh, a young lady of great Worth and Parts, who departed this Life about three years ago, for whom the Dean had no small Value." In this the wording of the Dublin edition (No. 1) is preserved, but the ten lines as found in No. 3 are added.

5. " Cadenus and Vanessa, a Poem, to which is added a true and faithful Inventory of the goods belonging to Dr. S——t, &c., by Dr. S——t. The fourth edition. London. Printed for N. Blandford [as No. 2] 1726." 8vo. p. 31, and the Inventory p. 1.

6. " Cadenus and Vanessa, a poem. Sixth edition. London. 8vo. [mentioned by Mr. S. Lane-Poole as in the Bodleian, &c.], 1726."

We have thus six editions published in 1726, and evidently from two distinct manuscripts. It is, I think, plain that it was not printed before that year, and if I am correct in thinking that the Dublin edition (No. 1) was really the first, the question naturally arises whether the MS. then printed came from Vanessa's executors ? If it did, why is it that it does not contain the ten lines ? and is it clear that she ever received the amended copy containing them ? The Van Homrigh correspondence, said to have been suppressed, was recovered by Sir Walter Scott, and published in his edition of Swift's Works, xix. 317, 78, but this throws no light upon the subject. Swift in one letter, dated May 12, 1719, promises to send her her verses when his thoughts and time are free ; and again on

August 12, 1719, he says, "What would you give to have the History of Cd—— and —— exactly written?" To which Sir Walter adds, "this second part was never completed."

EDWARD SOLLY.

Pedigrees of Huguenot Families.

THE whole history of the lamentable events which culminated in the massacre of the French Protestants on St. Bartholomew's Day, 24th of August, 1572, and the Revocation of the Edict of Nantes by Louis XIV., is one which has yet to be exhaustively written in this country.

Even the French people themselves do not possess a trustworthy history of this great religious persecution. There are many works by many authors relating to it, but no one can be relied upon alone as an authority. This gap, however, is being filled up, though the process is a very slow one, by MM. Eugène and Émile Haag's work, "La France Protestante," which, when completed, will include a valuable work on the sad history of the Huguenots. It will prove of incalculable use to genealogists tracing the pedigree of a French Protestant family. I have myself been busily, and perhaps fruitlessly, at work in endeavouring to bridge over an hiatus of a century and a half in the history of a family of Huguenots who fled over from Normandy to this country to save their bare lives, for their goods had been confiscated, their houses burned and ransacked, their families cruelly tortured and outraged by that perjured prince, Louis XIV., his ministers and emissaries.

No little difficulty arises from the fact that it will often be found that in one family there were some who were Huguenots and others who still adhered to the Catholic faith of their ancestors, and meekly performed those barbaric deeds to which they were instigated by the Pope for the good (*sic*) of the Church. The terrible inhumanities of St. Bartholomew's Day, too, were celebrated by a medal struck at Rome by the order of another Pontiff, Gregory XIII.

When M. Weiss, in 1853, wrote and published his "Histoire des Refugiés Protestants de France," the Americans not only followed our example in favourably reviewing the book and writing pretty little sensational articles upon it and the painful scenes which it portrayed, but they translated it, and added an appendix containing some important and authentic documents. The appendix is written by a descendant of one of those Huguenots who had settled in America.

In this country we have done nothing of the kind ; and it is only in rare instances that it is felt how great the want is that exists for a decently-written and circumstantial history of the various families of Huguenots who settled in England, more especially in London and the eastern and south-eastern counties.

Mr. Smiles has, of course, written a very readable History of the Huguenots, and has vaguely dealt with some of those few refugees who rapidly rose to distinction here and intermarried with prominent families of our English aristocracy ; and it was not necessary to do more for the purposes of his book.

In 1829 a History of the Huguenots during the sixteenth century was produced by Mr. Browning, but it is of very slight use for any genealogical purpose, though it is a gracefully and interestingly written statement of the Huguenot politics.

I have referred to the fact that there are various—indeed, numerous—instances of one family being religiously divided against itself; the best example of such a case that I can quote is the following :—

The family are described in a standard French work on heraldry and genealogy—" Aubert de la Chenaye des Bois' Dictionnaire de la Noblesse." Some of the family were Catholics and remained true to that faith ; others were converted to the " Réligion Prétendue Reformée." They were not only separated by reason of their religious differences, but they met in fight with their respective partisans. The Huguenots, among whom was one brother X, were attacked by the Catholics, among whom was another brother X.

Being hard pressed, the Huguenots seized the house which belonged to the Catholic X in order to hinder the enemy and to cover their retreat. They were successful; but they pillaged and burnt the house before they left it. The account given by De la Chenaye des Bois is as follows :—

" À la requête de noble X Ecuyer qui atteste ques les Catholiques étoient en guerre avec ceux de la Réligion Prétendue Reformée ; dans une affaire, on commandoit le Seigneur ——— les Huguenots, tenant et occupant la ville de ——— furent assiégés avec tant de bravoure et de courage par les Catholiques, qu'après plusieurs reprises et attaques, ils emporterent la place. Les assiégés, pour le soustraire à la poursuite de l'ennemi, fortirent promptement ; et trouverent, dans leur suite précipitée, une maison forte appartenant à noble X, Ecuyer, qu'il jugerent, au premier coup d'œil, propre à leur servir de retraite pendant quelque instans ; et se trouvant suivis de très-après par un detachment de Catholiques, s'y refugièrent en toute diligence, pour se mettre à l'abri de la poursuite de cette troupe, qui, déjà fatiguée les y attaqua, sans pouvoir les contraindu d'en fortir . . . . . ils en partirent dans la nuit même, après avoir pillé et incendié la maison qui leur avoit servi de retraite."

This, however, is merely *en passant.* Take an instance, for example, of a person desirous to obtain information enabling him to draw up the pedigree of a family ennobled in France, and bearing the surname of " Blanc," " de Blanc," " du Blanc," or " le Blanc." To start with, the name is, I suppose, next to Martin, about the most common to be met with, and one has not, as a rule, much ground to go on as a basis, but is left to divine inspiration. Further than this, all work for a time is speculative, and any chance of future success which may have been entertained, is hardly enhanced by such a note as the following :—

Haag, in speaking of a family in which there were both Catholics and Huguenots, says : " Les jugemens de la noblesse que nous ont fourni la généalogie de cette famille *passant sous silence celui de ses membres qui précisément nous intéresse le plus."*

This is highly gratifying, and it requires a good deal of philosophical calmness to appreciate it properly. It sheds, however, a very brilliant light upon the worthiness of French peerages generally, and reflects great credit upon the versatile talent of the Frenchman, enabling him to get out of a difficulty in a simple but efficacious manner.

The difficulties, however, do not by any means exist only on the other side of the Channel. It is most appalling to contemplate the ingenious manner in which a perfectly plain and intelligible name has been murdered here in England. Thus, for instance, the name "Sise" has been variously given as " Six," " Syx," " Sais," " Saies," and " Syce." " Blanc," beyond the difficulty created by the refugees themselves, who transformed the name into White and Albus, is to be met with as " Blanck," " Blank," " Le Blon," and " Le Blans." There are numerous other instances which Mr. Smiles mentions.

The safest book decidedly is Haag's " La France Protestante " (2nd edition), but this work has progressed only to the letter " C " at present.

The Report of the French Committee, issued in 1705, will be found most serviceable as a ground upon which to start tracing the history of a refugee, supposing his name to be in the report at all. To carry the subject further, unless the inquirer has family papers or information to go upon, is a laborious but interesting work, and the result is problematical. The British Museum contains sufficient literature for a month's work, seeing that the French books are grossly defective in the way of indexes. Let me recommend Lichtenberger's "Encyclopédie des Sciences Religeuses," and Haag. The Lambeth Library and the Search-room at Somerset House should both be visited.

There are several reasons, which it would be as well to recapitulate, which greatly increase the apparent difficulties of such researches : they may be summed up as follows :—

(*a*) Refugees often changed their surnames for their equivalents in the country in which they settled, or where they retained their own proper names, the latter were so barbarously contorted as to be utterly unrecognisable:

(*b*) The apparent incongruity of members of the same family fighting against each other, and pillaging each other's property.

(*c*) The practice of the French genealogists of the time which led them, in enumerating a family, purposely to omit such as had joined the Huguenot party.

(*d*) The apparent incompatibility of a member of a noble family becoming a small and obscure tradesman ; this is explained by the fact that every other form of employment, save trade, was closed to a member of the Réligion Prétendue Reformée.

The surest guide is to be found in armorial bearings ; they were of great significance in France a couple of centuries since, and often afford considerable help.

Since writing the foregoing, I have discovered that "Phiz," the late Mr. Hablot Brown, was a descendant of a Huguenot family who came over here after the Revocation of the Edict of Nantes, when they changed thair surname from "Le Brun" to Brown.

M. GWYNNE-GRIFFITH.

MR. W. ST. CHAD BOSCAWEN commenced on Wednesday, December 3, at the British Museum, a series of six lectures on the history and antiquities of the Assyrian and Babylonian Empires. The subject of the opening lecture was the "Origin, Development, and Decipherment of the Cuneiform Inscriptions," and that of the second lecture, on December 10, was "The Land of Nimrod." The remaining four lectures of the course were announced to be delivered on the following dates :—December 17 and 31, and January 7 and 14, commencing each day at 2.30 p.m.

King Alfred in Somerset and the Legend of St. Neot.

By Mrs. C. G. Boger.

PART I.

IN the early history of Alfred, as well as in that of his father Ethelwulf and his mother Osburga, are related various incidents, which it is difficult to reconcile with known historical facts. To make legend assist history, and out of apparent contradictions to form a consistent whole, and at the same time to mark the connection of the most picturesque incidents in the life of the greatest of our kings with Somerset, is the object of these papers. The difficulties to which reference has been made, and which are slurred over or inadequately explained by historians, are as follows. First, the personality of the young Sub-Regulus Athelstane, whose disappearance after the battle of Sandwich in 851 is not satisfactorily accounted for, and who is variously described as brother and son of Ethelwulf. Secondly, the dropping out of Osburga's name in history, and its reappearance in the tales of Alfred's first learning to read, and of his refuge at Athelney in Somerset. (Historians, by the way, get over this last difficulty by substituting his wife for his mother.) Thirdly, the marriage of Ethelwulf and Judith, and consequent rebellion of Ethelbald; and, fourthly, the identity of Prince or King Athelstane with Alfred's friend and spiritual adviser, St. Neot.

To make the story clear, it will be necessary to go back to the days of the great King Egbert. Egbert had two sons : the eldest—whose name presumably was Athelstane—died, and the heir to the throne was Ethelwulf, who had been brought up as an ecclesiastic, if not as a monk ; he had been appointed, if not actually consecrated, to the Bishopric of Winchester. On the death of his brother, however, a release from his vows was asked and obtained. Ethelwulf returned to the world, and married Osburga, daughter to the King's butler, and was put in possession of the kingdom of Kent (consisting of Kent, Sussex, and part of Surrey), which was then looked upon as the appanage of the heir to the throne. At the death of Egbert he succeeded to the throne of Wessex and the over-lordship of the rest of Britain, resigning Kent to his eldest son Athelstane.

I cannot resist here giving Ethelwulf's genealogy as it is to be seen in the Anglo-Saxon Chronicles. Ethelwulf was the son of Egbert, Egbert of Elmund, of Eafa, of Eoppa, of Ingild; Ingild was Ina's brother, King of the West Saxons, he who held the kingdom thirty-seven years, and afterwards went to St. Peter and there resigned his life, and they were the sons of Kenred, of Ceolwald, of Cutha, of Cuthwin, of Ceawlin, of Cynric, of Cerdic, of Elesa, of Esla, of Gewis, of Wig, of Freawin, of Frithogar, of Brond, of Beldeg, of Woden, of Frithowald, of Frealaf, of Frithuwulf, of Finn, of Godwulf, of Geat, of Tœtwa, of Beaw, of Sceldi, of Heremod, of Itermon, of Hathra, of Guala, of Bedwig, of Sceaf, *that is the son of Noah : he was born in Noah's Ark;* Lamech, Methusalem, Enoh, Jared, Mahalaleel, Cainion, Enos, Seth, Adam the first man, and our Father, that is Christ. Amen.

The young Sub-Regulus was, like his grandfather, of small stature, but he had withal a brave soul and a large heart. The Danes were making their piratical raids on the country. In 835 they had in conjunction with the West Welsh (the Britons of the South-Western Peninsula) invaded Wessex ; they were put to flight by Egbert, but he died the following year. From this period, year after year, we read of the incursions of these barbarians. In 845 " the Army," as it is always called in the Saxon Chronicle, landed at the mouth of the Parret, near Bridgewater ; they were valiantly withstood by the Somersætan under their Ealdorman, and the men of Dorset under Bishop Ealstan of Sherborne, and their Ealdormen. The Danes were defeated, and the West Saxons gained a complete victory.

But these ruthless invaders were repulsed at one point only to appear again at another; and in the year 851 they appeared on the Kentish coast ; the young King Athelstane flew to defend his charge. Willing to save his kingdom from fire and sword, he fought the first naval battle on record since the time of Carausius. He went out to meet them on their own element, slew a great number of the enemy, put the others to flight, and took nine of their ships. But, alas ! in spite of his victory, we are told that for the first time they wintered in Kent. Was it as a mark of gratitude to the God of battles, who had given him this great victory, or was it disappointment at the small results of it, that caused Athelstan in the flush of his triumph to dedicate himself entirely to God's service, forsaking the world, its duties and its rewards, its pleasures and its troubles? He left his father, his kindred, his military glory, and his succession to the Crown ; and retiring to the Abbey of Glastonbury, chose for himself the humble and toilsome, yet peaceful duties of a simple monk. In order to prevent any special respect being paid to him on account of his rank, he dropped his own name and assumed that of Neotus. How Athelstane won over his father to consent to his taking the vows from which Ethelwulf himself had been released, does not appear ; he may possibly have stolen away, and that may account for the mysterious silence which history maintains with regard to him after his victory at Sandwich. It may be that he pleaded earnestly with both his father and mother, that he dwelt on the happiness of giving up the world, and devoting himself in his youth to the service of his Creator and Redeemer ; that he touched probably upon the examples of his ancestor, Cædwalla, of Ina and his wife Ethelburga, who gave up their thrones, and, making a pilgrimage to Rome, there died. Such pleading may have had, and probably did have, great effect upon Osburga and Ethelwulf. And now Osburga disappears from authentic history. What can be more likely—especially by the light of what followed—than that she, like Ethelburga, the wife of Ina, determined to retire from the world ? And that she should feel specially drawn toward Somerset, where her first-born had betaken himself, was only natural. At the same time, her youngest son Alfred, a child of rare promise, was sent to Rome with an honourable escort both of nobles and commons. Here he remained till after his father's death. In 855 Ethelwulf himself set out in great state for the Eternal City, and there can be little doubt that he went with the idea of resigning the world and re-dedicating himself to a religious life. At Rome he would find his little son, who, though receiving no special instruction, must have had, from all he saw and heard, his remarkable intelligence ripened, and his mind opened by all the wonders that he beheld.

But, in passing through France, Ethelwulf paid a visit to the Court of Charles the Bald, Emperor and King, and there saw his beautiful and bewitching daughter. But she could not be for him. Osburga was still alive ; he himself was—all but—revowed to a monastic life. But he could not forget her, and, as he continued his journey, he probably warped his own mind by the specious argument that, as Osburga was dead to the world, she was dead to him ; that, as he had been released from his ecclesiastical, he might also be from his matrimonial vows. He hastened on to Rome. Did he equivocate ? Did he mystify Pope Leo ? or, did he bribe him to ask no questions by offering to settle on the Church the tenth part of the royal demesnes ? Certain it is that he returned through France, and that he married Judith, and carried her to England. The marriage was solemnised by Hincmar, Bishop of Rheims. The laxity of the French kings with regard to their marriage vows was so great that it is likely enough that neither King nor Bishop saw any reason for objecting.

But the news of the old man's crime and folly had gone before him.* Ethelbald, who had looked upon his immediate succession to the throne as certain and imminent, found his father returning again to claim it, and as if to justify his unnatural rebellion was insulting his mother by bringing another wife to take her place. He set up his standard, and was joined by Ealstan, Bishop of Sherborne, and Eanwulf, Earl of the Somersætan. Ethelwulf knew himself to be verily guilty, and from the very weakness and gentleness of his nature shrank from bringing on the land the horrors of civil war ; he offered, therefore, as a compromise, to exchange kingdoms with his son, and he retired to the little kingdom of Kent. One thing only was he determined upon. The doating old man, probably incited thereto by Judith, insisted on her holding the position of Queen, a dignity to which Osburga had never aspired, as it was against the Anglo-Saxon laws. Ethelwulf survived his ill-omened marriage only two years, and Ethelbald, treating her former marriage as a thing of nought, took the shameless siren Judith as his wife.

Meanwhile Alfred remained at Rome ; and when the Pope heard of his father's death, he confirmed Alfred, who was his godson, and at the same time, with a prophetic instinct, anointed him King. It was probably after this that Alfred returned to England, being then between eight and nine years old.

Osburga, in her retreat in Somerset, gathered her sons at times around her, especially the two younger, Ethelred and Alfred, and the impression of her teaching, and that of St. Neot's, was seen in the saintliness of Ethelred and the public and private virtue of Alfred's whole life. To this time, then, we may refer the tale of Alfred's being incited to read by his mother. Ethelbald, in his bold defiance of the laws of God and man, she would weep and pray for. Ethelbert had succeeded to his brother's and father's kingdom of Kent, and was therefore far removed from her ; but to these younger ones she might devote herself, and she saw in Alfred a character unsuited for the retirement of the cloister, and yet far too lofty to spend his energies in nought but hunting and fighting. So she encouraged him to study ; and, though his difficulties at that time were great in finding

---

* It is fair to say that Osburga's dedication to a religious life and the *motive* for Ethelwulf's journey to Rome are purely conjectural ; but, if this view is accepted, it would remove all the puzzling difficulties and account for such loyal subjects as Ealstan and Eanwulf joining in Ethelbald's rebellion.

teachers, yet his energetic spirit overcame them all. During the reigns of Ethelbald and Ethelbert it seems probable that Alfred spent great part of his time in Somerset, dividing his time between study, devotion, and the chase, of which latter, like all his race—even the saintly Confessor—he was passionately fond, and which he could enjoy to the full on the Mendip hills or in the wild woods of Exmoor.

But it is time to return to his brother, St. Neot—once Athelstane, who was destined to have so great an influence on the life of his more famous brother. At Glastonbury he studied and prayed, and became famous for his learning and piety. He would rise at the dead of night, and, leaving his hard pallet bed, would offer praise and thanksgiving, mingled with intercessions for his country and those he held dear; and, that none might know of these extraordinary devotions, he would change his garments, disguising himself as the meanest of secular penitents. Thus watching till day-break in the church, he would then steal back to his cell and resume his ordinary habit. Step by step he set himself to climb the path of holiness; he strove to gather from each person with whom he came in contact the particular virtue for which they were most esteemed. The fame of his piety was so great that it reached to the bishop of the diocese, who sent for him and insisted on his undertaking the office of deacon; and after this he was appointed sacristan. Before the usual time of probation he was raised to the priesthood; and he then, knowing it was the priest's office to teach, went about amongst the people. They flocked to him for advice, and none who sought him ever went away empty. His sympathy, too, was ever ready to "weep with those that wept," whilst at the same time he "rejoiced with those that rejoiced."

About this time occurred the first miracle we have recorded in the life of this saint. It was the custom of the monks at midday to retire to their cells for private prayer and meditation; or it may be for sleep, as their night's rest was disturbed by keeping "the hours." At this time no communication whatever was allowed between the brethren. Neot, who was the porter, and whose cell therefore was nearest to the monastery gate, was disturbed one day by a violent knocking; on repairing to the gate to learn the cause, he found a person, who might not be refused, in haste for admittance. He hurried to the gate, but not having with him his iron stool, which on account of his small stature he used when celebrating mass, he could not reach the lock. In great distress he lifted up his heart, when the lock gently slid down to the level of his girdle, and he was enabled to open it without further difficulty.

The lock ever continued in the same place, and people flocked from all parts to see it in its new position. William of Malmesbury, three hundred years afterwards, testifies to having seen *in loco* both the lock and also the iron stool.

But again was the saint called, for the love of God and the promotion of His glory, to tear himself from all he held most dear; he was selected as a missionary to the West Welsh of Cornwall, to endeavour at once to reconcile the British Church to the Saxon, and also to rouse the slumbering faith of the people, who, cut off as they were in their narrow peninsula from Briton and Saxon alike, had apparently fallen into a state somewhat resembling the apathy and semi-infidelity from which they were aroused in the last century by the preaching of Wesley and Whitefield. He was called upon by external authority to leave the glassy isle which had been his home for so many years, and, taking his pilgrim's staff, and accompanied by his faithful servant Barius, he left the stately monastery embosomed in fair orchards, looking bright and peaceful as it lay in the sheen of the summer sun with the (then) not far distant murmur of the Severn sea,* and made his way across the rich plains of Somerset.

Then, we may follow him, climbing (it may be) the glorious mass of Dunkery Beacon, glowing with its gorgeous tapestry of purple heath and golden gorse, from whose summit the eye can discover sixteen counties, he took one last loving look over the fair kingdom of Wessex, and strained his eyes eastward towards his own dear land of Kent, though in imagination only could his eyes pierce the distance. His past life seemed spread out before him—the early days when he was his father's heir, his young brothers growing up around him, the troubles that gathered on his county, his famous victory at Sandwich. And then, gradually, his mind and eye came home again to what had been his resting-place and home of late years; a happy time of praise, and prayer, and earnest work; and then, with one last loving, lingering look at Glastonbury, that home of heroes and of saints, he resolutely turned away, and crossing the Exmoor Forest —still, even now, the home of the red deer and the black cock—he passed the beautiful district of North Devon, and made for the wild Cornish moors, where he settled, as directed by a vision, on a spot

---

* The sea at that part of Somerset has receded greatly within the last few centuries.

formerly inhabited by the good St. Guerryer, but henceforth through all time to be known as St. Neots.

Here we must leave him,* for Neot's life is no further connected with Somerset, save as it affects the life of Alfred. The deaths of Ethelbald and Ethelbert placed Ethelred on the throne, and this drew Alfred from retirement; for, though he does not appear to have been appointed Sub-Regulus of Kent, yet it became his duty to assist his brother in his defence of the country against the Danes. In one year nine pitched battles were fought against these marauders. But the greatest fight was that at Ashdown, or Essendune. The combatants were parted by night coming on. As morning dawned, Alfred was ready at his post, but the King lingered at his devotions, nor would he hurry them, although urged by a message from his brother that the heathen were rushing forward with unbounded fury. The English were giving way, and even bordering on flight, for the heathen were pressing down upon them from the higher ground, when the King himself, signed with the cross of God, unexpectedly hastened forward, dispersing the enemy and rallying his subjects. The Danes, terrified equally by his courage and by the Divine manifestation, consulted their safety by flight. Here fell Oseg their king, five earls, and an innumerable multitude of common people. But the struggle was too harassing to be continued, and Ethelred, worn down with numberless labours, died and was buried at Wimborne.

It was in 871, or the following year, that Alfred, a youth of twenty-one, succeeded to the toilsome labour of guiding the helm of the State. Ardent, impetuous, even cruel—it is said—in his vengeance on his enemies, yet with cultivated tastes, he despised the slow minds and sensual habits of his subjects, and took no care to conceal his contempt of them. For nine years the struggle with the enemy was continued, and at last was so far successful that the Danes left Wessex, and, crossing the Thames, visited London, Mercia, and East Anglia. And now came a pause and a period of comparative rest; but Alfred, instead of striving to heal the wounds of his suffering people, and comfort them in their afflictions, showed naught but disgust at their ignorance and their evil habits and coarse tastes; he would not listen to his subjects' complaints, nor help them in their necessities, or grant them relief from their oppressors; instead of

---

* Those who wish to continue the life and legends of St. Neot may consult Hunt's "Popular Romances of the West of England;" Butler's "Lives of the Saints;" Whitaker's "Cathedral of Cornwall;" Gorham's "History of St. Neot;" or, "The Lives of English Saints," published by Toovey.

this he repulsed them and paid no heed to their distress. It was not unnatural that Alfred should compare to their disadvantage his own pure and stainless life with the low animal pleasures of his people; but he was not left without warning, and his impatience and self-righteousness were rebuked.

(*To be continued.*)

The History of Gilds.

By Cornelius Walford, F.S.S., *Barrister-at-Law.*

PART IV.

(*Continued from Vol. VI. p.* 275.

Chapter XXXVII.—*The Gilds of Northumberland.*

THE Gilds of this most northern county of ancient Britain are fairly numerous, and are full of interest. They bear traces of the early Border feuds.

Berwick-upon-Tweed.—The Gild of this ancient Border town and county—which may now be appropriately included in Northumberland—possesses a feature of special interest, as illustrating the process of absorbing many separate fraternities into one Corporate Gild. This event occurred in A.D. 1283-4—indicating necessarily an earlier existence for the Gilds so absorbed. I shall give the substance only.

Statutes of the Gild ordained by the pleasure of the burgesses, so that, where many bodies are found side by side in one place, they may become one, and have one will, and in the dealings of one toward another have a strong and hearty love. All separate Gilds, heretofore existing in the borough, shall be brought to an end. The goods rightfully belonging to them shall be handed over to this Gild. No other Gild shall be allowed in the borough. All shall be as members having one head, one in counsel, one body, strong and friendly. Brethren shall bequeath something to the Gild if they make wills. Men, not being brethren, making a bequest, shall have the benefit of the Gild. Foul words to incur fine, and if repeated, other penalties. Heavy fines shall be paid for bodily hurt done. Weapons shall not be brought to Gild meetings. "Commit no nuisance." New members, not sons or daughters of Gildmen, to pay 40s. Whoever shall fall into old age or poverty, or into hopeless sickness, and has no means of his own, shall have such help as the Aldermen, Dean, and Brethren of the Gild think right, and such as the means of the Gild enable to be given. Doweries shall be given to poor maidens, either on marriage or on going into a religious house. Poor brethren shall be buried at the cost of the Gild. Help shall be given to brethren charged with wrong-doing. Burgesses who disclaim the Gild shall not be helped by it. All brothers shall come to meetings at the sounding of the trumpet. No lepers shall come into the borough, a place being kept for them outside the town. No dung nor dust-heaps shall be put near the banks of the Tweed. "Silence in Court." Every well-to-do burgess must keep a horse-Handmills are not to be used—the miller must have his share. No townsman (out of the Gild) shall trade in wool or hides unless he is free of the Gild; but stranger-merchants may do so. Underhand dealings in the way of trade shall be punished. The market shall not be forestalled as to ship-borne food-stuffs. If anyone buys goods, misled by false top samples, amends must be made. The price of mutton was fixed for the varying seasons of the year. Butchers shall not speculate in wool or hides. The price of ale was also fixed. Brokers to be chosen by the Town, to which they were to present a cask of wine every year; their names to be registered. Goods for consumption shall not be bought up by hucksters before the bell rings. Forestalling the market not allowed; wool and hides not to be engrossed by a few buyers. No burgess to get an outsider to plead for him against a neighbour. The Gild shall be one and undivided. How the commonalty of Berwick shall be ruled. The Mayor and Provosts shall be chosen by the commonalty. Bewrayers [betrayers] of the Gild shall be heavily punished. No skinner nor glover shall cut any wool from the skins during the summer months, but all skins to be sold as they are. Buyers of herrings shall share and share alike. Regulation for carriage of wine casks. Regulation as to quantity of beer to be brewed by alewives. Butchers shall not forestall the market. Leathers must be sold in open market. No one shall have more than two pairs of mill-stones. Local custom as to sharing goods bought. The place and times for buying and taking away sea-borne goods. Dues from foreign merchants to go to the Gild-stock. Out-dwelling brethren of the Gild must deal in the town on market-days.

This is probably the best type extant of the restrictions of the Town or Corporate Gilds of the Middle Ages.

Newcastle-upon-Tyne.—In this ancient borough (once a stronghold of the Roman invader) there are traces of early Gilds. I shall here present in outline a few of the more important.

Merchant Adventurers.—King John, in the 17th year of his reign (1215)—it is to be observed, one year before his grant to the merchants of London—constituted a Society or Gild of Free Merchants ; the members of which (amongst other privileges) were exempted from pleading anywhere without the walls of the town, to any plea but that concerning foreign tenures. He released them also from the duties of toll, lastage, pontage, and passage, in all the sea-ports of his dominions at home and abroad—empowering the Mayor of New-castle, or Sheriff of Northumberland, to give them reparation for whatever injury they might sustain. This Charter was afterwards confirmed by Henry III., Edward II., and Edward III., with the addition of new privileges.

This Gild assumed at an early period to regulate the trade of the town and port. When in 1281 an Italian merchant was found making shipments of wool and leather, attention was called to the fact that members of this Merchants' Gild ought to have like privileges. So again, when, in 1343, other burgesses in the town were permitted to purchase merchandises at prime cost out of ships in their port, for their private use, the Gild regarded this as an infringement of its privileges.

But the importance of the Gild came into greater prominence when Edward III. removed the staple of English wool from the Flemings—for then Newcastle became one of the nine staple towns, and all wools of the growth of Northumberland, Cumberland, West-moreland, Durham, and Richmondshire, were commanded to be shipped for foreign ports there. Richard II. in 1397 granted leave to the merchants of this Gild to carry woolfels, and other commodities, to any other foreign port besides Calais, on paying custom and subsidy. Newcastle, at this date, carried on a considerable trade with the Baltic ports.

In 1480 the Society of Merchants in Newcastle subscribed a written agreement for the better government of the body, under which they bound themselves to meet and hold their courts monthly at the Maison Dieu Hall, on the Sandhill, and their annual gather-ing on the Thursday next after " Mid-fast" Sunday. The Society to go in procession on Corpus Christi Day. Those members holding rank, as the Mayor, Sheriff, and Aldermen, were to attend with their officers and servants upon the Holy Sacrament ; and according to seniority of office were to be the principals in the solemn procession, in which the latest made burgess was to walk foremost. A play was annually enacted. In 1504 the privileges of the Gild regarding the shipment of north-country wools to various parts of Europe were enlarged.

In 1546 Edward VI. granted a Charter to this Gild, under its expanded title of " The Governor, Assistants, Wardens, and Fellowship of Merchant Adventurers of the Town and County of Newcastle-upon-Tyne." They had at an earlier date been known as " Merchant Venturers in the Ports of Brabant beyond the Seas."

A peculiar feature of this Gild was that it consisted of three principal branches of members, viz. :—

1. *Drapers*, or merchants in woollen cloth. In an Ordinance for the government of the town confirmed by Edward III. in 1342, this branch is referred to as one of the " Twelve Mysteries." There is in the records of the town an Ordinance under date 1512 which throws some light upon the constitution of this branch. In the following century the parent Gild was disposed to claim the more important privileges of the branch, and to treat its section of members as being entitled to inferior privileges.

2. *Mercers*, or merchants of silk. There seems to be no available date for determining the distinct fellowship of the members of this branch of the Gild.

3. *Boothmen*, or merchants of corn. Here again no distinct records seem to exist determining the separate existence of this branch. There are some scattered references.

I think the strong inference is that the twelve mysteries or trades had a separate existence earlier than the Charter of King John, and that they were consolidated by that charter, or some earlier one, into this Merchants' Gild or Company. It seems, however, equally probable that but three of the early mysteries so united ; for there were yet nine other Gilds claiming separate existence, which I now proceed briefly to notice. It is more than probable that the twelve ancient mysteries had descended direct from the Roman period.

The Merchant Gild still exists. As recently as 1823 its Hall or Court, above the Maison Dieu, on the Sandhills, was pulled down and rebuilt. This must be one of the oldest incorporations now existing in Great Britain.

Skinners & Glovers.—The earliest known Ordinance of the Skinners is dated January 20, 1437. The fellowship were to meet on the Tuesday after Michaelmas every year, unless that festival should fall on a Monday, and then on the Tuesday seven-night following, to choose their stewards and pass their accounts. Amongst the different orders it promulgated and recorded was one forbidding the use of tobacco at its meetings, under a penalty of 3d. for every offence. The Ordinance of the Glovers, dated January, 1436, enjoined them to go together in procession at the feast of Corpus Christi, in a livery, and play their play at their own charge; to choose annually three stewards; that apprentices should serve seven years, on pain of forfeiting 6s. 8d. "to the light of the said craft;" that no Scotsman born should be taken apprentice, nor allowed to work in the town, under a penalty of 40s.

The fusion of the two Gilds took place at a later date. They were existing, in an attenuated form, early in the present century.

Taylors.—The oldest known record of this fraternity is dated October 8, 1536. It enjoins that every brother, at setting up his shop, should pay a pot of oil to the fellowship; as also 3d. a year to the stewards for "our Lady-light;" and that each apprentice or person hired by the week should pay 4d. per annum, and each hireling 3d. a year to their play when it should be performed; also that any person born a subject of the King, and free of Newcastle, might set up a shop on payment of £40, with a pound of wax and a pot of oil, on his admittance; as also 13d. to our Lady-light, and 8d. to the play which exhibited the Descent into Hell. That no taylor should work on Saturdays after 8 o'clock in the evening, and should keep holy the Sundays, vigils, and festival days, on pain of 6 lbs. of wax for every default. That the Society should pass its accounts on St. John's Day in every May, and having chosen twelve electors, the said twelve should choose the four stewards, the searchers, and auditors. It further ordered that every brother should be at the procession on Corpus Christi Day, before it passed the New-gate, on pain of forfeiting a pound of wax; and that each brother should attend in his livery. And that the common light of the fraternity should go before the corpse of every brother when it was carried to church for interment, and continue there lighted during mass time, and till the body was interred; but if there be a dirge, then the light to be extinguished during the dirge.

There are later Ordinances, which, however, throw no new light upon the Ordinances of this Gild, which was existing in the early part of the present century, having a considerable income from real estate.

It appears that the members of this Gild took prominent part in supporting the rights of the freemen to the open spaces of this town during the last century; and in 1773, on a victory being obtained by a legal process, this Society presented to each member of the committee who conducted the cause of the burgesses, a gold ring, in the signet of each of which, under a crystal, was represented Liberty stepping out of her temple, with a label proceeding from her mouth, inscribed, "Town moor saved Aug. 10, 1773."

Saddlers.—The oldest Ordinance of this Gild is dated March 6, 1459. It enjoins the brethren to go together in procession, in a livery, at the Feast of Corpus Christi, and perform their play at their own cost; and that each brother should be at the procession when his hour was assigned, under pain of 40d. That no Scotsman born should be taken apprentice, or suffered to work within the town, under a penalty of 20s. It further ordered that no apprentice should be taken under the term of seven years, on the pain of 6s. 8d., enjoining civil behaviour to each other at their meetings, the observance of holidays, &c. There were but a small number of members in this fraternity at the beginning of this century.

Bakers and Brewers.—The making of bread and beer being a corporate monopoly (says Mackenzie, "History of Newcastle," ii. 674), this mystery was, in remote times, specially protected by the government of the town. It was agreed at full Gild of the town, held at St. Mary's Hospital, on the Friday before Valentine Day, 1342, and confirmed by the King October 20 in that year, that "the assizes of bread and beer be held according to law. The master bakers, and not their servants, to suffer penalties ordained by Statute. Measures, ells, and weights to be proved twice a year, or at least once." By an inquisition taken at Newcastle January 4, 1446, it appears that the common baking and brewing for sale were restricted to that town, and nowhere else within the port of the Tyne.

This Gild had an Ordinance, under date 1583, to which various references are made in their records. In 1661 it was agreed that the membership meet yearly on November 23, unless it should fall on a Sunday, and then the day after, to elect twelve of the Society and four wardens, who were empowered, by the name of the Wardens of the Art and Mystery of Bakers and Brewers, to prosecute, sue, and implead, and be prosecuted, sued, &c. only within the courts of Newcastle-upon-Tyne; to make laws for the government of the Society, impose fines, &c., forbidding any brother to strike another at any meeting with fist, hand, elbow, dagger, staff, stick, rod, or otherwise, on pain of 20s.; and ordering that no apprentice should be taken under seven years, nor a second until the first had served six years ; as also that the Society should attend the burials of their brethren, on pain of a penalty of 3s. 4d. for every omission. The Gild was much reduced in numbers towards the end of the last century.

Tanners.—This fraternity was anciently called the *Barkers.* By an Ordinance dated November 8, 1532, the brotherhood was enjoined to come yearly in their best array and apparel, at the feast of Corpus Christi, and go in procession, set forth their pageants, &c., on pain of forfeiting a pound of wax. Not to take any Scot by birth for an apprentice under a penalty of 20s. That each brother should have but one butcher to buy slaughter of, on pain of £10, and not to buy above eight fothers of bark, or forty trees, on pain of 6s. 8d. ; also to supply each other with bark, &c.

This Society had grown comparatively rich, but had very few members at the end of last century.

Cordwainers.—This Gild was incorporated in the 17 Henry VI. (1439). Another Ordinance, dated 17th of Dec., 1566, mentions their meeting house in the then recently dissolved monastery of Blackfriars. It enjoins that every apprentice should serve ten years, five of which to be expired before a second could be taken ; and that foreigners might be admitted into the Company on payment of £5, one half to go to the fellowship and the other to the reparation of Tyne Bridge.

The " Cobblers " seem to have carried on a species of trade warfare with this Gild. There is a record of a grant from the Common Council of the Borough, under date 2nd of June, 1617, reciting that " divers persons for years, under colour of exercising the trade of a cobbler, who should only mend old shoes that are brought to them to be mended, do buy great numbers of old shoes mended and made fit to be worn at London and elsewhere, and cause them to be brought to Newcastle-upon-Tyne, and in the Cobbler's houses, and in the market within the said town, sell them to the best advantage : whereby the fraternity of Cordwainers of Newcastle aforesaid is much impoverished." The Common Council then proceeds to empower this Gild to fine the aforesaid Cobblers, in view of the preservation of its " ancient customs, rights and privileges." The Gild, early in the last century, granted to twelve persons the right to follow the calling of Cobblers, in retail and not in bulk, on payment of 6d. each per annum. This was known as the " Cobblers' Bond."

The Gild followed the old Corporation practice of sharing in each other's purchases of leather ; and a special book records these transactions.

Early in the present century this Gild had a considerable fellow-ship, and was also in possession of considerable property.

Butchers.—An Ordinance of this Gild dated 20th of July, 1621, enjoined the brethren to meet every year on Ash Wednesday, to choose their two Wardens ; that apprentices should serve at least eight years, five of which were to expire before a second could be taken ; that no brother should be a partner with any foreigners called " crockers," on pain of forfeiting £5 ; that none should kill after nine o'clock on Saturday night, nor keep open shop after eight o'clock on Sunday morning ; that no brother should buy, or seek any licence to kill flesh in Newcastle during Lent, without the general consent of the fellowship, on pain of forfeiting £5 ; that none should kill either at Lent or at any other time within the liberties of the High Castle, " being in the County of Northumberland," on the like pain for each offence ; but that any butcher, though not a brother, might expose good meat for sale in the market from the times of eight in the morning till four in the afternoon.

There was an Order in the Gild that no free brother should blow a calf's pluck, or any part of a calf, except calf's close-ear, nor any other goods but a cow's udder, under a penalty of 6s. 8d. unforgiven.

The Gild was flourishing in the first quarter of this century.

Smiths.—The oldest known Ordinance of this Gild, dated 14th of January, 1436, enjoins that the brethren should go together in pro-cession on the Feast of Corpus Christi, and play their play at their own expense, attending at the hour appointed, on pain of forfeiting a pound of wax ; that every brother should be at St. Nicholas' Church, at the setting forth of the procession on St. Loy Day, on the like penalty ; that no Scotsman born " should be taken apprentice or suffered to work, on pain of the forfeiture of 40s., half whereof to go to the Chamber of the town, and the other half to the fellowship ; " that no brother should sell " seyme and coff " by weight, under 3s. 4d. a hundred, on pain of forfeiting 6s. 8d. for each offence.

Another Ordinance, dated September 25, 1664, exhibits the Society as consisting of the different branches of blacksmiths and farriers, blacksmiths or anchor-smiths, and locksmiths or white-smiths.

Another, dated August 17, 1677, empowered the fraternity to be a body politic in law ; enjoined them to meet yearly, on St. Loy Day, to choose four wardens, of whom one, at least, was to be an anchor-smith ; that the twelve of the Company should consist of four anchor-smiths, four blacksmiths and farriers, and four lock-smiths, to choose four searchers; that apprentices should serve seven years; and that no brother should come to meetings, or attend the public Gild of the town with his apron on, but with a decent cloak or coat, on pain of forfeiting 6d. for each default.

The Gild was still flourishing in the earlier part of this century.

Fullers and Dyers.—The members of this fraternity were originally designated "Walkers." An Ordinance dated May 6, 1477, enacted that no brother should stain cloth upon the tentor to deliver it with the short wand, on pain of forfeiting 4 lbs. of wax; nor tentor cloth on a Sunday, nor "wend to the walk mylne" with any raw cloth on that day, on pain of forfeiting 2 lbs. of wax; that they should take no Scotchman born to apprentice, nor set any such to work, under a penalty of 20s., half whereof to go to the Society, and half to the support of Tyne Bridge; that no apprentice should be taken under seven years; that no brother should work carsey under 2d. the yard; to work no broad-cloth of colour under 4d. a yard, nor any wadded blue under 2d. the yard; to "dight" (*i.e.*, clean) no gown under 4d. on pain of half a pound of wax; not to sheer a dozen yards of tilled cloth under 3d., on pain of 2 lbs. of wax, or fustian under 1d. a yard, or broad-cloth under 3d. for the like quantity, on penalty of forfeiting 1 lb. of wax for each.

The Ordinance also provided that they should attend the weddings and burials of the brethren in their livery; that they should meet in their livery in Carlel Croft, on St. John's Day in May at six o'clock in the morning, and upon St. John's Day at Christmas at one o'clock in the afternoon; that none of the Company should fail at being at the setting forth of the procession on Corpus Christi Day, on pain of forfeiting 1 lb. of wax; that each brother should pay 6d. to the processions and play yearly; that they were to choose twelve, who were to be sworn and elected wardens, auditors, and searchers, two to attend the Mayor and Chamber for the year, &c., &c. The Gild was still existing in a small way in the early part of this century.

All the foregoing were Craft Gilds, and their Ordinances show how much the element of Trade protection was aimed at. There were, in addition to these, fifteen bye-trades, or lesser fraternities, which I shall notice in another chapter.

(*To be continued.*)

Forecastings of Nostradamus

By C. A. WARD.

PART V.

(Continued from Vol. VI. p. 214.)

ＴHE most remarkable prophecies relating to England have
already been given, but a good many others more or less
intelligible are enumerated in a pamphlet of 1715 by D. D.*

CENTURY IV. QUATRAIN 96.

La sœur aisnée de l'isle Britannique,
  Quinze ans devant le Frere aura naissance.
Par son promis moyennant verifique,
  Succedera un Regne de Balance.

"The elder sister, heir to the British island, shall be born fifteen years before
her brother. Verifying her conditional promise, she shall succeed to the kingdom
that sways the Balance (of Europe)."

This relates to Mary, who followed Edward VI. to the throne, and
in fulfilment of her vow she reinstates all the Papists, and causes Elizabeth to be committed to prison on a charge of conspiracy. She died
1558, in the fifth year of her reign. It is to be remarked here that
she was not born fifteen, but twenty-one years before her brother,
and as this was actually an event contemporary with Nostradamus, he
might easily have rendered it conformable to the facts of history.
One may learn from this that our prophet acted quite independently
of external aids by methods and ways of his own, and received what
he noted down in a sort of unconscious manner, more as an
amanuensis than as being personally responsible for anything he
wrote. The explanation of D. D. upon the passage is very singular,
and to those who study the human mind without private prejudice
highly interesting. He says :—

"But if he has not known it, then has he either overheard it *in
raptu*, whilst his genius dictated unto him one year and three *Heptades*, or forgot it *post raptum*, and did write one year and two
Heptades. The *Lingua Dæmonum* uses *Septenarios in numerando* as
we do *Denarios*."

The phrase *Regne de Balance* is one of those pithy, pregnant sentences for ever and anon dropping instinctively from the pen of

---

* "The Prophecies of Nostradamus concerning the fate of all the Kings and
Queens of Great Britain since the Reformation, and the succession of his present
Majesty King George, and continuation of the British Crown in his most serene
Royal House to the last day of the world." Collected and explained by D. D.
1715.

Nostradamus, on all topics treated by him or glanced at. The whole bent of England's policy from Henry VII.'s day to the Treaty of Vienna has been to maintain a European equipoise, that no state might grow so strong as to overwhelm the rest. The wise counsels of Elizabeth were all directed to fortify it, and it was never seriously infringed till the Partition of Poland. The permission of that unjust act blinded England, and hired publicists soon sprang up in abundance, who confused the moral sense of Europe. It was pretended that the Poles could not govern themselves. But the fourth article in Peter the Great's will shows that they were not to be allowed to govern themselves, but to "be kept in continual jealousy," whilst the other Powers were to be corrupted by gold and a share of the plunder till Russia could retake it all. The publicists succeeded so well that the very phrase "Balance of Power" became a topic of ridicule in common conversation, and excluded its obvious rationality from any chance of a fair hearing. The Navigation Laws and Protection have both been treated in the same way in our time, and with the same revolutionary consequences and loss of English supremacy. At Vienna the *Regne de Balance* passed away, I fear for ever, from the sceptre of England.*

---

* Hume has very ably handled this important question in his Seventh Essay (Hume's Philosophical Works, iii. 373, Edinburgh, 1826). He there sets out that it is no modern invention as some have maintained, for the Asiatics combined against the Medes and Persians, as Xenophon shows in his "Institutions of Cyrus." Likewise Thucydides exhibits the league formed against Athens, which led to the Peloponnesian war, as being grounded on this principle. Afterwards, when Thebes and Lacedæmon disputed the supremacy, Athens always threw her strength into the lighter scale to preserve the balance. She was for Thebes against Sparta till Epaminondas won at Leuctra, and then she immediately changed sides, as of generosity, but really jealous to preserve the balance. If you will read Demosthenes, he says in the Oration for the Megapolitans you may "see the utmost refinements on this principle that ever entered into the head of a Venetian or English speculatist." On the rise of the crafty Macedonian he again bugled the alarm to Greece, which brought the banners together that fell at Chæronea. The principle was right, but the too great delay had knit Fate's smile into a frown. Envy (if you like to call it so, but I call it a jealous prudence) must in a community of States prevent any one from overtopping, as Athenian ostracism expelled the citizen who grew too lush and vigorous for a communion in equality. Hume points out with perspicuous beauty how England went too far. Her emulous antagonism to France made her so alert to defend her allies, that they could count upon her as a force of their own. The expenses consequent upon this imprudent course led to funding, *i.e.*, the *National Debt*, and that has led us into an absurd meekness, a dread of war, and the peace barkings of Quaker Bright ; so that England dares not fire a howitzer when Russia, contrary to her most solemn pledges, annexes Merv, Bokara, and Khiva, and cannot find a word to say when Germany has her foot on the throat of France. Blunders in extravagant advocacy, blunders in parsimonious neglect of a principle do not diminish its importance, they only emphasize it. With a prophecy out of dry reason Hume says it will become "more prejudicial another way, by begetting, as is usual, the opposite extremes, and ren-

Century VI. Quatrain 74.

" La dechassée au regne tournera,
  Ses enemies trouvez des conjurez ;
  Plusque jamais son temps triomphera,
  Trois et septante, sa mort, trop asseuré."

The last line in Ed. 1558 reads, " Trois et septante à mort trop asseurrez."

" The rejected one shall at last reach the throne, her enemies found to have been traitors. But her period shall more than ever be triumphant. At the age of 70 she goes assuredly to death, in the third year of the century."

Trois stands with Nostradamus for 1603. He often drops the thousands and hundreds from a date. We shall have shortly another instance in the case of the Fire of London, 1666, when he describes the doomed city as, " Bruslé par fond, de vingt-trois les six."

Queen Elizabeth proved a thorn in the side of Popery. She over-threw the Armada, crippled Spain, despoiled her of a large tract of land in America ,called Virginia, and under Essex in 1596 inflicted on her a loss of twenty million ducats, or pieces of eight, in the Bay of Cadiz, to which the following seems to refer.

---

dering us totally careless and supine with regard to the fate of Europe." That is how we now stand. In a very recent French cyclopædia, *l'équilibre Européan* is said to be quite a modern idea, with nothing corresponding to it in antiquity. The writer pretends that it originated with the Church, and that Podichad the King of Bohemia sent Marini to Louis XI. to point out the necessity there was for a *Parliament of Kings* to adjust matters between the Church and people. This may be the first form of a Congress. Francis I. carried on the same policy, and Henri IV. extended it to an idea of a Christian republic of federated nations, as against a universal monarchy. This idea enabled Cromwell to meddle as European arbiter, whereas he ought only to have acted as moderator and equaliser of parties. Leibnitz called the House of Hapsburgh a continual conspiracy against the rights of the people, and Richelieu got the *equilibrium* established at the Treaty of Westphalia, and introduced as a principle of the law of nations, with its concomitant of *Congresses*. The princes so assembled plotted against Poland, as might have been anticipated, and in the course of seventy years have been enabled entirely to break up the Balance of Power in Europe. Cromwell, Richelieu, Napoleon, and Bismarck, by force, finesse, chicane, and brutal bluntness, have overturned the very groundwork of the principle. The English, having at first stirred up war by means of subventions, have now tumbled only too laxly into the stupid doctrine of non-intervention. Congresses should never have been allowed. These " Parliaments of Kings " can only do mischief, as they have no controlling power to refer to. They lack a *King* above the Parliaments, and as that is *impossible* Congresses can only meet for evil. The strongest are irresistible in such congregations. The weaker can get no justice and no sympathy. If they take the field everybody is against them, if they submit they are despoiled without hope of a remedy : whereas, formerly, a wrong done might excite a feeling of justice in a neighbour, and so induce him to help ; or where justice was weak, fear of similar treatment might opportunely bring forth the required aid.

CENTURY VIII. QUATRAIN 94.

" Devant le lac on plus cher fut getté,
De sept mois, et son ost descomfit ;
Seront Hispans, par Albanois gastez,
Par delay perte en donnant le conflict."

" Before the Bay [of Cadiz, where the English fell in with and destroyed thirteen ships of war and forty huge South American galleons, part of the great ' silver fleet or plate fleet'], where the rich fleet was stranded [in its own harbour], after a seven months' voyage, and all its host discomfited. The Spaniards shall be worsted by the English [Albanois*], giving battle after the chances are lost by delay."

This may reasonably enough be interpreted of the attack made in June, 1596, by Essex, Howard, and Raleigh on Cadiz, as above stated, when the Duke De Medina set fire to the ships to prevent their capture. No doubt the Spaniards were very supine † at Cadiz, and if they had attacked instead of awaiting the onset of the English, they might have beaten the English off, or at least kept them out of the harbour. The bay and harbour of Cadiz may very well be called a lake, being twelve miles one way and at least six the other, whilst the entrance to it, from Rota to the Castle of St. Sebastian, is a good six miles. When Essex got possession of the Castle of Puntales he commanded the whole town and harbour.‡

CENTURY VI. QUATRAIN 22.

" Dedans la terre du grand temple Celique,
Nepueu á Londre par paix feincte meurtry ;
La barque alors deviendra schismatique,
Liberté feincte sera au corn, et cry."

" In the country of the great heavenly temple, the nephew is murdered by her who comes to London under a feigned truce. The ship (of Peter) will then become schismatic, and feigned Liberty become the hue and cry everywhere."

This refers to the murder of Henry Stuart, 1567, and the final establishment of the Reformation. The temple of heaven means,

---

* Garencières translates this "*Albaneses*, a nation between the Venetians and Greece," *i.e.*, what we now style Albanians, but it is far preferable to understand it as English = Albanies or Albions.

† "The Spartans and Spaniards have been noted to have been of small despatch : "Mi venga la muerte di Spagna,' Let my death come from Spain, for then it will be sure to be long in coming." (Bacon's Essay on Dispatch.) Oddly enough, this proverb is not given in Collins' Spanish proverbs. But not the Spartans only procrastinated. "Business to-morrow," said the Theban Polymarch, in Plutarch, as he laid some dispatches relating to a conspiracy under his pillow, and was killed. The copy-slip was never better verified : such "Delays are dangerous " indeed.

‡ The idea of lake is actually expressed in the very name of Cadiz, which is derived from a Punic word *Gaddir*, an *enclosed place.* This the Greeks corrupted into Γάδειρα or γῆς δειρή, neck of land. The Romans made this or the Punic into *Gades*, and the Spaniards, with their Arabic guttural, into *Xerez*.

D. D. thinks, the kingdom of the *angeli* or *angels*, Angles, English. *Celique*, however, may stand for Celtique. If we read .Celtique, " la terre du grand temple Celtique " would be the island in which there is the great Druid temple of Stonehenge; but in any case we must assume it to mean Scotland more especially. Instead of interpreting *La barque* as the *Ship of Peter*, it would be best to understand it as the Ship of State, which having become schismatical, the Puritans will make a great hue and cry about liberty of conscience. The Puritans were very troublesome in England and Scotland both, all through the reigns of Elizabeth and Mary Stuart. Here D. D. points out what it is the business of his book to establish, that the settlement of the House of Hanover on the throne of England is one of the distinct prophecies of Nostradamus. James I. was the great-grandfather of George I. His daughter Elizabeth, sister of Charles I., married Frederick the Elector Palatine, and had issue the Princess Sophia, Electress of Brunswick-Lunenburgh, the mother of George I.

(*To be continued.*)

Collectanea.

A BOOK-WORM.—We quote the following from the *Publishers' Circular:* "A *Book-Worm* is described in the dictionaries as 'a great reader or student of books,' and also as 'a worm that eats holes in books;' despite its large ravages the worm itself is very rare. We confess that, although quite familiar with the little circular tunnel to be met with in bound books as well as in 'quires,' we have never before seen the engineer that so scientifically performs this destructive kind of work. He is not at all what our fancy painted him. We had always imagined a dark-coloured, tough, wiry *worm*; but he is a white, wax-like little fellow; he so exactly resembles those little white maggots to be seen in a well-decayed 'Stilton' that one is inclined to regard him simply as a 'Stilton' maggot with a taste for literature, in fact (like his prototype) a 'student,' or, perhaps, it is better to say a rodent of books. His history will be found in the following note: 'Booksellers are often made aware, in a manner that is more painful than pleasant, that there are such things as book-worms in existence. However, it is not many booksellers that have ever seen one, for, despite its large ravages, the worm itself is very rare. Mr. G. Suckling discovered three at Messrs. Sotheran's Strand house a few days ago. They were half-way through a bundle of quires, and were evidently on their second or third journey, judging from the number of perforations made in the paper.' Mr. Blades devotes, in his 'Enemies of Books,' some space to a description of this destructive but withal interesting species of worm."—A. J. BOWDEN (Messrs. Sotheran & Co.), 136, Strand, W.C.

Reviews.

A Smaller Biblia (Biblion) Pauperum. T. F. Unwin, Paternoster-square. 1884.

THIS is a reprint, on a reduced scale, of a work which was given to the public at the Caxton Exhibition of 1877, where it created no little interest. It is a sort of *Diatesseron*, or epitome of the four Gospels, the text being taken from Wycliff's version, and illustrated on the alternate pages with rough and bold engravings from wood-blocks, which, as we are told in the preface, were cut a few years before Caxton set up his press in Westminster Abbey, but, from some reason or other, do not appear to have been used. Having been allowed to lie stowed away for three centuries or more, the blocks were bought seventy years since by a gentleman in the north of England, from whom we gather they came into the possession of Messrs. Unwin, who, in a prefatory note, state that these blocks "cannot be recognised as belonging to any *printed* book," and that the artist's mark, which appears on one of the plates, "is unknown to any Bibliographer." The blocks form a kind of "Biblion Pauperum"—the Bible of the Poor—illustrative of the life, miracles, parables, and sayings of our Saviour, and, occasionally, typical subjects from the Old Testament are introduced. There are altogether seventy-eight subjects represented on the thirty-eight plates. A date is engraved on two of the plates; but it would seem that the figures are transposed, for it is stated that authorities at the British Museum agree in reading the date as certainly 1540, but suggest that it is difficult to refer the artistic composition to that period, as "it clearly belongs to the end of the previous century." By the kindness of Messrs. Unwin we are enabled to reproduce one of the wood-blocks as a frontispiece; it is illustrative of the miraculous casting out of evil spirits by the Saviour (St. Mark v.). The educational value of such illustrated "biblia" as these in the days before the art of printing had become known, is made the subject of a short introductory essay by Dean Stanley. We can only say that the book, with its quaint old English typography, its handsome rough-edged paper, and its antique parchment cover, does very great credit to the firm to whom this reproduction is due; and we hope sincerely that it will meet with the sale which it deserves.

The Lay of St. Aloys (Eyre & Spottiswoode) is almost the only "Christmas book," out of those on our table, which we care to notice specially. All readers of "Tom Ingoldsby" will recognise in it one of his most amusing legends; but they will see their old friend in a new guise, the text being given in old English letters, after the best antiquarian patterns, and illustrated by Mr. Ernest M. Jessop in a manner quite in keeping with the text. His monks, his priests, and his bishops, their mitres, their copes, their habits, and their shaven crowns are all given with spirit, and yet with a faithful adherence to ancient patterns which is really wonderful. The initial letters and ornamental scrolls are studies in their way. The book would make an excellent New Year's gift.

The December number of *English Etchings*, Part xliii. (D. Bogue, 27, King William-street, Strand), contains three strikingly-executed examples of the etcher's art. "Roman Remains in Milan," by Mr. W. H. Urwick, shows the Colonne di San Lorenzo, which, according to Murray, is "the most considerable vestige of Roman Milan," consisting of " sixteen white marble columns of the Corinthian order, mouldering, fire-scathed, shattered by violence ;" much care, however, seems to be expended in supporting these interesting ruins. "A Castled Crag," by Mr. H. Pope, is a spirited drawing of the ruins of Deganwy, "the fort of the Conway," which are situated on a bold projecting mass of rock between Conway and Llandudno. The castle is supposed to have been erected soon after the Norman Conquest.

Obituary Memoirs.

" Emori|nolo ; sed me esse mortuum nihil æstimo."—Epicharmus.

MR. ROBERT A. C. GODWIN-AUSTEN, F.R.S., F.G.S., &c., died on November 25. He was the eldest son of the late Sir Henry E. Austen, of Shalford, Surrey, and married the only daughter and heiress of the late General Sir Henry T. Godwin, K.C.B., whose name he assumed. He was a gentleman well known in the antiquarian world, and most distinguished as a geologist. His writings date back to 1835, when he contributed to the *Philosophical Magazine* a paper on a raised beach near Torquay. "Mr. Godwin-Austen's views on the lacustrine origin of the old red sandstone," remarks the *Athenæum*, "though strongly opposed at the time by Murchison, were warmly espoused by Prof. (now Sir A.) Ramsay, and are at present accepted by almost every geologist." In 1862 the Geological Society awarded to him the Wollaston Medal.

MR. JOHN ASKEW ROBERTS, of Oswestry, a well-known antiquary, died on December 10, after a long illness. He was the founder of the *Oswestry Advertiser*, and down to his death edited an antiquarian column of that journal called "Bygones." He was also the author of several antiquarian papers and other works of local interest.

DR. KARL MAYER, formerly Librarian to the Prince Consort, who died at Berlin, December 9, was well known as an authority on philology, and distinguished for researches in the Celtic languages.

MR. JAMES BUCKMAN, F.G.S., F.S.A., &c., Professor of Geology and Botany at the Royal Agricultural College at Cirencester, died on the 23rd November. He was the author of several well-known works, including "The Geology of the Cotteswolds," "Our Triangle: Letters on the Geology, Botany, and Archæology of the Neighbourhood of Cheltenham," "The Ancient Straits of Malvern; or, an Account of the former Marine conditions which separated England and Wales," and "The Remains of Roman Art." Mr. Buckman enriched Cirencester with a fine museum of Roman antiquities, and with a large collection of fossils. The former are deposited in the Corinthian Museum and the latter at the Royal Agricultural College.

M. VASSILY VASSLIEVICH BAUER, Professor of Modern History in the University of St. Petersburg, died on the 18th Nov. The *Athenæum* states that besides his treatises on the Athenian hegemony and on the government of the Greek Tyranni, M. Bauer has left a series of remarkable essays, among which may be particularly noted "Russia's Relations with the Emperors of the Holy Roman Empire in the 15th and 16th Centuries," and a criticism of Gruber's " Der Jesuiten-Orden."

THE REV. ABRAHAM HUME, LL.D., Honorary Canon of Liverpool, and a well-known archæologist and traveller, died in November at his residence at Liverpool. Dr. Hume was a Fellow of the Royal Society of Northern Antiquaries at Copenhagen, and of the Society of Antiquaries and Statistical Society, London, and an honorary and corresponding member of several other learned societies of the kingdom. He was for six years president of the Historical Society of Lancashire and Cheshire. Dr. Hume was the author, *inter alia*, of "Sir Hugh of Lincoln ; or, An Examination of an Ancient Tradition respecting the Jews," "Ancient Meols; or, Some Account of the Antiquities found on the Coast of Cheshire," "The Growth of the Episcopate in England and Wales during Seventeen Centuries," "The Ecclesiastical History of Liverpool," &c. Many of his writings have appeared in the transactions of learned societies and in periodical publications on history and archæology, topography, and general literature.

Meetings of Learned Societies.

BRITISH ARCHÆOLOGICAL ASSOCIATION.—*Nov.* 19, first meeting of the Session 1884-5 ; Mr. T. Morgan, F.S.A., in the chair. The election of twenty-five new associates was announced by Mr. L. Brock, and Mr. De Gray Birch read a long list of books lately presented to the library of the Association. Mr. Brock exhibited some fragments of fine old painted glass from Westbeare Church, near Canterbury, which he purposed replacing in a "harlequin" window. Mr. Myers exhibited some curious rings, fibulæ, and other articles of personal adornment, which he had lately procured in a foreign tour. Mr. Worthington Smith exhibited a curious hammer-head of stone, found in North Wales, and also another stone implement, probably a pestle, discovered by a labourer in Epping Forest. A letter was read from Mr. C. Roach Smith, describing a curious old British entrenchment near Hayling Island. Mr. C. H. Compton read an elaborate paper on the remains of the old Roman bridge across the Trent, near Newark, which he showed to correspond as nearly as possible with the statements of the "Iter Antoninum." A portion of these remains, partly of stone and partly of wood, had recently been blown up by dynamite as interfering with the navigation of the River Trent. Mr. H. Rolfe, C.E., sent some interesting drawings showing the construction of the piers of the bridge, two of which were found to be strongly framed of oak ; the spaces between the timbers of the piers were packed with freestone similar to Ancaster stone. Mr. A. Cope exhibited some beautiful examples of ancient bookbinding, and read some illustrative notes of the rise and progress of the bookbinder's art. Mr. G. R. Wright, F.G.A., described the brass of Sir W. de la Haye, of early fourteenth century date, in Oakwood Chapel, Surrey ; and Mr. W. Myers, F.S.A., exhibited a collection of bronze fibulæ from Treves and other European localities.—*Dec.* 3, Mr. Thomas Morgan, F.S.A., in the chair. Mr. C. Roach Smith, F.S.A., communicated the discovery of a curious Anglo-Saxon bucket found in North Wales. It has three bronze rings, and on the woodwork between these have been scratched mystic inscriptions. It had been deposited in the ground near an upright stone pillar, placed apparently to mark the spot. Dr. Woodhouse exhibited some medals relating to the Reign of Terror in France, and of the period of the Russian Alliance. Mr. Romilly Allen, F.S.A. (Scot.), reported a remarkable discovery in Yorkshire. During some works of enlargement of the gardens of the Rose and Crown Hotel at Ilkley, whilst an old wall was being demolished, there was noticed in the foundation a large stone, which, on being raised, was found to bear sculpture and an inscription. It is doubtless a Roman sepulchral stone, having the figure of a female seated, with two long plaits of hair, one falling on each side of the face. There are four lines of inscription, the sepulchral character of which is shown by the common termination H.S.E. The stone had been used as old building material, but had evidently been removed from the cemetery of the old Roman station of Olieane. The Chairman then read a paper on the results of the recent Congress at Tenby. After describing the large amount of local interest that had been taken in the proceedings, the lecturer reviewed the places visited, including those seen during the extra days (see vol. vi. pp. 239—242). A discussion followed, in which Mr. E. Walford and Mr. Wright took part. A paper was then read by Mr. George R. Wright on the "Royal Bounty Distributions," particularly that of Maunday at Whitehall. The ceremony of the distribution was described, and various articles used on the occasion were shown. Among them were a large wooden bowl, cups, red and white purses, and some marked linen. In illustration of the paper a collection of Maunday money was exhibited by Mr. A. Cope. A discussion ensued, in which Messrs. Bidwell, Compton, Birch, and Chasemore took part.

SOCIETY OF ANTIQUARIES.—*Nov.* 27, Dr. J. Evans, F.R.S., V.P., and subsequently Dr. E. Freshfield, V.P., in the chair. Mr. A. Nesbitt exhibited two fragments of Roman glass, probably portions of two plates or dishes, which he believed may have been used as architectural decorations. Mr. Niblett exhibited five Roman cinerary urns, of the usual type, found in Gloucestershire, on the line of the old Ermine Street. Mr. J. H. Middleton contributed the first part of a paper on "The Temple and Atrium of Vesta at Rome, and the adjacent Regia." The Regia, or residence of the Pontifex Maximus, was said to be the oldest existing example of domestic architecture in Rome.—*Dec.* 4, Dr. Edwin Freshfield, V.P., in the chair. Mr. R. S. Ferguson contributed a variety of "Archæological Notes" from Cumberland, and the remainder of Mr. J. H. Middleton's paper on recent excavations in Rome was read. This paper, which was illustrated by diagrams and sectional plans, minutely described the recently-discovered Rostra at Rome, and the Græcostasis with the "Umbilicus Romæ and Milliarium Aureum;" it was read by the Secretary, in the author's absence. It appears from this paper that nearly the whole of the *suggestus* of the platform and of the *rostra* in the Forum, from which Cicero and other orators spoke in the days of the Republic, have been brought into the light of day, thus carrying one step more nearly to completion the great work commenced by the late Mr. J. H. Parker, that of unburying the early history of Rome.—*Dec.* 11, Dr. E. Freshfield, V.P., in the chair. Mr. G. Lambert exhibited the civic maces of Tenby, Pembroke, and Haverfordwest, which were, he said, of early date, viz., 1630—40, and had been found, on the recent visit of the British Archæological Congress to Pembrokeshire, to be in a very battered condition. They had now been carefully repaired and restored—a proof of the local advantages to be derived from the summer congresses of our leading archæological societies. Mr. J. P. Earwaker exhibited a collection of curious ecclesiastical and civil seals, which were explained in detail by Mr. C. S. Perceval. Mr. Everard Green, in a paper entitled " O Sapientia !" gave a learned and elaborate account of the antiphons used in the services of the Roman Catholic Church, and which varied at different dates and places ; apparently they were never less than seven, nor more than ten, and they were all taken out of the Holy Scriptures. The Rev. Dr. A. T. Lee expressed a hope that no steps would be taken by the Government to remove parish registers out of the charge of the clergy, and also suggested that the open space on the west side of Westminster Hall might be utilised as a repository for national monuments now that the Abbey was more than full.

ROYAL ARCHÆOLOGICAL INSTITUTE.—*Dec.* 4, Mr. J. Bain, vice-president, in the chair. Mr. W. H. St. John Hope read a paper on "The Augustinian Priory of the Holy Trinity at Repton," which he had lately examined, and where he had carefully excavated the ground plan of the church and the adjoining buildings. Mr. Hope gave an interesting account of the Priory, showing that it was originally founded as an establishment subordinate to the mother-house of the order at Cork ; and he gave a brief account of what is known of its history down to the dissolution of religious houses ; and "The Menhir Autel at Kernuz, Pont l'Abbé, Brittany," formed the subject of a paper by Admiral Tremlet, which was read in his absence by the secretary.

HISTORICAL.—*Nov.* 20, Lord Aberdare in the chair. Mr. Oscar Browning read a paper "On the Commercial Treaty between France and England in 1786." The eighteenth article of the treaty of Versailles (1783) contained a provision that a commercial treaty should be concluded between France and England within the space of two years from January 1, 1784. Jealousy of France prevented anything being done until the time had nearly expired. Mr. William Eden, afterwards Lord Auckland, was sent to negotiate, twelve months' delay having been accorded. The French wished for free trade pure and simple, the English for reciprocity. Eventually the duties on French wines, brandies, and vinegars were reduced, and English hardware, woollens, and cottons were admitted into France on terms of reciprocity. The French Revolution practically abrogated the treaty, and prevented its effect from being visible ; but the general opinion was that the balance was in favour of England. The treaty remains a monument of the liberality of the French Government under Louis XVI. and De Vergennes, and of the enlightened commercial principles of Pitt. Mr. Browning showed the original copy of the treaty, lent for the occasion by Lord Auckland. A discussion followed, in which Messrs. Hyde Clarke, J. Heywood, G. Hurst, and Lord Aberdare took part.

NUMISMATIC.—*Nov.* 20, Dr. J. Evans, president, in the chair. Archdeacon Pownall exhibited several medals of Popes Calixtus III., Paul II., and Sixtus IV., and Mr. Copp another in gold of Innocent XII. Mr. Montagu made some remarks on the angels of Henry VI., issued during the short period of his restoration, and imitating similar coins struck by Edward IV. Of these he described four new unpublished types, specimens of which he exhibited from his own collection. Mr. C. F. Keary read a paper "On the Morphology of Coin-Types." The subject had been first approached by the President in his "Coinage of the Ancient Britons," and subsequently enlarged upon, in reference to the same class of coins, in a lecture delivered by him before the Royal Institution "On the Coinage of the Ancient Britons and Natural Selection." The study, Mr. Keary showed, might be carried through the whole range of numismatics, and would be one of great use not only to the numismatist, but to the ethnologist, who was often obliged to conjecture the epoch of any implement or ornament by reference to the variations which it could be seen to have undergone.

ROYAL SOCIETY OF LITERATURE.—*Nov.* 26, Mr. J. Haynes in the chair. A paper was read by Mr. C. H. E. Carmichael " On the Border-land of the Middle Ages and of the Renaissance." Taking the fifteenth century as the period which constituted this borderland, Mr. Carmichael drew attention to some of its principal historical and literary features, noticing briefly Shakespeare's treatment of this period and the contemporary English and French historians and chroniclers, and dwelling particularly on the excellence and value of the memoirs of Philip de Comines. Mr. Carmichael also described the religious, social, and political characteristics of the age, the reforming councils of Constance, Basle, &c., and the state of the national literature in the chief European countries. In conclusion, he dwelt on the special interest attaching to the fifteenth century from its varied life, its activity in thought, together with the discoveries by sea and land, and the striking contrasts presented by its leading men.—*Athenæum.*

BIBLICAL ARCHÆOLOGY.—*Dec.* 2, the Rev. St. Vincent Beechey, Hon. Canon of Manchester, in the chair. The following papers were read : " On the Egyptian Belief concerning the Shade or Shadow of the Dead," and " On some Egyptian Rituals of the Roman Period," by Dr. Samuel Birch.

ROYAL HISTORICAL SOCIETY.—*Dec.* 18, Lord Aberdare, President, in the chair ; Mr. Robert Walker read a paper on " Fiji : its Peoples, Traditions, and Customs."

PROVINCIAL.

CAMBRIDGE ANTIQUARIAN SOCIETY.—*Nov.* 10, Mr. J. W. Clark, M.A. (President), in the chair. The Master of Peterhouse exhibited and presented to the Society a shilling of James I. which was lately found in digging a drain in the Lodge garden; *obv.* IACOBVS ˙MA˙ BRI ˙ FRA ˙ ET ˙ HI˙ REX crowned bust to right XII : *rev.* QVÆ ˙ DEVS ˙ CONIVNXIT ˙ NEMO ˙ SEPARET˙—in memory of the Act of Union. Professor Hughes gave an account of the opening of a tumulus at the north-western side of Upper Hare Park, *i.e.*, at the eastern end of the four-mile Racecourse, Newmarket. He also described the camp at Whitley, near Alston, and the portion of the Maiden Way south of that town. He thought that the characters of a Roman camp were well known, and—even allowing for such differences as might be expected in the mode of entrenchment adopted by troops of such different nationalities as were pressed into the service of Rome—that there was a uniformity of plan in all proved Roman camps. They were the camps of an aggressive people, holding their own in an enemy's territory. Theirs was a system which could be readily carried out by advancing forces quite irrespective of the natural features of the ground. All known British camps also showed a common mode of construction—a selection of strong positions, and an arrangement of the entrenchments so as to take advantage of natural features and to strengthen the weaker points. They are essentially the camps of native tribes well acquainted with the strong places and acting on the defensive. Having described in greater detail the characters referred to, he pointed out that the camp at Whitley was in all essential points British. He had found Roman pottery within the entrenchments, and had seen

Roman inscribed stones said to have been found close by. This he accounted for by supposing that the Romans had occupied a British strong-hold—as he had on a previous occasion shown they had done at Peny-gaer and Cissbury. Dr. Bryan Walker, in commenting upon the *Inquisitio Comitatus Cantabrigiensis*, observed that it was discovered amongst the Cottonian MSS. in the British Museum, and published in 1876, having evidently been overlooked by Sir H. Ellis when he included the *Inquisitio Eliensis* in the third volume of the Domesday publication. It gives for the whole of Cambridgeshire, except a small portion where the MS. is defective, the full particulars which Domesday only states for Norfolk Suffolk, and Essex. It is arranged according to townships, Domesday being arranged according to the names of the tenants-in-capite; and gives the total hidage of each township, which Domesday does not give; and comparison of these totals with the items enables us to detect errors of considerable importance in the Great Record; the transcriber having frequently omitted to note when he changed from one *vill* to another. The Saxon hidage in all cases tallies with the tabulation of the component holdings in the vills; the Norman does not, and where there is a variation, the Norman estimate is generally the lower, indicating the growth of Beneficial Hidation, or remission of taxation. The parcels being often expressed in acres, and the total in hides and virgates, we find that a hide was usually 120 acres, but sometimes 100, 96, or 80; these latter instances, however, are few, being only six or seven in number, whilst in 23 cases the hide is 120 acres. This clearly means 120 acres, whatever these acres were, in corn-crop each year, and therefore taxable; with another 60 in fallow or *warecta*, therefore paying no tax. In the 80-acre hides, cultivated in two shifts, 80 similarly in corn, and 80 waiting in fallow. Whether the intermediate hides of 96 and 100 were two-shift or three-shift, it is impossible to say from our existing data. The spelling of local names varies greatly in the "Inquisitio" from that in the Domesday. The word *sol* is used for *hida* in two places, Bassingbourne and Melbourne; and *Consul* as an equivalent for *Comes* in four instances. *Sol*, he observed, seems connected with the *solin*, or *sullung*, a name for hide, used generally in Kent, and occasionally in Essex, Sussex, and Berks. The "Inquisitio" always specifies "carucæ villanis" where the Domesday has "carcucæ hominum;" whence it is to be argued that the "villani" and "bordarii" alone had ploughs and oxen, which they used to cultivate the land in demesne as well as their own plots, and this is confirmed by reference to the Hunts. Domesday, where the regular entry is "tot car. in dominico; *x* villani et *y* bordarii habent tot car." Professor Skeat explained the word *sol* to mean a plough, and said that it was still so used in Devonshire. After a few remarks from Mr. Pell, Mr. Cunning-ham expressed his great interest in the paper, and his hope that Dr. Walker's analysis of the "Inquisitio" might soon be in their hands, so that they might be able to use it side by side with the Domesday. The President exhibited and described two fine specimens of the Bison priscus and the Bos primogenius, dug up in the Fens of Cambridgeshire.

HAILEYBURY COLLEGE ANTIQUARIAN SOCIETY.—*Oct.* 13, the Rev. G. E. Jeans, President, in the chair. The Rev. H. C. Wright gave some account of the doings of the Art Section during the past year. Mr. H. R. Ford read a paper on some places of antiquarian interest in Middlesex, including Tottenham, Hadleigh, Kingsbury, Heston, and Enfield. At the last-named town, the chief among many places of interest are the remains of the Palace, which was built by Edward VI. for the Princess Elizabeth, who often stayed there. The present building is only a part of the original, being a portion of the centre and south wing. In White Webb's Park may be seen White Webb's House, which fell under suspicion at the time of the Gunpowder Plot, on account of Guy Fawkes having been in the habit of visiting it before his apprehension. The President then proceeded to narrate some "holiday experiences." Beginning with Cambridgeshire, he spoke of the very fine Early-English church at Cherry-Hinton. Passing on into Norfolk, he dealt with the church of St. Margaret, at Lynn, which is almost unique among parish churches in the possession of two western towers, both of different date. He also described the Priory at Castle Acre and the Church, which contains a very fine font cover, a very good specimen of the beautiful woodwork that forms a special feature of Norfolk churches. He next mentioned the parish church at West Walton, the tower of which—standing at a distance of thirty-six feet from the church itself—forms a gateway. He also spoke of the Priory Church at Dunstable, which has a Norman nave and Early-English west front ; the famous three spires of Coventry ; Glasgow Cathedral, which is the most important Early English church in Scotland ; Leicester Abbey and Town ; and the Church of Wheathamstead, in Hertfordshire, which possesses a lantern tower.

LANCASHIRE AND CHESHIRE ANTIQUARIAN SOCIETY.—At a conversazione held at the Town-hall, Manchester, on Dec. 11, Dr. E. A. Freeman delivered an address in which he urged antiquarians to remember that their local researches tended to clear up the history of England, and the history of England was only part of a still greater whole—the history of Europe. There was hardly any kind of local research, down to the very smallest, which could not in some way help in that direction. They would find that every district and town had something in its curiosities and history characteristic of itself. It would be almost possible for the chief districts and cities of England to give a kind of definition, marking out the great facts in their history which distinguished one from another. For instance, while Carlisle was a city which was in ruins from the Danish invasion to the latter end of the eleventh century, Exeter had gone on from the very earliest times without any break. The county of Chester, again, stood out as having a greater degree of separation and independence from the mass of the kingdom than any other part. Then in Domesday there was no such county as Lancashire. It was Cheshire to the Ribble, and it was Yorkshire beyond. With regard to chief towns, one of the differences between France and England was that in France the oldest towns of the country—those which were the greatest in olden times—had remained the greatest, while in England the exact contrary was the case, with the two obvious exceptions of Paris and London. The greatest towns in France to-day were the oldest cities ; Marseilles dating from the sixth century B.C., and Lyons, so intimately associated with the Roman power in Gaul. But in England the oldest and most famous cities were no longer the greatest. In the history of the newer places— Manchester, Liverpool, Birmingham—there was much that was instructive. There were few places in England which had absolutely sprung out of the ground as many towns had in America. The three towns which he had mentioned, though modern in their importance, had existed from early time.

PENZANCE ANTIQUARIAN SOCIETY.—The Penzance Natural History and Antiquarian Society have had three nights' conversazione at Mowab House, Penzance, on December 4, 5, 6. The newly-elected President,

Rev. W. S. Lach-Szyrma, opened the proceedings with a few remarks on the first night. A series of about a dozen papers on various scientific subjects, by Messrs. Ralfs, Marquand, Magor, Barnett, Tregellas, and Baily, were delivered during the three evenings.

ROYAL HISTORICAL AND ARCHÆOLOGICAL ASSOCIATION OF IRE-LAND.—The quarterly general meeting was held in the Town Hall, Sligo, Oct. 1, Colonel Cooper, D.L., of Markree Castle, in the chair. Colonel Wood-Martin, hon. local secretary, read the minutes of the last quarterly meeting held at Armagh, which were signed by the chairman. Mr. W. F. Wakeman represented the Rev. James Graves, hon. general secretary, who was unavoidably absent through indisposition. Colonel Wood-Martin read his paper on "The Battlefield of Northern Moytura," now known as Moytirra, which is situated fifteen miles from Sligo, on a high tableland overlooking Lough Arrow. A carefully executed map of the district, prepared by Mr. C. B. Jones, C.E., County Surveyor of Sligo, member of the Association, accompanied by a series of etchings and plans prepared by Mr. Wakeman, showing the various mounds, stone circles, cromlechs, and other monuments which still remain on this historic site, illustrated the paper, and were exhibited to the meeting. The covering stone of one of these cromlechs is computed to weigh at least seventy-five tons. Some gold and bronze antiquities have been found amongst these monuments, though whether they had any immediate connection with these or not has not as yet been decided. The battlefield of Northern Moytura has been supposed by Petrie, Wylde, O'Donovan, and others to have been on a totally different site, which Colonel Wood-Martin's researches now show to have been an entirely erroneous supposition. Mr. Wakeman made some remarks on the status of the County of Sligo as being one of the most interesting localities in the British Isles, containing, as it does, a complete and unbroken series of monuments of all kinds—military, ecclesiastic, and domestic—from the earliest period known to Irish history down to the seventeenth century. He referred in particular to the collection of antiquities on the Island of Innismurray, which lies about four and a half miles off the coast of Sligo in the Atlantic Ocean. Here, within the bounds of a pre-historic fort, similar in almost every respect to the great duns on the Islands of Arran, are grouped together a number of ecclesiastical structures, churches, houses, and beehive-shaped cells erected as early as the sixth century. The founder (St. Molaise) was a friend and contemporary of St. Columba of Iona, the apostle of the Picts. One of the churches still styled *Teach Molais* remains as perfect as the day it was built, retaining even its stone roof. The cemeteries on the island, of which there are a considerable number, retain numerous *leaghts* or monumental stones inscribed in the characters of the sixth and following centuries, with the names of the early ecclesiastics who were buried beneath. Mr. Wakeman also read a paper on some ancient churches and other structures which the County of Sligo contains. After the meeting the members and their friends visited Sligo Abbey, where they examined the various points of interest in connection with that historic structure. The next place visited was the Deer Park adjoining Hazlewood Demesne, where the wonderful rude stone monument, unique in Ireland, which has been happily called the Irish Stonehenge, comprising three well-marked trilithons, was carefully examined and its possible character discussed. An excursion was also made to Drumcliffe, where the interesting stone crosses and the remains of Sligo's only round tower were visited, terminating the meeting.

Antiquarian News & Notes.

THE annual meeting of the St. Paul's Ecclesiological Society will be held on January 31.

POPE LEO has issued a bull declaring the bones of the apostle St. James, discovered some years since in the Cathedral of Santiago, to be genuine.

THE 125th anniversary of Schiller's birth has been celebrated at Weimar.

MR. SAMUEL RAWSON GARDINER, B.A., of Christ Church, Oxford, who has just been elected a Fellow of All Souls' College, has undertaken to write anew the History of England 1642-9.

THE REV. W. H. SEWELL, Vicar of Yaxley, Suffolk, announces for publication with the new year the first number of a cheap monthly parish magazine, called *Yaxley Bells*.

IT appears that there is some doubt whether the museum promised conditionally by Mr. Ruskin to the town of Sheffield will not find instead a home at Evesham.

THE site of the old Horsemonger-lane Gaol, having been laid out as a public recreation ground, has been " taken over " by the vestry of Newington Butts.

THE Basilewsky collection of objects of art and curiosity, long one of the best known in Paris, has been acquired by the Russian Government for, it is said, 500,000 francs.

MR. A. C. SWINBURNE possesses the copy of Wither which belonged to Lamb, and which Lamb annotated copiously. Mr. Swinburne has made the volume the subject of an article in the *Nineteenth Century*.

OWING to official etiquette, application must be made at the Bethnal-green Free Library for the illustrated catalogue of silver plate (from the collection of Mr. Joseph Bond) now on view at the Bethnal-green Museum.

THE HON. D. A. BINGHAM, author of " The Letters and Dispatches of the First Napoleon," has finished a " History of the Bastille." He has also in preparation " The Marriages of the Bourbons," as a sequel to his previous work on " The Marriages of the Bonapartes."

MESSRS. LONGMANS & CO. will shortly publish the first volume of a series of "Lives of Greek Statesmen," by Sir G. W. Cox. The series, which will be brought down to the dissolution of the Achaian League, will be completed probably in four volumes.

THE Trappist Fathers of the Abbey of the Three Fountains, near Rome, says the *Weekly Register*, have obtained a diploma of honour at the Turin Exhibition, for their labours in draining the Campagna around Rome.

" A HISTORY OF THE PARSEES," by Mr. Dosabhai Franigi Karaka, S.I.C., has been published by Messrs. Macmillan & Co. in two volumes. The Prince of Wales has been pleased to accept the dedication of the work.

THE articles bought by a Syndicate at the sale of the Fontaine Collection, have, with two exceptions, been repurchased by the British Museum and the South Kensington authorities. The exceptions are a pair of Palissy candlesticks, said to be worth £1,500.

A VOLUME of papers bearing on Biblical archæology and criticism, read at the Monday meetings at the lodgings of the Regius Professor of Hebrew, Oxford, will be published by the Clarendon Press.

Professor J. Wordsworth, Canon Driver (Regius Professor of Hebrew), Professor Sanday, Dr. Edersheim, and Dr. Neubauer are among the contributors.

THE noble banqueting hall of the celebrated Norman keep at Castle Hedingham, in Essex, the stronghold of the De Veres, presented an animated appearance on Nov. 25, when it witnessed the annual dinner of the Hinckford Conservative Club, which had been held within its walls only once before, on the occasion of the visit of Lord Beaconsfield (then Mr. Disraeli) in 1849.

EXTENSIVE remains of a Roman dwelling have been discovered in a field near Purwell Mill, Hitchin, Herts. A room with a tessellated pavement of red and white in a fair state of preservation has been opened to view. The dwelling consisted of several rooms, and in one place there had been a hypocaust. The walls were built chiefly of large flints which had been roughly squared. A lane, which in Roman times probably connected this district with ancient Verulam, runs close by the dwelling.

THE sale of the Syston Library, formed chiefly by the late Sir John Hayford Thorold, at the end of the last and beginning of the present centuries, commenced on Friday, December 12, and extended over eight days. An account of the sale is unavoidably deferred to our next number. The Mazarin Bible was knocked down on the second day to Mr. B. Quaritch, of Piccadilly, for £3,900, a sum larger by £700 than a copy has ever realised before.

A STRIKING discovery has been made at Alresford, near Colchester, of a complete Roman villa. Excavations made on the 24th November resulted in several tessellated pavements being laid bare, extending over a space of some 300 feet. Several cinerary urns, &c., were discovered at the same time. This find is of special interest in view of the scarcity of Roman remains hitherto unearthed to the west of Colchester (*Camulodunum*).

FRESH results from the Essex earthquake of last spring have now come to light, in addition to the antiquarian losses recorded in our June number. One of the massive arches of the grand old ruin of St. Botolph's Abbey was thrown to the ground. The tower of Greenstead Church, near Colchester, has been severely damaged, and though of no architectural interest, its repair has led to the interesting discovery of some of the original holes made by Fairfax's cannon-balls in the famous siege of 1648. The tower of St. Mary's-at-the-Wall, Colchester, has also been injured, like so many others, at the summit. The upper part of this tower was completely battered down by Fairfax in 1648, and not rebuilt till 1729.

ON December 3 an ancient civic custom was observed at Guildhall, when, according to usage, gifts of black cloth (4½ yards each) were dispatched to the Lord Chancellor, the Lord Chief Justice, the Master of the Rolls, the Lord Chamberlain, the Vice-Chamberlain, the Lord Steward, the Treasurer and Comptroller of Her Majesty's Household, the Home Secretary, the Foreign Secretary, the Attorney-General, the Solicitor-General, the Recorder, and the Common Serjeant. The Town Clerk received a gift of six yards of black cloth and six of green, and his principal clerk four yards of black and four of green cloth. The cloth is called "livery cloth," and the custom has its origin from the time when the liverymen of the various Guilds used to wear the distinctive garb of their Companies.

IN view of the impending sale of a portion of the French Crown jewels, the following particulars about them will be read with interest. When they were valued just after the Revolution of 1789, they were estimated at £840,000, and they consisted of 7,482 diamonds, 506 pearls, 230 rubies, 150 emeralds, 134 sapphires, 71 topazes, eight garnets, and three amethysts. They were stolen from the Treasury, in which they had been deposited, and only a very small portion recovered, but the purchases made by Napoleon and the Bourbon Kings brought the total of the Crown jewels up to £900,000 when they were valued in 1832. When a fresh inventory was taken in 1875 it was found that the Crown jewels consisted of 77,486 stones, weighing over 19,000 carats, and a part of these will shortly be sold. It is a mistake, however, to suppose that all the objects of historical interest will be reserved, for many of the jewels which belonged to the Duchess Anne of Brittany, and became an appanage of the French Crown when she married Charles VIII., are to be disposed of, as also several articles bequeathed by Cardinal Richelieu.—*Times*.

Antiquarian Correspondence.

Sin scire labores,
Quære, age : quærenti pagina nostra patet.

All communications must be accompanied by the name and address of the sender, not necessarily for publication.

"GREEK FOLK-SONGS."

SIR,—Miss Garnett's "Greek Folk-songs from the Turkish Provinces of Greece" having been advertised for publication last spring, inquiries are constantly being addressed to me as editor, through home and foreign publishers and booksellers and others, as to the cause of the delay. Will you, therefore, kindly allow me to publicly answer these inquiries, which it would take a great deal of time to reply to privately and separately? The cause of the delay is simply this : the publisher, Mr. Elliot Stock, has declared that he will not "go on with the book" unless certain large payments are made to him which are not only not in accordance with, but, as we are advised, excluded by, the terms of the agreement ; and he has latterly announced that he has "put the matter into the hands of his solicitor to compel Miss Garnett to carry out her part of the agreement." As it is not known what part of her agreement Miss Garnett has, as alleged, "failed to carry out," Mr. Stock's threat was promptly answered by Miss Garnett's solicitor, who is also the solicitor to the Incorporated Society of Authors, and who informed Mr. Stock that he was ready to accept service of process on Miss Garnett's behalf. Nothing more has since then been heard from Mr. Stock, nor can anything, therefore, be said as to when the book will be published, though—to quote a letter of the printer's—"it has already been all set up six months, and the greater part of it nine months." I may add that, by the terms of the agreement, Mr. Stock takes *all* the profits from an edition of 500 copies, and that the book has been largely subscribed for. J. S. STUART GLENNIE.

Athenæum Club, Dec. 10, 1884.

[Mr. Stock's conduct in respect of this book ought to surprise no one who has read Mr. E. Walford's letter to Lord Talbot de Malahide.—ED. A. M. and B.]

"PORT" OR "GATE."

Sir,—As an interesting illustration of the identity or synonymous character of the terms " Port " or " Gate," permit me to call attention to the fact that these terms are used indiscriminately, and their identity is thus acknowledged, by the translators respectively of the Bible version and of the Prayer-book version of the Book of Psalms.

In the Bible version, Psalm ix. 14, we have the rendering, "In the *gates* of the daughter of Zion ;" whilst in the Prayer-book version we have, "In the *ports* of the daughter of Zion," thus showing that the translators considered it quite immaterial which term they employed. This authority for the identity of the terms must be regarded as valuable, and it is obviously quite as permissible to *apply these terms* in their synonymous character *to the laws of Athelstan* as to anything else, to use them as is done, for example, in the passage just cited, or to apply them, as is done by Sharon Turner, to the word *port-reeve* itself. And all that I have done is merely to make a similar use of these terms. The passage in the laws of Athelstan, to which *I applied them* in their synonymous character, *is not*, and never professed to be, a "*quotation.*" This must be apparent even to the merest tyro by the absence from it of inverted commas, whilst it will as readily be seen that inverted commas mark the *actual quotation* from the laws of Athelstan which immediately follows, *e.g.*, "every marketing must be within the port." Here, then, it will be observed that the synonym or "*gate*" is not introduced, in order in this case to leave the exact words of the *quotation* untouched, and thus clearly to show the difference between this and the preceding passage. *The application* thus made of the terms "port " *or* "*gate*" to the passage in the laws of Athelstan, will, I feel assured, be recognised as perfectly legitimate by everyone who is capable of appreciating the synonymous character of the terms in question.

Taunton, December, 1884.   James Hurly Pring, M.D.

Catalogues of rare and curious books, most of which contain the names of works of antiquarian interest, have reached us from Mr. J. Stillie, 19, George-street, Edinburgh ; Messrs. Fawn & Sons, 18, Queen's-road, Bristol (including a small library of French books) ; Mr. Charles Hutt, Clement's Inn-gateway, Strand, W.C. ; Messrs. Robson & Kerslake, 43, Cranbourne-street, Leicester-square (including a complete uncut set of the first edition of Berwick's works, a decorated MS., described in Dibdin's Reminiscences, &c.) ; Mr. W. P. Bennett, 3, Bull-street, Birmingham ; Mr. W. Downing, 74, New-street, Birmingham (containing a portion of the library of the late Canon the Hon. W. H. Lyttelton, Rector of Hagley) ; Mr. G. P. Johnston, 33, George-street, Edinburgh ; Mr. William Withers, Leicester ; Mr. Andrew Iredale, Torquay (including special lists of works relating to Devonshire and witchcraft) ; Mr. H. Edwardes, 20, Drury-court, Strand ; Messrs. Meehan, 32, Gay-street, Bath ; Mr. U. Maggs, 159, Church-street, Paddington-green, W. ; Messrs. Reeves & Turner, 196, Strand, W.C. ; Messrs. Taylor & Son, Northampton ; Mr. Jonathan Nield, Old Town-street, Plymouth ; Mr. Walter Scott, Bristo-place, Edinburgh ; Mr. George Harding, 19, St. John-street, Westminster ; Von Albert Cohn, Berlin ; Mr. George Redway, York-street, Covent-garden ; Mr. Francis Edwards, 83, High-street, Marylebone.

TO CORRESPONDENTS.

THE Editor declines to pledge himself for the safety or return of MSS. voluntarily tendered to him by strangers.

Books Received.

1. John Wycliffe and his English Precursors. By Prof. Lechler, D.D. Religious Tract Society. 1884.
2. Palatine Note-book. No. 47. Dec., 1884.
3. John Hopkins University Studies. Second Series, No. 11. Nov., 1884.
4. Bradford Antiquary. Part iii. Sept., 1884.
5. Le Livre. No. 59. Paris. Nov., 1884.
6. English Etchings. Part xliii. D. Bogue, 27, King William-street Charing-cross.
7. Miscellanea Genealogica et Heraldica. Second Series. Vol. i. No. 12. Dec., 1884.
8. Western Antiquary. Edited by W. H. K. Wright Nov., 1884.
9. Journal of the Hellenic Society. Vol. v. Nos. 1 and 2. Macmillan & Co. 1884.
10. Publications of the Pipe Roll Society. Vol. ii. 1884.
11. British Almanac and Companion for 1885. Edited by C. Mackeson. Stationers' Company.
12. Japanese Enamels. By J. L. Bowes. Sotheran & Co. 1884.
13. Japanese Marks and Seals. By J. L. Bowes. Sotheran & Co. 1884.
14. Mr. William Shakespeare's Tragedie of Romeo and Juliet. Published according to the True Originall Copies. Simpkin, Marshall & Co. 1884.
15. Second Annual Report of the Metropolitan Public Garden, Boulevard, and Playground Association. 1884.

Books, &c., for Sale.

Archdall's *Monasticon Hibernicum.* Apply to Rev. James Graves, Stonyford, co. Kilkenny.

Works of Hogarth (set of original Engravings, elephant folio, without text), bound. Apply by letter to W. D., 56, Paragon-road, Hackney, N.E.

Original water-colour portrait of Jeremy Bentham, price 2 guineas. Apply to the Editor of this Magazine.

A large collection of Franks, Peers' and Commoners'. Apply to E. Walford, 2, Hyde Park Mansions, N.W.

Books, &c., Wanted to Purchase.

Antiquarian Magazine and Bibliographer, several copies of No. 2 (February, 1882) are wanted, in order to complete sets. Copies of the current number will be given in exchange at the office.

Dodd's Church History, 8vo., vols. i. ii. and v.; Waagen's Art and Artists in England, vol. i.; East Anglian, vol. i., Nos. 26 and 29. The Family Topographer, by Samuel Tymms, vol. iii.; Notes and Queries, the third Index. Johnson's "Lives of the Poets" (Ingram and Cooke's edition), vol. iii. A New Display of the Beauties of England, vol. i., 1774. Chambers' Cyclopædia of English Literature, vol. i. Address, E. Walford, 2, Hyde Park Mansions, Edgeware-road, N.W.

E

EARLY READING AND WRITING MATERIALS.

Etched by W. B. RYE.

The *Antiquarian Magazine* *& Bibliographer.*

Early Reading and Writing Materials.

 N a previous volume of the ANTIQUARIAN MAGAZINE * we gave an illustration of a "horn-book," one of those curious aids to learning out of which our great-grandfathers and great-grandmothers learnt, not only their alphabets, but the first elements of religion. These "horn-books" appear to have been in use as far back as the early part of the sixteenth century, and to have become very common during the Elizabethan period; but, in consequence of the absence of dates upon the examples which are still met with, it is difficult to assign any precise date to the manufacture or issue of each. Two or three horn-books are preserved among the treasures of the British Museum; and references to the subject may be found in the pages of the "Journal of the British Archæological Association," vol. ix. 1854; Willis's "Current Notes," Oct. 1855; John Timbs' "Things not Generally Known," 1856; Chambers' "Book of Days," vol. i., and a few other works.

At a meeting of the British Archæological Association in 1853, a horn-book of the time of Charles I. was exhibited by Mr. Thomas Bateman, of Youlgreave, Derbyshire. It was found in taking down an old house at Middleton, near Youlgreave, in 1828; and Mr.

---

* See Volume ii. pp. 165—169.

Halliwell favoured the Association with the following observations respecting it : " Horn-books are, perhaps, the most curious relics of the educational system pursued by our ancestors that have been preserved to our times ; and yet we can scarcely say that, absolutely obsolete as they now are, they belong exclusively to any early period, for they were in current use till the commencement of the present century. They are now, however, so little known, that few persons are aware of their exact character; and on that account, the very curious specimen in the possession of Mr. Bateman, here engraved, is extremely worthy of notice. . . .

Horn-books of this early period are of the highest degree of rarity, and perhaps the specimen in Mr. Bateman's possession may be considered amongst the most curious known. It is a curious fact, that in after ages the rarity of a book or tract is almost invariably in inverse ratio to the extent of the impression. Thus, of tracts of the Elizabethan period, those which were circulated by thousands are now either lost, or exist in unique or very rare copies ; while books of a serious nature, of which only small numbers were printed, may be easily met with." By permission of the Council of the British Archæological Association we are enabled to give a *fac-simile* of one side of the Caroline horn-book above referred to. The portrait of King Charles will be easily recognised.

The plate prefixed as a frontispiece to this number has been kindly placed at our disposal by Mr. W. B. Rye, formerly of the British Museum, by whom it was etched many years ago. It exhibits, first, an English black-lead pencil-case of the date of 1565 ; secondly, a school-boy with horn-book, dated 1504 ; and, thirdly, a portable writing-desk of the twelfth century, with ink-horn, penknife, reed-pens, and sponge. The first subject, the pencil-case of 1565, Mr. Rye writes, is taken from Conrad Gesner's " De Rerum Fossilium,

Lapidum, et Gemmarum Figuris," &c., 1565 ; it is described at page 104 as follows :—

"Instrumenta varia diversorum artificum è diversis metallis fiunt. Stylus inferius depictus, ad scribendum factus est, plumbi cujusdam (factitii puto, quod aliquos Stimmi * Anglicum vocare audio) genere, in mucronem derasi, in manubrium ligneum inserto."

Beckmann, in his "History of Inventions" (Bohn's edit., vol. ii. p. 390), observes : "The antiquity of black-lead pencils cannot be determined by the help of diplomatic documents. It might be traced out with more ease were it known by what mineralogical writer, *plumbago*, and the uses of it, were first mentioned. . : . . The first author in whose writings I have as yet found certain mention of *plumbago* is Conrad Gesner, a man whose name can never be mentioned without respect. In his book on fossils, printed at Zurich in 1565, he says that people had pencils for writing which consisted of a wooden handle, with a piece of lead, or, as he believed, an artificial mixture, called by some *stimmi Anglicanum* [Anglicum]. Such pencils must at that time have been scarce, because he has given a figure of them in a wood-cut. To judge by this, the pencil seems to have had a wooden sheath or covering."

The boy with the horn-book is from the border of the title-page to the "Margarita Philosophica" of Georgius Reisch, printed at Strasbourg, by Joannes Grüninger, in 1504. The work is a kind of encyclopædia, and has numerous curious wood engravings. The author was Prior of the Chartreuse at Friburg, and Confessor of the Emperor Maximilian I. The most important of Grüninger's illustrated publications are noticed in Didot's "Histoire de la Gravure sur Bois," 1863, p. 98, &c.

The desk is taken from a French archæological publication, and the following extract relating to it has been supplied by Mr. Rye :—

"Pupitre du xii. siècle. Petit pupitre portatif, que l'on mettait sur les genoux pour écrire : l'encrier fixé sur le côté, simplement une corne insérée dans un trou, l'un a de plus le canif, les instruments de transcription et une petite éponge. Ces instruments sont des bouts de roseau dont se servent encore tous les Orientaux pour écrire."

---

* Stimmi, from the Greek στίμμι, Antimony. Ainsworth's Latin Dictionary, where the reader is referred to Pliny, xxxiii. 6.

Forecastings of Nostradamus.

By C. A. WARD.

PART VI.

(Continued from p. 34, ante.)

CENTURY III. QUATRAIN 70.

" La grande Bretagne comprinse l'Angleterre,
Viendra par eaux si fort à inonder.
La Ligue neufve d'Ausonne fera guerre,
Que contre eux ils se viendront bander."

"When England goes under the name of Great Britain, a great inundation of water will come. The new alliance made in Italy will make war against anyone who shall make war against them."

Of course, England was called Great Britain when Scotland became united with her, in 1603.

D. D. says that there was a great inundation in the third year of James I., and after the *Union* alluded to by Nostradamus. In the year 1526 an alliance, called *Liga Sancta,* was entered into between the King of France, the Pope, and the Venetians, and in 1606 they concluded a second alliance, which was but defensive. In 1607 the sea overflowed a vast tract of land in Somerset.

Charles I., born in 1600, Nov. 18, at Dunfermline, when Mercury, Lord of the Horizon, was combust and following Saturn cosmically with the sun: the sun leaning to conjunction with Mars, and the moon in her worst location, in quadrature with Mars.

In 1625, Charles I. succeeded to the throne, and of the ominous constellation Nostradamus writes thus :—

CENTURY V. QUATRAIN 93.

" Soubs le terroir du rond globe lunaire,
Lorsque sera dominateur Mercure :
L'isle d'Ecosse fera un luminaire,
Qui les Anglois mettra à déconfiture."

This D. D. translates oddly enough thus :—

"In regione aëris sublunari,
Mercurius shall govern,
When a light shall be born in Scotland,
Which will put England into great disorder."

More literally, it will run :—

"Under the jurisdiction of the round globe of the moon, dominated by the influence of Mercury, the island of Scotland will produce a luminary (or prince) that will greatly discomfort the English people."

If we suppose this to refer to Charles, it wants no further determination.

In 1609 James I. tried to induce the Scotch to conform to some sort of uniformity in Church ceremony, but he stopped short of endeavouring to enforce it. Archbishop Laud, in 1637, advised Charles to introduce the English Liturgy into the churches of Scotland, *auctoritate regis*, with the rashness of a madman flying in the face of Fate, Quem Deus vult perdere prius dementat.

It was established by royal mandate the 23rd July, 1637, and by royal proclamation of 20th June, 1638, withdrawn, undertaking that no English ceremonies should be forced on the Scotch Church. This came too late, and the Scotch entered into a Covenant never to permit the establishment of the English Ritual ; or, as they called it, the English *Service Book.* In 1643 England, urged Puritanically, went further, and established the Solemn League to like effect.

In 1641 the discontent had spread to Ireland, and, as usual in such cases, English reasoning and Scotch logic quickly developed into blood on the other side of St. George's Channel. The English are often content with black ink, but an Irish Celt must always write the record of his dissent in a rubric of blood. In the first four months of their antagonism 150,000 Protestants massacred by Papists could be reckoned up by name. " Tantum religio potuit suadere malorum," is D. D.'s comment on this.

Laud expiated his mistake with his head on Tower Hill, and the King himself was to follow five years later at Whitehall, and after being yielded up (as Nostradamus puts it, ii. 53, " Le juste sang, par prix damné sans crime)" by the Scotch to the English. In 1624 Prince Charles favoured the impeachment of Cranfield, Earl of Middlesex, at which King James grew angry, and told him he " would yet have his bellyful of impeachments." The old King hardly knew that Westminster Hall would ring to the impeachment of royalty itself.

Century VIII. Quatrain 40.

" Le sang du juste, par Tore et les Torads,
Pour se venger contre les Saturnins :
Au nouveau lac plongeront la Menade,
Puis marcheront contre les Albanins."*

---

* This verse is given somewhat differently in the edition of 1558, but it appears to be less interpretable than the above.

"The blood of the righteous, for Torah and Torees sakes, cries for vengeance against the *Saturnine* rebels, who will plunge the priestess of Bacchus, *la ménade*, into the sea of their novelties, and march afterwards against the Scotch."

His remarks on "Tore et les Torads" are so curious that I subjoin the whole in a foot-note;* suffice it here to say that he interprets them to stand for Royalists, whilst the "Saturnins" are Roundheads. For the sake of the law-abiding people (the Torah and Torees) the King's blood cries for vengeance against the Saturnian or Titanic Roundheads. The intoxicated people shall plunge into a new course of wickedness (*Au nouveau lac plongeront la Ménade†*) and then will march against the Highlanders. This was all fulfilled, says D. D., in 1650, when King Charles II., after the conclusion of his capitulation with the Scotch at Breda, was in the north with an army consisting chiefly of Highlanders. On 3rd Sept., 1650, at

---

* "Some people stick to the Church of *England* discipline, even to a superstition, and to their last breath. These people had the nick-name of *Tories*, cast on them by the Cromwellites; which is as much as to say some have the law of the Church put upon them, from the Hebrew *Torah*, which signifies the *law*, or the *law of the Church of God*. Perhaps did Cromwell himself, or some of his confident advocates and ministers, designedly invent that cursed name; as it is likely from what happened in the year 1651, when the Parliament ordered the law-books to be translated out of *Latin* into *English*, wherein the lawyers took a great deal of freedom by using the *verbalia passiva* very frequently, and almost on all occasions, according to their own fancy and pleasure. As, for instance, Apellans and apellatus, they made an *Apealer* and an *Apealee*; the *Arrestans* and *Arrestatus*, the *Challenger* and the *Challengee*; as likewise the *Warranter* and the *Warrantee*; the *Voucher* and the *Vouchee*; the *Leaser* and the *Leasee*; in which manner they used likewise the terms of *Torer* and *Toree*; a *Torer*, in the first place—that is, a promoter of the Common Prayer and Church of England service; and an imposer of human traditions, instead of God's law; and, in the second place, a *Toree*; that is, one that submits, and suffereth such laws to be imposed upon him. Which *nomina verbalia passiva*, so much in vogue amongst the English lawyers, are not at all English but meer French, and the *Participium Passivum* itself; and more proper to the neat *French*, than the corrupted *Provincial Dialect*; which last our Nostradamus very often mixes with his style; wherein they commonly use to say, *Les confirmads, les restads, les escilads*, instead of *les confirmez, les restez, les exilez*, etc. And according to this *Dialect* one must say, LES TORADS, instead of LES TOREZ, and thus does our Poet."

† Ménade. The μαινάδες were Baccantes, the priestesses who celebrated the festivals of Bacchus. Stephanus says, that it is to be explained not only as Bacchic, but as frantic, and this is unquestionably the meaning here. The Greek word appears to be connected with the Sanscrit *man*, to think, and thence the word *Manyu*, anger, is derived. They used to run dishevelled, half-naked, and, brandishing the thyrsus, in their fury they would kill and behead men whom they encountered by the way, and carry off their heads leaping with rage and joy. According to Nonnus they were virgins so careful of their chastity, that they slept with a cincture of serpents. Juvenal attributes no such severity of virtue to them, but their pretensions to such superlative purism renders them all the fitter emblems of the canting Puritans, who won Cromwell's battles for him, practically blaspheming the name of the Lord. To *speak* ill of God hurts religion less than to *do* ill to man in the sacred name of Heaven."

Dunbar, Cromwell, short of provisions, and with an army numbering barely half as many as the Scotch, gave the attack not far from Edinburgh, and defeated them completely. He treated the Highlanders worst, shipping them to America *to be there sold as slaves*. He sent the Great Seal of Scotland as a trophy to London. This seems accomplished in

CENTURY VIII. QUATRAIN 56.

" La bande foible la terre occupera :
 Ceux du *haut lieu* feront horribles cris :
Le gros troupeau d'estre coin troublera,
 Tombe près d'Edinbro: descouverts les escrits."

"The weak army shall occupy the field [after the battle]. The Highlanders shall raise horrible shouts [before the engagement and after the defeat]. The larger force shall be hampered for lack of space from being cornered [d'estre (en) coin ?], and fall close to Edinburgh, and their papers fall into the victor's hands."

"Ceux du *haut lieu*" comes very near to the *Highlanders*.

Also Cromwell captured the whole of the papers of the Scotch War Office, as well as the Great Seal, on this occasion.

All that was done here, however, could not prevent Charles from being crowned on January 1, 1651, at Scone, in Scotland, and in the next summer he penetrated into England, followed up by Cromwell and his Ironsides.

Following on this comes Quatrain 57, which has been interpreted of Cromwell, but unless it be a type of two handles of the old ecclesiastical sort, I think it will apply better to the Bonaparte commonly called *Great*, and who is intellectually great if placed in comparison with Victor Hugo's *Le Petit*. In Nostradamus the succession of the quatrains commonly means no more than that they lie together as one bean touches another in a bushel measure. So we may pass freely, dropping No. 57, to—

CENTURY VIII. QUATRAIN 58.

" Regne en querelle aux frères divisé,
 Prendre les armes et le nom Britannique
(Tiltre Anglican) sera tard avisé,
 Surprins, de nuict mené á l'air Gallique."

"When a kingdom in quarrel divided between two brothers takes up arms and the name of Great Britain (which is then the title of England), his action under advice shall prove too tardy, and surprised, he will be driven to seek the air of France under the shelter of night."

The two brothers here are to be taken as being the two nations of England and Scotland. Prince Charles had a doubt about the fealty of the Scotch, and when finally he made up his mind to risk the great effort the Parliamentary side had developed into a strength that he was quite unequal to cope with. On September 3 he was so over-powered at the Battle of Worcester, that he could scarcely effect his escape, but under the cover of night he managed to get from the city of Worcester, though he had to fly from place to place for weeks, till at last, on October 20, he got well shipped for Dieppe, and finally reached his mother safely at St. Germain.

(To be continued.)

King Alfred in Somerset and the Legend of St. Neot.

By Mrs. C. G. Boger.

PART II.

(Continued from p. 21.)

IT was some years since Alfred had visited his brother—who now, indeed, by his retirement into Cornwall, was removed further from him—possibly he shrank from meeting the stern and unsparing criticism of that true friend ; but at last he betook himself once more to him for friendship and counsel. In the interim St. Neot had visited Rome ; he had left his solitary cell and founded a monastery. It was nine years since the brothers had met, and Neot, though receiving Alfred honourably as his Sovereign, and lovingly as his brother, reproved him sharply, "for he grieved from the bottom of his heart" for his sin, and his prophetic spirit foretold what must befall him as a recompense for his pride of heart ; nevertheless, he regarded not the reproof of the man of God, and refused to receive his words. Yet his conscience must have been awakened, for he went to his house in awe and great fear, and from that time came frequently to see the saint, and seek from him advice and counsel. At last came the last earthly interview, and the prophecy of final vengeance.

"Thou seest, O King!" said St. Neot, " what now thou sufferest from thine enemies, and thou shalt suffer more hereafter ; for in thy kingdom thou art proud and tyrannical, whereas before the eyes of the Divine Majesty thou oughtest rather, with the King and Prophet David, to have shown thyself meek and humble. Therefore, by a foreign nation that knoweth not Christ, thou shalt be driven thence. Alone shalt thou escape from thine enemies, and shall be concealed under the hands of God, and so for thy sins shalt thou remain many days. Nevertheless I have obtained for thee, by my prayers, that if thou wilt turn from thine iniquities God will yet have mercy on thee and restore thee to thy state and sceptre; and behold I go the way of all flesh, but when Divine Providence shall have fulfilled its purpose concerning thee, and shall have rightly punished thee for thy misdeeds, then be thou of good heart, and put thy trust in Him who rulest all things, and pray for His assistance, and Almighty God shall hear thy prayers and restore thee again to thy place."

And so it came to pass; Alfred had alienated the love of his subjects; and when, in the year 878, the Danes made a sudden irruption into Wiltshire and the adjoining districts, some of the inhabitants submitted; others fled into the Isle of Wight; and Alfred, deserted by all save a small band of trusty followers, found himself driven to take refuge in the marshes formed by the confluence of the Thone and the Parret; and on a spot slightly elevated above the surrounding country, since called the Isle of Athelney, he took refuge for several months. Yet in this, his deepest distress, William of Malmesbury tells us the people of Hampshire, Wiltshire, and Somerset, " held fast by their allegiance."

We are not told how he disposed of his wife, Elswitha, and their children at this time; but evidently for greater security—perhaps for both—he was alone, save for his aged mother, Osburga. It is likely enough that the Danes had destroyed the religious home in which she had taken refuge; at any rate, here we find her with him in Athelney. It was perhaps before his mother joined him that the story of Alfred and the cakes, which has been repeated *ad nauseam*— and yet which *must* be told again amongst the legends of Somerset— though legend it scarcely is, for it appears in the pages of that most scrupulously truthful of all historians, Asser, in his Life of Alfred. We give it in his own words :—

" At the same time the above-named Alfred, King of the West Saxons, with a few of his nobles, and certain soldiers and vassals, used to lead an unquiet life among the woodlands of the county of Somerset in great tribulation; for he had none of the necessaries of life, except what he could forage openly or stealthily, by frequent sallies, from the Pagans, or even from the Christians who had submitted to the rule of the Pagans, and, as we read in the Life of St. Neot, at the house of one of his cowherds.

" But it happened, on a certain day, that the countrywoman, wife of the cowherd, was preparing some loaves to bake, and the King, sitting at the hearth, made ready his bow and arrows and other warlike instruments. The unlucky woman, espying the cakes burning at the fire, ran up to remove them, and, rebuking the brave king, exclaimed—

> " ' Ca'sn thee mind the ke-aks, man ; an' doossen zee 'em burn?
> I'm boun thee's eat 'em vast enough, az zoon az tiz the turn.' *

" The blundering woman little thought that it was King Alfred, who had fought so many battles against the Pagans, and gained so many victories over them."

Alfred bore her threats and abuse meekly ; it was part of his penance, he thought, and the woman must have soon learnt her mistake, if, as some say, her husband was the swineherd Denewulf, who, after receiving some training and education, became Bishop either of Sherborne or Winchester. In the times when Alfred could scarce find a priest south of the Thames who could read his own breviary, supposing him to have been a pious and godly man, the thing is not so extraordinary as it appears at first sight ; but all this was mended in the King's later years.

Whilst Alfred remained in this enforced seclusion at Athelney he thought much, studied much, and prayed much. The second book which he studied (the first being the illuminated book of poems given him by his mother) was a volume containing a selection from the Psalms, with the daily prayers according to the ancient usages of the Church ; and the perusal of this volume, which he always carried in his bosom, afforded him, we are told, constant comfort and support. But the time was now come when this great and good man was to emerge from the fire of affliction, and, like gold seven times tried in the fire, was to appear purified from earthly dross, and shining with a clear and undimmed light in the world.

It became gradually whispered about, amongst those who re-mained faithful, where Alfred was ; and the men of Somerset gathered around him. Then he built a fort at Athelney, and from here he sallied out, when he had the opportunity, and made frequent attacks upon the Pagans. But as the numbers of his followers increased it became more and more difficult to supply them with food, the Danes having eaten up or destroyed all the produce of both field and fold. Wild fowl and fish from the meres was all that could be found, and that only in scant measure.

Now it happened one day that all his followers had scattered them-

---

* In a note to Dr. Giles' translation of Asser's " Life of Alfred," he says the original is in Latin verse ; it may, therefore, be rendered into English verse such as every housewife in Somersetshire would understand.

selves in search of necessary supplies, and he and his mother were in the fort alone, when a poor man came to the door begging an alms. They wondered much how he could have found his way to this secluded and jealously-guarded spot. Osburga told him that they were as poor as he was ; but the King, who was reading, desired his mother to give him bread. She answered that they had but one loaf left to them, which would not suffice them for provision for the day, yet he prayed her to give half of it to the man, bidding her trust in Him who had fed the five thousand with five loaves and two fishes.

As they were awaiting the return of their companions, both Alfred and his mother lay down to rest, and as they slept the same vision appeared to each of them. Cuthbert, former Bishop of Lindisfarne, appeared, and thus addressed the King : " I am Cuthbert,* if ever you heard of me ; God hath sent me to announce good fortune to you ; and since England has nearly paid the penalty of her crimes, God now, through the merits of her native saints, looks upon her with an eye of mercy. You, too, so pitiably banished from your native kingdom, shall shortly be again seated with honour on your throne, of which I give you this extraordinary token : your fishers shall this day bring home a great quantity of fish in baskets, which will be so much the more extraordinary because the river, at this time hard-bound with ice, could warrant no such expectation, especially as the air, now dripping with cold rain, mocks the art of the fisher. But when your fortune shall succeed to your wishes, you will act as becomes a king if you conciliate God, your helper, and me, His messenger, with suitable devotion." Saying this, the saint divested the sleeping King of his anxiety, and comforted his mother also with the same joyful intelligence. When they awoke, they repeatedly declared that each had had the self-same dream, when the fishermen, entering, displayed such a multitude of fishes as would have been sufficient to satisfy the appetite of a numerous army.

But the vision was to receive a still more glorious fulfilment. News was brought that Hubba, the fierce Danish leader, with twenty-three ships, after much slaughter of the Christians, came from the country of Demetia (South Wales),† had sailed to Devon, where, with twelve hundred others, he met with a miserable

---

* It is remarked as a sort of confirmation of this legend that a church in Wells is dedicated to St. Cuthbert, a north-country saint. (*Vide* Freeman's Old English History.)

† Asser. It should be noticed that Asser, himself a Briton, never of course speaks of Wales or the Welsh, for he could scarcely allow them to be foreigners. He generally makes no distinction, save that of Pagans and Christians.

death, being slain while committing his misdeeds, by the King's servants, before the Castle of Cynuit (Kynwith, on the River Taw) into which many of the King's servants, with their followers, had fled for safety. The Pagans, seeing that the castle was altogether unprepared and unfortified, except that it had walls in its own fashion, determined not to assault it, because it was impregnable and secure on all sides except the eastern, as we ourselves have seen, but they began to blockade it, thinking that those who were inside would soon surrender either from famine or want of water, for the castle had no spring near it.

But the result did not fall out as they expected; for the Christians, before they began to suffer from want, inspired from Heaven, judging it much better to gain victory or death, attacked the Pagans suddenly in the morning, and from the first cut them down in great numbers, slaying also their king, so that few escaped to their ships, and there they gained a very large booty, and, amongst other things, the standard called Raven; for they say that the three sisters of Hingwar and Hubba, daughters of Lodobrok,* wove that flag, and got it ready in one day. They say, moreover, that in every battle, wherever that flag went before them, if they were to gain the victory a live crow (? raven) would appear flying on the middle of the flag; but, if they were doomed to be defeated, it would hang down motionless. And this was often proved to be so.

Great, therefore, was the dismay amongst the Danes when they heard of this terrible disaster—of the loss of men and leaders; but, above all, of their magic banner. In a corresponding degree were the hearts of the English raised. And now awoke the cry from Alfred, their King; he knew well that this was the moment to take advantage of the Danes' dismay; and, besides, had not St. Cuthbert promised him success? So, sending his faithful followers secretly in every direction to gather together the men of Hampshire, Wiltshire, and Dorset, he made a tryst to meet them with his faithful Sumorsætas at " Petra Ægbryhta," Egbert's Stone,† which was on the borders of Selwood Forest, which means in Latin *Silva Magna,* the great wood, but known in British as Coit-Mawr.

Meanwhile, determining to do nothing rashly, he would learn something of the state of the Danes and the watch they kept; so disguising himself as a glee-man, and taking his harp (of which he was as fond as King David) he started alone for their camp, which

---

* Leather breeches.   † Now called Brixton Deverill.

was in another part of Selwood Forest. He easily gained admittance, and, assuming the character of a Danish scald or bard, delighted these fierce men by singing them their favourite war-song. Whilst he stayed there for some days, he went from tent to tent watching and carefully noting their entrenchments, the position of their leaders, the careless watch they kept, &c. &c. Having carefully observed all he required to know, he made his way back to Athelney, and, assembling his companions, pointed out the indolence of the enemy, and the easiness of their defeat ; he then joined the rest of his army at Ægbryht's Stone. It was now nearly Whitsuntide ; and from thence he went to Iglea, or Iley. Here they halted for the night, and, as Alfred lay in his tent, his anxious mind not letting him rest, St. Neot appeared to him ; his form was as an angel of God ; his countenance beaming with glory ; his raiment white as the driven snow. He thus addressed him : " Rise up in haste and prepare for victory. When thou camest hither I was with thee—I supported thee. Now, therefore, on the morrow, go forth, thou and thy men of war, to the fight, and the Lord shall be with you—even the Lord strong and mighty — the Lord mighty in battle, who giveth victory to kings. And, behold, I go before you to the battle, and thine enemies shall fall by thy arm before mine eyes, and thou shalt smite them with the edge of the sword."

The Danes were at Ethandune (we do not know for certain the exact spot ; three places are mentioned by different authors, but all agree that it was not in Wiltshire, but on the borders of Somerset), and were in careless security ; so rapid and energetic had been Alfred's movements that he himself brought the tidings of the rising. The morning mist hung over the camp ; not a watch-dog barked ; not a note of alarm was given, while troop after troop of Saxons filed silently over the hill. Alfred made a stirring address to his people, promising them the success of which he had been assured. The word was given, and down rushed the host upon the foe. The Saxon army was as nothing to the great Danish host ; but God and the Saints fought for the Christians against the heathen Danes. As the battle was doubtful, St. Neot himself appeared ; he seized the standard ; he fought by Alfred's side ; he secured the victory. Thousands upon thousands fell, and the terrible carnage had not ceased when the sun went down. The name of Slaughterford marks the spot where the battle was fiercest. Never again was St. Neot seen on earth !

(*To be continued.*)

Ⓐ Ⓕourteenth Ⓒentury Ⓛibrary.

By J. H. ROUND, M.A.

THERE is preserved among the "Additional Manuscripts" at the British Museum, a copy of a very curious list of books of the reign of Richard II. The prices affixed to some of the books impart to it a peculiar value; and if, as I presume, it has not yet found its way into print, its contents will doubtless prove acceptable.

The list commences with an extract from the inventory of the goods of Sir Simon Burley, both at the Mews and at Baynard's Castle, taken at the time of his fall, Nov. 8, 1387. The fate of this brilliant but ill-fated knight lends it a touching interest. The valiant companion of the Black Prince, and the tutor of his youthful heir, he lived to fall a victim to the popular reaction against the glittering extravagance and shallow chivalry that characterised the court of the aged Edward. His position as one of the trusted counsellors of his pupil, Richard II., is represented by his "Livre de Governement de Roys et de Prynces," while the excessive proportion of romances in his library typifies the chivalrous but unpractical mind of the friend of Froissart and the Black Prince.

Les Livres : —
Primerement j. livre de Romans et de ymagery de Buys et de Aigrement.
It. j. graunt livre de la bible oue les histoire escolestre.
　　j. autre livre de Romans en prose covere de blanc cuer.
　　j. livre de Sidrak.
　　j. livre de Romans oue ymagery covere au peel de veel.
　　j. livre novelle de x. comandementz covere de cuer rouge.
　　j. livre de governement de Roys et du Prynces.
　　j. livre de Romans de William Bastard covere de blanc.
　　j. livre de philosophie rumpue covere de cuer rouge.
　　j. livre de vies de seintz covere de cuer rouge.
　　j. livre du Romans du Roy Arthur covere de blanc.
　　j. livret q. comence "miserere mei deus."
　　j. autre livre de x. comandementz covere de Rouge.
　　j. livre de papier oue diverses paroles de diverses langages.
　　j. livre doles propheties de Merlyn.
　　j. livret de Romans oue un ymage al comencement.
　　j. livre de Romans de Meisᵣ covere de blanc.
　　j. livre de Englys del Forster et del Sangler.
　　j. livre de Latyn covere de noir.
　　j. livret de bruyt.
　　j. livret de Romans de Maugis cuvere de rouge cure.

This catalogue is followed in the copy by the miscellaneous list below :—

Wyne Wyk ⎰ j. portors covre de quir rouge iiij*li.*　⎱
　　　　　 ⎱ j. messal covere de quir blaunc iiij*li.*　⎰ x*li.* xiii*s.* iiii*d.*
　　　　　 ⎩ j. legentz de seintz—Liii*s.* iiii*d.*　⎭

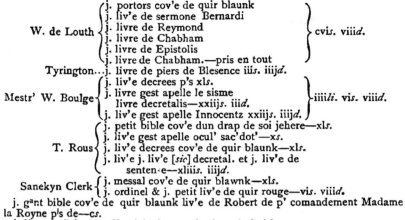

W. de Louth
- j. portors cov'e de quir blaunk
- j. liv'e de sermone Bernardi
- j. livre de Reymond
- j. livre de Chabham
- j. livre de Epistolis
- j. livre de Chabham.—pris en tout
} cvi*s*. viii*d*.

Tyrington...j. livre de piers de Blesence iii*s*. iiij*d*.

Mestr' W. Boulge
- j. liv'e decrees p's xl*s*.
- j. livre gest apelle le sisme
- livre decretalis—xxiij*s*. iii*d*.
- j. liv'e gest apelle Innocentz xxiij*s*. iiij*d*.
} iiij*li*. vi*s*. viii*d*.

T. Rous
- j. petit bible cov'e dun drap de soi jehere—xl*s*.
- j. liv'e gest apelle ocul' sac'dot'—x*s*.
- j. liv'e decrees cov'e de quir blaunk—xl*s*.
- j. liv'e j. liv'e [*sic*] decretal. et j. liv'e de senten·e—xliii*s*. iiij*d*.

Sanekyn Clerk
- j. messal cov'e de quir blawnk—xl*s*.
- j. ordinel & j. petit liv'e de quir rouge—vi*s*. viii*d*.

j. g^nt bible cov'e de quir blaunk liv'e de Robert de p' comandement Madame la Royne p's de—c*s*.

j. livere a Johan de Kendale de constitutions de la Messe—v*s*.

j. livere quest apelle Speculu' Marie & iiij autres xxv*s*.

It. j. livre apelle Sydrak viii*s*.

[NOTE IN A LATE HAND].—"The above books belonged to Sir William de Walcote, who had been an officer in Queen Isabella's household, and whose goods were sold to pay a debt owing the Queen about the 22 of Edward the Third."

The History of Gilds.

BY CORNELIUS WALFORD, F.S.S., *Barrister-at-Law.*

PART IV.

(Continued from p. 29.)

CHAPTER XXXVIII.—*The Gilds of Northumberland* (*continued*).

NEWCASTLE-UPON-TYNE.—I have now to notice the Gilds of the Lesser Fraternities of this ancient town. There is one of them of very great interest, and this I shall proceed to mention first.

Gild of the Fraternity of the Blessed Trinity of Newcastle-upon-Tyne.—In 1492 this body purchased the site of their present house, for which a red rose was to be paid yearly, if demanded, at Midsummer for ever. About 1530 the fraternity had conferred upon it the duty of primage and pilotage. Henry VIII., on October 5, 1536, granted a new charter of incorporation to this Gild, which then consisted of men and women, to have a common seal, implead and be impleaded, with licence to build and embattle two towers—the one at the entrance to the haven of Tyne, and the other on the hill adjoining, in each of which a light was to be obtained every night; for support whereof they were empowered to receive 4d. for every foreign ship, and 2d. for every English vessel entering the port of Tyne. This charter was confirmed by Edward VI. in 1548, and by Mary in 1553.

In 1584, Queen Elizabeth, by charter, refounded this society under the designation of the *Master Pilots and Seamen of the Trinity House of Newcastle-upon-Tyne*. Another charter was granted by James I., in 1606, constituting this society, under the above name, a body politic, and appointing a Master, twelve elder brethren, two elder Wardens, with two assistants, and two younger Wardens, also with two assistants. They were to have a common seal, and their jurisdiction was extended to Blyth, Sunderland, Hartlepool, Whitby, and Staithes. Power was given to impose fines on offending brethren, and to appoint pilots for the river Tyne, with its creeks and members. The pilotage dues to be 12d. for every foot a laden vessel should draw, and 8d. for unladen vessels. The duty of primage was confirmed, after the rate (for vessels coming from beyond the seas into the river) of 2d. per ton of wine, oil, and other things sold by the ton—fish killed and brought in by Englishmen excepted ; and 3d. per last of flax, hemp, pitch, tar, or other things sold by the last. Lightage was also confirmed to them ; of every English born owner's ship 4d. each time, and of every ship owned by an alien 12d. The buoying, canning, marking, and beaconing of the river Tyne was also confirmed to them, for which they were to receive of each ship whose owner was English, and burden above 20 chaldron of coals, 4d. ; of the same, when under 20 chaldron, 2d. ; and of every alien, 6d. They were also empowered to hold lands and tenements under £30 per annum clear value.

In 1687 James II. granted a new charter to this fraternity, with an addition of Pilotage. After this period the body became active in the maritime affairs of the nation. In 1800 the Master and bretheren, assisted by a committee of shipowners, applied to Parliament for extended powers. They represented that the pilotage fixed by the Charter of James II. had become an insufficient compensation for the labour, peril, and industry of the pilots. It was also proposed that toll be levied upon vessels sailing northwards for the maintenance of beacons and buoys at Holy Island. In the Session of 1801 there was enacted (41 George III. c. lxxxvi.) " An Act for extending and enlarging the powers and increasing the rates and duties of the Corporation of the Trinity House of Newcastle-upon-Tyne, and for better regulating the Port of Newcastle," conferring many of the powers sought. The income of the Corporation Gilds, which in 1796 had been £1,406 7s. 1¾d., had by 1817 increased to £3,866 17s. 6d.

About the year 1820 the fraternity was supporting within their house twelve men and thirteen widow pensioners, each having an allowance of 28s. per month, with a coat and hat to the men, and a gown and petticoat to the women, once in two years. They were provided with coals and medical attendance, with an allowance of wine when sick. There were two classes of out-pensioners. Of the first or master's class there were sixty, each of whom received £7 per annum, and 20s. extra for each child under fourteen years of age. The second class is limited to forty pensioners, of whom there were twenty-three upon the list, each receiving £5 per annum, and 20s. extra for each child under fourteen. The total number of bretheren in this Society was then 340.

Coopers.—The Ordinance of this fraternity, dated Jan. 20, 1426, enjoined them to go together yearly at the feast of Corpus Christi in procession, as other crafts did, and play their play at their own charge; that none should take a Scotsman born to apprentice, nor set any such to work, under a penalty of 40s. No brother to take more than one apprentice in seven years. All turners and pulley-makers coming to Newcastle to be bound by the same Ordinance. An after clause forbade the employing of any Dutchman. An Ordinance of the 17th Elizabeth consolidated the Fraternities of Coopers, Pulley-makers, Turners, and Ropemakers; and it was ordained "that none of these Companies shall take any apprentice but one in four years, except the children of the bretheren," penalty £10; or for any apprentice taken during the servitude of another, £5. In 1699 the Mayor of Newcastle granted to this fraternity the power to search all herrings, &c.

Barber-Chirurgeons, with Chandlers.—The ancient Ordinance of this conjoint fraternity, dated October 10, 1442, enjoined that they should go together in procession on Corpus Christi day, in livery, and afterwards play the "Baptizing of Christ," at their own expense. That no alien born should be taken apprentice, or allowed to work within the town or without, under a penalty of 20s.; that the society should uphold the light of St. John the Baptist, in Nicholas Church, as long as they were of ability; that no barber, apprentice, nor servant should shave on a Sunday, neither within the town, nor without by a mile's space. Another Ordinance, dated 1671, confirmed the former, and enacted that when any brother had taken a cure in hand, no other should meddle with it till it was completed, on pain of certain forfeits, one-half of which to go to the brother first called in. In 1648 the fraternity petitioned the Corporation for a site whereon to build a meeting-house, with land for a garden to be planted with medicinal herbs; and the grant was made on conditions. On June 14, 1742, ordered "that no brother shave John Robson, till he pays what he owes to Robert Shafto." Early in the present century the fraternity consisted of forty-five members.

Slaters.—The Ordinance was dated March 12, 1451, enjoined them to go together in a livery yearly at the feast of Corpus Christi to play their play, at their own expense. No apprentice should serve less than seven years, or a second be taken until the first had served six years; no brother should take a Scot apprentice under fine of 40s. If any brother took a slate quarry, or any place to cover with slates, none should undermine him. No brother to work upon St. Catherine's Day. Order dated 1460 that no brother should take less than 6s. 8d. for handling a rood of slate covering.

An Ordinance dated September 28, 1579, united the Slaters and Bricklayers. They were to play annually at Corpus Christi, "The Offering of Isaac by Abraham."

An Ordinance dated March 16, 1677, separated them from the Wallers, Bricklayers, and Dawbers *alias* Plasterers, and made them a Company by the name of Slaters and Tylers; ordered them to meet yearly on St. Catherine's Day; to work no kind of black mortar or clay, but to make ovens and chimneys, or funnels.

Early in the present century the fraternity consisted of thirty-five members.

Weavers.—The earliest known Ordinance of this fraternity is dated August, 1527. By the authority of the Mayor, Sheriff, and Aldermen, Justices of the Peace, with the consent of their own body, it enjoined them to assemble yearly at the feast of Corpus Christi, go together in procession, and play their play and pageant of "The Bearing of the Cross," at their own expense. To take no Scotsman born to apprentice, nor to set any to work under a penalty of 40s., wherein half to go to the fellowship, and half to the work of Tyne Bridge, "without any forgiveness." To admit any person who had served an apprenticeship with a brother of the society, a member thereof, on the payment of 13s. 4d. and 12d. for a pot of ale; as also any man of that craft, being the King's liege man, with power to set up a shop, on payment of £20, and 12d. for a pot of ale. The searchers to search four times a year at least. That any brother falling into poverty should be supplied out of the common box, at the discretion of the Steward and the twelve; and that any brother misbehaving at meetings should forfeit six pounds of wax for every default. That any brother lying in wait to beat, slay, or murder any of his bretheren, should be put out of the society for ever; that any brother calling another " Scot," " Mansworn" in malice, should forfeit 6s. 8d., without any forgiveness; that every apprentice should serve seven years, and pay at his entrance a pound of wax. The accounts to be settled, and officers elected, every year. The prices for certain kinds of work fixed. An Ordinance dated August 12, 1608, provided that foreigners and persons not free should take no work to the prejudice of the fraternity. A warrant was yearly granted to seize bad yarn, and to receive tolls from pedlars who kept booths on the Sandhill. The fraternity was very small in 1725.

Flumbers, Pewterers, and Glaziers.—The Ordinance of this fraternity (which anciently consisted of the Goldsmiths, Plumbers, Glaziers, Pewterers, and Painters), dated September 1, 1536, enjoined them to go together on the feast of Corpus Christi, and maintain their flag, " The Three Kings of Coleyn [Cologne];" to have four Wardens, one goldsmith, one plumber, one glazier, and one pewterer or painter, to be sworn on admission not to interfere with each other's occupation; that no Scotsman born should be taken apprentice, or suffered to work in Newcastle, on pain of forfeiting 3s. 4d., one half of which to go to the upholding of Tyne Bridge, the other half to the fraternity.

Amongst the orders occur the following: 1598, That none of the Fellowship be permitted to " worke or sell his own glasse under seven-pence one foot;" 1615, " No brother to work any Normandye glasse under eight-pence the foot. September 7, 1830, " No brother to lend his diamond, except to a free brother of the Company, on pain of forfeiting 6s. 8d."

1546. *Felt-makers, Curriers, and Armourers.*—The Ordinance, dated October 1, 1546, enjoined them to go together in procession at the feast of Corpus Christi, bear the charges of the lights, pageants, and play. None born out of the King's dominions should work with them, unless he were denizen, or for urgent causes, to be admitted by the Mayor and Justices of the Peace, on pain of paying £40 sterling. They were not to work on holidays, or on Saturdays later than five o'clock. The three associated trades were not to work at each other's occupations. March 27, 1671, order for seizure of French hats, except such as were sold by members of the

Company. 1719, ordered that no Quaker should be taken apprentice, on pain of forfeiting £100. Early in the present century there were fifteen members.

Milners or Millers.—The Ordinance of this fraternity, dated September 20, 1578, cites another of older date, constituting twenty free millers into a fellowship, with perpetual succession, and enjoining them to choose two Wardens every year, who might sue and be sued &c., in the Courts of the town; and, that when the general plays should be performed, they should play the one anciently assigned to this fellowship, called "The Deliverance of the Children of Isrell out of the Thraldome, Bondage, and Servitude of King Pharo," on pain of forfeiting 20s. for absence; that no stranger or alien-born should be taken apprentice or set to work under pain of 6s. 8d., and that apprentices should serve seven years; that no corn should be ground on Sundays; that each miller in the counties of Northumberland and Durham, who brought corn from Newcastle market, should pay the fraternity an acknowledgment of 6d. per annum; and pay 2s. 6d. every time he should be found in the wheat or malt market before two o'clock in the afternoon on market day, unless to fetch away the corn which his customers had bought there; and that none such foreign millers should buy corn there, under a penalty of 2s. 6d. for each default. The Wardens were to make oath in the Town Chamber concerning the fines, half whereof to go to the support of the Newcastle part of Tyne Bridge.

On April 8, 1672, an order was made that if any brother attended the funeral of another with a black hat he should be fined 6d. for every such default. The gild had but fourteen members in 1820.

House Carpenters, anciently called Wrights.—An ordinance of this society dated July 3, 1579, constituted the House Carpenters and Joiners a body corporate of themselves, with perpetual succession, and power to sue and be sued in the Courts of Newcastle. It was ordered that the fraternity should meet yearly and choose three wardens, two of whom were to be house carpenters and the third a joiner. That whenever the general plays of the time called Corpus Christi plays should be played, they should play the "Burial of Christ," which anciently belonged to their fellowship; that no apprentice should serve less than seven years; no Scotsman to be taken as such under a penalty of 40s., nor to be made free on any account. It was also defined which branches of work the carpenters and joiners should respectively follow. In 1589 the Joiners were and Bibliographer. 71

separated from the House Carpenters and made into a Gild by themselves, with ordinances, &c.

Masons.—The Ordinance of this fraternity, under date September 1, 1581, constituted it a corporate body, with perpetual succession ; enjoined them to meet yearly to choose two Wardens, who might sue and be sued in the Courts of Newcastle, make bye-laws, &c. Whenever the Corpus Christi plays were performed, they were to play "The Burial of our Lady St. Mary the Virgin." Every absent brother to forfeit 2s. 6d. No Scotsman to be taken apprentice under a penalty of 40s., nor ever be admitted into the Company on any account whatever. That at the marriages and burials of bretheren and their wives, the craft should attend to the church such persons to be married or buried ; that one half of their fines should go to the maintenance of the great bridge, the other half to the fellowship. The fraternity had but fifteen members early in the present century.

Shipwrights.—The Ordinance of this fraternity, dated August 8, 1636, probably in continuation of an earlier one, enjoins the members to meet yearly on December 27, to choose two Wardens, and the like number of overseers ; prohibiting them from working on Sundays and holidays observed by the Church, giving them powers to make bye-laws, and restricting apprentices from working tide-work till they had served three years. A later Ordinance, dated 1674, was of the same character. In 1825 the fraternity consisted of twenty-two members only.

Colliers, Paviors, and Carriage-men.—The Ordinance of this fraternity, composed of several crafts, was dated 30th July, 1656, and appears to have been a mutual agreement between themselves, pending proper authorisation from the magistrates of the borough. It ordered that no stranger, not having served an apprenticeship to their calling, should be set to work, penalty 40s., and that any brother working a day's work privately should forfeit 6s. 8d. for each default ; that they should choose a Warden yearly on the feast of St. Mark, who should keep the books of the Company. They had a box-master and two key-keepers. About 1825 there were ten members.

These were known locally as the "Fifteen Bye-Trades" of New-castle—by fusion the number had become reduced ;—and I draw the preceding details largely from Mackenzie "History of the Borough." There are yet some other Companies to be mentioned.

(*To be continued.*)

The Syston Library Sale.

THE sale in December, 1884, of the fine library of Syston Park, near Grantham, formed chiefly by the late Sir John Hayford Thorold, at the end of the last and beginning of the present centuries, adds one more to the dispersions which have made the last few years remarkable above all of former times in this country, in the sales of the famous Sunderland Library of Blenheim Palace, and the Hamilton-Beckford library of the other great ducal palace. The Syston library was sold at the rooms of the auctioneers, Messrs. Sotheby, Wilkinson & Hodge, during the eight days beginning on Friday, December 12, and the prices realised for some of the treasures far exceeded the sums which had hitherto been paid for such works. Those who admire the magnificent *editiones principes* of the classics from the famous early presses of Italy and France, when the printer was the rival of the painter in the love and worship of his art, here found an ample feast of delight in reviewing a collection wonderfully fine for condition and remarkable beyond most for completeness. Many were the choice editions of the Aldines and Elzevirs, several on vellum or large paper, generally in exceptionally good condition and in superb bindings, from the libraries of such high historic repute as those of Lorenzo de Medici, Marguerite de Valois, Diane de Poictiers, Barbarigo, Doge of Venice, and Catherine de Medici, Thuanus, Maioli, De Menars, Grolier, and more modern collectors.

In the limited space at our disposal it will be impossible to name more than a few of the most important books disposed of, with the sums realised. The first book which reached three figures was Æsopi (Airani et Remecii) Appologi sive Mythologi cum quibusdam Carminum Additionibus Sebastiani Brant, from Maroli's Library, bound in the Grolier style by Nicholas Eve, £170 (Quaritch). Æsopi Fabulæ et Vita, numerous woodcuts, fine copy, in olive morocco, covered with gold tooling, by Clovis Eve, a beautiful specimen of Marguerite de Valois' Library, 16mo., Lugduni, 1582, fetched £120 (Quaritch); America Verardi (Caroli), Historia Baetica et Regni Granata Obsidio, Victoria et Triumphus Accedit Christoperi Colom. Epistola de Insulis nuper Inventis, woodcuts (including ship of Columbus), fine copy, in red morocco, by C. Lewis, small quarto, 1494, £125 (Quaritch); Anthologia Græca Literis Capitalibus (cura J. Lascaris), printed on vellum; the last seven leaves in *fac-simile* are so beautifully executed as almost to defy detection, the first page is surrounded by a superb border exquisitely illuminated in gold and colours, displaying in the form of seven old cameos the gymnastic games of ancient Greece, wrestling being represented by Hercules strangling Antæus, magnificently bound by Roger Payne, small quarto, 1494, £122 (Quaritch); Balbi de Janua's Catholicon, two vols., first edition, and fourth book printed with a date, folio, Moguntiæ J. Gutenberg, 1460, a splendid specimen of Gutenberg's typographical skill, £400 (Maitland).

The first Bible put up was the " Biblia Polyglotta " of Cardinal Ximenez, in six volumes, a very fine copy, with the Cardinal's arms emblazoned in silver and colours on the titles, bound in red morocco, by Lewis, folio 1514—15—17. This is the earliest Polyglot Bible issued, and when complete and in fine condition is very rare. In it appeared the Greek New Testament printed in 1514 for the first time, although not published for several years after. This splendid book was secured by Mr. Quaritch for £176. Shortly after came the celebrated Mazarin Bible, described in the catalogue as follows : Biblia Sacra Latina e Versione et cum Præfatione S. Hieronymi, two vols., the first edition of the Bible, and the earliest book printed with metal types, by the inventors of printing, splendidly bound in blue morocco, a magnificent copy folio, Sine Nota Sed Moguntiæ, per J. Gutenburg et J. Fust, circa 1450—55. This rare work has been called the Mazarin Bible ever since the discovery by Debure of a copy in the library of Cardinal Mazarin. It is a superb work of printing on paper as thick and rich in tone as vellum, with glossy ink, intensely black, and very uniform in the impression; in double columns, the letters large and similar to those written by scribes of the Church missals and choral books. The bidding for the Mazarin Bible commenced at £500, and after a spirited contest it was finally knocked down to Mr. Quaritch for the enormous price of £3,900.

Another expensive Bible was the Biblia Sacra Latina, two vols., first edition, with a date beautifully printed on vellum, a splendid and magnificent copy in old blue morocco, with the large arms of Prince Eugene in gold on sides, folio, Moguntiæ, per J. Fust and P. Schoiffer, 1462, £1,000 (Ellis). Boccace (Jean) Les Cent Nouvelles traduit en François per Maistre Laurens du Premier fait, printed on vellum, with capital letters, and 101 miniatures, illuminated in gold and colours, red morocco, folio, Paris, circa 1500, £670 (Quaritch) ; Natalles (Pierre de) Cathalogue des Sainctes et Sainctes, translated en François, par Guy Breslay, two vols., printed on vellum, ornamented with 948 large and small miniatures of saints, and with 1102 capital letters illuminated in gold and colours, each volume with the arms of Jean de Bourbon emblazoned in gold, silver, and colours, folio, Paris, Galliot Du Pré, 1523-24, unique, the gem of the Meerman library, £530 (Quaritch) ; Ovidii Metamorphoses, numerous woodcuts, bound by Clovis Eve, 16mo., Paris, 1587, from the library of Marguerite de Valois, £113 (Quaritch); Pausaniæ Decem Regionum Veteris Græciæ Descriptio, two vols.; Marguerite de

Valois' copy, in olive morocco, by Clovis Eve, 16mo., Lugduni, 1559, £203.

The magnificent vellum-printed Lives of the Saints, in two volumes, one of the most perfect and beautiful illuminated books of the 16th century work, with miniatures, which once belonged to Jean de Bourbon, amply justified the large price of £530 given for it by Mr. Quaritch.

The climax of the sale was reached when the rare Psalmorum Codex of 1459 changed hands. For this magnificent work of the typographic art of Fust and Schoeffer the extraordinary price of £4,950 was obtained, after a very keen contest between Mr. Quaritch and Mr. Ellis. It was fully anticipated that this noble volume, being in so exceptionally perfect state, to say nothing of its rarity as one of only ten copies on vellum known, would bring a very large sum, and sums from £2,000 to £3,000 were named as possible, but no one dreamt of its beating the Mazarin Bible. Indeed, few but the more accomplished students of the history of typography are aware of the high interest that attaches to any work of this date. This Codex is, after all, a rarer and a grander book than the Mazarin Bible, and being in one volume complete, it has certain advantages in the eyes of a collector. This fine vellum folio has been accused by some of being only a reprint of a splendid predecessor of 1457 (two years earlier), of which the copy in the Royal Library at Windsor is one—a volume which has long been one of its chief treasures. "But there is not the slightest doubt," remarks the *Times*, "that this Codex of 1459 is a new edition, and such is its rarity in public sales that Mr. Quaritch says that in his experience of over forty years he has never had one through his hands, although he has had no less than four Mazarin Bibles. His commission from America for this Codex was high, but it was far below that which he held for an English client, which was, however, only £3,000, so that he has ventured to exceed his commission by a very considerable margin ; but it cannot be said for a moment that the book is not worth the money, as it was evident that Mr. Ellis's client had an equally high opinion of its value."

This lot was described in the catalogue as " Psalmorum Codex, Latinè, cum Hymnis, Oratione Dominicâ, Symbolis, et notis musicis, folio, Moguntiæ, Fust et Schoeffer, 1459, printed on vellum, with fine painted capitals and initial letters in red, the second book printed with a date, containing the Athanasian Creed, printed for the first time." Only ten copies of it printed on vellum are known, and it is almost as rare as the edition of 1457, of which only eight are known. This identical copy was in the MacCarthy sale, and brought 3,350 francs, and it sold again in Sir Mark Sykes's sale for £136 10s. It is bound by Staggemeier in red morocco, and is in an exceptionally fine state. The book was now put up, with a brief eulogy from the auctioneer, Mr. Hodge, at £500, and the biddings steadily advanced to £4,950, at which it was knocked down to Mr. Quaritch.

The next lot of any importance was "Shakespeare's (Mr. William) Comedies, Histories, and Tragedies. Published according to the true originall copies, folio, printed by Isaac Iaggard and Ed. Blount, 1623," with portrait by Martin Droeshout, and the verses by Ben Jonson very neatly inlaid. In the title-page the " Mr. William " is supplied in fac-simile entirely, while the last five letters of the name " Shakespeare " are also in fac-simile. The tails of the letter " g " in the name of the printer, and of the figure 3 in the date, have also been added. The impression of the portrait is an early and very fine one, with the curved hatchings over the forehead, before the straight cross hatchings were added in later impressions. The size of the paper is the largest known, measuring 13⅜ in. by 8¼ in., many of the leaves having the edges partly uncut. The top margin is ¾ in., the front 15-16 in., and the bottom 1¼ in. ; the printed part measuring 11⅝ in. by 7 in. It has, therefore, been cut as slightly as possible by the binder. The paper, however, is thin, and in some few places there are small defects which have caused the loss of a letter in different places over three leaves, about eight to ten in all, as stated in the catalogue. The copy of this first folio in the library of Lady Burdett-Coutts, which is perfect, and was purchased in Mr. G. Daniel's sale for £716 2s., measures 13¼ in. by 8½ in., and is, therefore, ¼ in. shorter. It was put up at £500, and, after a few advances of £10, was knocked down at £590 (B. F. Stevens). It was understood that this purchase was made on commission for an American library.

" To the last lot," remarks the *Times*, " this Syston sale maintained its surpassing interest as a collection of the rarest early printed books, which in the cases of the Mazarin Bible and the Psalmorum Codex has now assumed a historic celebrity in the annals of bibliography. No other private library similar in extent ever sold for so large a sum—£28,001 15s. 6d. Compared with those sold during the past two years, which happen to have been of exceptional importance—the Sunderland Library of Blenheim Palace, sold during 57 days at Messrs. Puttick & Simpson's, realising £56,581 6s. ; the Hamilton Palace, including the Beckford Library, at Messrs. Sotheby's, 40 days, £73,551 18s. ; Lord Gosford's, at Puttick & Simpson's, £11,318 5s. 6d. ; and Sir R. Colt Hoare's (the Stourhead Library), at Sotheby's, 8 days, £10,028 6s. 6d.—the Syston far exceeds any of them. The total of these recent great book sales forms an astonishing sum as representing the value of the splendid private libraries of England ; it amounts to no less than £179,481 11s.; and if the large sum paid by the German and French Governments for the Ashburnham manuscripts be added, we have something considerably over a quarter of a million expended upon precious books and manuscripts during this brief period. But the account by no means stops here, for it was announced by the auctioneer, Mr. Hodge, at the end of the Syston sale that the next great private library which would be offered at auction would be that belonging to the Earl of Jersey, so long preserved at Osterley Park. This is well known as an exceedingly fine collection, and celebrated for some rare manuscripts, and above all for no less than 11 Caxtons. This, then, is another most interesting sale in the future, and it is expected to come off early in February. As to any results of these heavy dispersions in diminishing the literary treasures of the country, it would seem from all that can be learnt from the great dealers that the taste and the ample means of English gentlemen still command the market against the world. The choice books from the libraries of Marguerite de Valois and Catherine de Medicis, and a few others of special interest to French collectors, have been carried off by M. Morgand; but we have good reason to believe that the Mazarin Bible and the still rarer Psalmorum Codex, with many other of Mr. Quaritch's purchases, will remain in English libraries. It is said that the commission in the hands of Mr. Ellis for the Codex was from the Berlin Library, which has long been envious of the Vienna Imperial Library having both the first of 1457 and the second edition of 1459 of Fust and Schoifher's Codex Psalmorum on vellum. The first has always been of such rarity that, quite in the primitive epoch of book sales, it is recorded by Brunet, in his invaluable 'Manual de Libraire,' as bringing 12,000 francs (£480) in MacCarthy's sale at Paris (about 1810), when the Codex we have just seen sold for £4,950 was also sold, but only for 3,350 francs. There is, we have heard, a 1459 Codex in the library at Wulfenbattel, but in a very damaged state. These are trifling additions to make to the admirable sale catalogue compiled by Mr. John Bohn, without which it would have been impossible at the time to give such full and interesting information as can only be got by much research and reference, enlarged by the knowledge of an expert and the experience of a long life devoted to the service. All who have a feeling for bibliography and a reverence for the splendid works of the first printers must recognise the value of such contributions to book lore as the Hamilton, the Beckford, and the Syston catalogues, which are, in fact, the supplement to Brunet and Lowndes."

Reviews.

Japanese Marks and Seals. By JAMES L. BOWES. Sotheran & Co.
*Japanese Enamels, with Illustrations from the Examples in the Bowes
Collection.* By JAMES L. BOWES, Liverpool. Printed for private
circulation. 1884.

BY means of the exhibition of several of the industrial arts of Japan at the
International Health Exhibition last year, the public gained a certain
amount of knowledge of the handiwork of the Japanese people ; and
now we have another exhibition of Japanese industries opened to the
public at Knightsbridge, in what is called the "Japanese Village,"
where native artisans and others may be seen following their several
avocations. *Apropos* of these exhibitions, we may speak of the two
handsome volumes now before us, by the joint author of " Keramic Art
of Japan." Japanese art, Mr. Bowes tells us, was practically unknown
in Western countries a quarter of a century ago, and the only examples
to be found in Europe were the decorated porcelain known as "Old
Japan," and a few specimens of lacquer ware ; and even the former of
these consisted " of vessels more European than Japanese in their form,
and the character of the decoration was unmistakably influenced by
European feeling." Of the real Art of Japan little was known beyond
the confines of that country. The visits of Commodore Perry and Lord
Elgin to Japan led to the opening of certain ports to foreign trade in
1859, but it was not until 1867, when the Japanese collection was displayed at the Paris Exhibition, that Europe became aware of the
marvellous diversity and extraordinary beauty of the art works of the
" Land of the Rising Sun." At the sale at the close of that Exhibition,
many of the Japanese objects found their way into the Bowes collection ;
but the main portion of the objects noticed by Mr. Bowes in the volume
before us was gathered together between the years 1867 and 1874. It
comprises examples of Cloisonné enamels both Japanese and Chinese,
and embraces specimens of each of the three classes with regard to date
—the Early, the Middle Period, and the Modern. The work, it may be
added, is profusely illustrated with photographs of the most important
objects described.

" Japanese Marks and Seals" treats exhaustively of marks on pottery,
on illuminated MSS. and printed books, and on lacquer, enamels, metal,
wood, ivory, &c. It also includes the Zodiacal cycle and year periods.
Both volumes are beautifully printed, and each has the advantage of a
copious index.

Ancient Battle-fields in Lancashire. By CHARLES HARDWICK.
Simpkin, Marshall & Co.

IN his preface to the book before us the author remarks that " human
nature is influenced in its action, quite as much by its faiths, beliefs, and
superstitions, as by the more exact knowledge it has acquired." That
sentence strikes the key-note of his work, in which he has striven to
disentangle, to use Mr. Matthew Arnold's term, literature from dogma.
Many a cherished superstition is destroyed in his four chapters, notably
in the first, in which is discussed the origin of Arthurian legends.
The writer divides his notices of battles not chronologically, but
according to the localities where they occurred. In the chapter which
deals with the legend of the Winwick Wild Boar, " the monster in former
ages which prowled over the neighbourhood of Winwick, inflicting injury

on man and beast," there is a graphic description of the various boar superstitions, and some ingenious speculation on the history and modern survival of the old tribal "totems." The Royal Welsh Fusiliers, however, would be surprised to learn that the goat which precedes the regiment when on march, is as much a "totem" as any Chippeway Indian's badge. The whole book can be cordially commended and recommended. Mr. Hardwick has been a venturous diver in the deep waters of our old chronicles, and found much to reward his search.

Boswell's Life of Johnson. A new edition. Edited by the Rev. R. NAPIER. 6 vols. Bell & Sons. 1884.

THIS publication is well-timed; and it may be hoped that it will help to keep alive the fame of the learned Doctor, the centenary of whose death our nation was too busy to celebrate last December. This edition is to a very great extent a republication of the celebrated edition of Boswell, with notes by John Wilson Croker, which was so terribly chastised by Macaulay in the *Edinburgh Review.* But it is Croker with all his good points, many as they were, and without his blunders and mis-statements. Mr. Napier has exercised a very sound discretion alike in those portions which he has excised and in those which he has allowed to stand; and he has done wisely in relegating the "Journal of Johnson's Tour to the Hebrides" to the end of the work, instead of interpolating it in the narrative, as Croker persisted in doing. The notes added by Mr. Napier are all marked as by "the Editor," and so their amount and their value can be duly estimated. The 6th volume is devoted to a series of sketches and reminiscences of Dr. Johnson by other hands than Boswell's, and collectively termed "Johnsoniana." The majority of these are already familiar to English readers; but two, at all events, will be new to most of them, namely, Dr. Campbell's "Diary of a Visit to England in 1775," which, having reposed no one knows how long in a legal office in Australia, has been once more made to see the light, and is now for the first time printed in England. In this 6th volume the Editor's labours have been shared by his accomplished wife, Mrs. Robina Napier. We may add that, in his account of the various portraits of Dr. Johnson, Mr. Napier acknowledges his indebtedness to the pages of this Magazine, July, 1883, for making him acquainted with one more copy of Sir Joshua Reynolds than was previously known to exist, and that he ascribes to Opie the Overstone portrait of the Doctor, which figures in the Grosvenor Gallery this season as by Gainsborough.

The January number of *English Etchings* (D. Bogue, 27, King William-street, W.C.) contains an admirable example of the etcher's art, by Mr. W. H. Borrow, "Hastings from the Minnis Rock." Here we have the entrance to the valley in which lies the old town, with the weather-beaten tower of All Saints' Church on the hill to the left, and the irregular roofs of the houses rising one above another. To the right we catch a glimpse of the West Hill, and the ruins of the Castle. Mr. A. W. Bayes contributes a spirited etching of a picturesque bit of Old London, often said, (though falsely, as we happen to know), to be the house of little Nell, "The Old Curiosity Shop." It stood at the corner of Portsmouth-street, Lincoln's Inn Fields, and was doomed to be demolished about a year ago in consequence of its dangerous condition. It was occupied by a man named Tissiman, who sold forged autographs, and practised on the belief of the credulous.

The first number of *The East Anglian* (Pawsey & Hawes, Ipswich), which appears under the editorship of the Rev. C. Evelyn White, not only gives good promise, but shows good performance. The account of the old stone crosses, once so common, but now so rare in the East of England, and that of the Roman remains lately found at Felixstowe, are useful contributions to archæology.

MR. G. WRIGHT, F.S.A., the "Congress Secretary" of the British Archæological Association, has published with Messrs. Jarvis, of King William-street, a volume of "Local Lays and Legends," which will be welcome to many antiquarian friends who have enjoyed his sallies of wit, which have enlivened the Congress afield, and will enable them to travel over old ground again by their firesides. The book is dedicated to his (and our) old friend, Mr. J. O. Halliwell Phillipps, F.R.S. and F.S.A.

MR. HENRY FROWDE, of the Oxford University Press Warehouse, Amen-corner, has just published a handsome edition of the Holy Bible in quarto, with several illustrations not unlike those with which the last generation was familiar in the edition known as "Doyly & Mant's." Along with it he has published a large type edition of "Helps to the Study of the Bible," comprising epitomes of the historical events of the Old and New Testaments, maps of the Holy Land, Egypt, &c., a complete Concordance, with essays on the geography and topography of the sacred volume, the names of plants, animals, &c., mentioned in its pages, lists of proper names, and of obsolete words occurring in Scripture. Each of the two books would form an appropriate present for the New Year.

Obituary Memoirs.

"Emori nolo ; sed me esse mortuum nihil æstimo."—*Epicharmus.*

MR. EDWARD KNOCKER, F.S.A., late of Dover, died at Torquay, on December 25, in his 81st year. He was an ardent antiquarian, and published "A Lecture on the Antiquities of Dover," a work on "The Archives of Dover," and several papers of local interest. He was also the author of "The Grand Court of Shepway of the Cinque Ports," and other works. Of late years Mr. Knocker had acted as honorary librarian to the Corporation of Dover, and he arranged the ancient records of the borough, and presented many valuable documents to his native town.

MR. ALFRED TYLOR, F.G.S., F.S.A., who died December 30, at Shepley House, Carshalton, Surrey, was connected with many learned societies, and was an active supporter of the London Institution. Mr. Tylor's papers are to be found in the *Journal of the Geological Society*, the *Geological Magazine*, the *Journal of the Anthropological Institute*, &c. One of his latest publications is a description, in the *Archæologia* (vol. xlviii.), of some remarkable Roman remains excavated in Warwick-square, Newgate-street, and now deposited in the British Museum. Mr. Tylor was the author of several lectures on archæological subjects.

MR. RICHARD MAKILWAINE PHIPSON, F.S.A., died December 30, at Norwich, aged fifty-seven. As an architect he was largely employed in the work of church restoration in Norfolk and Suffolk. He took great interest in the local Archæological Association, to whose journal he was an occasional contributor, his latest paper being on the subject of "Carrow Abbey."

MR. JOHN WHICHCORD, F.S.A., died on the 9th January at his residence in Inverness-terrace, Hyde Park. He was the author of " The History and Antiquities of Christ Church, Maidstone," " The History and Antiquities of St. Mary's, Aldermanbury," " Polychromy of the Middle Ages," and other works. He contributed many papers to the Royal Institute of British Architects. Mr. Whichcord was president of that society in 1879-81.

MR. HENRY CHARLES COOTE, F.S.A., the learned and distinguished author of " The Romans of Britain," died on the 4th of January. The youngest son of Dr. Charles Coote, a celebrated advocate of Doctors' Commons, author of " Sketches of the Lives and Characters of Eminent English Civilians," the subject of this notice was born in 1814, and practised for many years as a proctor and solicitor in the Probate, Admiralty, and Ecclesiastical Courts, and his works on the practice of those Courts have passed through many editions ; but it was as an antiquary that Mr. Coote was best known in the world of letters. In 1840 he printed in the *Gentleman's Magazine*, under the signature of H. C. C., a series of papers entitled " A Neglected Fact in English History," which he expanded in 1878 into his important historical work, " The Romans of Britain." He has since published in the *Transactions* of the Society of Antiquaries and of the London and Middlesex Archæological Society, the " Cuisine Bourgeoise of Ancient Rome," " Centuriation of Roman Britain," " The Milites Stationarii considered in Relation to the Hundred and Tithing of England," " Ordinances of some Secular Guilds of London from 1354 to 1496," " The English Guilds of Knights and their Socn," and other papers. Mr. Coote was a member of the Folk-lore Society from its foundation in 1878, and had frequently contributed to its *Journal*. He was also an occasional contributor to the *Athenæum* and *Notes and Queries*. As an archæologist Mr. Coote was highly commended at the last meeting of the London and Middlesex Archæological Society. He was a Vice-President of both the London and Middlesex Archæological and the Folk-lore Societies.

Meetings of Learned Societies.

METROPOLITAN.

SOCIETY OF ANTIQUARIES.—*Jan.* 8, Dr. Freshfield, Vice-President, in the chair. This was a meeting for business purposes, and the ballot for the election of Fellows. The following were elected :—Mr. F. Brent, Rev. G. T. Harvey, Mr. G. F. France, Mr. G. F. Bodley, A.R.A., and Mr. F. E. Sawyer. There was exhibited a series of 150 sketches of the Roman works between the Tyne and Solway Firth, executed by Mr. J. I. Coates. —*Jan.* 15. Dr. C. S. Perceval, treasurer, in the chair. A communication was read from the Rev. Robert Jenkins, of Lyminge, Kent, giving an account of sundry discoveries made by recent excavations in and around his churchyard and church, the foundations of which are believed to be Roman. Mr. Cooper-Cooper, of Toddington, Bedfordshire, gave also similar accounts of discoveries which had been made in the neighbourhood of Dunstable. Mr. J. C. Robinson exhibited two specimens of heraldic carvings on large oak panels, which were interpreted by Mr. Everard Green to be the achievements of a member of the Blount family, and the alliances of that house among the squires of Herefordshire. The chairman read a paper, by himself, entitled, "Remarks on an Early Seal," which was followed by a discussion, in which Mr. Milman, Mr. Winkley, and other Fellows took part.

BRITISH ARCHÆOLOGICAL ASSOCIATION. — *Jan.* 7, Mr. George R. Wright, F.S.A., in the chair. Mr. C. Lynam sent a cast of the inscription on the cross at Carew, and drawings of another cross at Penally, visited during the recent Congress. Mr. J. H. Whieldon sent further details of the Roman bridge at Collingham, which will be published in the next part of the *Journal*. The Chairman referred to some seventeenth century carvings which were taken down from Goathurst Church, Somerset, although still in the building. now for sale. The importance of retaining these in the church was urged by many speakers. Mr. Loftus Brock, F.S.A., referred to the collection of balluster shafts—probably of Roman workmanship—found in the walls of Jarrow Church during the rebuilding. and now preserved in the porch. The discussion upon the charities of the Royal Almonry, adjourned from the last meeting, was brought to a close. The Sub-Almoner defined the word "Deodand," as relating to chattels which had caused the death of a man. forfeited to the Crown. Mr. de Gray Birch, F.S.A., referred the derivation of the word "Maunday" to the art of eating, and instanced its occurrence in an Anglo-Saxon document of 832. Mr. Arthur Cope rendered some curious notes as to the practice of claiming deodands. If a man lent his sword and murder was committed, the sword was a deodand, and was not returned to its owner. If a horse threw its rider into a stream and he was drowned, the horse was not a deodand, since it was the water which slew the man. Mr. C. H. Compton referred to the old Mosaic Law, and in modern times to a railway engine being a deodand. Deodands were only finally abolished by Lord Campbell's Act. Mr. Walford traced the word from the Latin *deodandum*, which exactly defined its meaning. A paper was then read by Mr. C. Lynam, on the recent excavations on the site of the Abbey of Hulton, Staffordshire. The whole arrangement of the church and the conventual buildings have been recovered, and the site has been again filled in after careful measurement, the plans being produced

SOCIETY OF BIBLICAL ARCHÆOLOGY.—*Jan.* 13, Dr. Samuel Birch, President, in the chair. After the transaction of some formal business the Secretary's report for 1884 was read, from which it appears that the number of members is steadily on the increase ; and that in the communications submitted to the society in the form of both letters and papers printed in the Proceedings, the language and antiquities of ancient Babylonia and Assyria formed a large portion. The mounds scattered about the plains of Mesopotamia have yielded many valuable records, descriptions of some of which have appeared during the past year in the publications of the society. The report having been adopted, and the officers and council for the current year elected, Mr. T. G. Pinches read a paper entitled, "The Babylonian Kings of the Mythical Period," which was followed by a discussion.

LONDON AND MIDDLESEX ARCHÆOLOGICAL SOCIETY.—*Jan.* 12, Mr. Alfred White in the chair. The Chairman, in opening the proceedings, deplored the death of the late Bishop of London, who had been the patron of the society, and Mr. Henry Charles Coote, who studied every question of archæology, and made himself perfect master of every subject which he took in hand. Professor Hales read a paper entitled, "Notes on the Anglo-Saxon Charters Relating to Hampstead," in the course of whieh he said that the old Anglo-Saxon charters which were now accessible, cast important light on the social life and customs of ancient England. Especially they made us thoroughly realise how very old were the boundaries of property in this country, even at a period so remote as 1,000 years ago. They heard at the present time a great deal about the boundaries of boroughs, and it was a curious fact that what was now to be the borough of Hampstead had existed within the same boundaries as the Manor of Hampstead 100 years before the Norman conquest. The first charter relating to Hampstead was granted by King Edgar, and the second by King Athelred. The date of the first was 986, it had been known for many years, and the original itself existed in the archives of Westminster. The second charter, which had been only lately known, was amongst the Ashburnham manuscripts, which had been secured to the nation, and were now in the British Museum. Park, in his history of Hampstead, had supposed that the charter of Athelred was a forgery, but he (Professor Hales) thought they might fairly believe in its genuineness. It bore the signature of the king's wife Elfrida, and granted the manor of Hampstead to a certain person named Mangola, whose identity had not hitherto been traced. The second charter confirmed the grant of the first, which set out the limits of Hampstead, a name well known in the tenth century. A discussion followed, in which Mr. Waller, Mr. Kershaw, Mr. E. Walford, Mr. Finch, the Chairman, and other gentlemen took part. Mr. E. Walford said that the society was deeply indebted to Professor Hales for his valuable paper, which had cleared up several hitherto obscure matters connected with the early history of Hampstead, the substance of which would be embodied in the revised edition of Park's History, which was now in preparation by himself, and which would be published by Mr. Bogue in the course of the summer. Mr. Seaton also read a paper on excavations made in connection with the Inner Circle Railway.

VICTORIA INSTITUTE.—*Jan.* 5. A paper on the "Aboriginal Tribes of India" was read by Professor Avery.

NUMISMATIC.—*Dec.* 18, Dr. J. Evans in the chair. Mr. Roach Smith exhibited two gold coins of Allectus, one of which had for reverse type a lion, probably a copy of a similar coin in silver of Gallienus. Mr. T. W. Greene communicated a paper on Renaissance medals in relation to antique gems and coins, in which he showed that many Italian medallists of the fifteenth and sixteenth centuries not only were gem engravers. but occasionally made use of such works for the designs of their medals, these objects being at that time much prized by collectors. Mr. W. Wroth communicated a paper on the Santorin find of 1821, with which he connected several unclassed coins in the British Museum. These coins appear to have been issued in Ægina and the other Ægean Islands.

ROYAL HISTORICAL SOCIETY.—*Jan.* 15, Mr. Hyde Clarke in the chair. Major-Gen. Sir F. J. Goldsmid, C.B., read a paper on the "Perplexities of Oriental History."

ST. PAUL'S ECCLESIOLOGICAL SOCIETY.—*Nov.* 25, Mr. Charles Browne in the chair. Mr. T. Francis Bumpus read a paper entitled "Stray Notes on some London Churches erected since the Reformation, with especial reference to those of the Revival," describing in detail a large number of modern London churches.—*Dec.* 9, Mr. H. R. Gough, F.R.I.B.A., in the chair. Mr. John D. Sedding, F.R.I.B.A., read a paper entitled "Some Remarks upon Modern Ecclesiastical Art," in which he advocated a greater freedom and more natural treatment of Gothic. Mr. Sedding contended generally for more originality and a less slavish following of antiquity, as antiquity. He was in favour of the Renaissance style being adopted for town churches, while the Gothic style might be still used for village churches.

ANTHROPOLOGICAL INSTITUTE.—*Dec.* 9, Prof. Flower, President, in the chair. Sir J. Lubbock read a paper "On Marriage Customs and Relationships among the Australian Aborigines."

NEW SHAKSPERE.—*Dec.* 12, the Rev. W. A. Harrison in the chair. Miss Leigh Noel's third and last division of her paper "On Shakspere's Garden of Girls" was, in the absence of the writer, read by Mr. S. L. Lee, the characters treated being the "wild flowers"—Miranda, Perdita, Katharine, &c. Mr. F. J. Furnivall read some notes, by Mr. W. G. Stone, "On the Textual Difficulties in 'Measure for Measure.'" Mr. Furnivall called the attention of the meeting to the subject of those prose passages in Shakespeare which contained obvious verses, and asked for opinions as to the propriety of printing such passages as verse when the rhythm was undoubted.

PROVINCIAL.

ROYAL HISTORICAL AND ARCHÆOLOGICAL ASSOCIATION OF IRELAND. —*Jan.* 7. Annual meeting, the Right Rev. the Bishop of Ossory in the chair. From the report, which was read by the Secretary, the Rev. H. Graves, it appeared that there had been an increase of 44 new members in the course of the year. It was stated that the annual volume of the Association for the current year would be a "Monograph of Inishmurray," dealing with its churches, cloghans, crosses, &c., edited by Mr. W. F. Wakeman, Fellow of the Association, and Local Secretary for Dublin. The President, officers, and committee were then unanimously re-elected, with some additional Vice-Presidents as follows:— Ulster—The Very Rev. the Dean of Armagh and the Rev. Canon Grainger. Leinster—Lord Clermont and John P. Prendergast, B.L. Munster—The O'Donovan and the Rev. Canon Hayman, M.A. Connaught—The Hon. Gerald Dillon and Richard Langrishe, M.R.I.A.I. Colonel Vigors presented and explained some interesting "rubbings" from monuments in Old Leighlin Cathedral. Mr. W. Grey sent a paper with illustrations to appear in the next number of the society's Journal, on "Cromlechs of Antrim and Down." Mr. Day, of Cork, sent a paper on "Book-plates engraved in Cork." Mr. John P. Prendergast sent a transcript of a poem taken from a volume which was in the possession of the great Lord Charlemont, 1675. Its title was "The Moderate Cavlier," and it gave a graphic picture of the state of things after the Cromwellian settlement in Ireland. The Chairman exhibited photographs of a tablet to Tiglath, King of Assyria, telling of his wars with King Ahaziah, and how he crushed King Pekah, about 700 B.C. Another photograph was shown by his lordship of a terra-cotta cylinder containing much that was interesting about Esar-Haddon, King of Assyria B.C. 680.

HAILEYBURY COLLEGE ANTIQUARIAN SOCIETY.—*Oct.* 27. Mr. S. F Williams read a paper on Dunmow, Essex, treating of the curious custom of the "Flitch of Bacon," and the parish church. The paper ended with a discussion on the different styles of architecture exhibited in the building. The President (Rev. G. E. Jeans) read some extracts from a paper on "The Church Bells of Norfolk," sent to the

Society by the Rev. Dr. Raven. Some illustrations, copied from the paper by Yeates, were handed round.—*Nov. 10.* Mr. B. A. Snell read a paper on the "General History of Signboards," and Mr. W. Kennedy one on "The Destruction of Rome."

Antiquarian News & Notes.

C. SATHÁS has completed the fifth volume of his "Monumenta Historiæ Hellenicæ."

THE bi-centenary of Ludvig Holberg, the "father" of Danish literature, was celebrated in December at Copenhagen.

CARDINAL DU FALLOUX, who died in June last, has left to the Vatican a valuable collection of Moyen Age furniture and other objects.

A COLLECTION of casts from Greek and Roman works has been added to the South Kensington Museum.

THE Mayor of Taunton has presented a badge and chain of office to be worn by future Mayors of the ancient borough.

LORD EGERTON has presented to Chester Cathedral an antique marble font, specially obtained from Italy.

MR. JOSEPH BRIGSTOCKE SHEPPARD, antiquarian and historian, of Canterbury, has received the Lambeth degree of Doctor of Laws.

TWO art exhibitions were opened in January, namely, the Old Masters at Burlington House, and the Gainsborough collection at the Grosvenor Gallery.

MR. BOND, principal librarian of the British Museum, and Mr. George Scharf, F.S.A., director and secretary of the National Portrait Gallery, have been nominated Companions of the Bath.

A CLASSICAL prize has been founded at the Charter House School, in memory of the late Mr. Gordon Whitbread, a member of the Governing Body.

MR. JAMES BRYCE'S essay on "The Holy Roman Empire" is being translated into Italian by Count Ugo Balzani, and will be published in the spring by Signor Vallardi, of Naples.

M. ALEXANDRE DUMAS has presented to the Comédie Française the only known example of the handwriting of Molière, an act of one of his plays, with his signature appended.

MR. GRIGGS's fac-simile reprint of Richard III. (1597) is now ready for delivery to subscribers. The introduction is by Mr. P. A. Daniel, one of Mr. Furnivall's collaborators.

A. PAPADÓPULOS KERAMEUS has printed a part of the catalogue of the MSS. which he has lately examined in the Monastery of Leimon, in the Island of Lesbos.

THE Queen has subscribed £25 to the fund for the restoration of Queen Eleanor's Cross at Northampton. The members of the Northampton Architectural Society are interesting themselves in the matter.

THE present year witnesses the centenary of the deaths of the following illustrious persons : John Sebastian Bach, George F. Handel, Giovanni B. Cipriani, Fra Sebastian del Piombo, and Sir David Wilkie.

The Editor of the Journal of the Faversham Institute has lately added a column of local "Notes and Queries," thus helping to educate the young people of Kent, at all events to the extent of encouraging in them a spirit of historical inquiry. All such efforts should be supported.

THE fifth centenary of the death of Wycliffe, the Reformer, on December 31, passed off at Lutterworth, the scene of his labours and death, without any special ceremony being observed in his honour.

CAPTAIN R. C. TEMPLE, by his collection of the legends of the Punjab and the publication of Punjab notes and queries, is doing much to remove the reproach that England is indifferent to Punjabee literature.

THE municipal records of Bath, from Richard I. to Elizabeth, are being prepared for publication by Messrs. Austin J. King and Benj. V. Watts.

WITH the new year was published the first number of " The Manx Note Book," a quarterly journal of matters past and present connected with the Isle of Manx. It is edited by Mr. A. W. Moore, M.A.

A NEW edition of Mr. Thomas Fairbairn's " Relics of Ancient Architecture and other Picturesque Scenes in Glasgow," is in preparation. The book has long been out of print. Messrs. Annan, of Glasgow, are to issue the work.

THE Rev. J. Halford, vicar of Brixworth, Northampton, has reported the discovery in that parish of an earthenware vase—probably a Roman cinerary urn—and other articles of pottery, spearheads, &c. The objects were found about 3 ft. below the surface.

THE Ashburnham manuscripts have arrived safely at Florence, and were delivered at the Laurenzian Library by Professor, or, as he must now be called, Senator, Villari on December 3. The thirty cases which contained them were sent from Ostend in a special waggon, fastened with locks and seals. They were insured for £23,000.

MR. JOHN BRIGHT, M.P., has bought, for £4 10s., at Messrs. Puttick and Simpson's auction rooms, the original certificate on parchment of the marriage of Abraham Ellis, of Jewin-street, London, and Elizabeth Hudson, of Cripplegate (Quakers), which was solemnised on the 25th of February, 1691.

MESSRS. KEGAN PAUL & CO. announce, under the title of " Raphael and the Villa Farnesina," an account, by M. Charles Bigot, of Raphael's decoration of the famous villa, illustrative of the stories of Psyche and of Galatea, with fifteen etchings. The edition consists of 150 copies only, all numbered and signed.

DURING the renovations and cleaning of St. Peter's Church, Sudbury, Suffolk, the remains of an ancient fresco over the chancel arch have been re-discovered. Thirty years ago the painting was found under layers of whitewash ; but, only a central and two side figures being partially visible, it was again coloured over. It represented " The Last Judgment."

AMPTON HALL, near Bury St. Edmunds, the seat of Mr. John Paley, was burnt down on January 3. It was a large brick-built mansion, of the Tudor period. Swakeleys, near Uxbridge, Middlesex, a fine old Elizabethan mansion, narrowly escaped destruction by fire in December : one valuable picture was destroyed.

The Phonetic Journal for January contains the address of the President of the Shorthand Society, Mr. T. A. Reed, delivered at the meeting in December. It is entitled " The Early History of Professional Shorthand Writing in England," and gives much interesting information concerning the practice of it from the middle of the sixteenth century.

MESSRS. MACMILLAN & BOWES, of Cambridge, have announced the publication of an etching, by Mr. Robert Farren, of Samuel Cooper's portrait of Oliver Cromwell in the lodge of Sidney College ; also forty etchings, by Mr. Farren, of the cathedral cities of Ely and Norwich, with an introduction by Mr. Edward A. Freeman, D.C.L.

THE late Dr. Angus Smith's library, consisting of 3,500 volumes, has been purchased and presented to Owens College. The division containing the rarest and most valuable books, the Celtic, with 490 volumes, is said to be the most important collection in existence of works relating to the Celtic language and the history of Scotland.

THE Rev. J. W. Ebsworth is hard at work upon the sixth volume of the "Roxburghe Ballads," which he is editing. Mr. Ebsworth has still the two remaining volumes, including the huge general index of the entire work, to complete. He has also on hand his still heavier editorial work, "The Civil War; Protectorate and Restoration Ballads and Political Poems, 1637—1661."

MR. RICHARD JACKSON, of Leeds, has announced for publication, by subscription, "The Costumes of Yorkshire; or, Manners, Customs, Industries, and Dress of Yorkshire in 1814." The work will be edited by Mr. Edward Hailstone, F.S.A., and will contain engravings illustrative of Yorkshire life and character seventy years ago.

WHILE two men were engaged recently in cutting a drain on land belonging to Mr. Ferguson, near Beaumont, Cumberland, they came upon a large quantity of coins of Edward I. and King David I. of Scotland. The coins were buried beneath a round stone close to the surface, and had evidently been enclosed in a bag or some other covering.

THE issue of the "Key" to the abbreviations used in the Early Pipe Rolls, which it was anticipated would be ready in time to forward with the second volume of the Pipe Roll Society's publications for 1883-4, is unavoidably postponed for a short period, the Council having decided to include in the work some important additional matter.

MR. MURRAY'S January list of publications contains, inter alia, Professor Brewer's "Reign of Henry VIII.," edited by Mr. J. Gairdner; Cook's "Origin of Language and Religion;" Mr. A. S. Murray's "History of Greek Sculpture;" and new editions of Dr. Schliemann's works— "Troja," "Ilios," and "Mycenæ and Tiryns," and a uniform edition of Dean Stanley's works.

MESSRS. LONGMAN will publish shortly a work by Mr. J. Theodore Bent, entitled "The Cyclades: a Life among the Insular Greeks," containing accounts of folk-lore and archæological researches during two winters spent on these islands. Mr. Bent will shortly continue his explorations among the Sporades. The antiquities which Mr. Bent brought from the pre-historic graves in Antiparos have been purchased by the British Museum.

MR. AUSTIN DOBSON has completed for the Clarendon Press a volume of selections from the essays of Steele upon the model of Mr. Arnold's selections from Addison. Mr. Dobson's selections will include papers from the *Tatler, Guardian*, &c. The volume will be annotated and introduced by a memoir embodying some fresh items of information which it is proposed to use in a larger Life.

THE Emperor of Austria has publicly opened the new buildings at the University, Vienna, in the presence of the authorities. The Rector said that five centuries ago Duke Albert III. of Austria, by adding a Theological Faculty, had completed the institution founded by his brother, Rudolph, as a *Universitas Literarum*. Successive Sovereigns had raised new buildings, and His Majesty had given the site of the present fine structure.

THE restoration of the west front of Lichfield Cathedral is fast progressing, and several of the still vacant niches will shortly be filled with the statues intended to replace the old series. The arcade of kings, which forms a striking feature in the front, will be soon completed, those of Penda, Wulfere, Ethelred, Offa, Egbert, Ethelwolf, Alfred the Great, Edgar, Canute, Edward the Confessor, Richard II., &c., being *in situ*, to be followed by those of King David, William I., and II., Henry I., II., and III., and Edward I.

THE large chambered mound discovered in the parish of Stenness, in west mainland of Orkney, has now been fully opened and explored by Mr. Clouston. Among implements of the Stone Age found are a flint arrow-head and a stone knife and some fragments of pottery. A number of pieces of bones and human skulls were also found, but so broken and scattered as to be of little value. Altogether there are six large chambers and one small chamber in the mound, the larger chambers ranging in size from 4 ft. by 5 ft. to 5½ ft. by 6 ft.

A PARLIAMENTARY Committee has been sitting to decide what shall be done with the western front or side of Westminster Hall, which it is feared will decay if exposed to the weather ; but no report is expected till the spring. Meantime, a controversy rages in the daily papers as to the desirability of lengthening the windows and raising the roof of the hall, so as to increase the light in its interior. The controversy has led to an expression of much architectural feeling, which appears to be settling in favour of a one-storied cloister, leaving the carved corbels and flying buttresses exposed to view as at present. It appears that the floor of the hall was lowered by Mr. Sidney Smirke, in 1836.

THE rebuilding of the Lanthorne Tower, as one of the main features of the Tower of London, has just been completed. It has been built upon the original foundations of the old Lanthorne Tower, which were discovered a few years since, and from drawings made from old sketches, a portion of the materials being those which formed the old building. The structure is situated midway between the Wakefield Tower and the Salt Tower, and is connected with the latter by a massive ballium wall. Immediately on the north side of the wall a flight of steps is carried up to the level of the castellated battlements leading on to a parade extend-ing to the Salt Tower. The parade rests on a series of Gothic arches.

WITH reference to the present dearth of fish, Mr. W. O. Chambers, Secretary to the National Fish Culture Association, writes : " The cost of pond construction in the first instance is small, and when once they are made and properly stocked with fish the expense of maintenance is nominal. During the middle ages the monks and abbots of the monasteries, together with the occupiers of old manor-houses, reduced the culture of fish and the construction of stews to a science, chiefly on account of the difficulty of transporting sea-caught fish from the coast to inland towns and villages."

AT an early date will be published by subscription an elaborate work on " Monumental Brasses on the Continent of Europe," with brief descriptive notes by the Rev. W. F. Creeny, M.A., Vicar of St. Michael, at Thorn, Norwich. The book, which will be imperial folio, will be a valuable addition to our archæological literature. It will contain thirty full-page illustrations, comprising in all eighty examples of the most im-portant and elaborate brasses from Denmark, Sweden, Germany, Poland, Silesia, Bavaria, Switzerland, Holland, Belgium, France, and Spain. Rubbings of many of the brasses have been exhibited at meetings of the Society of Antiquaries, &c.

AN archæological discovery only to be compared to that of the Scipios' tomb in 1780 has been made in the building land lately bought for the Bonaparte family by the Banca Romana outside Porta Salara, at Rome. It is the tomb of four noble persons of the family of Licinius Crassus, concerning whom we find many pages of mention in Tacitus and Suetonius, not to speak of references of minor importance in Seneca, Pliny the Younger, and others. Three out of these four persons were assassinated, the first by order of Claudius ; the second by that of Nero ; and the third by that of Otho. Pompey's epitaph mentions his imperial father-in-law, at whose hands he met his death.

IN clearing the northern wing of the Roman Villa at Brading, in 1881, was found a well which at the time was cleaned out to the depth of 75 ft., at which point the work had to be given up on account of the rapid inflow of water, but at the close of last year a further attempt was made to reach the bottom of the well, which was found just over 90 ft. from the surface. In the excavation three years ago several objects of interest were discovered, worked stones, Roman pottery, tiles, burnt wood, and portions of a human skeleton. In the last 15 ft. the only things found were boulders such as were used in the construction of walls, flints, and a few pieces of Roman pottery.

CATALOGUES, containing articles more or less of an antiquarian character, have reached us from Messrs. Jefferies & Sons, Redcliff-street, Bristol ; Mr. John Taylor, Northampton, (mostly referring to the history of Northamptonshire) ; Messrs. Jarvis & Son, 28, King William-street, W.C., (comprising MSS., scarce editions of Shelley, Keats, Byron, and Shakespeariana, &c.) ; Mr. William Downing, New-street Birmingham ; Mr. Henry Gray, Cathedral-yard, Manchester ; Mr. J. Salisbury, 48, Paternoster-row ; Mr. W. P. Bennett, Bull-street, Birmingham (in which will be found some purchases from the Syston Park Library) ; Mr. A. B. Osborne, 11, Red Lion-passage, W.C. (including the " Duke of Hamilton's Tracts " and Burton's " Cromwellian Diary.")

THE Basilerski collection of objects of old Christian art, which has been purchased for five and a half million francs for the Emperor of Russia, is about to be added to the treasures of the Hermitage Palace, and will be placed in the two rooms of the upper story hitherto occupied by the numismatic collection. This latter collection will be transferred to the rooms on the ground-floor that were formerly used for the Council of State. Very many of the objects in the Basilerski collection are of German workmanship, and date from the 13th and 14th centuries. Such are two remonstrances, and some carved figures of saints in wood. There are also carvings by German artists of the 15th century, stained glass, and some articles of iron work. The collection ranges from the second to the sixteenth century, and is particularly rich in objects of the Renaissance period.

A BAGFUL of historical documents relating to the proceedings which led to the siege of Carlisle in 1644 and 1645, says the *Standard*, has been found under a beam in the triforium on the north-west side of the choir of Carlisle Cathedral, by the workmen who were making some repairs. The documents bear the dates of 1642 and 1643, and they must have been hidden under the beam 240 years ago. They have been taken possession of by the Dean and Chapter. The siege of Carlisle by the Scots, after the battle of Marston Moor, forms one of the most interesting episodes of the history of the city. The place was invested on all sides by Lieut.-General Leslie, and his force numbered 4,000 horse and foot. The garrison consisted of about 700, 200 of whom had come with Sir Thomas

Glenham, commander-in-chief of King Charles's forces. The siege lasted many months, the Scots finally getting possession of the city on June 25, 1645.

THE Royal Academy of Sciences at Berlin is in communication with the Prussian Government for the purpose of obtaining a more perfect exploration and survey of the supposed site of the catastrophe which overwhelmed the Roman legions under Varus, A D. 9. The circumstance which set the Academy in motion was a communication from Professor Mommsen, about some Roman treasures found in the last century near Osnabrück, and containing a large amount of Roman coins, some of a late date. The alleged site of the discovery of this treasure is near the place which tradition has assigned for the battle. The Government has deputed Dr. Menadier, of the Royal Cabinet of Coins, to report on the coins found near Osnabrück. It will subsequently be decided whether a full survey of the supposed site of the disaster of Varus is desirable.

THE following articles, more or less of an antiquarian character, appear among the contents of the magazines for December and January:— *Blackwood*, "John Wycliffe, his Life and Work;" *Contemporary Review*, "Würzburg and Vienna," "Ancient Palestine and Modern Exploration," "The City Companies," and "Dr. Johnson;" *National Review*, "The Myths of Romeo and Juliet;" *Magazine of Art*, "The New Forest, historical." "Oriental Brasswork," "Hatfield House," "Early Sculptural Stones in England," and "Francis I., Architect and Amateur;" *English Illustrated Magazine*, "Thomas Gainsborough," "St. Guido," "Clovelly," and "Shakespeare's Country;" *Tinsley's* "The Altar-piece of St. Romain," and "A Ramble through the Metropolis;" *The Century Illustrated Magazine*, "Dublin City;" *Fortnightly Review*, "Samuel Johnson," and "Eastern Notes;" *Quarterly Review*, "Dr. Johnson and his Era;" *Edinburgh Review*, "Recent Excavations at Rome."

IT is known that a great Roman road led from Mayence, by Worms, to Spires and Strasburg, but its exact line has been ascertained in only a few places. Lately the accident of the carrying out of some alterations and extensions at a manufactory at Worms brought to light a portion of the old pavement, and 400 mètres (about a quarter of a mile) have been laid bare. A large collection of antiquarian objects has been found. Among them are a large number of "pieces" (*latrunculi*) for playing the game of draughts, made of earthenware, slate, glass, marble, ivory, &c. and two figures of terra-cotta. representing matrons on horseback, much broken in the process of digging out. Some time ago some workmen found in the road, near Mayence, a small carved tablet, a companion to which was dug out a few days since. The two together form a Roman military commission, bearing date Oct. 27 (vi. Kal. Nov.) of the year 91 of our era. This interesting relic has been placed in the Paulus Museum at Mayence.—*The Times*.

THE extensive and valuable collection of ancient books, deeds, maps, and other documents, forming an almost complete historic record of Hackney from the days when it was a mere "vyllage neare London" to the present time, has been handed over by its donor, the Rev. R. D. Tyssen, rector of South Hackney, to the special committee appointed by the Hackney Vestry for its reception. One of the large rooms in the Town-hall has been set apart for the purpose, and as soon as the preparation of the catalogue, itself no inconsiderable task, shall have been completed, the library, under certain regulations, will be open for inspection and reference by the parishioners of Hackney on Tuesday evenings.

The Vestry has resolved to effect an insurance on the library for £1,000, but that amount does not represent the value of the documents, which Mr. Michael Young, chairman of the committee, describes as "above price," and likely to prove of service to local historiographers.

THE late Mr. W. Russell's collection of drawings by the Old Masters, and engravings and water-colour drawings, have been sold by auction by Messrs. Christie. Among the most interesting specimens of the Old Masters were Michael Angelo Buonarotti, study of a female sleeping, black chalk, £57 15s. ; whole length figure of a man, pen and ink, with a contemporary copy, from the Denon Collection, and an engraving, after the original by Fabbri (3), £47 5s. ; Correggio, the Virgin and Child, red chalk, from the Cosway Collection, £25 4s. ; Vandyck, the Crucifixion, in bistre, £5 ; Holbein, three heads of priests, from the Uvedale, Price, and Myles Collections, £8 ; Giorgione, warrior in armour, £5 ; J. Van Huysum, vases with flowers, water colours, £13 ; N. Poussin, Administering extreme unction, and Christ delivering the keys to St. Peter, pen and bistre, £8 8s. ; Domenichino (after Raphael), the Three Graces, with Cupid, from the ceiling of the Farnesina, red and black chalk, £5 15s. 6d. ; Raphael, A Papal Procession, composition from the "Heliodorus," black and coloured chalk, £105 ; The Virgin, Child, and St. Anne, a small cartoon, black chalk, £10 10s. ; Giulio Romano, the Battle of Constantine (after Raphael), in water-colours, £7 17s. 6d. ; Rubens' Jupiter and Cupid, from Raphael's fresco on the ceiling of the Farnesina, red chalk, £10 10s. ; A. Vandyck, Samson and Delilah, water-colours, £16 5s. ; Titian, landscape, with sheep and herdsmen piping, pen and bistre, twice engraved, £12 1s. 6d. The total proceeds of the sale, which lasted three days, was over £2,300.

WE have received the first Report of the Oxford Historical Society. It was started on January 1, 1884, with more than 400 members, now increased to 500. The text of four volumes is ready for the press ; but the operations of printing and binding will delay the issues for 1884 until the first quarter of 1885. It is hoped that such delay will not occur again. The publications for 1884 will be (1) Vol. i. of an edition of Hearne's Diaries, edited by C. E. Doble, M.A., of Worcester College. This first instalment will include *all* the matter contained in the first fifteen volumes of the MS. diaries, which can be regarded as of permanent value. A special and, perhaps, unique feature of this edition is that Hearne's correspondence is calendared on the same page with the record of each day, so that we shall not only follow his movements and literary labours, but also take note of the budget of letters received and sent out, which must have largely influenced his daily life. 250 pages out of about 420 are already in type, and only the index and notes remain to be composed. (2) The records of degrees conferred by the University between 1448 and 1463, and from 1505 to 1564, edited by the Rev. C. W. Boase, Fellow of Exeter College. This work is nearly finished, and will present in chronological order, with an alphabetical index, the entire series of degrees of which records remain, up to the register of Matriculations in 1564. It may be expected that some interesting identifications will result from the publication of these lists. (3) Mr. James Parker's Account of Early Oxford, enlarged from the private issue of 1871. This will include all the extracts about the city which are contained in the old chronicles and in the manuscript life of S. Frideswide, and touching on the early legendary history. These three volumes will contain about 900 pages, and the committee feel able to pledge themselves that the three will be ıssued *before* Easter, 1885. The accounts of the Society will be made up, audited, and sent round to members soon after the close of the year. The Society regrets the loss of two distinguished members of the Council, H.R.H. Prince Leopold, and the Rev. Mark Pattison, late Rector of Lincoln College.

THE intended issues of the above Society for the present year are : (1) Dr. Bloxam's collection of documents relating to the attempt of James II. to force a President of his own nomination on Magdalen College. (2) Vol. i. of a series of Memorials of Merton College, containing short biographies of the Wardens and Fellows up to the seventeenth century, based on the papers of Antony a Wood, Astry, and Kilner, edited by the Hon. the Warden, and prefaced by his lately-delivered lectures on the state of the College at successive periods. (3) A volume of Collectanea, edited by C. R. L. Fletcher, Fellow of All Souls' College. The component parts may be the following, which are arranged in chronological order :—*a.* Oxford coroners' inquests (early thirteenth century), edited from MSS. in the Bodleian, at Bridgewater, and in the Public Record Office, by James E. Thorold Rogers, M.P. ; *b.* A fourteenth century catalogue of Oriel College Library, edited with a preface by C. L. Shadwell, Fellow of the College ; *c.* Early letters relating to Oxford, edited from the originals in the British Museum and Public Record Office, by C. Trice Martin, M.A., F.S.A. ; *d.* The daily ledger of John Dorne, bookseller in Oxford, 1520-21, believed to be unique of its kind, edited from a C.C.C. (Oxf.) MS. by F. Madan, M.A. ; *e.* The building accounts of Wadham College, edited by the Rev. J. Griffiths, D.D., Keeper of the Archives ; *f.* The account-book of James Wildinge, a student at Oxford, 1682-87, edited by E. G. Duff, an undergraduate of Wadham College ; *g.* Dr. Wallis's account of life and studies at the University at the close of the seventeenth century, edited from a Savile MS. by Major-General Gibbes Rigaud, M.A.

ST. MICHAEL'S at Coventry is the largest parish church in England with the exception of St. Nicholas at Great Yarmouth, which is said to exceed its area by one or two square feet. The steeple is the highest among those of parish churches, while it is surpassed by only two of our cathedrals, Salisbury and Norwich. " It is probably unrivalled," writes Mr. J. O. Scott, " in the perfect gracefulness which marks its design." The time has now come that this grand pile must be restored, and the citizens of Coventry have set to work in earnest to raise the means ; the estimated cost is £35,000, but with £30,000 in hand or promised the work will proceed. Towards this sum £29,000 has been raised within the last few months, including one donation from a generous parishioner of £10,000. The restoration committee, of which the Bishop of Worcester is President and Lord Leigh Vice-President, feel assured that they will not appeal in vain for help to complete the amount required from the many who know of St. Michael's, Coventry, as one of " the glories of our land." The tower and steeple, which together are 303 feet high, were commenced in A.D. 1373, and the tower was completed in 1395 at the cost of William and Adam Botoner, Mayors of Coventry, and in a few years after the spire was built with a great enlargement of the church by their sisters, Ann and Mary Botoner. The great value of the structure on account of its high architectural merits gave it the character of a public monument ; and Sir Gilbert Scott in a report upon the structure some years since goes on to say : " The design is in every way excellent ; every detail is designed and carried out with the most careful study. It is of the earliest variety of the

Perpendicular style—a vigorous and manly style, intended no doubt as a falling back upon more massive and nervous forms after the too great softness and flexibility of treatment which had characterised the architecture of the middle of the fourteenth century." Fortunately, the interior of the church was restored some thirty years since. In the present restoration of the exterior under Mr. J. O. Scott, there will be *no deviation* from original lines, the intention being not to innovate, but to "restore" the building to its original beauty.

THE dispute between the Dean and the Restoration Committee of Peterborough Cathedral and the Bishop and Chapter has been submitted to arbitration. A meeting of the Restoration Committee was held on Dec. 17, the Dean presiding, for the purpose of considering the question of raising the tower, and a resolution which had been passed by the Chapter to the effect that, considering the generally depressed state of trade, the Chapter did not feel justified in altering the present contract in respect to the central tower. This resolution the meeting did not endorse, but the following resolution was carried, fourteen voting for it and five against: "That the Restoration Committee is of opinion it is desirable that the Dean and Chapter should adopt the first stage of Mr. Pearson's modified plan for rebuilding and raising the central tower, and that the work be at once proceeded with; the Committee recognising that a special fund be raised to defray the additional expenditure involved by this deviation from the original plan." Dr. Leonard Cane, a member of the Restoration Committee, writes that "during the work of demolition enough of the original Norman arcading has been discovered to enable the architect to restore the tower to its intended height; and this was stated by Mr. Pearson in his report issued to the subscribers in January, 1884, when a further appeal was made for subscriptions towards the completion of the works recommended by the architect, which distinctly included 'the raising of the central tower.' As for reproducing the historical character of a great part of the Cathedral," adds Dr. Cane, "surely it is not necessary to reproduce the errors of the fourteenth century builders, who were compelled by the rotten state of the piers to put up the low and lightly-constructed lantern tower. Let all who wish to see a complete restoration of Peterborough Cathedral rally round the Restoration Committee, who at their last annual meeting recommended to the Dean and Chapter that Mr. Pearson's plan should be adopted." In a letter to *The Times*, in January last, Mr. Turner, the Secretary of the Society for the Protection of Ancient Buildings, writes: "The Dean and Chapter and the Restoration Committee entered into a contract with the public to rebuild the tower of Peterborough Cathedral, 'stone for stone,' exactly as it stood before it was by them pulled down. To that contract we hold them still in honour to be bound, and to them we appeal to let nothing whatever, no pressure of opinion, public or other, induce them to give way." The work has given rise to much newspaper controversy, clearly showing that architects, like doctors, sometimes disagree. Professor Freeman says that owing to the noble western front added to Peterborough Cathedral, being the main feature of the building, the central tower becomes of minor importance, and ought to be kept as a subordinate part of the work, in order to give the church that peculiar character which the addition of the portico originally conferred upon it. Sir E. Beckett thinks that this view is absurd, and recommends the rebuilding of the central tower in such a way as that it may carry an octagon or even a spire, and declares that the historical unity of a cathedral is all moonshine. The Dean writes in favour of a more elevated tower, and suggests that after all it would be best to go on with other works, and to adjourn the completion of the tower till rival experts have come to an agreement.

THE reports of the Commission appointed to inquire into the condition of our cathedral churches have been issued in the case of Lichfield, Salisbury, and Winchester. The Commissioners for Lichfield—Lord Cranbrook, the Bishop of Carlisle, Lord Blachford. Mr. Beresford-Hope, Lord Northbourne, Mr. C. Dalrymple, Dean Bickersteth, and Canon Lonsdale—preface their report by a brief sketch of the history of the cathedral, which is of the old foundation, from the establishment of the see in A.D. 656, its erection into an archiepiscopal see in A.D. 789, its subjection to Canterbury in A D. 803, its removal to Chester and to Coventry, the building of the cathedral in 1129 and its enlargement 170 years afterwards, and its completion in 1375. The Commissioners add to their report the full code of statutes, which the Dean and Chapter, by prescription of 700 years, have the right of repealing, altering, and framing ; and the Commissioners have not deemed it incumbent upon them to frame a new code of statutes. The present code was last revised in 1875, in the time of Bishop Selwyn. The Commissioners make certain recommendations with regard to the livings attached to the Chapter, and especially that the income of the Dean should be at least £1,200 a year. Appended to the report is a list of the questions addressed by the Commissioners to Cathedral Chapters and the answers given by the Chapter of Lichfield. These questions concern all matters relative to the cathedral, the position, duty, and emoluments of all officers, clerical and lay, the library, schools, residences, rotation of preachers, the whole income and expenditure, the fabric fund, the number and condition of the buildings, and several other such matters. From the answers we learn that the gross annual income paid by the Ecclesiastical Commissioners is £5,500, of which sum the Dean receives £1,000 a year, and the Canons residentiary £500 each. The Commissioners for Salisbury are the same as those for Lichfield, except that the Dean of Salisbury and Canon Lear take the places of the corresponding dignitaries of the other diocese. This see is also of the old foundation, and its charter, dated A.D. 1091, was drawn up by Osmund, the first bishop, whose ordinal formed the base of the famous "Use of Sarum." The code of statutes, still binding, was drawn up in A.D. 1319. The Commissioners in this case think it desirable to supplement the old code by a body of new statutes which they submit to Her Majesty. From the answers given to the Commissioners' questions by the Chapter, we find that the income of the cathedral is £6,133 3s. 7d., of which the dean and four canons receive £3,213 6s. 7d., and £270 is paid each year to the Fabric Fund. which amounts, from all sources, to about £1,160 yearly. The Commissioners for Winchester, after reviewing briefly the history of the capitular body, observe that since 1879, owing in large part to the agricultural depression, the income of the Cathedral has fallen off very seriously. Their recommendation, therefore, that the canons residentiary should be bound to be in residence for eight months in each year must be taken to be made on the supposition that the income of a canon will not fall below the amount settled between the Ecclesiastical Commissioners and the Chapter in the year 1861.

Antiquarian Correspondence.

Sin scire labores,
Quære, age: quærenti pagina nostra patet.

All communications must be accompanied by the name and address of the sender, not necessarily for publication.

"PORT OR GATE."

SIR,—It may be as well, in the interest of philology, to explain how Dr. Pring has been, no doubt unintentionally, misled by the fact that the terms "port" and "gate" "are used indiscriminately," as he truly observes, by the translators of the Book of Psalms.

If he will refer to Professor Skeat's, or indeed to any decent English Dictionary, he will learn that the "port" which was so used in the sixteenth and seventeenth centuries, was derived from *the French* "porte," a gate. I may remind him, that if he had read my papers with care, this would have been made clear to him. I there explained this usage, and alluded to its survival in such a word as "porthole." To quote Dr. Pring's own expression, it "must be apparent even to the merest tyro" that *this* "port, of *French* extraction, can have nothing to do with the "port" of Æthelstan's day, which, indeed, he himself contends was derived directly from the *Latin*. Whether Æthelstan's "port" be derived from *porta* or *portus*—whether, even if derived from *porta*, it meant, as Dr. Stubbs says, a market-town, or, as Dr. Pring says, a gate, —all this is matter of opinion. But what is a matter, not of opinion, but of certainty, is that the "port" of the Psalms, derived from the French, can have nothing in the world to do with the "port" of Æthelstan's laws, derived from the Latin, and extinct ages before the French "porte" was adopted into the English tongue. The argument from the Psalms to the Laws of Æthelstan is therefore so far from being "perfectly legitimate," as to be a desperate attempt to represent the latter as prejudging the question, which in the word "port" they leave so absolutely open.

Colchester. J. H. ROUND.

MITHRAIC RITES IN BRITAIN.

SIR,—Lord Southesk has opened a subject of considerable interest, but of great obscurity—*i.e*, the existence of Mithraic superstitions in Britain during the third, and it may be fourth, centuries. It is curious that much of the Cornish tradition of British heathenism—*e.g.*, the references in the last discovered MS., "Berinans Meriasek," and elsewhere, in Cornish dramas (written in the old Cornish language), might refer to Mithraism as much as to any other system. The idea of a heathen among the old Cornish appears to have been a worshipper of the sun and of fire. Did Mithraism supersede older systems before the conversion of the Britons to Christianity? W. S. LACH-SZYRMA.

THE PROPOSED JOHNSON CENTENARY.

SIR,—Although there has been no centenary commemoration of the death of Dr. Johnson, which occurred on the 15th December, 1784, there are, however, two steps which might, perhaps, be taken, with little trouble or expense, to render the memorials of the Doctor already existing at St. Paul's Cathedral and Westminster Abbey more noticeable than they now are by the thousands of his countrymen who visit those sacred buildings.

Dr. Johnson was buried in the south transept of the Abbey, near the foot of Shakespeare's monument, and his grave, as Boswell tells us, was covered with "a large blue flagstone," on which were recorded simply his name and age and the date of his death.

This stone is unfortunately cracked across, in the part where the inscription is. Still, the interest attaching to it seems to forbid the substitution of another stone until the change shall be absolutely necessary. Such was, I have reason to believe, the feeling of Dean Stanley. But, without any change of the stone, it would much facilitate the reading of the inscription if the letters could be filled in with brass. This was done in the case of the tombstone of David Garrick, which is alongside that of Dr. Johnson.

Garrick has likewise a conspicuous mural monument at the Abbey. Nothing of this kind seems to be necessary for Dr. Johnson ; but a small mural tablet might be placed (to the left of Shakespeare's monument), with a few words indicating the locality of his grave. At present, perhaps, not one in a hundred of the visitors to the Abbey notices the grave. It would then be comparatively conspicuous.

At St. Paul's Cathedral (near the choir) is a cenotaph monument to Dr. Johnson, a colossal semi-nude figure on a pedestal, on the front of which is the Latin epitaph that was composed by Dr. Parr. Is it likely that one in a thousand of those who look at the monument can understand the epitaph ? Perhaps the Dean of St. Paul's could cause a brief English inscription to be placed on a side of the pedestal for the benefit of the myriads who are not Latin scholars, and who miss the lesson that the epitaph ought to teach. L.

[The attention of the Society for Preserving the Memorials of the Dead has been drawn to the state of Dr. Johnson's memorial slab.—ED. *A. M. & B.*]

MONKTON CHURCH, PEMBROKESHIRE.

SIR,—In reading your account * of the visit of the British Archæological Association to my church, I was pleased to note the following, referring to the roofless Monk's Choir and Lady-chapel :—"But it is hoped that the former may ere long be turned to good account, and be restored so as to form a chancel to the nave." It is my wish to have, not only the choir, but also the Lady-chapel restored ; but difficulties have presented themselves, and of such a nature as not to be easily overcome.

First, the antiquarian difficulty; you refer to it in your magazine : it is the wall existing between the nave and the roofless choir. There is one point about this wall on which all are not agreed, and to which, with your kind permission, I would like to call the attention of your readers. What is the date of its erection ? Is it as old as the nave? Is it older ? One gentleman, a prominent member of the B.A.A., gave it as his opinion that the nave was pulled down (why ?) and enlarged, while the east wall was left standing. Why this was left standing remains to be explained. If this is correct, it would be interesting to know how the arch of the north transept was built, as the north end of this wall covers the lower part of the east section of the arch. Others are of opinion that the wall is not as old as the nave ; that it was built at a subsequent period—a fair inference to draw from the fact of the wall resting on the arch. I should mention that the wall is not tied nor bonded, and is quite free of the north

---

* See vol. vi. p. 194.

wall. The arch, or opening, between the nave and choir is so rough and broken, and presents such a jumble of masonry, that it cannot be with any certainty declared to be Norman. The next difficulty (again antiquarian) is the "fresco," which is described as "not good enough to be preserved, and very much too good to be destroyed." Mr. Brock suggested that this might be pierced, and another arch made to correspond on the north side. Since the visit of the B.A.A., another society has taken an interest in my church, and has sent its secretary to examine and report on it. I have the report, and in few words it amounts to this—the "fresco" must not be touched.

Now, sir, the question is this, and it is a serious one : Is this wall, unsightly in the extreme, with a fine building to the east of it, which requires roofing, windows, and flooring, and which is capable of being restored and used as a chancel to the parochial nave, now without a chancel—is this wall to remain an obstacle in the way of reclaiming the whole building and restoring it to God's service ? I may be allowed to say this much for myself, that I have too great a veneration for ancient buildings to destroy any wantonly ; but when I find men advocating the retention of old walls "at any price," I confess I am in fear of losing a little of my enthusiasm. The desire for retention is, I think, at the present day carried to too great an extreme, I may say more now than at any period in the history of architecture ; for you cannot examine any ecclesiastical building without meeting features which puzzle the cleverest among clever architects and archæologists, some places filled in and others opened out. The fact is, I believe, in ancient days they built and treated buildings as circumstances required. That is what we ought to do now, and what we must do here in Monkton. The next difficulty is "funds." My parish is a very poor one ; there are but two resident gentry, a few farmers, and the rest all of the labouring class. We have accomplish d the internal restoration of the nave and windows and built a Sunday school, which have cost about £1,500, and this has been done without extraneous help. The work we are now contemplating is extra-parochial, and is quite beyond our "purse." Any help which any kind friend who takes interest in the preservation of ancient "Houses of Prayer," may be pleased to render in this instance will be thankfully received by

Monkton, near Pembroke.   DAVID BOWEN, Vicar.

WESTMINSTER HALL.

SIR,—Now that the question is under discussion as to how the space to the west of Westminster Hall should be best occupied, and in what manner its imperfect front should be restored, I venture, with your permission, to make briefly a practical suggestion.

The Abbey itself, its transepts, aisles, and desolate chapels, are more than incongruous and unedifying monuments, several of which—vulgar busts, more vulgar brackets and feeble recumbent figures, and many of these recently added—are more and more crowding up what little space remains, and are in no degree adding to the interest and remarkable architectural character of this very beautiful ancient building.

Let the new additions to Westminster Hall, therefore, be so arranged as that some suitable hall, cloister, or gallery be added, so that busts and tablets and nineteenth century memorial brasses might be there displayed.

The late Dean Stanley informed me several years ago that the difficulty of finding, not suitable positions, but any position for proposed monuments of this kind in the Abbey was even then so great as often to exclude memorials which, with available space, might have been properly admitted.

Here, then, seems to me an opportunity which ought to be seized. A suitable rectangular cloister, either closed or open, even of two stories, would provide much appropriate wall space, while a stately external staircase from the lower to the upper, of the type of that leading to the Ducal Palace at Venice, would not only be an effective architectural feature, but might suitably enough be made for additions of such an elevation as to break and relieve the monotony of the long unbroken roof of the Hall itself, and add a very practical feature to the proposed new buildings.

All Saints' Vicarage, Lambeth.   FRED. GEORGE LEE, F.S.A.

THE EARL AND COUNTESS OF HUNTLY.

SIR,—George Gordon, third Earl of Huntly, who fell at Corrichie Burn, in 1562, married the Lady Elizabeth Keith, sister to the Earl-Marshal of Scotland.

What became of the Countess after the death of her husband and the the proscription of the Gordons ?

Alluding to the fate of Huntly, a contemporary bard relates (correctly) that "dead suddeinly he downe did sincke ;" but he adds that his widow committed suicide.

Is it true that the Countess laid violent hands upon herself? If so, *when* and *where ?*   INQUIRER.

THE INNS OF CHANCERY.

SIR,—When the Serjeants-at-law, including many of the Judges, dissolved their Society a few years ago and sold the buildings in Serjeants'-inn and divided the proceeds among themselves, which it may be assumed they were entitled to do, they gracefully presented to the National Portrait Gallery the well-known collection of portraits of distinguished lawyers which had adorned the walls of their hall.

Is it too much to expect of the "Ancients" of Clements'-inn that they, too, should be content with having sold their brick and mortar, and that they should imitate the example of Serjeants'-inn, and give to our national collection the portraits of Sir Edward Coke, Sir Matthew Hale, Lord Coventry, and other great judges which were in Clement's-inn Hall until quite recently? The pictures deserve a better fate than to be knocked down to the highest bidder like Charles Surface's ancestors.

The public assuredly is very glad to know that the recent sale of Clement's-inn, Staple-inn, and Barnard's-inn is engaging the attention of the authorities of the Local Government Board. Perhaps I may be allowed to suggest that much interesting information on the subject will be found in "The Report of the Commissioners appointed to inquire into the arrangements of the Inns of Court and Inns of Chancery for promoting the study of the law and jurisprudence," signed by Vice-Chancellor W. Page Wood, Sir Alexander Cockburn, Sir Richard Bethell, and other eminent personages, and presented to both Houses of Parliament in August, 1855.   H. M.

"THROWING THE DART" IN CORK HARBOUR.

SIR,—A Cork correspondent, writing to a newspaper, draws attention to the recent observance of a very singular custom, which, he says, is periodically performed in Cork Harbour, and which is known as "throwing the dart." He describes it thus :—

"The Mayor and Corporation in their robes of office, attended by a numerous company of prominent citizens, proceeded in a steamer down the river to a certain point in the harbour. The Mayor then mounted the paddle-box, and cast an arrow into the sea—by which act he asserted his jurisdiction over the water to the point where the dart fell. The origin of this ceremony is somewhat obscure, but it is said to have come down from the time of the Danish occupation. It has been likened to the ancient Venetian custom of the Doge throwing a ring into the Adriatic."

Can any of your readers enlighten me as to the origin of this Irish municipal ceremony, and also as to whether a like custom exists elsewhere?   P. J. MULLIN.
Leith, N.B.

"SALLY, SALLY, WATER."

SIR,—In this part of Wilts, the girls at their school treats always play a game called "Sally, Sally, Water," which may be thus described:—

The girls join hands in a circle, and having placed one in the centre, dance round to the following refrain:—

> Sally, Sally, water sprinkle in the pan;
> And rice, Sally, rice for a young man.
> Choose the best, and choose the worst,
> And choose the one that you love best.

The one in the centre then picks her choice from the ring, which halts for this purpose. But as soon as they have retired hand in hand to the centre, the dance is recommenced to these words:—

> Now you're married, I wish you good joy,
> First a girl, and second a boy,
> Seven years after son and daughter;
> Pray you come shake hands together.

Can anyone throw light upon this curious game? Does not the mention of rice show that throwing of rice at marriage is an old, if very uncomfortable, custom in England?
Calne, October, 1884.   C. V. G.

ANTIQUARIAN LATIN AND GREEK.

SIR,—Last year I had occasion to draw your attention to some very bad Latin which I found in a certain publication called *The Antiquary*, of which it cannot be too far or too widely known that Mr. Walford was *not* the Editor after its 12th number, although he *was* its founder; and, if he had stood on his legal rights, was joint-proprietor. I should now like to be allowed to show up some bad Latin, and some worse Greek, which I find in two works which proceed from the same *officina* in "The Row." At the bottom of p. 14 of a newly-started periodical, called *Book Lore*, I am equally puzzled and amused at reading "*Non nobis tolum nati fumus*"! On page 21 I see some Latin Elegiac verses printed as if they were Hexameters, or at all events Pari-syllabics. Oh! shade of Macaulay's "Fifth form School-boy"! where are you?

But bad as is the Latin of this house in "The Row," its Greek is far worse, and such as would have earned for its writer a whipping in my old school days. Only think of such a word as ηυιδε in a Greek epigram which is sent to the editor as a corrected version! This occurs on p. 21, where the classical scholar will be able to refresh his eyes with the sight of such "accents" and "breathings" in the *Book Lore* Greek as I will venture to say he never saw before. Some of both the one and the other are "conspicuous by their absence;" the few that appear look as if they had been dropped at hazard out of a pepper-caster. Some are out and out wrong. There is no such Greek word as ἠχει; if there were, the *Echo* would be spelt *H*echo. Another book, proceeding from the same laboratory, is called *The Gentleman's Magazine Library*, and professes to be edited by a F.S.A. ! But alas! for the standard of scholarship among the Society of Antiquaries, if old-fashioned Greek "ρ" is constantly confounded with "long o." Thus the word πεσσοί, dice, is spelt page after page ωεσσοι, and κατα παν figures as καταωαν, printed in one word instead of in two! And, finally, I cannot help suspecting that when Mr. G. L. Gomme, F.S.A., tells his credulous readers, on the authority of "Ingulphus," that King Alfred translated "Æsop's Fables" from the Greek into the Saxon, he is mixing up that ancient worthy with a far different person—a learned bishop, whose name has the same second and third syllables, though not the first. We have heard of "the schoolmaster abroad;" it would be well, I think, if he kept a little "at home."

Hyde Park Mansions, N.W.   E. WALFORD, M.A.

❖❖❖❖❖❖❖❖❖❖❖❖

TO CORRESPONDENTS.

"GREEK FOLK SONGS."—In reply to Mr. Stuart Glennie's letter in our last number (see *ante*, p. 46), complaining of the non-publication of Miss Garnett's "Greek Folk-Songs," Mr. Stock writes to us declaring Mr. Glennie's statements untrue, but adduces no facts in support of that assertion. It is very easy to "give the lie," and very safe—now that horsewhippings and duels are both out of date.—ED. *A. M. & B.*

MUS RUSTICUS.—Denton, in Huntingdonshire, was the birthplace of the eminent antiquarian Sir Robert Cotton, who rebuilt its little Norman church. For further particulars about it see *Notes and Queries*, Dec. 3, 1864 (iii. Ser. vi. p. 449).

THE Editor declines to pledge himself for the safety or return of MSS. voluntarily tendered to him by strangers.

❖❖❖❖❖❖❖❖

Books Received.

1. Boswell's Life of Johnson and Johnsoniana. With Notes and Appendices by Alexander Napier, M.A. Six vols. Bell & Sons. 1884.

2. Western Antiquary. Part vii. Plymouth: W. H. Luke. December, 1884.

3. The Sunday Service-Book for 1885. Helps to the Study of the Bible. Holy Bible, illustrated. Henry Frowde, Oxford University Press Warehouse, Amen-corner.

4. Catalogue of Richmond Free Public Library. 1884.

5. Miscellanea Genealogica et Heraldica. Vol. i. No. 13. Hamilton, Adams & Co. January, 1885.

6. Johns Hopkins University Studies. Second Series, No. 12. Dec., 1884.

7. Phonetic Journal. No. 1, vol. xliv. Jan. 1885.

8. East Anglian. New Series. Vol. i. Part i. Ipswich: Pawsey & Hayes. January, 1885.

9. History of Aylesbury. Part xii. Aylesbury : Robert Gibbs.

10. Le Livre. Nos. 60, 61. Paris : 7, Rue St. Benoit. December, 1884, and January, 1885.

11. Journal of the National Society for Preserving the Memorials of the Dead. No. 4. December, 1884.

12. St. Lawrence, Reading. By the Rev. Charles Kerry. Published by the Author. 1883.

13. Palatine Note-book. No. 48. January, 1885.

14. English Etchings. Part xliv. D. Bogue, 27, King William-street, W.C.

15. The Genealogist. New Series. Vol. ii. No. 5. Bell & Sons. January, 1885.

16. Fourteenth Annual Report of the Leeds Public Library and Museum. 1884.

17. Historical Reprints. No. 5. "No Blinde Guides." Privately Printed. Edinburgh. 1884.

18. Collectanea Adamantæa—II. "Kempe's Nine Daies Wonder." Edited from the original MS. By Edmund Goldsmid, F.R.H.S. Privately printed. Edinburgh. 1884.

19. Bibliotheca Curiosa. "The History of Reynard the Fox." Two vols. "On the Origin of the Native Races of America." Privately printed. Edinburgh. 1884.

20. Hakluyt's "Voyages and Discoveries." Vol. i. Parts ii. and iii. Edited by Edmund Goldsmid. F.R.H.S. Edinburgh : E. and G. Goldsmid. 1884.

21. A Fac-simile of the Celebrated Forged Letter from General Monk to Charles II. (Reprint). Edinburgh : E. and G. Goldsmid. 1884.

22. Colchesters Teares (Reprint). Edinburgh : E. and G. Goldsmid. 1884.

Books, &c., for Sale.

Archdall's *Monasticon Hibernicum.* Apply to Rev. James Graves, Stonyford, co. Kilkenny.

Works of Hogarth (set of original Engravings, elephant folio, without text). bound. Apply by letter to W. D., 56, Paragon-road, Hackney, N.E.

Original water-colour portrait of Jeremy Bentham, price 2 guineas. Apply to the Editor of this Magazine.

A large collection of Franks, Peers and Commoners. Apply to E. Walford, 2, Hyde Park Mansions, N.W.

Books, &c., Wanted to Purchase.

Antiquarian Magazine and Bibliographer, several copies of No. 2 (February, 1882) are wanted, in order to complete sets. Copies of the current number will be given in exchange at the office.

Dodd's Church History, 8vo., vols. i. ii. and v.; Waagen's Art and Artists in England, vol. i.; East Anglian, vol. i., Nos. 26 and 29. The Family Topographer, by Samuel Tymms, vol. iii.; Notes and Queries, the third Index. Johnson's "Lives of the Poets" (Ingram and Cooke's edition), vol. iii. Chambers' Cyclopædia of English Literature, vol. i. Address, E. Walford, 2, Hyde Park Mansions, Edgeware-road, N.W.

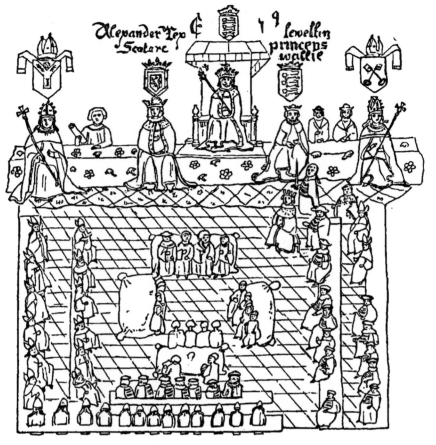

PARLIAMENT AT WESTMINSTER, 1278.

(*From " Chronicles of the Yorkshire Family of Stapelton "* (*see p.* 135).

The
Antiquarian Magazine
& Bibliographer.

𝕾𝔀𝔦𝔣𝔱'𝔰 𝕮𝔬𝔫𝔡𝔲𝔠𝔱 𝔬𝔣 𝔱𝔥𝔢 𝕬𝔩𝔩𝔦𝔢𝔰.

By Edward Solly, F.R.S.

N October, 1711, Swift composed that masterly pamphlet, so well known by name to all, yet read now by so very few, entitled "The Conduct of the Allies." The Tory Ministry sadly wanted strength ; the nation wanted peace ; the Whigs, who had long flourished on the war, clung to the great name of Marlborough and insisted on the continuance of war. The Queen, never very strong-minded, was gradually breaking down, worried by party squabbles, and yet more by the petty impertinences of her favourites ; troubled with many things, some of which, such as the question of succession and the schemes of the Jacobite party, appeared to grow just in proportion as her bodily and mental powers diminished ; whilst she keenly felt the great responsibility of her high position, was, in fact, in some things almost powerless. She could control neither her Ministers, her Parliament, nor her armies ; her force of mind was diminished, though her obstinacy was increased. Everything depended on the great question of peace or war, and one of the chief factors in the crisis was the position of the Duke of Marlborough. The prosperity of the country, probably, and the existence of the Tory Ministry, certainly, depended on two things—the declaration of peace, and the curtailment of the Marlborough influence. It was to aid in this that

Swift wrote his pamphlet, and he probably designed that it should be published soon after the meeting of Parliament, which was to assemble on the 7th of December. From his " Journal," we know that he was finishing the pamphlet on the 24th of November, and had no doubt been rather hurried in doing so by the return of the Duke of Marlborough on the 18th, who, of course, by his presence raised the hopes and increased the activity of the Whig party. Swift pressed on the printers, and the first copies of the " Conduct of the Allies " were sent out on the 26th of November. This was probably some weeks before the time he had originally intended for its appearance ; he mentions on page 78 that " he had two reasons for not sooner publishing this discourse "—one being that he had to speak of things " the discovery of which ought to be made as late as possible, as at another juncture it might not only be very indiscreet, but perhaps dangerous."

The foundation of the pamphlet may be summed up in a very few sentences, all pointing to the grossest and most culpable negligence on the part of England's " Domestic Enemies." The writer says : " Against all manner of Prudence or common Reason we engaged in this War as Principals, when we ought to have acted only as Auxilliaries. We spent all our vigour in pursuing that part of the War which could least answer the end we proposed by beginning of it ; we made no efforts at all where we could most have weakened the common Enemy, and at the same time enriched ourselves ; and we suffered each of our Allies to break every article in those Treaties and Agreements by which they were bound, and to lay the burthen upon us." Starting from this as a general statement, Swift gave a rapid and masterly sketch of what the former Ministers had done, and also of what they might have done, but neglected to do, every now and then bringing in with great skill the various subsidiary facts and statements best suited to his purpose.

"The Conduct of the Allies " was in the hands of the Ministers on the 26th of November, and was published on the 27th. It is a point of some bibliographical interest, if, as I believe, it came out bearing the date 1712. It has already been pointed out that circumstances made it necessary to bring it out before the period originally contemplated, and this may perhaps account for the fact of the date.

Mr. Stanley Lane Poole, in his " Notes on the Bibliography of Swift," in the *Bibliographer* for November, 1884, gives " 1711, The Conduct of the Allies, and of the late Ministry, in beginning and carrying on the Present War. Lond. 1711. (Scott gives date 1712)."

As Mr. Poole does not mention a copy of this as to be found in any one of the seven great libraries to which he has referred, it is to be presumed that he had not then seen or examined one; the first noted in his list being the second edition, of which he says there are copies in the Bodleian, Trinity College, Dublin, and Forster collection, South Kensington. The title of what I believe is the first edition is:

1. The Conduct of the Allies and of the Late Ministry in Beginning and Carrying on the Present War. Motto: " Partem tibi Gallia nostri," &c. London : Printed for John Morphew, near Stationers' Hall, 1712. Title; preface three pages; pp. in all, 96.

Swift states in his " Journal," that the edition was 1,000 copies, and that it was all sold in two days. On the 29th of November, therefore, a second edition was set in hand, and was published on Saturday, the 1st of December. Swift says in reference to this second edition, " Lord Treasurer [Harley Lord Oxford] has made one or two small additions," and adds, " the pamphlet makes a world of noise, and will do a great deal of good. I have added something to this second edition." This was—

2. Title as before. Second edition, corrected. London : Printed for John Morphew, near Stationers' Hall, 1711. Paging as before, in all pp. 96.

Swift's pamphlet was published; it was a triumphant success, and he or Lord Oxford made an addition for the second edition, and this addition was one of some interest; it is to be found on page 46, where Swift is speaking of the King of Spain, and is as follows :

" I shall add one example more to show how this Prince has treated the Q——n, to whom he owes such infinite obligations. Her Maj—ty borrowed Two hundred Thousand Pounds from the Genoese, and sent it to Barcelona, for the payment of the Spanish Army. This money was to be re-coined into the current species of Catalonia, which by the allay is lower in value £25 per cent. The Q——n expected, as she had reason, to have the benefit of this re-coinage, offering to apply it all to the use of the War; but King Charles, instead of consenting to this, made a grant of the Coinage to one of his courtiers, which put a stop to the work : And when it was represented that the Army would starve by this delay, His Majesty only replied, ' *Let them starve !* ' and would not recal the grant."

Whether this paragraph was added by Lord Oxford or by Swift it would, perhaps, now be difficult to determine; but it is impossible not to be struck by the curious, one may say half-prophetic character of the statement. The evil here charged to the King of Spain found its counterpart in history twelve years later, when George I., to please a favourite, gave the contract to William Wood for coining debased money in Ireland; and it fell to the lot of Dean Swift to denounce the thing in his celebrated Drapier's letters. The point of immediate interest now, however, is the fact that this sentence is to be found in the second and all subsequent editions of Swift's pamphlet, but not in the first, with the erroneous date of 1712. The second edition, then, came out on the 1st of December, and was sold off in five hours; and a third edition was brought out on the 3rd of December.

3. Title as before. The Third Edition, corrected. London: Printed for John Morphew. Paging as before; pp. 96.

At the end there is a note referring to a very unfortunate misprint in the second edition, showing in what great haste the work was driven through the press. This was on page 20, where it is said: " We did not do all we could to injure our enemies, and at the same time enrich *ourselves;*" the last word was by mistake printed *our allies*, thus totally perverting the sense of the argument. This third edition was sold out as quickly as the two former ones; and on the 5th of December a fourth was printing.

4. Title as before. The Fourth Edition, corrected. London: Printed for John Morphew. Paging as before; pp. 96.

At the end of this was added a short but rather important postscript. Great exception had been taken to a passage in the first three editions, which, though its purpose was very clear, was eagerly seized on by the Whigs as treasonable and Jacobitish. This was on page 39, where, after speaking of the absurdity of our asking the Dutch to guarantee the succession to the British Crown, Swift had concluded, " Thus putting it out of the power of our own Legislature to change our succession without the consent of that Prince or State who is guarantee, how much soever the necessities of the Kingdom may require it."

This was certainly an unfortunate expression, and might be read in two ways. He therefore, in the fourth edition, changed the last line into " however our Posterity may hereafter, by the Tyranny and Oppression of any succeeding Princes be reduced to the fatal Necessity of breaking in upon the excellent and happy settlement now in force." In the postscript Swift remarks on this: " It is pleasant to hear those People quarrelling at this, who profess for themselves for changing it as often as they please, and that even without the consent

of the entire Legislature." He further takes notice of the replies to the
" Conduct," and " faithfully promises to fully answer any objection of
moment he can find in them, in the fifth edition." This was already
in the printer's hands, and two or three days later came out, but the
promise was not fulfilled.

5. Title as before. The fifth edition, corrected. London: Printed
for John Morphew. Title; preface two pages; pp. in all, 48.

This was the last edition before the close of the year; and the pamphlet, as may be readily supposed, had created a great sensation. Swift,
with great confidence in his own powers, terribly feared the weakness
and supine action of the Ministry, and his "Journal" of the week
shows this strongly. Writing on the 15th he says: " I look upon
the Ministry as certainly ruined; and God knows what may be the
consequences. This will be a memorable letter, and I shall sigh to
see it some years hence." But the " Conduct " continued to be read,
and was gradually producing a good effect; Dr. Sheridan [Life of
Swift] says that 11,000 copies were sold within the month. Early in
the new year there came out two more editions, namely—

6. Title as before. The sixth edition, corrected. London: Printed
for John Morphew, 1712. Title; preface two pages; pp. in all, 48.
This edition was of 3,000, and was all sold by January 28.

7. Title as before. The seventh edition, corrected. London:
Printed for John Morphew, 1712. Title; preface two pages; pp. in
all, 48. Mr. Poole states that there was a quarto issue of the seventh
edition, which is in the Bodleian. The effect of Swift's work was
seen and felt when the affairs of the Allies came before the House, on
February 3, as we learn from the oft-quoted Letters to Stella: " Those
who spoke drew all their arguments from my book, and their votes
confirm all I writ; The Court had a Majority of a hundred and fifty.
All agree that it was my book that spirited them to these resolutions."

There do not seem to have been any other London editions
published in the year 1712. The pamphlet was, however, again
reprinted early in the following year.

8. Title as before. The eighth edition, corrected. London;
Printed for John Morphew, 1713. Title; preface two pages; pp. in
all, 48. To all of the last three editions there is added a brief
postscript, drawing attention to the correction of the paragraph which
had been objected to as Jacobitish, and which was first modified in
the fourth edition.

It is a curious circumstance that in the collections of Swift's
works, both those published in his lifetime and also those printed

after his death, the " Conduct of the Allies," as a rule, is taken from the first edition, that with the erroneous date, 1712. This is the case in Faulkner's subscription edition, published at Dublin in 1738 ; in the collection of Swift's political writings, published by Davis in London, 1738 ; in Hawksworth's quarto of 1755, and his octavo of 1766 ; in Nichols' edition of 1801 ; and in Scott's two editions of 1814 and 1824. In all these it is distinctly stated on the title-pages that the tract was *written* in 1712, when in truth it was published in November, 1711. As a necessary consequence, none of the editions of Swift's works introduced or took any notice of the paragraph in relation to the King of Spain, which was first added in the second edition ; Nichols and Scott, however, introduced the anti-Jacobin correction, which first appeared in the fourth edition, in notes.

In the postscript to the fourth edition Swift promised to reply to all his answers in the preface to the next issue ; but this he did not do. He found it more convenient to reply in independent pamphlets, of which there were two ; one entitled " Some Remarks on the Barrier Treaty," which he wrote himself; and " An Appendix to the Conduct of the Allies," which was compiled under his direction and printed in the *Examiner* of January 16, 1713. In the former Swift pointedly refers to the anti-Jacobite addition in the fourth edition : " I was assured that my L——d C——f J——e affirmed that Passage was Treason: one of my answerers, I think, decides as favourably ; and I am told that Paragraph was read very lately during a Debate, with comment in very injurious terms, which perhaps might have been spared. That the Legislature should have power to change the succession whenever the necessities of the Kingdom require, is so very useful towards preserving our Religion and Liberty, that I know not how to recant. The worst of this opinion is, that at first sight it appears to be *Whiggish ;* but the distinction is this, the Whigs are for changing the succession when they think fit, although the entire Legislature do not consent ; I think it ought never to be done but upon great Necessity, and that with the sanction of the whole Legislature."

A little further on, when referring to the various pamphlets written in reply to " The Conduct," Swift says, " And I solemnly declare that I have not wilfully committed the least Mistake. I stopt the second Edition, and made all possible enquiries among those who I thought could best inform me, in order to correct any Error I could hear of ; I did the same to the third and fourth editions, and then left the Printer to his Liberty. This I take for a more effectual answer to all Cavill, than a hundred pages of controversy." From the

"Journal" it is plain that the stopping of the second edition chiefly meant submitting the proof to the critical consideration of the Lord Treasurer Oxford, and Swift was evidently well pleased that Harley made some alterations in it.

Speaking of one of his answerers, who printed four letters in reply, Swift says, with conscious satisfaction, "My Book did a World of Mischief(as he calls it) before his first part could possibly come out; and so went on through the Kingdom, while his limped slow after; and if it arrived at all, it was too late; for People's opinions were already fixed."

It is probable that no man either previously or subsequently ever rendered to a Ministry services so important as Swift did to the Ministers in 1711, by the publication of the "Conduct of the Allies;" and it is certain that no one who has rendered aid at all similar in magnitude has been so meanly rewarded. They gave him the poor Deanery of St. Patrick, and practically exiled him from the country which he loved and had served so well.

As this is only a bibliographical note in reference to the English edition of the "Conduct," it would perhaps be out of place to go into several other matters of interest in relation to it; one may, however, be very briefly referred to. Two years later Steele brought out the "Crisis," and this led to a reply from Swift, which may be said fairly to have extinguished Steele's pamphlet. It was entitled, "The Public Spirit of the Whigs," and in it Swift did not hesitate to say, "The author of the 'Conduct of the Allies' writes Sense and English, neither of which the author of the 'Crisis' understands."

DURING the progress of the works of repair of the Tol-house, Great Yarmouth, some interesting discoveries have been made, consequent upon the removal of the old rough-cast and cement work which once entirely covered the walls. Not only have the angle quoins and the original face of the walling been laid open to view, but the forms of some of the original windows have been recovered. These will be repaired and filled in with tracery as near to the original pattern as possible. On the wall beneath the little open gallery of the porch being taken in hand, the removal of the rough-cast laid open a series of neatly wrought trefoiled arches, supported upon moulded corbels. Below these the original arched opening has been met with, which afforded light and air to the common prison, or "hold," into which the prisoners appear to have been thrust. These features will be carefully repaired. The architects are, Mr. Loftus Brock, F.S.A., of London, and Messrs. Bottle & Olley, of Great Yarmouth. The work in progress will open out for inspection the ancient features of this unique building, which will appear more like an old one at the conclusion than it did at the commencement. It may be added that funds are still required to carry on the work. (For a description of the Tol-house, with an illustration, see vol. vi., pages 3-5).

England in 1689.*

PART I.

Communicated by JAMES GREENSTREET.

THORSDAY, *November* 22, 1688.—Set sail out of Boston Harbour about an hour by Sun [before sunset], with a very fair wind.

*   *   *   *   *

Friday, Dec. 21.—Little wind and that is Northerly. See many Porpuses. I lay a [wager] with Mr. Newgate that shall not see any part of Great Britain by next Saterday senight sunset. Stakes are in Dr. Clark's hand. *Satterday, Dec.* 22, wind is at North-East, at night blows pretty fresh. This day a Gannet was seen, and a Purse made for him that should first see Land, amounting to between 30 and 40ˢ N[ew] England Money. I gave an oblong Mexico piece of Eight.

Monday, Dec. 24.—Wind remains right in our Teeth. See a Ship to Leeward most part of the day, which stood the same way we did: but we worsted her in sailing. *Tuesday, Dec.* 25, see two Ships, one to windward, 'tother to Leeward. About 10, *m.* a Woodcock flies on board of us, which we drive away essaying to catch him.

Sabbath, Dec. 30th.—Spake with a Ship 7 weeks from Barbados, bound for London, tells us he spake with an English Man from Galloway, last Friday, who said that the King was dead, and that the Prince of Aurang [Orange] had taken England, Landing six weeks agoe in Tor Bay. Last night I dreamed of military matters, Arms and Captains, and, of a suddain, Major Gookin, very well clad from head to foot, and of a very fresh, lively countenance— his Coat and Breeches of blood-red silk, beckened me out of the room where I was to speak to me. I think 'twas from the Town-house. Read this day in the even the Eleventh of the Hebrews, and sung the 46th Psalm. When I waked from my Dream I thought of Mr. Oakes's Dream about Mr. Shepard and Mitchell beckening him up the Garret-Stairs in Harvard College. *Monday, Dec.* 30th (*sic*), contrary wind still, speak with our Consort again. *Tuesday, Jan.* 1 [168⅞], speak with one who came from Kenne-

---

* Being extracts from a Diary written by Samuel Sewall, the American Judge. (Printed by the Massachusetts Historical Society, Boston, U.S.A., 1878).

beek [?] in Ireland 8 day's agoe : says there are Wars in England. Prince of Aurang in Salisbury Plain, with an Army Landed with fourscore and 5 Men of War, and above two hundred Fly Boats, has took Plymouth and Portsmouth, &c., and is expected at London daily. Read Hebrews 13th.

Wednesday, Jan. 2.—Last night about 12 aclock the Wind comes fair, so that by morning the word was, Steady, Steady. The Lord fit us for what we are to meet with. Wind veered from East to South, and so Westerly. This day eat Simon Gates's Goose. *Thorsday, Jan.* 3, wind comes East again. A gray Linnet and a Lark, I think, fly into the Ship. *Friday, Jan.* 4, wind not very fair. Some say they saw a Robin-Redbrest to-day.

Sabbath, Jan. 6.—See Capt. James Tucker, Commander of the *Betty* of London, about 120 Tons, whom spake with, this day sennight. Saith he saw the Light of Silly last Thorsday night. We carry a light and keep company. *Monday, Jan.* 7th, Mr. Clark goes on Board our Consort, and brings Oranges and a Shattuck [shaddock]. So steer in the night E. and East and by South. We had no Observation. Capt. Tucker saith he had by a forestaff, and Latitude 49.30. Reckons we shall be abrest with the Lizard by morning. Wind So. west. *Tuesday, Jan.* 8, *mane,* a brisk west wind. We sound and have 55 fathom : speak with our Consort, who saith he had Lizard Soundings, and would now have us steer East and by N. They were a little to windward of us, and a little astern. By and by they all gathered to their Starboard side, and looking toward us made a horrid Outcry, Land ! Land ! We looked and saw just upon our Larboard Bow, horrid, high, gaping Rocks. Mr. Clark imagined it to be the French Coast. We asked our Consort. He said, Silly ! Silly ! Trim'd sharp for our Lives, and presently Rocks all ahead, the Bishop and Clarks, so were fain to Tack, and the Tack not being down so close as should be, were afraid whether she would stay [not miss stays]. But the Seamen were so affected with the breakers ahead, that the Mate could not get it altered, or very little. But it pleased God the Ship staid very well, and so we got off and sailed in Bristow Channel toward Ireland, winding Nore, N. West, and N.N.W., westerly. Just when we saw the Rocks it cleared a little, and when fix'd in our course thicken'd again. Blessed be God who hath saved us from so great a Ruin. Saw the Light-House, that look'd slender, about the height of a man, and a Rock with a cloven top, not altogether unlike a Bishop's Mitre, which I therefore take to be the Bishop.

Wind would have carried us between Silly and the Lands End, but durst not venture, and could not speak to our Consort, who probably knew better than we. And we Tacking, he Tacked.

Tuesday, Jan. 8, 168⅞.—About Noon our Consort being astern, Tacked, and we then Tacked, and stood after him, hoping to wether Sylly and its Rocks. Just before night we were much in fear by reason of many Rocks, some even with and some just above the water under our Lee, very near us, but by the Grace of God we wethered them. In the next place we were interrogated by the Bishop and his Clarks, as the Seamen said, being a Rock high above the water, and three spired Rocks by the side of him, lower and much lesser, which we saw, besides multitudes at a remoter distance. The breach of the Sea upon which made a white cloud. So I suppose the former Rocks near the Land of Sylly not the Bishop. Sailed Souwest, and S.W. by S. At night our Consort put out a Light, and about 8 o'clock began to hall away South-East. We imagined we saw some Glares of the Light of Sylly, but could not certainly say.

Wednesday, Jan. 9th.—As soon as 'twas light the word was they saw of Man of War, which put us into as great a consternation almost as our yesterday's Danger. Puts out his Ancient [ensign]; coming nearer speaks with us: is a Londoner from the Canaries, who by dark wether for several days had not made the Land, and lost his Consort last night. We told him we came from Sylly last night. He told us that five weeks agoe a Ship told them the Prince of Aurange was Landed in England before they came from Portland. This was at Canaries. Said also, the King not dead. Suppose ourselves abrest with the Lizard. Our Gunner said he saw it. Sail along 3 of us pleasantly, *Laus Deo.*

In the night the Londoner carries two Lights, one in 's poop, the other in 's round Top.

Thorsday, Jan. 10, 168⅞.—Very fast wind, sail along with four or five more ships. About Ten o'clock saw the Isle of Wight plain, which is the first Land next to Sylly that I have seen. Next to that saw high white Cliffs: but then Clouds and Fogg took away our Sunshine and Prospect. The Ile of Wight makes a long space of Land, Hills and Valleys.

Friday, Jan. 11.—A pretty while before day, a vehement North wind comes up, so that fain to ly by, and great confusion by reason that the 6 or 7 Ships were so near together that ready to fall fowl one of another. In the morn see that we are over against Beachy

[Head]. In a while Tack about to try to gain the Wight, but cannot. A little before night tack again ; Seven Cliffs. Make thus cold wether.

[*Saturday*,] *Jan.* 12.—Meet with a Pink 14 days from Liverpool : tells us Prince of Aurange landed about the 29th Nov. [really on the 5th] in Torbay, with 50 Thousand Men, Six hundred Ships : Sea-Commanders all yielded to him : no bloud shed : King and Prince of Wales gone to France somwhat privatly. Bought three Cheeses of him. He sent us some Bottles of very good Beer, and we him one of my Bottles of Brandy. About 12 o'clock the wind springs up fair, and about 6 in the even we take our leave of Beachey. Saith the occasion of Prince's coming in, that apprehends King James has no Legitimate Son, that that of Pr. Wales is a Cheat. Told us there were Englishmen found dead, drowned, tied back to back : so put us in great fear, because he intimated as if French Men of War were cruising with English Commissions. *Sabbath, Jan.* 13. Goe ashoar at Dover, with Newgate, Tuttle and Sister. Hear 2 Sermons from Isaiah, 66. 9.—Shall I bring to the birth? *Monday morn. Jan.* 14th, view the fort at the west end of the Town and the Castle : went into the Kings Lodgings. The Town is like a Bow, only the two Ends the thicker parts and the back the thinner, being built as the Sea and Cliff would suffer it. A small River runs that helps to clear the Dock of Shingle : the Peers also defending. Houses of Brick covered with Tile generally : Some very good Buildings. A handsome Court-House and Market-place, near which the Antwerp Tavern, where we drunk coming out of Town.

Got this night to Canterbury time enough to view the Cathedral, and Kentish Husbandry as went along.

(From Contemporary Pocket Book.)

Sabbath, Jan. 13, 168⅞.—Through God's Grace landed at Dover about 9 or 10 aclock with Mr. Newgate, Mr. Tuthill and his Sister Mary and Monsier Odell. Mr. Newgate and I went and heard one Mr. Goff in a kind of Malt-House. In Afternoon all went. His text Isa. *ult.* v. 9th, *vid.* Sermon-book.

Monday, Jan. 14.—Rode in a Coach to Canterbury, after had view'd at the West, King's Lodging &c. 'Tis a piece of work that at first cost Labour and Expence, but now much decay'd. Getting to Canterbury a little before night view'd the Cathedral, which is a very lofty and magnificent building, but of little use. Visited Aunt Fissenden, her son John and three daughters

Mary, Elisabeth, and Jane, as I take it. Cousin Jn° sup'd with
us at the Red Lion.   I should have said before that Dover is a
large Town like a Bow, only the back is thinnest, reaching from
the Fort to the Castle.   A convenient Market-place and Court
Chamber.   The Harbour is not altogether unlike Boston Dock
but longer.   Two Peers to keep off the small shingle or stones,
and that also clear'd in some measure by a small River whoes
head is several Miles towards Canterbury, on which two or
three villages and Water-Mills for Corn.   The Town built chiefly
of brick.   Houses, most of them old, some very fair buildings.
Town built as the Cliff and Sea would admit back of the Bow
toward the Cliff.   A very handsom square of Warehouses, and
another little range, both more newly built, on the Beach, which
made a good shew as we came ashore in one of the Boats that
came for a Pilot.

Tuesday, Jan. 15.—Came to Rochester through Sittingburn
(where din'd) and Ranam with other little places.   No room in
the Inn by reason of Souldiers, so lodg'd at a Coffee-House
over against the Assize-House that is now building.

[*Tuesday,*] *Jan.* 15—To Chatham and Rochester, which make a
Long Street of Good Houses.   A fair Assize-House now building,
just over against which we lodged at a Coffee House : no room in
the Inn.   Dined at Sittingburne.

Wednesday, Jan. 16th.—To Dartford, where had a good Goose to
Dinner.   'Tis a considerable place.   A river runs into the Thames
under a Stone Bridge of four Arches.   To Southwark, where we
drink and reckon with the Coachman.   Hire another Coach for
18d to Cousin Hull's.   *Thorsday, Jan.* 17th, went to the Exchange.
[*Wednesday,*] *Jan.* 30th, went to the Temple and to White-hall.
Saw Westminster Abbey: Henry 7ths. Chapel.   Heard Dr. Sharp*
preach before the Commons, from Psa. 51.—Deliver me from Blood
guiltinesse, &c.   Saw St. James's Park.

[*Thursday,*] *Feb.* 7.—A Minister who lives at Abbington earnestly
invites me to his House with Mr. Mather, and he will goe and shew
us Oxford.   Mr. Brattle shewed me Gresham Colledge, by Mr.
Dubois his kindness and Cost.   Afterward went to Smithfield, and
the Cloisters of the Blew Coat Boys [at Christ's Hospital].
Gresham-Colledge Library is about one Hundred and fifty foot long,
and Eighteen foot wide.

---

* Dr. Sharp, at this time Dean of Norwich, died Archbishop of York.   See,
in Macaulay's History of England, chap. x., an account of this sermon.

[*Saturday*,] *Feb.* 9, 168⅞.—Guild-Hall I find to be Fifty yards long, of which the Hustings take up near seven yards, Measuring by the same yard-jointed Rule, Mr. Brattle and I find the breadth to be Sixteen Yards.

[*Monday*,] *Feb.* 11ᵗʰ.—Mr. Brattle and I went to Covent-Garden and heard a Consort of Musick. Dined to-day with Madam Lloyd and Usher.

[*Tuesday*,] *Feb.* 12.—Saw three Waggons full of Calves goe by together. At the Star on the Bridge, Mr. Ruck's, saw the Princess * pass in her Barge, Ancients [Ensigns] and Streamers of Ships flying, Bells Ringing, Guns roaring. Supped at Mr. Marshal's.

(FROM THE POCKET BOOK.)

[*Tuesday*,] *Febr.* 19.—Went to Winchester into the Hall and Arbour to see the choice of Knights of the Shire. Jarvis, Henly, and Fleming stood. It came to the Pole, I offer'd my Voice, but was refus'd because I would not lay my hand on and kiss the book, though I offer'd to take my Oath.

My Rapier was broken short off, I suppose coming down the steps into Hall. View'd the king's [troup ?].

Thorsday, *Feb.* 21 [at Baddesly].—Cousin Jane Holt came in the morn to invite me to dinner. I went with my Aunt Alice and Cousin Nathˡ. Had very good Bacon, Veal, and Parsnips, very good shoulder of Mutton and a Fowl rosted, good Currant suet Pudding and the fairest dish of Apples that I have eat in England.

Monday, *March* 18.—Went and saw the Jews burying Place at Mile-End : Some Bodies were laid East and West ; but now all are orderd to be laid North and South. Many Tombs. Engravings are Hebrew, Latin, Spanish, English, sometimes on the same stone. Part of the Ground is improv'd as a Garden, the dead are carried through the keepers house. First Tomb is about the year 1659. Brick wall built about part. Ont's two sides 5444, Christi 1684, Tamuz 21, June 23, as I remember.— I told the keeper afterwards wisht might meet in Heaven : He answerd, and drink a Glass of Beer together, which we were then doing.

[*Wednesday*,] *March* 20.—Went and saw Weavers Hall and

---

* On her passage from Holland, she had taken barge off Greenwich and was going up to Whitehall.

Goldsmiths Hall.   Went into Guild-Hall and saw the manner of chusing the Mayor.   About 16 were put up, though I think but four were intended.   Pilkington and Stamp had by much the most Hands, yet those for fatal Moor* and Rayment would have a Pole, which the Court of Aldermen in their Scarlet Gowns ordered to be at four o'clock.   They sat at the Hustings.   Sheriffs in their Gold Chains managed the Election.   Common Sergeant [counsel of the Mayor and Aldermen] made a speech.   When the People cry'd, a Hall, a Hall, the Aldermen came up two by two, the Mace carried before them, came in at the dore opposite to the Street dore out of another apartment.   I stood in the Clock-Gallery.

(FROM THE POCKET-BOOK.)

[*Thursday*,] *March* 28, 1689.—With Mr. Mather and his son Sam. went in the Coach of Abbington to Hounslo, so to Colebrook and to Maidenhead 22 miles from London. Sam. and I went to Bray-Ch. and writt out 2 Epitaphs by Candlelight. I din'd alone at Colebrook with a Bullock's cheek. About 6 o'clock Mr. Mather, Son and I sup'd on two Dunghill fowls.

Satterday, *March* 30.—Mr. Mather and we ride in the Coach to Oxford 5 miles, little ones [from Abingdon], costs us 12s. of which I pay 5 and Mr. Mather the rest. See the Colledges and Halls, New Colledge, Maudlin and Christ Ch. do most excell. At New-Col. eat and drank Ale, Wine, Lent Cakes full of Currants, good Butter and Cheese, by means of Mr. Benj. Cutler the Butler, to whom Dr. Woodward sent a Letter on my behalf. Saw the Theatre and Schools Congregation-House.

[*Monday*], *Ap*. 15.—Come to Wickam, where dine in K. Ch. 2d Bedchamber, 4 Men, so we pay for the 2 Maids 12d. apiece. Rid through Uxbridge where drunk some Kans of Ale, from thence to London about 7 o'clock. Passengers shew'd me the House where Uxbridge Treaty was held and say 'tis now haunted that none dare dwell there. A lovely Stream

---

* The parties to the contest were Sir Thomas Pilkington, who was elected in 1689 ; Sir Thomas Stamp, Mayor in 1692; Sir Jonathan Raymond ; and probably Sir John Moore, who had been Mayor in 1682, or some relative of his. In the year 1682 there was a severe struggle at the election of Sheriffs. Kennet says : "This great struggle put the Court upon considering, and in a manner resolving, to take away the election of Sheriffs out of the power of the City ; and no other expedient could be found but by taking away their Charter." This may account for the epithet "fatal" attached to Sir John Moore's name.

runs throw the Town-House, compass'd with a Brick Wall :
Great part of the House now pulled down.

[*Saturday,*] *April* 20.—Went on foot to Hackney, through
Brick-Lane, about ½ a mile long, and dined with Mr. Tho. Glover his
Son, Read, Thompson, their wives, Mr. French, and several Grand-
children. Eat part of two Lobsters that cost 3s. 9d. apiece, 7s. 6d.
both.

[*Monday,*] *April* 29.—Went to Greenwich with Mr. Mather,
Whiting, Brattle, Namesake : Supped at the Bear. Went through
the Park to Mr. John Flamsted's, who shewed us his Instruments
for Observation, and Observed before us, and let us look and view
the Stars through his Glasses.

[*Tuesday,*] *April* 30.—Come to Deptford, where breakfast with
Cheesecakes : from thence to Redriff upon the River's Bank, where
Dr. Avery's Cousin had us to a Gentleman who showed us many
Rarities, as to Coins, Medals, Natural and artificial things : from
thence by water to Tower Stairs, about 10 o'clock.

[*Thursday,*] *May* 2ᵈ.—Went with Capt. Hutchinson, and saw the
Crown, Scepter, Armory, Mint (none to see the Milling), Lions,
Leopard.

Tuesday, May 7.—Went to Windsor. [*Wednesday,*] 8ᵗʰ, Eaton,
Hampton Court, and so home.

[*Thursday,*] *May* 9.—Went to H[ampton] Court, to wait on the
King and Council. As we came home were entertained by Mr.·
Stephen Mason with Cider, Ale, Oysters and a Neat's Tongue, being
ten of us, or 11. This house is at Clapham, wherein Col. Bathe
did dwell.

Satterday, May 11ᵗʰ.—Declaration of War against France comes
out. *Wednesday, May* 15. Went and dined with Fish at Capt.
Kelly's upon Mr. Partrige's Invitation. Capt. Hutchinson, Clark,
Appleton, Brattle, Hull, in company. Went to a Garden at Mile
End and drunk Currant and Rasberry Wine ; then to the Dog and
Partrige's, and plaid Nine Pins. At the house a Souldier was shot
by his drunken companion the night before. Sir Samuel Dashwood
has by the Poll 1,000 and odd, and Sir Wm. Ashurst 1,700 and odd,
for a Citizen to sit in Parliament.

Thorsday, May 16.—Went to the Old Bailey, the Court was
holden by Pilkinton, Mayor, Lord Chief Justice Holt, Lord Chief
Justice Pollixfen, Chief Baron Atkins, and 7 more Judges. Sat till
3 o'clock, in which time the London Jury returned and brought in
four Verdicts, which they were charged with at once.

[*Saturday,*] *May* 18.—Goe to Hampton Court in company of
Capt. Hutchinson and Jo. Appleton;   . Mather, Sir Sam. Tomson,
Mr. Whiting, and Mr. Joseph Tomson ridd in another Coach.   Cost
21s. apiece, besides money to the Drivers.   Were dismissed *sine Die*.
Mr. Ward and Hook our Council.   Entertain Mr. Humphrys too.
Just now about a virulent Libel * comes out against N[ew] E[ngland],
the day Mr. Wharton was buried.

(To be continued.)

King Alfred in Somerset and the Legend of St. Neot.

By Mrs. C. G. Boger.

PART III.

(*Concluded from p.* 63.)

AFTER the conflict was over, the scattered remnants of the
Danish army gathered together under Guthrum and took
refuge in their entrenchments.   Here they were blockaded
by Alfred during fourteen days.   No succour could reach them from
their countrymen, and at last, being well-nigh hunger-starved, they
were compelled to accept such terms as Alfred imposed.   They
asked for peace, and Alfred granted it on such conditions as they had
never accepted before—viz., that they should give such hostages as
the King pleased; while he should give them none in return.   After
which the Pagans swore that they would immediately leave the kingdom; and their King, Guthrum, promised to embrace Christianity
and receive baptism.

But Alfred, though victorious, could not expel the Danes from
England.   He ceded East Anglia to them, and they were to hold it
as vassals under Alfred, so that it would be to their own interest to
keep the country free from fresh marauders; and those who would
not submit to Christian baptism left the kingdom, and Guthrum and
thirty of his chiefs were to be baptized at once.

Three weeks passed, while Guthrum and his thirty selected followers were placed under instruction in order to prepare for holy

---

* This was doubtless the pamphlet called "Considerations," &c., to show that
the charters of the colonies were taken away for good cause, which is printed in
the third volume of the "Andros Tracts."   Mather wrote a rejoinder.

baptism. Then at Aller, not far from Alfred's refuge at Athelney, Alfred presented his conquered foe as a candidate for baptism. Bishop and priest, and the mingling crowd of Saxons, Britons, and Danes, so lately foes, were there. The church doors opened, and a lengthened procession passed in, two and two.

Foremost, with every eye upon them, came the majestic figures of the two kings. Alfred led the Danish chief, and stood at the font as his godfather, and witness of his vows. When asked to name his son in the Faith, Athelstane was the name he chose, and so, bathed in the waters of purification, and signed with the sign of the cross, he rose up, no longer Guthrum, but Christian Athelstane. That name, dear to Alfred as his brother, his teacher, his deliverer, he now chose as the name of his reconciled enemy, trusting that it might bring a blessing upon him.

In like manner were his thirty warriors admitted into Christ's Church, and then they turned and took the oaths of fealty to England's sovereign. Twelve days did Guthrum-Athelstane and his followers wear the white robes of their baptism, and the chrisom cloth or white fillet which was bound round their heads at confirmation, a rite which then followed immediately after baptism. And during those twelve days of retirement and holy quiet, we may suppose that Alfred often instructed his godson in Christian truths, in Christian graces, and in Christian duties. Then, when the twelve days' "retreat" was over, Alfred took his guests and friends to his palace at Wedmore, and there he held the christening feast with holy and chastened joy; and there they loosed the chrisom, and laid aside their baptismal garments.

It was at Alfred's palace at Wedmore that the treaty was signed which gave peace to England for many years. By this agreement, Guthrum-Athelstane and his people were to cross the Thames and live in East Anglia, subject to Alfred and his laws, but all those Danes who refused to leave their heathen gods had to cross the sea, and it is said they joined the host of Hastings, which went to ravage the fair lands of France. And Alfred sent his new subjects to their homes with great gifts.*

Alfred did not forget his " Isle of Refuge;" he built at Athelney a fair monastery on the site of his fort, and thither we may well believe he would retire at times for rest and repose from the toils and

---

* There is still shown at Aller a large ancient font, which was dug out of a pond in the vicarage garden, and is now replaced in the church ; it is said to be the same in which Guthrum and his followers were baptized.

troubles of sovereignty. In order to defend the island, and yet render it attainable, a bridge was built between two heights, and at the western end of the bridge was constructed a tower of beautiful work, and in this monastery he collected monks of all kinds from every quarter. John, a priest and monk (an old Saxon by birth— meaning that he came from Saxony on the Continent), was first abbot. It seems that this motley assemblage of monks brought from different nations did not live well together, and two monks of Gaul laid a wicked plot to murder their abbot, and bring his name into disgrace. This abominable scheme was, however, happily frustrated by his attendants being roused by the scuffle, and coming to his aid.

We must remember the state of fearful ignorance into which the country had fallen, and in inviting learned monks over from other countries, Alfred's object was to provide fit teachers in the monastic schools for his subjects.

One interesting memorial of Alfred's residence in Athelney still remains. In the seventeenth century, an ornament made of gold and enamel was found there, entire and uninjured. It bears an inscription, " Ælfred het meh gewircan," " Alfred caused me to be worked." It is now preserved at Oxford in the Ashmolean Museum.

Alfred's will once more connects his name with Somerset, that land which, though the place neither of his birth nor his death, yet seems in a special manner to have been his school in self-denial and tenderness, and as though from it and the bitter, though loving dis- cipline he then underwent, he went forth armed and equipped for the grand life which was thenceforward to be devoted to God and his country. In his will, which, according to the custom of those times, he brought before the Witenagemot to be ratified during his life— probably about the year 885—he makes mention of a great number of slaves, particularly on his estates at Cheddar and Domerham, in Somerset, whom he had raised to the condition of free tenants, only making his petition to them, that they would, after his death, con- tinue to cultivate those lands, with his son Edward for their landlord, rather than take to a new occupation.

From the peace of Wedmore, in 878, the glory of Alfred's reign may be dated. It was not that he had no troubles, anxieties, cares, and sorrows ; but that all worked together for good, his own good and that of his people. His life was henceforth one of constant progress towards the complete and full perfection to which he more nearly attained in this life, than any other king in any age or place. But all this belongs to general history, and not in any special way to Somerset. But when we know all that he accomplished, it is difficult to believe that Alfred finished his course at the comparatively early age of fifty-two.

It is scarcely possible to bring these legends to a close without comparing and contrasting the lives of the two great heroes, British and Saxon, who, alike in their patriotic struggles against foreign invasion and heathenism, yet were in their results so different. Arthur's brilliant career lighted up with a glorious blaze the expiring struggles of a decaying cause, while Alfred's represented a young and vigorous nationality, throwing off the evils that beset it, and rising stronger from each contest. A blessing rested on his work, and with the one exception of Edwy, his successors down to Ethelred had glorious and successful reigns. Both alike made Somerset their rallying point, and the fairest and most graceful legends connected with the career of each have their local habitation in our county.*

The Burial-Place of Malcolm I.

IN the library of Fetteresso Castle, Kincardineshire, is a curtained recess, within which is a coffin or chest with a glass lid. This mysterious repository contains a few crumbling human bones, some dust, and two documents. By the kindness of Mr. R. W. Duff, M.P., the proprietor of this interesting old castle, I am permitted to publish for the first time the contents of the MSS.

The first paper is an account of the discovery of an ancient tomb. It was drawn up at the time by the Rev. George Thomson, minister of Fetteresso.

On Friday, January 4, 1822, some labourers, digging gravel for the repair of a road, discovered on the farm of Ferrochie, near Stonehaven, the property of Mr. Duff, of Fetteresso, one of those ancient sepulchral repositories which antiquarian research or accident has occasionally laid open in various parts of this island. The field in which the present discovery was made includes a natural ridge, or hillock, terminating abruptly towards the north-east, but previously rising, at this extremity, into an apex, or mound, on which there was till lately a cairn of stones, now composing the walls of the farm build-

---

* Authorities: William of Malmesbury, Asser's "Life," Lives of St. Neot, Histories of Glastonbury, "Anglo-Saxon Chronicle," &c. &c., Butler's "Lives of the Saints," Dugdale's "Monasticon," "Lives of English Saints," published by Toovey, &c.

ings. At this extremity the labourers had commenced an excavation, and it had been carried forward horizontally for several yards, through a bed of gravel, when the stratum, in which they were digging, assumed an artificial appearance ; and, at length, about the centre of the apex, their progress was impeded by several large stones sunk at unequal distances, and seemingly placed for the protection of some-thing below. These were removed, and under them, at the depth of six feet from the surface, was found a coffin four feet four inches long, two feet wide, and twenty inches deep, of which the sides and ends were composed of four unhewn stones, placed on edge, and the lid of one rude slab, seven feet long and four feet broad, the bottom, as afterwards appeared, being laid with small white pebbles, evidently gathered from the sea-beach, about a mile and a half distant. On removing the ponderous lid of the coffin, which was done with great care, under the immediate directions of Mr. Duff, it was found that on what it contained the work of time was nearly accomplished. Sufficient was left to show that, rude as was the sepulchre, it must have enclosed the remains of a person of consequence.

The first object that arrested the eye were the mouldering vestiges of a pall, or shroud, composed of fine network, in which were curiously-formed oval figures, or compartments, with the elegance displayed in a modern lace veil. The colour of it was dark brown, but the nature of the materials it was impossible to ascertain, as the slightest touch reduced it in semblance, as in reality, to dust. By taking up along with it part of the black and once animated earth on which it was incumbent, one compartment, near where the head had been, was raised entire, and it is now in the possession of Mr. Duff. A small hemispherical box next attracted notice, the circular lid of which, in tolerable preservation, was of a mahogany-coloured wood, flat, and neatly polished as a piece of cabinet work of the present day, and had been by minute stitches united to the body, which was about the size of a cocoa nut, but in the last stage of decay. The contents, whatever they had been, were no longer distinguish-able from the mass of black earthy matter in which the box was found embedded. The head of the corpse had been laid towards the south-west, on a pillow of turf which now bore only the print of the skull, marked by a reddish dust, into which time had dissolved the bones. A profusion of fine auburn hair still remained on the turf, in nearly the same state of decay as the pall, and near it a remnant of some vegetable substance, of the appearance of decayed flowers, still of a green or yellowish hue, which may have formed a chaplet for departed valour. Some of the hair and the hemispherical box are now in Mr. Duff's possession. The only portion of the corpse not totally decomposed was part of the bones of the legs, to which was laterally attached a small quantity of that white, fatty substance into which animal matter is in certain circumstances known to change. The spinal bones, however, had retained their form in their transmutation to a fine reddish-coloured earth, slightly unctuous, sufficiently adherent to admit of one of the vertebræ of the back being raised entire, but falling into powder on the smallest pressure. The dimensions of these vertebræ indicated that this was the grave of a full-grown person, and from their situation, relatively with the bones of the legs, it was evident that the corpse had been laid on its right side, with the knees bent to accommodate it to the length of the coffin. On the 9th of January, the labourers working in the same place again accidentally discovered, within two or three yards of the coffin, a small stone box, filled with mould, intermixed with small pieces of bones, which had undergone the operation of fire. This repository was formed, like the coffin, of unhewn stones, but of much less dimensions, and it differed from it also in being deposited within little more than a foot of the surface of the ground.

In what age this tumulus was formed, or to what nation belonged the person of whose body the stone coffin was the repository, it is for the learned antiquary to determine. But it may aid the speculations of the curious to advert that it was found within two miles of the Grampian Hill, now known by the name of Reedikes, on which are very legible the remains of an extensive encampment, supposed by some antiquaries to have been that of Galgacus, on the occasion of his last conflict with Agricola; while nearer the sea there remained, till lately, traces of what was considered a camp of the Romans. The Roman practice of burning their dead may in some degree operate against a supposition that the coffin in this tumulus belonged to that nation. But, on the other hand, the exquisite workmanship of the pall and box found in it, forces a conviction that it belonged to a people well advanced in arts and civilisation. Burning their dead, too, does not seem to have been on all occasions a part of Roman sepulture. It began to be departed from so early as the reign of Numa, who left orders that his body should not be burnt, but buried in a stone coffin. May it not on these grounds be considered as a conjecture not extravagantly improbable that this was the sepulchre of a follower of Agricola, possibly of Aulus Atticus,

the only man of note whose fall in that battle is noticed by Tacitus?
If so, this tomb has now been explored, after the lapse of more than
seventeen hundred years!

In sending this account to Professor John Stuart, of Aberdeen,
Mr. Thomson accompanied it with a letter, which is, unfortunately,
lost. The purport of it may be gathered from Professor Stuart's
reply, viz., that this was probably the sepulchre of Malcolm I. The
second paper is Professor Stuart's acknowledgment, and is of
considerable interest.

Copy letter Professor John Stuart, Aberdeen, to the Rev. George
Thomson, Minister of Fetteresso, Stonehaven.

College, Aberdeen, January 15, 1822.

DEAR SIR,—I have just been favoured with your pacquet, and am
much obliged to you for the very great trouble you have taken in
describing the curious ancient tomb so lately discovered at Fetteresso,
and in sending me specimens of the contents. You are so well
founded in your conjecture of its being the sepulchre of Malcolm I.,
that on receiving Mrs. Duff's note I had not the smallest doubt of it,
being previously informed, on good authority, that he was killed
there. My authority was and is Father Inness's " Critical Essay on
the Ancient Inhabitants of Scotland " (by far the best book we have
on these subjects), vol. ii., Appendix, p. 787, copied from one of the
Pictish Chronicles found among the Colbertine MSS. The account
of Malcolm I. ends thus : " Et occiderunt viri na Mocrore Malcolaim
in Fodresach in Claideom." What occasioned me to mark the
passage and remember it the better was a dispute that I had several
years since with the well-known Mr. Pinkerton about this very word
" Fodresach," which he would not allow to be Fetteresso until I
showed him that place so spelled in an old map of Scotland. He
was obliged to acquiesce, but neither of us could make anything of
the other word "Claideom." Perhaps you who know the names of
the neighbouring places so much better may be more fortunate, and
discover this also.

This, then, may be considered as most direct and satisfactory
evidence of its being the grave of Malcolm, which is corroborated
still more by the extreme degree of care and trouble taken about the
interment. I have little doubt of your being also correct about the
materials found with the body, though they appear too much decayed
to ascertain precisely the texture or fabric of any of them, unless
the hair and the acorns. Nor am I surprised at any part of the

ornamental work you describe, considering that from our number of religious houses, at first chiefly filled by foreigners, we may be said to have been at that period in the possession of all the arts of Europe.

The most extraordinary circumstance attending the discovery, I think, is the head being wanting, which is the most indestructible of all the bones of the human body, as we see every day in all the oldest mummies ; and this, I imagine, may be accounted for by supposing that when our historians always repeat " Sepultus est in Iona," instead of carrying the whole body from the most distant parts of the kingdom to that sacred and remote island, they had been contented with carrying only the head or heart, as Robert Bruce ordered his heart to be carried to the Holy Land. Whatever may have been the case, the whole discovery is so curious that some account of it ought certainly to be drawn up by you for insertion in one of the public journals, or the transactions of the Antiquarian Society, which I am persuaded will be reckoned highly interesting. I beg leave to present my best respects to Colonel and Mrs. Duff, and also the compliments of the season for yourself and Mrs. Thomson, and always am with much regard, dear Sir,

Most sincerely yours,

(Signed). JO. STUART.

Professor Stuart communicated the discovery to the Society of Antiquaries, Scotland. His paper was reprinted in the volume of " Essays, chiefly on Scottish Antiquities," but the full account of the opening of the tomb has never been printed as recommended by him.

The human remains in the coffin, with the glass lid, are those discovered in the sepulchre, and it may be that the remains of one of Scotland's early kings are sheltered by the hospitable roof under which lodged a late aspirant to the Crown.

Can any reader of the *A. M. & B.* throw any light on the word " Claideom " ?

J. P. EDMOND.

A LOAN exhibition of pictures, drawings, and other works of art was opened at Norwich in January, with the object of raising funds to pay off the debt on St. Peter Mancroft Church, which was elaborately restored some years ago by the late Mr. Street. The exhibition contains a large number of specimens of the " Old Masters," especially those of the Norwich school, together with a few fine pieces of old antique plate, and Mr. Edward Joseph's well-known collection of old French fans, and of miniatures by Cosway and his contemporaries.

The History of Gilds.

BY CORNELIUS WALFORD, F.S.S., *Barrister-at-Law.*

PART IV.

(*Continued from p. 71.*)

CHAPTER XXXIX.—*Gilds of Newcastle-upon-Tyne* (*continued*).

THE following fraternities were not considered to be included in the Fifteen Bye-Trades of the Borough, already described, although some of them appear to have sought admission thereto by various devices at different periods.

Hoastmen.—This was one of the earliest fraternities in Newcastle, and has existed from time immemorial. By a clause in the great charter granted by Queen Elizabeth to the town, they were incorporated as a free and distinct fraternity. Forty-eight persons were named therein for the better loading and disposing of pit coals and stones upon the Tyne, and for their own better support as a society, with the title of Governor, Stewards, and Brethren of the Fraternity of Hoastmen in the Town of Newcastle-upon-Tyne, a common seal being awarded. The Governor and Stewards were to be annually elected on the 4th January.

Power was given to the Hoastmen to load and unload anywhere on the Tyne between Newcastle and Sparhawk, yet as near to Newcastle as they could. In return for these privileges the Hoastmen granted to Her Majesty and her heirs for ever 1s. for every chaldron of coals shipped in the port of Tyne for home consumption.

During the reign of Charles I. great abuses and extortions crept into the coal trade, chiefly under Royal authority. Other local and serious complaints followed. In 1674 the Hoastmen endeavoured to obtain an Act of Parliament to regulate their affairs and avoid the abuses complained of. In 1682 they made the admission into their fraternity more exclusive than formerly. In 1690 they made an order that the custom of gift coals to the City of London should be abrogated. In 1697 the mayor of the borough granted a warrant to seize on coals, grindstones, and rub-stones sold by foreigners, *i.e.*, persons not free of the town and Hoastmen's Company. In 1706 a fruitless attempt was made to rid the Hoastmen of Newcastle of the duty of 12d. per chaldron which had been granted by that society to Queen Elizabeth and her successors, Queens of England, for ever. In 1824 the fraternity, which was still regarded as one of the highest respectability, consisted of 29 members. It was computed that 839 persons had in the whole been admitted to the freedom of the company.*

Bricklayers and Plasterers.—The earliest record preserved by this Craft Gild is one dated " the viith day of Nouember, in the yere of ouyr Lord God A thousand four hundreth and four and ffyffty," enjoining them to meet yearly at the feast of Corpus Christi, to go together in procession as other crafts did, and play at their own charge two plays, viz., " The Creation of Adam " and " The Flying of our Lady into Egype." After the plays the Wardens were to be chosen by the common assent of the fellowship ; each man of the said craft to be at the procession when his hour was assigned him ; that they should not take any to apprentice, nor set any to work either within the town or without, but such as be the King's liegemen, on pain of 20d., one half thereof to go to the fellowship, and the other half to Tyne Bridge ; that no Englishman, not being a freeman, should work in the town, on pain of a pound of wax ; that if any free brother, or his wife, should die, all the lights of the fellowship should be borne before them, according to the custom of the said fellowship.

It was ordered, October 2, 1637, "by the consent of the Company of Waulers and Bricklayers, that every brother of the said fellowship shall pay sixpence each weeke, towards the maintaineing of a suite against forreners."

It was ordered March 17, 1645, "and agreed uppon with the consent of the most pte. of the Company of Wallers and Bricklayers, that Thomas Grey shall be a ffree brother amongst us, and ffree of the said Company. In consideration whereof we have received of him xxs., and he ingaiges himself to pay fforty shillings more ; twenty shillings thereof on Martinmas Day next, and the other twentie shillings the 17 March, 1646 : besides he is to make a breekfast for the said Company, and give every man a pare of gloves, according to the custome of the said Company."

On February 24, 1659, Thomas Coates and John Wann were appointed *Searchers*, whose duty consisted in examining buildings and reporting to the Company that such were sufficient. St. Luke's Day, 1659, Robert Robson and Richard Garbut fined each 3s. 4d. " for working insufficient worke." Many other instances of a similar kind are also recorded.

Another Ordinance of the fraternity, dated January 19, 1660,

---

* The origin of this fraternity clearly dates back to a period when strangers visiting the Port were placed under the charge of Hoastmen (*i.e.*, persons to look the " Hoasts "), who took charge of them during their stay.

constituted them a fellowship with perpetual succession, who should meet on the 24th February in every year, and choose two Stewards, who might make Orders, plead, and be impleaded, &c., in the Courts of Newcastle; that they should not be molested by the Company of Masons, or the Slaters; that no foreigner should work in the town, under a penalty of 6s. 8d.; that none should employ an alien born, under the like penalty; that apprentices should serve seven years, and that no second should be taken until the first had served three.

Porters.—The first known Ordinance of this fraternity is dated in 1528. On September 25, 1648, the Common Council of New-castle made an order to revoke the Ordinance of the craft for refusing to go down and lend their assistance, on the revolt of Tynemouth Castle.

On September 27, 1667, a second Ordinance was granted, which constituted the fraternity a body politic, sixteen in number (vacancies in which by death and removal were to be filled up by the Mayor of Newcastle), and ordered them to meet on Michaelmas Day, and choose two stewards, with power to make bye-laws, sue, &c., in the Courts of Newcastle, accompanied with a table of wages. On January 1, 1670, another Ordinance was granted to this body; and on December 14, 1704, a new table of wages was appointed them by the Common Council.

There is reason to suppose that the Free Porters' office was a position of some consequence originally, both as to responsibility and profit; and that they were anciently properly the body guards of the magistrates, or perhaps of the town. As late as George I. they were armed with a sword and a dagger, in addition to the halbert, which is the only weapon they now carry when they attend the magistrates, &c., on the day the Mayor is elected, and the Sheriff at the execution of criminals. (*Vide* note quoted by Mackenzie, ii. 703.)

On January 21, 1691, an Order was made by the Corporation of Newcastle-upon-Tyne, that the Slaters and Tylers should not exercise the trade of bricklaying and plastering, otherwise than in making and mending chimney-tops above the slates and plastering them; but that the annual acknowledgment from them to this society should cease to be paid in future.

The end of this confraternity, assuming it was the end, was a remarkable one, as narrated by Mackenzie (ii. 700): "The Society consists of 111 members. On enrolling the indenture of an apprentice, £20, £10, and latterly £6, was paid; but some of the members refusing to comply with this charge—2s. 6d. being all that could be demanded by law—the Company, in a hasty fit of resentment, resolved to sell its property, to prevent those apprentices who paid only the legal sum for enrolment from enjoying any benefit therefrom. Accordingly, in 1826 their property in the Bird and Bush Yard and Silver Street was sold for £1,090."

Meters.—The Ordinance of this fraternity, dated August 3, 1611, enjoined them to meet on the 20th of September in every year, and choose four Wardens, who were to pay accounts and make an equal division of their money on the day following. There was a card, or table of rates and duties of the same date. On October 18, 1670, upon the alteration of measures, another Ordinance was granted to the craft; and on June 30, 1726, a new card, or table of rates and duties, was appointed by act of Common Council.

The Free Meters claimed and exercised the exclusive privilege of *measuring* of grain imported and exported, for which they made rather extravagant charges, particularly to non-freemen and foreigners. Their charges were 5d. a last for freemen, 10d. for non-freemen, and 1s. 10½d. for aliens.

These charges were resisted, and the matter was brought to a legal issue at the assizes in 1827, when material modifications were agreed to by mutual consent.

Rope Makers.—An Ordinance of this fraternity, dated April 14, 1648, citing one of more ancient date, made them a fellowship with perpetual succession, to meet on June 6 every year and choose two Wardens, who, with the fellowship, should make bye-laws, sue and be sued, &c., in the Courts of Newcastle. Ordered that they should not be molested by the Company of Coopers, Pulley-makers, and Turners; that no brother should set an alien to work; that they should take apprentices only once in four years, but put their own children to the business at their pleasure; and further enjoined that they should not impose upon the public by excessive prices.

There is an order in the books, under date January 30, 1695, that every brother should pay a fine of 6s. 8d. for every hundred-weight of hemp, unsound " for rope yards for either shipp, keel, water-gins, cole pitts, or lead-mines."

Early in the present century the Company consisted of about forty members, and its average annual income was about £115.

Sail Makers.—The Ordinance of this fraternity, dated December 18, 1663, constituted five persons of the occupation and fellowship, with perpetual succession, and enjoined them to meet yearly on August 10, and appoint two Wardens, who, with the fellowship, might sue and be sued in the Courts of Newcastle, and have power to make bye-laws ; that apprentices should serve seven years ; that every brother should attend at meetings ; and that none but those who were free of the town, and this fellowship, should exercise their trade. The Ordinance was confirmed by the judges, August 15, 1664. About 1825, the Gild consisted of fourteen members.

Goldsmiths.—I have shown in a previous chapter that this ancient Company was incorporated with the Plumbers, Glaziers, Pewterers, and Painters in 1536, and separated from them in 1717.

Scriveners.—The Ordinance of this fraternity, dated September 13, 1675, appointed eight scriveners a fellowship, with perpetual succession. The business of a scrivener then consisted principally in making leases, writings, and assignments, and procuring money on security. The Gild was nearly extinct at the commencement of the present century.

Cooks.—The Ordinance of this craft, dated September 10, 1575, cited a still more ancient one. They received dues of all persons that cut or sold fish, or dealt in pies or pasties ; and were bound to keep up the bonfires on the Sandhill on Midsummer or St. Peter's Eve. The Company probably became extinct about the close of the seventeenth century.

Girdlers and Keelmen.—This craft is mentioned in a Star Chamber decree, under date May 2, 1516. It is now extinct. There is a body of Keelmen on the Tyne, having Parliamentary powers.

Waits or Musicians.—A very ancient fellowship, now extinct. Originally they were musical watchmen, who paraded the streets during winter to prevent theft or robbery. They were also the privileged minstrels at weddings and feasts. The Corporation provided them with instruments, and in the reign of Queen Elizabeth paid " five waites sallary £20."

There were other crafts, such as *Spicers, Furbishers, Bronzers, Fletchers, Spuriers, Vintners*, and all now extinct.

Upholsterers, Tinplate Workers, and Stationers.—The Ordinance of this fraternity, under July 22, 1675, constituted six Upholsterers, three Tinplate Workers, and two Stationers, a fellowship, with perpetual succession ; and ordered them to meet annually on the 25th day of July, and choose four Stewards, two Upholsterers, and one of each of the other branches, who, with the Society, shall have power to make byelaws, impose fines, &c. ; that apprentices should serve seven years, and no second taken until the first had served three ; that they should not interfere with each other's callings ; and that no person not free of the town and this Society should exercise their trade in Newcastle.

The craft early in the present century consisted of fifteen members.

Proposed British School of Archaeology at Athens.

A MEETING of the general committee and subscribers for the promotion of the proposed British School of Archæology at Athens was held at the rooms of the Royal Asiatic Society, Albemarle-street, on Monday, Feb. 2, the Bishop of Durham, President of the Hellenic Society, in the chair.

The report stated that the French school and the German institute at Athens have long rendered valuable services to science, and that in 1882 the joint action of several American colleges provided similar aids for students proceeding to Greece from the United States. For many years a desire had been felt among scholars and archæologists in this country that advantages of the same kind should be afforded to our students. At length, in May, 1883, a definite plan for the establishment of a British school at Athens was brought before the public. The Prince of Wales signified his interest in the proposal, and presided over a meeting invited to consider it at Marlborough House on June 25, 1883. At a meeting of the general committee held on October 17, 1883, an executive committee had been appointed. Mr. Escott and Professor Jebb were appointed honorary secretaries of the executive committee, and Mr. Walter Leaf honorary treasurer. The report went on to state that in the autumn of 1882 the Greek Government had generously offered, through the English Foreign Office, to give a piece of ground at Athens for the proposed British school. This offer had been gratefully accepted by the committee. The site given by the Greek Government was in the immediate vicinity of Athens, on the southern slope of Mount Lycabettus, west of the Monastery of Asomatos ; it had an extent of somewhat less than two acres, and was valued at about £2,700. The upper part of the sloping ground commanded a view of Mount Hymettus in front, while the Bay of Phaleron and the Island of Ægina were visible to the right. On May 18, 1884, the Greek

Government formally sanctioned an act of the Board of the Monastery of Asomatos giving the ground on Lycabettus to the British Archæological School to be established at Athens. On November 3, 1884, a contract was signed at Athens by which the ground was formally conveyed to Mr. Agg-Gardner, Mr. Ralli, and Mr. Waring as the trustees of the committee for the school, Mr. Arthur Nicolson, Her Majesty's Chargé d'Affaires at Athens, acting as attorney of the trustees.

The funds subscribed or promised in answer to the appeals made by the executive committee amounted to over £4,000. This sum would suffice to build a house of the kind contemplated, viz., containing accommodation for a resident director, and affording one good-sized room to serve as the library of the school. Besides building such a house, the sum of £4,000 would also, it was believed, suffice to provide a library of reference for the school, or at any rate the nucleus of such a library.

The report was adopted, and resolutions were carried to the effect that it is desirable to continue the Committee, and to entrust them with the funds for establishing a British school at Athens, and for erecting the school on the site given by the Hellenic Government, and that an appeal in aid of the school be made to the two Universities, the Royal Society, the Society of Antiquaries, the Hellenic Society, the Royal Academy, the Institute of British Architects, and other public bodies. The secretaries of this committee are Mr. Escott and Professor Jebb, and Mr. Walter Leaf, honorary treasurer.

Besides the Chairman, the meeting was addressed by M. Argyropoulos, the Greek Minister; Mr. Ford, the well-known British Minister, who has just quitted Athens; Professor Jebb, Mr. Newton, and others. As the last-named gentleman remarked, " a training at home, partly from the materials which exist in our museums, is essential before the student is to do any good as an excavator, explorer, or observer in Greece itself. On the spot, a student can dig and explore, can discover and decipher inscriptions, and by every such act he will do something to advance positive knowledge." Extraordinary additions to our knowledge of Greek life and history have been made by means of inscriptions. Little indeed was known thirty years ago about the organisation of Greek religion, or about the part which it played in Greek life; but Mr. Newton's essays have shown us how much has been learned quite recently on this subject, as on very many more, by the investigations at Delphi and elsewhere.

The advocacy of the proposed British School of Archæology at Athens has led to some correspondence, in which it is suggested that the cause of archæological research would receive far greater benefit from the establishment of a school on the other side of the Ægean, say at Smyrna. Mr. Leaf, the treasurer, calls attention to the fact that it is not so much large sums of money paid down that the committee require, as the promise of regular annual contributions, to the extent of £600 or £800 a year. Mr. J. T. Wood, whilst praising the generosity of the Greek Government, takes the opportunity of pleading the cause which he himself has in hand, namely the exploration of the site of the Temple of Diana at Ephesus, which for the present is at a standstill through want of funds.

Mr. G. A. Macmillan, Secretary of the Hellenic Society, in reply, maintains the superiority of Athens to Smyrna as a basis of educational operations.

Reviews.

A Genealogical History of the Dormant, Abeyant, Forfeited, and Extinct Peerages of the British Empire. By Sir BERNARD BURKE, C.B., Ulster King of Arms. Harrison, 59, Pall Mall.

AN apology is due, not only to the author of the volume before us, but also to our readers, for our delay in noting it. The work, we need scarcely say, is one of great value to genealogists, and, indeed, to all who take an interest in the history of the past. Although the nobility of the British Empire still exists in all its grandeur as it did in very remote ages, and includes in its roll the names of Howard, Nevill, Percy, Devereux, Grosvenor, Talbot, Douglas, Murray, and many others of equal fame, still it must be confessed that a large number of the most distinguished houses have so far passed away as to form now part of the " Dormant and Extinct Peerage." " It is a fact no less strange than remarkable," as Sir Bernard Burke writes in his preface, " that the more conspicuous a man is for his great mental powers, the more rarely does he leave a representative to perpetuate his name. Neither Shakespeare, nor Milton, nor Marlborough, nor Napoleon, nor Nelson, nor Walter Scott, nor Chatham, nor Edmund Burke, nor William Pitt, nor Fox, nor Canning, nor Macaulay, and, I may add, nor Palmerston, nor Beaconsfield, has a descendant, in the male line, living. May not the same observation be applied with equal truth to those families which stand out the most prominent in the pages of history? May not the splendour of race, like the splendour of mind, have too much brilliancy to last? Beauchamp, De Vere, Beaufort, De Clare, De Lacy, Dunbar, Bohun, De la Pole, Sydney, Holland, Tudor, Plantagenet, and Mortimer, are 'entombed in the urns and sepulchres of mortality.'" Scarcely a year passes by but what the names of one or more of our titled nobility becomes extinct. "The present House of Lords," Sir Bernard Burke tells us in his "Vicissitudes of Families," "cannot claim among its members a single male descendant of any one of the barons who were chosen to enforce Magna Charta, or of any one of the peers who are known to have fought at Agincourt ; and the noble house of Wrottesley is the solitary existing family, among the Lords, which can boast of a male descent from a founder of the Order of the Garter." That the utmost care and attention has been bestowed by the author in the revision and perfecting of his laborious work may be taken for granted ; but it strikes us as a pity that the several peerages which have been recorded are entered under the family name of the holder, instead of the more natural arrangement of the title : thus, for instance, Palmerston and Beaconsfield will be found, not under those heads, but under the names of Temple and Disraeli. The reader, how-ever, is assisted in his researches by a complete index of titles at the end of the volume.

The Early Genealogical History of the House of Arundel. By JOHN PYM YEATMAN, Esq. Mitchell & Hughes.

THIS is a large folio volume, of some 400 pages, giving an account of the origin not only of the Arundels, but of the families of Montgomery, Albini, Fitzalan, and Howard, and is based mainly on the early Rotuli Curiæ Regis and other rolls. In his researches through these early documents, as Mr. Yeatman tells us, he has been able to correct many erroneous statements relative to the pedigree of the Lords Arundel of Wardour, during the reign of Edward I., which have been given in Sir R. C. Hoare's " History of Wilts," Lyson's " Cornwall," and other works. The author has been enabled to trace the pedigree of the family to his own satisfaction, step by step, back to the time of the conquest of Normandy by Rollo the Dane, and to deduce it, not from the House of Montgomery, but directly from the House of Albini, which succeeded to the inheritance of the ancient Honor of Arundel. During the progress of the work, the author obtained unrestricted access to the very valuable collection of MSS. belonging to the Earl of Egmont, and to the collection of twelfth-century records belonging to the Duke of Rutland, at Belvoir Castle, and also was allowed to inspect and copy private records bearing on the subject in the possession of Lord Arundel himself at Wardour, and those in the hands of other noblemen. The work is one of especial interest to residents in Wiltshire and in Cornwall, in which latter county the Arundels until the middle of the last century were among the largest holders of broad acres and manors. It exhibits a vast amount of research, and it has the advantage of a copious index of names and places.

Chronicles of the Yorkshire Family of Stapelton. By H. E. CHETWYND-STAPYLTON. Bradbury & Co.

BY the genealogist, the herald, and the antiquary, this work will be warmly welcomed. The fruit of long and loving labour, it reflects on its author no small credit, and may be justly said to form a worthy memorial of the ancient House whose history it records. Every source of infor-mation has been explored, materials, both in print and in manuscript, ran-sacked, and the result is seen in a work, as interesting as it is valuable, which affords a striking contrast to the untrustworthy compilations too often put forth by antiquarian *dilettanti*.

The origin of the family is here, for the first time, clearly established. It first appears in Richmondshire, where it derived its name from the little village of Stapleton (or Stapelton)-on-Tees. From small beginnings it steadily advanced during the course of the thirteenth century, and attained in the fourteenth to splendour and renown. It was chiefly by war and marriage that the Stapletons pushed their fortunes, and in both they were peculiarly fortunate. The vitality of the family is really remarkable. The parent stem, Stapelton "of that ilk," ended in heiresses, as was too often the case, after attaining the honours of a Writ of Summons, but one of its cadets had, by marrying a Fitzalan heiress, founded the Bedale branch, which took its place, and which in turn gave way, in 1466, to the two well-known branches of Carlton and Wighill, both springing from one of its own younger sons, who with his elder brother, was among the earliest of the Knights of the Garter. Of these, the Carlton branch, now represented by Lord Beaumont, appears to have become extinct in the male line in 1707, but of the Wighill stock, through its Myton offshoot, there are still extant male descendants.

THE YOUNG MASTER AND HIS SISTERS.

Here, in short, we have a vivid picture of a typical English family. We trace the rise of its fortunes ; we are enabled to follow the doings of its members in their public and in their private capacities ; and we learn how the warriors of the fourteenth century developed into the squires of the eighteenth. Nor must we forget to mention the interesting and excellent engravings which serve to illustrate the text. Two of these we are enabled by the courtesy of the author to reproduce. The one at page 102 represents the Parliament of 1278, at which Nicholas de Stapelton was present in an official capacity ; the other is taken from an ancient MS. on the Comte d' Artois, and presents us with a domestic scene of the fifteenth century. The former of these is engraved in Longman's "Lectures on English History," p. 106, and the latter figures in Wright's "Domestic Manners and Customs," to both of which sources our author acknowledges his indebtedness.

A Book of Fac-similes of Monumental Brasses on the Continent of Europe, with brief Descriptive Notes. By the Rev. W. F. Creeny, M.A. Imperial Folio. Published at Norwich by the Author. 1884.

THIS work is unquestionably the most valuable, as regards illustrations, of any of the books on monumental brasses which have yet appeared. As the title informs us, the brasses of the Continent are here exclusively made the subject of Mr. Creeny's consideration, and no English examples are noticed, except by way of comparison. Anyone who is acquainted with the books on English monumental brasses published by Haines, Boutell, and Weale, will see how immeasurably superior, both in design and execution, are the foreign examples illustrated by Mr. Creeny, as compared with even the best of the numerous specimens remaining in this country. No less than eighty illustrations are given in this handsome volume, being photographic fac-similes of the heelball "rubbings" produced by the enthusiastic vicar of St. Michael, at Thorn, during the long and romantic tours made by him in quest of this particular class of memorial. When it is seen that these excursions took him, in a marvellously short space of time, to such places as Thorn, Posen, Gnezen, and Cracow, in Poland ; Ringstead, in Denmark ; Vesta A'Oker, in Sweden ; Nymwegen, in Guelderland ; as well as to the better known towns, Lübeck, Hildesheim, Nordhausen, Bamberg, Breslau, Bruges, Meissen, Amiens, Erfurt, and elsewhere, it will be seen with what zeal a modern antiquary can go in pursuit of his especial hobby.

The reproduction of the rubbings by photography is of infinitely greater value as a mode of illustration than the most careful of woodcuts, because by this means every line of the engraving is shown with the utmost fidelity.

Nearly all the specimens in this book belong to the class known in England by the generic term "Flemish ;" that is to say, they are mostly engraved upon a single surface of latten, the various figures and architectural features being separated only by an elaborate diaper, and not by the marble or stone upon which the plate is fixed, as is the case with our native memorials. The earliest is that of Bishop Ysowilpe, in St. Andrew's Church, at Verden, North Germany, which dates from 1231, and is believed to be the oldest brass remaining. The design is extremely early, and might well pass for twelfth century work. We cannot here allow space enough to review this book at length, so will merely call a'tention to some of the finest of the examples given. The memorial of King Eric and Queen Lugeborg, at Ringstead, 1319, claims attention as a regal monument of imposing size. It measures 9 ft. 4 in. by 5 ft. 6 in. The treatment of the figures, and the elaboration of the tabernacle work and background diapers, are masterly efforts of mediæval art. The brasses of Bishops Serken and Mul (1317, 1350), and Bishops Godfrey and Frederic de Bulowe (1314, 1375) at Schwerin, are also sumptuous specimens of this class, and of exceeding beauty. For superb examples of a later period *vide* the brasses of Martin de Visch (1452) at Bruges, and John Luneborch (1474) at Lübeck, the latter the work of an artist of great ability. The ducal family of Ludewig of Bavaria is represented by some beautiful sixteenth century memorials from Meissen ; while, of later times still, we have finely-engraved specimens from Brussels, Coburg, Cracow, Termonde, and Mechlin. The letterpress is instructive, though not indicative of deep archæological knowledge.

We sincerely hope that antiquaries, and all who are interested in archæological art, will support the author of this extremely interesting work, and so relieve him of the expenses incurred in producing, at so small a cost to the public, a volume which should be a valuable adjunct to any art library.

AN old-fashioned "coal-staith" on Tyne side, one of those picturesque "bits" so eagerly seized upon by etchers—and, indeed, by artists in general—forms the subject of one of the three plates in Part xlv. of *English Etchings* (D. Bogue, 27, King William-street, Strand, W.C.). It is the work of Mr. Herbert M. Marshall, R.W.S.

Obituary Memoirs.

" Emori nolo ; sed me esse mortuum nihil æstimo."—*Epicharmus.*

COUNT OUVAROFF.

NOT only in Russia, but also elsewhere throughout Europe, the death of Count Ouvaroff will be learned with deep regret, on account of his devoted pursuit of archæology, and his generous efforts, as President of the Moscow Society of Antiquaries, for the promotion of all that contributed to throw light upon his country's past. Aleksyeï Serghyëvich Ouvaroff, who died on January 10th, was the only son of S. S. Ouvaroff, the Minister of Public Instruction, who was one of the celebrities of his day, and whose name towards the close of his career became extensively associated with archæological studies, which were then beginning in Russia to attract more systematic attention. The late Count, his son, gave himself up to antiquarian researches from his youth, never relaxed his ardent pursuit of the study of the past, and was widely and, in Russia at least, almost unanimously recognised as one of the most able, competent, and experienced authorities in most matters of national archæology. On quitting the St. Petersburg University he betook himself to the shores of the Black Sea, so rich in the remains of the old civilisation of the Greek Colonies. A result of the Count's long studies in these regions was his very valuable book, " Researches into the Antiquities of Southern Russia and the Shores of the Euxine," which was published in 1851. A French edition of this work in a more complete form, in 1855, disclosed a mass of valuable information up to that time unknown to Western scholars. One who knew him well writes : " Ouvaroff's birth and fortune had given him social influence ; his book secured him authority in the antiquarian world. He united himself with the Moscow Society of Antiquaries, and was looked on as its head, and his efforts in the cause he and the Society had at heart henceforth became unremitting. The investigation of the sepulchral tumuli, or *kourgani*, wherewith so many Governments of Russia abound, now became the work which received his chief attention, and constantly employed as he was in superintending, directing, and carefully recording such labours and their results, he acquired an almost unparalleled skill in conducting excavations of this sort, and in drawing inferences from his discoveries. His next most important contribution to the literature of archæology in Russia was an outcome of his researches among the *kourgani*. This work was a treatise on the Stone Age; it may be said to mark an epoch not only in the author's career, but in the advance of Russian research. At the Congress of Archæologists held last autumn at Odessa, where the results of the last four years of antiquarian work in Russia were summed up and discussed, Count Ouvaroff was present at his post, but his manifest ill health was a source of anxiety to his personal friends, and to the wider circle of those who appreciated his scientific labours, and understood how hard it would be to fill the gap which his loss would create. Though, indeed, Russia now numbers a host of competent and experienced archæologists, there is no one so qualified to stand in the van of their body as the leader of whom they have just been deprived by death."

MR. WILLIAM STAVENHAGEN JONES, of Carlton Hill, N.W., a great writer on coins and other antiquarian subjects, and a constant contributor to *Notes and Queries*, died on the 8th of February, at the early age of 43.

M. CHARLES VATEL, a noted antiquary and historian, has died at Versailles. " His knowledge of the latter part of the eighteenth century," observes the Paris correspondent of the *Times*, " was unrivalled, and his last work, a ' Life of Madame Du Barry,' has superseded all previous biographies, and dispelled all legends and calumnies. On the famous Tennis Court at Versailles being restored and converted into a museum, M. Vatel was appointed keeper."

MAJOR-GENERAL GIBBES RIGAUD, a well-known antiquary, died on New Year's Day, at Oxford. A son of the late Mr. Stephen Peter Rigaud, Savilian Professor of Geometry and Astronomy at Oxford, he was born about the year 1823, and was formerly in the 60th Foot (King's Royal Rifle Corps). He was an Hon. M.A. of Magdalen College, Oxford, and took a lively interest in antiquarian subjects, and more particularly with regard to matters connected with the Oxford of the past, the results of which formed the subject of frequent communications in the pages of *Notes and Queries*.

COMTE A. DE LIESVILLE, a great collector of relics of the First Revolution, has recently died at Paris. The municipal museum in the Rue Carnavalet owes to him nine-tenths of its collection of coins, medals, pottery, engravings, and books connected with the Revolutions of 1789, 1830, 1848, and 1870. He also presented the model of the Bastille, carved out of one of the stones of that edifice, and books and newspapers to the number of 10,000. Sprung from a Legitimist family in Normandy, he was a warm admirer of the Revolution, and for twenty-five years rummaged all France for relics of it. On the remodelling of the Carnavalet Museum in 1879, the curator, M. Cousin, himself an ardent collector, induced him to present his collections to it. By his will he leaves his house at Batignolles and 50,000f. for a children's art school, while a valuable porcelain collection goes to the Sèvres manufactory.

M. DU SOMMERARD, son of Alexandre du Sommerard, founder of the Cluny Museum, died on February 5, aged 77. He became Curator of the Museum in 1843, since which time great additions have been made to its contents, particularly in mediæval objects. M. de Liesville, who collected relics of the Revolution, is also dead.

UNDER the title of " Old Times : a Picture of Social Life at the End of the Eighteenth Century," and dealing with the daily life of our great-grandfathers, Mr. John Ashton is going to issue a work similar to his " Social Life in the Reign of Queen Anne." Nothing is taken from the diaries or lives of the upper classes ; it aims solely to give a fair account of the life of the middle class. Mr. Nimmo is the publisher.—*Athenæum.*

Meetings of Learned Societies.

METROPOLITAN.

SOCIETY OF ANTIQUARIES.—*Jan.* 22, Mr. H. S. Milman, Director, in the chair. Mr. R. Day, jun., exhibited the following objects : (1) A pair of thin circular discs, about 2⅝ inches in diameter, pierced in the centre with two holes, and ornamented with concentric lines and a chevron pattern between. These plaques (the property of Mr. A. Forster) were found near Cloyne, co. Cork. (2) A gold bracelet from Mr. Day's own collection, found in the parish of Skreene (*i.e.* Shrine), between Ballina and Sligo, co. Sligo. It bore a corrugated pattern with dotted lines in each of its six depressions. It was fastened with terminal tubes soldered on, a mode of fastening not common on Celtic ornaments. (3) A bronze spearhead, dredged from the river at Blackrock, near Cork, and described in " Proceedings," second series, vol. viii. p. 202. The Rev. H. T. Armfield communicated an account of a Roman pavement and other remains, the existence of which had been revealed by the plough at Alresford, Essex, in a field lying in the angle formed by the estuary of the Colne and a creek running eastward towards Brightlingsea Church. The find also yielded some fragments of pottery and of metal, remains of the deer and of the ox. burnt ashes, charcoal, oyster and other shells. Mr. A. G. Hill exhibited some rubbings of marble slabs from the Catacombs, now in the Kircherian Museum, and comprising inscriptions and various devices and representations of a religious nature. One of the inscriptions ran as follows :—

DOMVSETERNALISAVRCELSIETAVRILARITATISCONPARIMEESFECIMVSNOB-
ISETNOSTRISETAMICISARCOSOLIOCVMPARETICVLOSVOINPACEM.

This inscription Mr. Hill said was unintelligible, but it was interpreted by Mr. E. Walford, with the exception of four letters : " The eternal home of Aur. Celsus and Aurelius his jovial companion. . . . We have made this for ourselves, and our relations and friends in Arcosolium with his dear little father let him go in peace."—*Jan.* 29, Dr. E. Freshfield, in the chair. Mr. E. Bellasis, *Lancaster Herald*, exhibited as a specimen of modern penmanship and heraldic painting a pedigree of the House of Orange, which had been prepared by the Count de Magny and offered to the King of Holland. Mr. E. Green, in connection with this exhibition, laid upon the table a " Blazonrie of the Royal Descent of the Green Family," as yet another specimen of modern heraldic painting, executed by a Cistercian monk. Mr. R. S. Ferguson exhibited two copies, of the fifteenth and sixteenth centuries respectively (one a most beautiful and costly specimen), the property of the Dean and Chapter of Carlisle, and gave a description of a large hoard of silver coins of the fourteenth century found at Beaumont, near Carlisle. Mr. A. G. Hill also exhibited a cope, now in use at a church in the west of London, on the orphrey of which were some very fine figures of saints, viz., St. Bartholomew, St. Anne, St. Peter, St. Paul, St. Andrew, and St. Catharine. On the morse was the figure of a wolf carrying a lamb in its mouth. Mr. Hill assigned to this cope the date of 1500 A.D.—*Feb.* 5, Dr. E. Freshfield, V.P., in the chair. Mr. R. Blair exhibited a photograph of a Roman sculptured stone, which had been found in two portions, at intervals of three years and 100 yards, and of which he had become the possessor. It represented a recumbent figure, that of the deceased, in the act of taking food from a vessel held in one hand, and in the lower portion of the stone was the figure of a youth holding up a vessel with some more food or drink. The inscriptions recorded that the stone was erected " To the divine shades of Victor, by nation a Moor. He lived twenty years, and was the freedman of Ninnerianus, a horseman of the first Ala of the Asturians, who followed him affectionately to the grave." The grammar and spelling of the inscription were open to criticism. The monument was 3 ft. 4 in. high by 1 ft. 11 in. wide. Mr. E. W. Godwin exhibited, by permission of Mrs. Chaworth Musters, of Annesley Park, Notts, an illuminated scroll, 27 ft. in length, giving a pedigree of the Royal family of England. It comprises nine skins of vellum, eight of which had been executed as early as the reign of Edward II., with a continuation (on the ninth skin) of the time of Henry IV. The drawings in their general character resembled those of Queen Mary's Psalter or the Arundel Psalter. Especially remarkable was a figure of Fortune in a representation of the wheel of fortune which headed the roll. Major C. Cooper exhibited two very curious clocks, one of which he had bought at Vevay and the other at Leighton Buzzard. Mr. St. John Hope exhibited impressions of the corporate seals of the borough of Lyme Regis, in the county of Dorset.

BRITISH ARCHÆOLOGICAL ASSOCIATION.—*Jan.* 21, Mr. G. R. Wright, F.S.A., in the chair. Mr. Worthington Smith exhibited a dagger of the bronze period, found at Ruthin, twenty feet below the surface, in a bed of peat. Mr. Cecil Brent, F.S.A., described a series of double-handled vessels, showing a curious similarity of form, although of very varying ages and nationalities, there being among them examples of Etruscan and Roman wares, some of later date, and some of modern times. He exhibited also portions of an ancient manuscript, containing the service for St. Agatha's Day. Mr. Loftus Brock, F.S.A., exhibited a curious collection of articles found at Aldgate, which showed the progress of the City of London. There was a portion of a prehistoric vase, probably of a date anterior to the Roman occupation, examples of many of the pottery wares of the Romans, a Saxon knife, fragments of Delft ware, Elers ware, and modern Wedgwood. These articles were found close together. A paper by Mr. C. Lynam on the inscription on the cross at Carew Castle, Pembrokeshire, was then read. The cross, which is 14 ft. 1½ in. high, stands by the roadway, the upper portion being in a separate stone to the lower, to which it is morticed. It is covered with interlaced work, there being no animals in the design. The inscription has been variously read by Professors Westwood and Rees and by Hubner. At the end of the paper, Mr. W. de Grey Birch, F.S.A., proceeded to show that the inscription was not Latin, as had been believed, but British, which he read, " Magy Gilteut Decettfy," the first portion being the most legible. He traced the resemblance of the wording to other similar names recorded by Hubner and others, and to the familiar British name of " Iltut," " Mac " being a common prefix. The inscription, which is of the eighth or ninth century, runs on a small slab, forming a portion of the design. A similar one, intended probably for an inscription, remains as originally formed. A paper was then read on St. Milburga of Wenlock, by Mr. H. Syer Cuming, F.S.A. (Scot.). After comparing some of the absurd legends about this Saint, he traced her life from authentic history, making, of course, a passing reference to the story of her having banished from Wenlock the geese which ate her grain. She is represented in but a few of our mediæval churches in the dress of an Abbess, and mostly with a flock of geese flying from her. The paper was illustrated by a clever drawing by Mr. Watling from a fifteenth century painting, formerly in a church, but which has now passed into private hands.—*Feb.* 3, Mr.

S. Tucker, Somerset Herald, in the chair. Mr. Cecil Brent, F.S.A., exhibited two Assyrian seals, in very good preservation. The Rev. Prebendary Scarth reported the discovery of the base of a pedestal at Park Farm, Tockington, Gloucestershire, with some fragments of tesselated pavements of Roman date. It was ornamented with a star pattern, and an adaptation of an egg and tongue moulding. Mr. Earle Way described a large find of Roman pottery and glass at St. Saviour's, Southwark, among which was the head of a remarkably large amphora. Mr. E. Walford exhibited a book of MS. prayers of the fifteenth century in German. Mr. C. Lynam described two plaster casts of portions of the Runic cross at St. Michael's, Isle of Man, worked in slate. Mr. Loftus Brock, F.S.A., drew attention to the mode of execution of the figures represented, which had evidently been cut by a chisel, although some authorities believe that all old work was executed by a pick or axe. The date is that of the ninth or tenth centuries. The first paper was by Mr. J. W. Grover, F.S.A., on "The Registers of the old Clapham Parish." These are fairly complete from 1551, except that those from 1691 to 1701 are missing. They indicate the early settlement of several families still resident at Clapham, or which have been there until recently. Among these, references to the following occur at early dates : Warfield, Winterbottom, Thornton, Pennington, Sydenham, Atkins, Thatcher, Franks, and many others. Some curious references to burials in woollen, to touching for the cure of King's Evil by Charles II., and to collections for special objects are referred to in the documents. In 1649 the first collection appears to have been made for the spread of the Gospel in New England. In 1689 for the Irish Protestants ; in 1691 for the relief of the inhabitants of Tinmouth, damaged by the French. In 1698 collections for the Vaudois. In 1690 the first stage coach is reported to have run from Clapham to Gracechurch-street. In course of an animated discussion, in which Mr. Walford, Mr. Wright, F.S.A., Mr. Brock, and the Chairman took part, the lecturer stated that the recent excavation of Mount Nod, Clapham, had only revealed that the mound was artificial, but nothing was met with to determine its date, although, contrary to expectation, it was probably no older than the large mansion which formerly stood on the site of the Cedar's Terrace. A portion of a paper was then read, by the Rev. G. F. Browne, on the remarkable cross now preserved in Leeds Church, found during the rebuilding. The remainder of the paper was deferred until the next meeting.

ROYAL ARCHÆOLOGICAL INSTITUTE.—*Feb.* 5, Lord Percy, M.P., President, in the chair. Admiral Tremlett sent a paper on "Pierres à Bassins," some remarkable excavations in Brittany, which were thought by the peasantry to have been used in the rites of the Druids, but which really are cavities artificially hollowed for the purpose of cutting out "querns" for grinding corn. These the writer showed to be at least ten centuries old. The paper was illustrated by drawings and diagrams. Mr. Somers Clarke read a paper, entitled "Notes on the Screen in Sandridge Church, Herts." This screen, Mr. Clarke observed, has in reality more the appearance of a substantial wall of brick and stone, pierced in the lower part, and cutting off the nave from the chancel in such a manner as almost to separate one from the other. A discussion followed the reading of each paper. Among the objects of antiquarian interest exhibited were a variety of patens from various churches in Norfolk, by the Rev. W. Manning ; some rubbings of brasses recently found in Norfolk, and formerly belonging to Heigham Church, in that county, by Mr. Wm. Vincent ; and a series of photographs of Megalithic remains, by Mr. Seidler.

LONDON AND MIDDLESEX ARCHÆOLOGICAL SOCIETY.—*Feb.* 10. Mr. J. G. Waller in the chair. Mr. E. W. Bradbrook read a paper by Mr. C. Roach Smith, Vice-President, on the late discoveries in the old " Wall of London." Mr. Smith supported the theory that the wall was coeval with the enclosing of London by the Romans, that this was the original wall, and that the semicircular projecting bastions were part of the original structure ; as in the case of examples to be found in France. This view was supported by the Chairman at some length. On the other hand, Mr. Alfred White and Mr. J. E. Price, the Secretary, were of opinion that there was an extension of the city, probably about the time of Alfred, and that the bastions were built at a period subsequent to the erection of the wall, out of the materials of-older buildings, for the purpose of strengthening it. Mr. E. Walford read a paper on Park's " History of Hampstead," which he said had been regarded as a valuable contribution to topographical literature. It went out of print soon after its publication in 1814, and he (Mr. Walford) was now contemplating its re-issue. Its author, Mr. John James Park, was a native of Hampstead, and died comparatively young, though not until he had been elected to the chair of English Law and Jurisprudence in King's College. Mr. Park's father, Thomas Park, F.S.A., the editor of Horace Walpole's " Catalogue of Royal and Noble Authors," of the " Harleian Miscellany," and of a long series of reprints of old English poetry, had long been a·resident in Church-row. As a child he had searched over and over again through the parish records, and had pored over the registers and charters in the keeping of the Dean and Chapter of Westminster, to whom nearly all Hampstead had once belonged, and this he had done with such good effect that, when he was only twenty years old, he produced a work quite equal in merit to Robinson's history of Tottenham and Hackney, and superior to Prickett's history of Highgate. Mr. Walford's paper on Hampstead was descriptive of its waters, its wells, its architecture, literary associations, &c. A discussion followed, and a cordial vote of thanks was accorded to Mr. Walford.

ST. PAUL'S ECCLESIOLOGICAL SOCIETY.—*Jan.* 13, Mr. G. H. Birch in the chair. A learned paper on Church Bells and Bell-founders was read by Mr. J. Ch. Stahlschmidt ; the paper was followed by a discussion, in which the Rev. Dr. Raven and Mr. E. Walford took part. The former said that the materials for an account of the church bells of Suffolk were at the disposal of any society who would publish them, and the latter illustrated *from his own experience* the means of preventing the destruction of church bells and church towers, as at Goring, in Oxfordshire, and at Sandwich, Kent, where the churchwardens, who had intended to sell the peal of bells, had met with an inhibition from the Archbishop of Canterbury.—*Jan.* 31, annual meeting, the Rev. H. C. Shuttleworth in the chair. The Council, secretary, and other officers were re-elected. From the report, which was adopted, it appears that the position and prospects of the society are in a highly satisfactory condition. During the past year ten meetings were held at the Chapter-house, St. Paul's, and papers on various antiquarian subjects read. Visits were paid to several churches in and near London, and an excursion was also made to Winchester, where Mr. Somers Clarke conducted the members over the Cathedral and the Hospital of St. Cross. Part V. of the Society's " Transactions," it was stated, was in the press, and would shortly be in the hands of members. It has been decided to reprint Part II. uniform in style with the other parts, and half the life subscriptions of the year have been devoted to a special fund for that purpose.—*Feb.* 5, Mr. C. H. Gough, C.E., in the chair. Mr. H. Roumieu Gough, F.R.I.B.A., read a paper, entitled, "Some Ecclesiastical Antiquities," in which he gave an historical and descriptive account of several of the most famous and interesting remains of ruined abbeys in England, Ireland, Scotland, and Wales, including Fountains, Furness, Tintern, Netley, Dryburgh, Melrose, Jedburgh, Roslyn, Boyle, Ardfert, Dunbrody, Moyne, Adare, and Muckross. The reading of the paper was accompanied by some photographic lime-light illustrations.

BIBLICAL ARCHÆOLOGY.—*Feb.* 3, Dr. Samuel Birch, President, in the chair. Several presentations of books to the Society were announced, and thanks ordered to be returned to the donors. A paper, entitled, "Notes on the Antiquities from Bubastis, in the collection of Mr. F. G. Hilton Price, F.S.A.," was read by the author. This ancient Egyptian city was of considerable importance as early as the time of the eighteenth dynasty, but increased in both size and magnificence under the kings of the twenty-second dynasty, and was at that time probably the most considerable place in the Delta. After the conquest of the Persians (B.C. 352), who dismantled its walls, the town was, as is proved by the antiquities discovered in the ruins. evidently occupied by the Greeks and Romans.—A paper, by Professor Sayce, on the "Karian Language and Inscriptions," was read.

SHORTHAND SOCIETY.—*Feb.* 4, Mr. W. St. C. Boscawen delivered a lecture on the subject of "Oriental inscriptions as illustrative of the growth and development of writing." At the commencement of his lecture, Mr. Boscawen said that it was difficult to realise, as we looked at a page of modern printing or writing, the fact that we had before us in the twenty-six simple characters of the Western alphabet the result of the labours of millions of minds during tens of centuries. The art of writing, the desire to give a graphic record of events in the personal or tribal life, or to convey some message to others, was one which was attained and practised at a very remote period in the history of the human race. The inscribed records of Egypt and Chaldea carried us back to a very remote period, to within, it might seem, an almost appreciable distance of the threshold of history. The laws which regulated the growth and development of writing from its rudest and most primitive stage of pure pictorial expression to the higher development of syllabic and alphabetical writing were now known, and, when applied to the chief systems of writing in use in the Oriental world, revealed the same process of growth and development in each. The hieroglyphics of Egypt, the cuneiform scripts of Mesopotamia, and the pictorial characters of the Hittites, had each passed through the various stages of word-building by compounded idiographs, of phonetic expressions by syllables, and even simplification to an alphabetic stage. In no case, however, were the various stages so fully represented and the periods of transition which connected them so well preserved as in the cuneiform inscriptions.

NATIONAL SOCIETY FOR PRESERVING THE MEMORIALS OF THE DEAD.—Meetings of the Executive Committee and Council took place on January 21, 22, and 23, under the chairmanship of Mr. Hellier Gosselin, the Ven. Archdeacon Harrison, F.S.A., and Mr. James Hilton, F.S.A., when reports as to the work of the Society were submitted and approved. These included the preservation of the Deane monuments at Great

Maplestead ; the Poll monuments, Snarford Church ; brasses in Cheam Church ; the Barnewall monument at Lusk, Ireland ; monumental slabs in Milford Church, and the church of St. Michael-in-Coslany, Norwich ; the Pedlar's Window, in St. Mary's Church, Lambeth ; the Pugin brass, Christchurch Church ; the Fewtrell monument in Easthorpe Church ; the helmets on the tomb of the Earl of Shrewsbury, in Sheffield parish church : and the monumental records in Ellingham Church.

ASIATIC.—*Jan.* 26, Sir F. Goldsmid in the chair. The Rev. Dr. Pope read a paper "On the Study of the Vernaculars of Southern India," in which he pointed out the importance and value of such labours, as the surest means of gaining a real knowledge of the character and feelings of the native population. Hindus, he stated, are not apathetic when once their interest is aroused. He then gave a sketch of the Tami*l* people and language, the latter of which has a valuable literature, in character chiefly ethical, independent of and antagonistic to Sanskrit. In confirmation of this view Dr. Pope gave an account of the three most famous Tami*l* works, the "Kurra*l*" of Tiruva*ll*uvar, the 400 quatrains called "Nâla*a*i," and the writings of the poetess Avvai.

ROYAL INSTITUTE OF BRITISH ARCHITECTS.—*Feb.* 2, a paper was read by Mr. M. B. Adams, Associate, on "Architectural Drawing," illustrated by an exhibition of more than 200 original specimens, the work of artists from Inigo Jones down to the present day. The exhibition was stated to be the best collection ever brought together within the walls of the institute.

NUMISMATIC.—*Jan.* 15, Mr. W. S. W. Vaux, V.P., in the chair. Mr. J. G. Hall exhibited a ducal and a testoon of the Grandmaster Giovanni de la Valette. Mr. H. Montagu read a notice on a jetton bearing a sprig of thistle and rose combined and the inscription BEATI PACIFICI. From its type and inscription Mr. Montagu attributed the piece to James I. Mr. H. A. Grueber read a paper on English medals, in which he gave an outline of the history of those objects, at the same time noticing the principal artists and their different styles of work.

NEW SHAKSPERE.—*Jan.* 16, Dr. R. Garnett in the chair. A paper "On the Authorship of Henry VIII.," by Mr. R. Boyle, was read by Mr. F. J. Furnivall. Mr. Boyle, accepting Fletcher as undoubted part author, and the scenes allotted to him by the New Shakspere Society as on the whole his, proceeded to deal with his partner in the work. Shakespeare had by the time the play was written abandoned co-partnership in writing for almost twenty years ; nor would he have let his work be spoilt by an inferior dramatist. The metre of the non-Fletcherian part dates the play as not earlier than 1612, and probably some years later ; and historical allusions in the play to 1615-17. The editors of the first folio of 1623, though including "Henry VIII.," were not to be trusted in the matter. But the complete failure of both male and female characterisation, and the want of plot, compactness, and proportion, as compared with other plays of his last period, were the strongest evidence against Shakespeare's authorship. Mr. Boyle considers that Massinger was Fletcher's partner. The Chairman, while acknowledging the ability and ingenuity of Mr. Boyle's paper, disputed his conclusions.

PROVINCIAL.

AYR AND WIGTOWN ARCHÆOLOGICAL ASSOCIATION.—This Society has, within the past twelvemonth, been very successful in its search after early Christian remains in its district, and its discoveries have led to some remarkable contributions to our knowledge of lake dwellings. The cavern and its monument unearthed last summer on the coast of Glasserton show that the spot is one of the deepest interest to antiquaries. St. Ninian's Cave has lately been the scene of the explorations of the Association, and a large number of antiquities—including no less than nineteen stone crosses and a font—have been discovered. It is satisfactory to record that Mr. Stewart, the owner of the soil, has caused good care to be taken of the relics which have been laid bare, by having caused an iron grill to be placed across the mouth of the cave, which is kept locked.

PENZANCE NATURAL HISTORY AND ANTIQUARIAN SOCIETY.—*Jan.* 16, a paper was read by the President, the Rev. W. S. Lach-Szyrma, on the "Folk-lore of the Sea," dealing with fishermen's superstitions of divers natures.* A curious thumb-ring was afterwards exhibited by Mr. T. Cornish, and also a muster-roll of the 4th Royal Cornwall Militia in 1809 by Mr. H. S. Hill.

Antiquarian News & Notes.

MESSRS. BLACKWOOD announce a new edition of the late Mr. J. H. Burton's "Book-hunter."

MESSRS. BELL have added to their art library the 6th vol. of Vasari's "Lives of the Painters."

MR. J. MURRAY has just published a new work by Josiah Gilbert, "Landscape in Art before Claude and Salvator."

THE concluding volume of the "Life of Raphael," by Messrs. Crowe and Cavalcaselle, is in the printer's hands.

THE claim of Mr. John Fraser, of Carnarvon, to the title and estates of Lord Lovat, will come before the House of Peers shortly.

THE Palace of Tiberius has been discovered at Capri. Some fine mosaics and three beautiful wall paintings have already been exposed.

THE 420th anniversary of the Horners' Company was celebrated by a banquet at the Guildhall Tavern on February 2.

MR. P. SMITH has added a new volume to Murray's "Student's Manuals," namely, the second volume of the "Student's Ecclesiastical History," containing the Middle Ages and the Reformation.

THE indefatigable Mr. William Andrews, of the Literary Club, Hull, has just completed a work on "Modern Yorkshire Poets," and is employed on four other antiquarian books.

DE AMICI'S "Holland and its People" is almost out of print. The work, which is published by Messrs. Putnam & Sons, of Henrietta-street, was limited to 600 copies ; so we fear that it can hardly be reprinted

A PROVINCIAL architect writes to the *Times* condemning the use of Chilworth and other perishable stone in the restoration of Westminster Abbey.

THE important collection of pictures formed by the late Mr. Christopher Beckett, chiefly from the Hamilton Palace sale, will be brought to the hammer at Messrs. Christie & Manson's in June.

MR. J. L. SIBLEY, for thirty years librarian at Harvard College, has, says the *Athenæum*, just completed the eightieth year of his age and the third volume of his biographical memoranda of Harvard graduates.

---

* We shall probably give the substance of this lecture as a separate article in a future number.

IT is proposed to raise a subscription for a portrait of Dr. Stubbs, now Bishop of Chester, to be placed in the Bodleian Library at Oxford.

THE Biblical fragments described by Dr. Harkavy in the "Mémoires" of St. Petersburg Academy, will, it is stated, be offered for purchase to the British Museum.

COLONEL RAMSAY lately died at Rome. It was at his suggestion that the municipality put up a tablet on the house in which Sir Walter Scott resided at Rome in 1832.

ACCORDING to the *Academy*, the Hon. D. A. Bingham, author of "The Marriages of the Bonapartes," has in preparation a work on the "Archives of the Bastille."

MR. W. S. ELLIS is engaged upon a book entitled "The Parks and Forests of Sussex, Ancient and Modern," which will describe about 150 parks and forests, as well as the castles, manor houses, and mansions.

THE Council of the Royal Historical Society have chosen as Fellows for life, "distinguished for services to historical science," Mr. Lecky and Professor Max Muller.

MESSRS. W. H. ALLEN will publish shortly a "History of Hindustan," by Mr. H. G. Keene, C.S.I., late of the Bengal Civil Service. The term "Hindustan" is taken in its strict sense as limited to Northern India—the country, in short, where Hindi is the vernacular language.

THE Rev. W. J. Loftie has accepted a commission from the Government to write a series of small and large guides to the Tower of London. He will also write "London" for Professor Freeman's series of "English Cities."

THE original autographs of several love-letters addressed by John Keats to Miss Fanny Brawne in 1819-20 will be sold by Messrs. Sotheby, Wilkinson & Hodge the first week in March, together with six unpublished autograph letters of Charles Lamb.

MR. REDWAY is issuing from the Chiswick Press "Hints to Collectors of Original Editions of the Works of Thackeray." In addition to an exact copy of every title-page and a collation of pages and parts, it supplies notes of differences between true and false editions.

THE library of the late Rev. R. Gibbins, D.D., Professor of Ecclesiastical History in the University of Dublin, originally bequeathed to his old University, has been lately sold in London by Messrs. Sotheby & Co., the testator having changed his mind.

THE annual blessing of the horses and mules took place on St. Anthony's Day, outside St. Anthony's Church, at Rome. It is to be hoped that such blessing will do good ; for in no part of the world are horses and mules treated more cruelly than in Italy.

MR. W. J. C. MOENS, of Lymington, Hants, has prepared for publication "The Registers of the Dutch Church, Austin Friars, London," extending from 1571 to 1874, with descriptions of the monumental inscriptions, and a short account of strangers and their churches.

MR. GEORGE A. AITKEN, of the Secretary's office, General Post-office, has been for some time preparing a collected edition of the works of Sir Richard Steele. Mr. Aitken has discovered various facts relating to the subject, and obtained many letters which have not been published.

MR. JOHN SOUTHWARD has recently issued a second and revised edition of his "Practical Printing," which has been supplemented by a treatise on "Book-keeping for Printers," written by Mr. Arthur Powell. Mr. Southward has devoted himself for several years to the study of the literature and antiquities of printing.

AT the demolition of an old house in St. Stephen's-square, at Vienna, a secret staircase was discovered in the wall on the ground floor. A pamphlet, entitled " A beautiful Song of grisly Death," illustrated with a skeleton, holding in one hand a spade and in the other a lantern, was found on the staircase. It bears date 1633.

PRINCE B. GIUSTINIANI has placed in the hands of the Pope, in the name of his friend Lord Ashburnham, a precious manuscript from the library of Ashburnham House. It contains letters by Innocent III., written during the years 1207 and 1209, and taken from the archives of the Holy See when at Avignon at the beginning of the fifteenth century.

ALL the casts from masterpieces of antique sculpture belonging to the Musée on the Trocadéro, Paris, are being placed in the hitherto un-occupied gallery on the Passy side of the building. It is proposed to open this collection to the public at Easter. The fine antiquities brought from Indo-China by M. Delaporte, are placed in two stages of the pavilion at the extremity of the same gallery.

MR. WILLIAM M. RAMSAY, M.A., Fellow of Exeter College, Oxford, has been elected first Lincoln Professor of Archæology and Art in the University. The Professorship is endowed by the Statutes of Lincoln College with the proceeds of one Fellowship, and "the Professor is to lecture and give instruction on the arts, and manufactures, monuments, coins, and inscriptions of classical antiquity, and on Asiatic and Egyptian antiquities, or some of those subjects."

MESSRS. BURNS AND OATES announce the publication, by subscription, in five volumes, of a " Literary and Biographical History, or Bibliographical Dictionary, of the English Catholics, from the Reformation, in 1534, to the Present Time," by Mr. Joseph Gillow. Though the scope of the work admits only of abridged and condensed notices, the antiquary and historical student will find in it much that will repay perusal ; as, until a very recent date all Roman Catholic books were almost surreptitiously published, and authors' names did not find their way into the ordinary catalogues.

IN digging the foundations for a new bank at Canterbury an interesting discovery has been made. At a depth of fifteen feet under the surface, the skulls of oxen have been exhumed, which, from the peculiar curvature of the horns, are pronounced to have belonged to the ancient British ox, the *Bos longifrons*. This species of horned cattle was not found earlier than the neolithic or polished stone implement period ; they formed the food of the ancient Britons, and disappeared at the Saxon invasion. The specimens are in the possession of the East Kent Natural History Society.

THE *Bombay Gazetter* describes the district of Belgaum, the history of which is carried back to the end of the fifth century. In 1472, Belgaum, then a fortress of great strength, surrounded by a deep ditch, and close to a pass defended by redoubts, was besieged and captured by a large Mussulman army, and was afterwards for a time dependent on the kings of Bejapore. On the decline of the Mogul's power the place passed into the possession of the Nizam, but the Mahrattas soon asserted their supremacy. Belgaum was a place of some importance during the wars with Hyder Ali, and after the fall of Peishwa, early in the present century, it passed into the hands of the British.

THE publications of the English Dialect Society for the year 1884, which have been delayed by unavoidable circumstances, consist of the third and concluding part of "English Plant Names," by Mr. James

Britten and Mr. Robert Holland ; "Upton-on-Severn Words and Phrases," by the Rev. Canon Lawson ; "A Word-list, illustrating the Correspondence of Modern English with Anglo-French Vowel-Sounds.' by Miss B. M. Skeat ; and Part I. of "A Glossary of Archaic and Provincial Words used in Cheshire," by Mr. Robert Holland.

LORD BUTE, being accused of subscribing, though he is a Roman Catholic, to a fund for republishing the works of Wyclif, states that he considers the Reformer's works as "of much historical interest." He adds : " If we are to abstain from printing matter of literary and historical interest because we don't agree with the sentiments expressed, philological and historical science would perish. I would subscribe without scruple to publish a critical text of Arius' *Thalia*, if anybody could find a Codex ; and I gave a copy of the Koran to a parish library the other day."

CATALOGUES, containing books more or less of an antiquarian character have reached us from Messrs. Taylor & Son, Northampton (including the MS. collection of John Cole, the antiquarian bookseller) ; Mr. W. Withers, Leicester ; Mr. James Thorpe, 53, Ship-street, Brighton ; Messrs. Reeves & Turner, 196, The Strand, W.C.; Messrs. Fawn & Son, Queen's-road, Bristol ; Mr. U. Maggs, 159, Church-street, Paddington-green ; Mr. W. P. Bennett, Bull-street, Birmingham ; Mr. J. Salisbury, 48, Paternoster-row ; Messrs. J. W. Jarvis & Son, 28, King William-street W.C. (including purchases from Mr. Herman's, and other recent sales) ; and Mr. Geo. Redway, 15, York-street, Covent-garden, W.C.

MESSRS. ANNAN, of Glasgow, have lately issued a new edition of the "Relics of Ancient Architecture and other Picturesque Scenes in Glasgow." The illustrations were drawn by Mr. Thomas Fairbairn, and the letterpress description was by the late Mr. James Pagan, editor of the *Glasgow Herald.* The work was originally published in 1849. The drawings were executed to the commission of the late Mr. James Bogle, Lord Dean of Guild in Glasgow. A general survey of the city having at that time been made, and many buildings having been condemned, Mr. Bogle desired to preserve memorials of such as were interesting in a picturesque or antiquarian point of view, and went over the city with Mr. Fairbairn to make a choice. Nearly all the subjects are now gone for ever, and the remainder are so much altered as to be scarcely recognisable. The original drawings are now the property of the City of Glasgow, and are preserved in the Corporation Galleries.

UNDER the presidency of Lord Enfield, a Society has been established, called the Middlesex County Record Society, for the purpose of publishing, under efficient editorship, such of the county records, or extracts therefrom, as may present matter of general interest with respect to the history of the county. These Records, relating to its civil and criminal history, commence with 1549, and are more or less complete down to the present time. Until recently, these records had been left in a condition which not only rendered examination impossible, but seriously endangered their existence. They have, however, now been placed in a newly-constructed muniment room at the Sessions House, Clerkenwell, and have been arranged, labelled, and indexed by order of the Court of Quarter Sessions. This important work has been carried out at a cost to the county of more than £1,000, under the advice and supervision of Mr. J. Cordy Jeaffreson, who was in the first instance deputed by the Historical MSS. Commissioners to examine and report upon the Records, and they are now made available for investigation and use.

MR. J. HALLIWELL-PHILLIPPS has printed for circulation among his friends a dignified remonstrance against the discourtesy with which he has been treated by Mr. C. Flower, of Stratford-on-Avon, after having gratuitously calendared all the ancient charters and other documents belonging to that ancient town in which rest the bones of Shakespeare. He also protests, and most justly, against a statement in the *Stratford Herald* to the effect that he allowed valuable papers entrusted to his charge to lie about " unclassified, uncalendared, and uncared for"—the real fact being, as he clearly shows, that he recommended to the Mayor and Corporation to bind such, and such only, as were of real historic value ; he also states that while Mr. Flower reflected on him for taking valuable documents to a house a few yards off, to be reproduced by the autotype process, the same Mr. Flower felt no scruple in sending up to London 119 records, and leaving them there for several months !

THE following articles, more or less of an antiquarian character, appear among the contents of the reviews and magazines for February : *Quarterly Review*, "The London Livery Companies ;" *Church Quarterly*, " The Seabury Centenary ;" *Westminster Review*, " On the Study of the Talmud," and " The Materials of Early Russian History ; *Scottish Review*, "Correspondence of Sir Robert Moray," and " A Letter from James Sharp to the Earl of Middleton, proving his Treachery in 1661 ;" *Art Journal*, " The Early Madonnas of Raphael ;" *Ladies' Treasury*, " The First Printed Bible," *Catholic World*, " Ecclesiastical Survivals," and " A Provincial Poem ;" *Longman's* " On the Antiquity of Jests ; " *Atlantic Monthly*, "The Quest of the Grail of Ancient Art;" *Home Chimes*, " Goldsmith," and " Folk-lore ; " *Macmillan*, ." The City Companies," *English Illustrated Magazine*, " Shakespeare's Country," and " Naworth Castle ;" *Edinburgh Review*, "Spencer as a Philosophic Poet," and " The Correspondence of Mallet Du Pan ; " *Illustrated Naval and Military Magazine*, "Volunteer Forces under George III."

Antiquarian Correspondence.

Sin scire labores,
Quære, age : quærenti pagina nostra patet.

*All communications must be accompanied by the name and address of the sender,
not necessarily for publication.*

THE EARLIEST LOCAL ANTIQUARIAN SOCIETY.

SIR,—I read lately in the *Newcastle Chronicle* the following paragraph : " 1813, Nov. 3. The members of the Antiquarian Society held their first meeting in apartments in the Old Castle (Newcastle-on-Tyne), which had been fitted up for their use by the Corporation." Is any local Antiquarian Society known to have existed before the above date ? I think not.
MUS RUSTICUS.

THE BIBLE IN SHORTHAND. ·

SIR,—I have a copy of the Bible in shorthand. The note at foot of what appears to be the Contents runs as follows : " Printed for the Author and Peter Story, and sold by Tho : Fabian at the Bible in Pauls

Churchyard. Dorman Newman at ye Kings Armes in the Poultry. Wm. Marshall at the Bible in Newgate-street. Thomas Cockerill of ye 3 Leggs over against ye stocks market. I. Lawrence at ye Angel in ye Poultry." There is no date. Can any of your readers tell me its date, and if of any particular value? The volume is bound in old green morocco, and is in perfect condition. GEORGE UNWIN.

Chilworth, Surrey.

MITHRAIC RITES IN BRITAIN.

(See vol. vi. p. 302 ; and *ante*, p. 94.)

SIR,—There is an idea that the worship of Mithras was never general in Britain, but was only confined to certain bodies of legionary soldiers quartered here during the Roman occupancy.

A fine altar has been found at Housesteads, near Haydon Bridge, Northumberland, the ancient Borcovicus ; the inscription (date about 252 A.D.) runs thus : " D.O.M.   Invicto Mitrae Saeculari," &c. ; a second is, " Deo Soli invicto Mitrae Saeculari."   One at Riechester or Rochesterward, in Elsdon parish, in the same county, runs : " Deo invicto Soli Socio Sacrum ;" this place was called Bremenium, in Redesdale ;, one at Chesters, near Hexham, called Cilurnum ; one at Castlesteads or Cambeck-fort, near Brampton, Cumberland, on the Wall, was Petriana ; others have been found at Chester, York, &c.

All this is local, not national, worship ; but the native Sun-god was called Sual or Sul, the Latin Sol ; thus Bath was named Aquæ Solis. May I urge your valued correspondent, Mr. Lach Szyrma, to produce an English version of these ancient Cornish dramas, the " Berinans Meria-sek," &c. ? A. H. GENT.

ANCIENT GUILDS.

SIR,—*Apropos* of Mr. Cornelius Walford's " History of Guilds," or " Gilds," as he chooses to spell the word—now appearing in your pages, the following note from the MSS. of Cole, the friend and correspondent of Horace Walpole, in the British Museum, respecting St. Clement's Guild, in Cambridge, may be acceptable to your readers : " And though our modern guilds, or clubs, may be too often instituted as a call to the ale house, and never, as the old ones used to do, with a devout intent both as to this life and that which is to follow, as is evident by their processions and masses, yet as they are of frequent use to sick members, whom they bury decently ; and as a religious deportment either in high or low life in our refined age would be highly ridiculous, any further parallel of one with the other is out of the question.   In one or two particulars I thought the institutions were so alike that I could not help thinking that they both arose from the same motive ; and that we still have our Guilds as far as is consistent with the pure and unspotted devotion of a Protestant faith.   Yet in candour and justice I must still hold that I really believe these superstitions.   Papists were much better Christians and subjects and neighbours than the enlightened generation of our days; and for this reason, that I sincerely think not one-half that outwardly profess themselves Christians are virtually so.   Neither do I believe that the refinements that our politics have gone through by those divine geniuses, Milton, Hobbes, Locke, and some others, have made us a bit better satisfied with our national establishment, or mended our notions in regard of society." D. W.

DR. JOHNSON'S PORTRAIT AND SIR JOSHUA REYNOLDS.

(See vol. iv. p. 1.)

SIR,—Without venturing to express an opinion as to the genuineness or non-genuineness of the portrait of Dr. Johnson lately acquired by you, I may yet usefully, perhaps, call your attention to one or two points that struck me upon closely examining the painting. I have no doubt that the work, by whomsoever executed, has passed through the cleaner's hands and has been denuded of some of the surface colours or glazing ; but, if I am not mistaken, the flesh-tints have this characteristic of most of Reynolds' authentic work—that they have naturally faded or sunk in the time that has passed since they were laid upon the canvas. In your picture this fading of colour has had the effect of bringing to light one of the initial processes employed by the painter in transferring his subject to the canvas, and this process has certainly been employed by Sir Joshua in some of the pictures bearing his name in the National collection. It was this : Before beginning to paint, the artist carefully laid down upon his canvas, in a series of *dotted lines,* the exact positions of the features, as well as the forms and boundaries of their shadows. I have not sought to determine whether these guiding marks were transferred to the canvas from a perforated drawing on paper, and I cannot at the moment remember whether Sir Joshua's method of working has been described by any of his biographers or critics ; but I have satisfied myself, by the examination of several of his well-known works, that he sometimes, if not habitually, employed exactly the same means of grounding his portraits as those to which the painter of your portrait had recourse. Of course, I do not for a moment insist that this analogy of procedure *proves* anything ; but I think it only fair that it should be taken into consideration as pertinent to the question at issue—as to the authenticity of the, in any case, highly interesting portrait in your possession.

CHARLES SMITH CHELTNAM.

8, *Frithville-gardens, Shepherd's Bush, W.*

TO CORRESPONDENTS.

THE Editor declines to pledge himself for the safety or return of MSS. voluntarily tendered to him by strangers.

Books Received.

1. Calendar of State Papers, Domestic Series, during the Commonwealth. Edited by Mary A. E. Green. Longmans & Co. 1884.
2. Fac-simile of Monumental Brasses. By the Rev. W. F. Creeny, M.A. Norwich. Published by the Author. 1884.
3. The Stratford Records and the Shakespeare Autotypes. By J. O. Halliwell-Phillipps. Brighton : J. G. Bishop. 1884.
4. The Life of the Buddha. Translated by W. Woodville Rockhill. Trübner & Co. 1884.
5. Chronicles of the Yorkshire Family of Stapelton. By H. E. Chetwynd-Stapylton. Reprinted from the Yorkshire Archæological and Topographical Journal.

6. Catalogue of the Medals of Scotland. Arranged by R. W. Cochrane-Patrick, Esq., M.P., F.S.A., &c. Edinburgh: Douglas. 1884.

7. Mythology, Greek and Roman. Translated from the German of F. Nösselt, by Mrs. Angus W. Hall. London: Kerby & Endean. 1885.

8. Pedigree of the Family of Conder, of Terry Bank, Westmoreland. Michell & Hughes. 1884.

9. St. Andrew's, Edburton, Sussex. Parish Register Book. 1558—1673. By Rev. C. H. Wilkie, M.A. Brighton: J G. Bishop, *Herald* Office. 1884.

10. History of England under Henry IV. By J. H. Wylie, M.A. Vol. i. Longmans & Co. 1884.

11. Western Antiquary. Plymouth: W. H. Luke. January, 1885.

12. Proceedings of the Fourth and Fifth Annual Meetings of the Library Association. Edited by Ernest C. Thomas, Hon. Sec. 1884.

13. The County Companion, Diary, and Directory. 14. Municipal Corporations Companion, Diary, and Directory. Waterlow & Sons. 1885.

15. Plant Lore, Legends, and Lyrics. By Richard Folkard, Jun. Sampson Low & Co. 1884.

16. Johns Hopkins University Studies. Baltimore. January, 1885.

17. Miscellanea Genealogica et Heraldica. Second Series. Vol. i. No. xiv. Hamilton, Adams & Co. February, 1885.

18. Journal of the Royal Archæological Institute. No. 164.

19. The Tolhouse at Great Yarmouth. By F. D. Palmer. Great Yarmouth: J. Buckle. 1884.

Books, &c., for Sale.

Archdall's *Monasticon Hibernicum.* Apply to Rev. James Graves, Stonyford, co. Kilkenny.

Works of Hogarth (set of original Engravings, elephant folio, without text), bound. Apply by letter to W. D., 56, Paragon-road, Hackney, N.E.

Original water-colour portrait of Jeremy Bentham, price 2 guineas. Apply to the Editor of this Magazine.

A large collection of Franks, Peers and Commoners; C. Knight's "Pictorial History of England," 8 vols., half-bound in calf. Apply to E. Walford, 2, Hyde Park Mansions, N.W.

Books, &c., Wanted to Purchase.

Antiquarian Magazine and Bibliographer, several copies of No. 2 (February, 1882) are wanted, in order to complete sets. Copies of the current number will be given in exchange at the office.

Dodd's Church History, 8vo., vols. i. ii. and v.; Waagen's Art and Artists in England, vol. i.; East Anglian, vol. i., Nos. 26 and 29. The Family Topographer, by Samuel Tymms, vol. iii.; Notes and Queries, the third Index. Johnson's "Lives of the Poets" (Ingram and Cooke's edition), vol. iii. Chambers' Cyclopædia of English Literature, vol. i. Address, E. Walford, 2, Hyde Park Mansions, Edgeware-road, N.W.

ABBEY COINS, COUNTERS, OR JETTONS.

W. DAMPIER, *del.*

The

Antiquarian Magazine & Bibliographer.

Abbey Coins, Counters, or Jettons.

 URING part of the Anglo-Saxon period, the Archbishops of Canterbury enjoyed the privilege of coining money. Pennies exist of Lambert, who presided over the see from 763 down to 790 ; of Æthilheard, who died in 803 ; of Wilfred, who succeeded in that year ; of Coelnoth, who died in 870 ; of Ethered, 871 ; and of Plegmund, who was Archbishop from 891 to 923. In Athelstan's laws two "moneyers" are allowed to the Archbishop of Canterbury ; but it is believed that no archiepiscopal coins of that reign are known, nor indeed any until the time of Archbishop Bourchier, in the reign of Henry VII. In the seventeenth century nearly every tradesman had his token, with his name and trade, or a device of some kind, engraved on it. Tokens, indeed, were as common as signboards, yet, if the following ditty be correct, they were not always within reach :—

> " For name's sake I gave a token
> To a beggar that did crave it ;
> More he need not me importune,
> For 'twas the utmost of my fortune."

It is not so generally known, however, that in the middle ages coins or tokens—sometimes called counters or jettons, and abbey-pieces—were current among the travelling monks, and appear to have been used by them in their business transactions one with another. A large number of these counters were made at Nuremberg, in Germany, and are mostly inscribed with the words "Rechen-pfennig." Many of the older kind were made of silver, and have been frequently found near conventual buildings. They seem to have been used by mendicant friars and pilgrims. The earliest known counters struck in England for the use of monasteries appeared first in 1272, and they continued till early in the sixteenth century.

There is undoubtedly a mystery hanging over the original use of these medals or tokens. Some writers believe they were circulated as money, whilst others conjecture that they were intended only for the use of monks and pilgrims, who travelled from one religious house to another, and that they were used as a kind of passport, without which a stranger would not be admitted or relieved. What-ever their origin or use may have been, they appear, at all events, to have been most frequently found in the ruins of old abbeys (hence their name); and if we may judge from the large numbers that have been exhumed in all parts of England, their circulation must have been very general.

From the great variety of types found, it is probable that each abbey had a token of its own, just as each had a distinctive seal. From the frequent occurrence of the *fleur-de-lis* upon them, and from the legends, "VIVE LE ROI," and "VIVE LE DOLPHIN DE FRANCE," &c., there can be little doubt that they were mostly coined on the other side of the Channel.

A few years ago a large number of these so-called abbey-pieces came under my observation, and I was enabled to make drawings of several of them. Half-a-dozen of these are figured on the accom-panying plate (see p. 154).

No. 1, which is the most common type, has on the *obverse* three *fleurs-de-lis* in a shield, with the legend in Lombardic letters, "AVE MARIA GRACIAM" (*sic*). *Reverse:* within a quatrefoil a floriated cross, with the initials A.M.A.M. in the quarters.

No. 2 has for device, on the *obverse*, a crown or coronet, the legend, a slight variation from No. 1, being "AVE MARIA GRACIA PLE." The *reverse* is somewhat similar to that of No. 1, but with the letters A.V.E.M. outside the quatrefoil.

No. 3 has on the *obverse* four *fleurs-de-lis* in a lozenge, and the legend "VIVE LE DOLPHIN DE FRAN[C]E"; and on the *reverse* an inscription, of which the meaning is, to say the least, somewhat obscure. The *reverse* shows, within a quatrefoil, a shield having a regal coronet, or crown, in base, and the letter D and a saltire or X, in chief; the legend, so far as can be made out, being, "DEVOLE · DEVON · DEVOL · EVI."

No. 4, which was found at Exeter, and would appear to have been used as a counter, shows on the *obverse*, within a lozenge, four *fleurs-de-lis*, and is surrounded by the old French legend, "GETTES ENTENDES AV COMPTE" (Get a knowledge of counting); the legend on the *reverse* being "GUARDES VOS DE MESCOMPTE" (Guard against miscounting).

No. 5 is a very peculiar coin. The legend on the *obverse* is, "AVE MARIA GRACIA TOURNAI;" and on the *reverse* "VIVE LE ROI DE FRANCHE." Between the "vive" and "le" are two human faces, and there is another in one of the quarters on the *obverse*. This token was found, during some repairs, under a stone at the top of an early Perpendicular church tower in Northamptonshire. As this token is as perfect as when first coined, and as it was most likely placed there when the tower was built, the end of the fourteenth century may be fixed upon as the date of the piece.

No. 6 has for device, on the *obverse*, three *fleurs-de-lis* in a trefoil; on the *reverse*, a cross moline in a quatrefoil, with the legend in Latin, viz.:—*Obv.*, LUDOVICUS FRANCORUM REX. *Rev.*, BENEDICTUM SIT NOMEN DNI. All the above-mentioned tokens have the legends in Lombardic letters; but about the middle of the sixteenth century other tokens of a similar type were coined with Roman letters upon them. W. D.

Swiftiana Published by Curll.

IN 1727 was issued from the press, but without either printer's or publisher's name, a book entitled "Miscellanea. In Two Volumes. Never before Published." From the "get-up" of the work, and from the fact that the end of the first volume has appended to it a list of Curll's publications, it is not unreasonable to conclude that the series in question was issued from a shop "over against Catherine-street, in the Strand." It is dedicated to "Henry Cromwell, Esq.," by the editor, addressed to whom is a letter from "his sincere friend, Corinna;" the preface is signed "VALE":—

> "*As to the fix't time*, the Tenth of June,
> *When ev'ry* Tory's *Heart's in Tune.*"
"Anno 1726."

It is believed that this "Miscellanea" of Curll is very rare; the

British Museum possesses only the first volume, in which there are some interesting MS. notes by Sir Charles Dilke, who presented the book to the Museum; and the second volume is in the possession of the writer of this paper.

The first volume contains :—

(1) Familiar Letters written to Henry Cromwell, Esq., by Mr. Pope.

(2) Occasional Poems by Mr. Pope, Mr. Cromwell, Dean Swift, &c.

(3) Letters from Mr. Dryden to a Lady [Corinna] in the year 1699. London : Printed in the year 1727. Price 5s.

The second volume contains :—

(1) An Essay on Gibing,* with a Project for its Improvement.

(2) The Praise of Women : in Answer to this Question : Whether the Company of Women is useful, or hurtful, to young Gentlemen at their first Setting out in the World ? Translated from the *French* original of Monsieur L'Abbé Bellegarde. By Mr. S. Macky.

(3) An Essay on the Mischief of Giving Fortunes with Women in Marriage.

(4) Swiftiana (*sic*). Consisting of Poems by Dean Swift, and several of his Friends. Never before printed.

(5) Laus Ululæ. The Praise of Owls. An Oration to the Conscript Fathers, and Patrons of Owls. Written in Latin, by Curtius Jaele. Translated by a Canary Bird.

The " Swiftiana," with which we now are alone concerned, contain the following :—

(1) The Broken Mug. A Tale. By Dean Swift. [This octosyllabic " tale " will be found printed on a " broadside " in the British Museum, under " Miscellanies, 839, *m.* 23," with this note : " This, considerably enlarged from the 1st part of a poem under the same name by Laurence White. 8vo. Dublin, 1742. 2nd Ed."]

(2) A Rebus on Dean Swift. By Vanessa. [The second line of the first verse runs thus :—

" And be the first Syllable only apply'd."

In both Faulkner's and Scott's "Swift" it is slightly different, *e.g.* :

" And let the first of it be only apply'd."]

(3) The Dean's Answer.

(4) A Riddle. By Dean Parnell.

(5) The Three *Gentle* Shepherds. By Mr. Pope.

---

* This is sometimes attributed to Swift. See British Museum Catalogue.

(6) A Riddle. By Dr. Delany. Inscribed to the Lady Carteret.

(7) The Same answered by Dean Swift.

(8) The Journal. By Doctor Swift, Dean of St. Patrick's, when at the Lord Chief Baron Rochfort's House. [This " Journal" consists of a hundred and thirty lines, and commences as follows :—

> " *Thalia*, tell in sober Lays,
> How *George, Nim, Dan, Dean* pass their Days ;
> And should our *Galls-Town* Wit grow fallow,
> Yet, *Neget quis* Carmina Gallo?
> Here (by the way) by *Gallus* mean I
> Not *Sheridan*, but Friem *Delany*.
> Begin, my Muse ; First, from our Bow'rs
> We issue forth at diff 'rent Hours.
> At seven the *Dean* in night gown drest,
> Goes round the House to wake the rest.
> At nine grave *Nim* and *George* facetious
> Go to the *Dean* to read *Lucretius*."]

(9) A Petition to his Grace the Duke of Grafton. [This commences thus :—

> " It was, my Lord, the dextrous shift
> Of t'other *Jonathan*, viz. *Swift*,
> But now St. Patrick's saucy Dean,
> With silver Verge, and Surplice clean,
> Of *Oxford*, or of *Ormond's* Grace
> In looser Rhyme to beg a Place.
> A Place He got, yclep'd a Stall,
> And eke a thousand Pounds withal ;
> And were he a less witty Writer
> He might as well have got a Mitre.
> Thus I the *Jonathan* of *Connor*
> In humble Lays my Thanks to offer," &c.]

(10) His Grace's Answer. By Dean Swift. [Of this " Answer" the first few lines are as follows :—

> " Dear *Smed*, I read thy brilliant Lines,
> Where Wit in all its Glory Shines ;
> Where Compliments with all their Pride
> Are by thy Numbers dignify'd ;
> I hope to make you get as clean,
> As that same, viz., *St. Patrick's Dean*."]

(11) The humble Petition of a beautiful young Lady to the Reverend Dr. Berkeley.

(12) The Answer of a Lady to a Gentleman after a long Courtship.

The most recent writer on Swift and Swiftiana, Mr. Stanley Lane Poole—to whom the publication was unknown—has been good enough to inform me that there is nothing in the volume above described from Swift's pen. It is, however, not without interest to students of Swift, and also to collectors of what may be styled " Curlliana."

W. Roberts.

Guy of Warwick.*

By the Rev. F. Conway, M.A.,
Member of the Royal Asiatic Society.

PART I.

AN American writer has compared the tale of Guy, Earl of Warwick, to the legendary "beggar-maid" whose loveliness,
though obscured by rags, was nevertheless patent to the critical eye of
King Cophetua. In so far as the tale, though it has never been worthily
told, nevertheless shows its exquisite pathos and intrinsic charms
beneath its mean attire, it resembles Zenolophon, as Shakespeare
tells us the beggar maid was named ; but the mendicant girl was
more fortunate than the story, for her humble attire was changed at
last to royal splendour ; but the legend is still left to languish in its
old clothes. This is the more unaccountable when we think of the
popularity which Guy's exploits once enjoyed. Three names in the
middle ages stood pre-eminent among English heroes of romance—
the names of Arthur, of Sir Bevis, and of Guy. But how different
is their present lot ! The silver cadences of the Laureate have chimed
the tale of Arthur to the world ; but Sir Bevis is a mere name, and
Guy's memory lingers only in local traditions. It is true we men
and women of Warwickshire cherish with affection these relics of a
glory which is past. We have most of us read a dreary ballad about
Guy, and some of us have tried to like it. We have visited Guy's
Cliffe to gaze upon the cave in which rumour says our county hero
passed the evening of his life, keeping out the cold with portentous
messes of porridge, and we are sure the tale is true because the porridge-
pot is extant to this day. The bladebone of the Dun Cow has also
obtained its fair share of attention ; and some of us have been to
Warwick Castle, and inspected Guy's armour, heedless of the revela-
tions of a Warwickshire antiquary, who tells us that "the armour
exhibited at the porter's lodge of Warwick Castle, as that of Guy,
consists of a steel cap of the time of Edward III. ; his breast-plates
are two shields—one of the 15th century, and the other of the time
of James I. ; his sword is of the time of Henry VIII., and his staff
is an ancient tilting lance." Yes, we people of Warwickshire do this
much, but in the rest of England Guy is either a mere name, or he
has been relegated to the nursery, to hob-nob with Mother Hubbard,

---

* This paper was delivered as a lecture before the Leamington Institute.

and condole with her on the freaks of her favourite dog. But Guy's time may yet come. Material for an elaborate epos which might move men's hearts more than the tale of Arthur moves them, lies embedded in these local traditions of Warwickshire, waiting only for the poet's hand. Cannot Shakespeare's county produce another bard?

But to turn from the possible to the actual—from the poems that may be written in the future, to the poems that have been written in the past—the earliest account of Sir Guy and his bride, which has come down to us, is a metrical romance of the 13th century, written in Norman-French, and discovered in 1842, in the Ducal Library at Wolfenbuttel, in Germany. A translation of this, certainly as old as the 14th century, is among the MSS. of a Cambridge college. In the 16th century Guy made his first appearance in print, in a curious black letter translation of the original French romance. Ballads were in fashion about this time, and the tale was accordingly condensed into that dreary doggrel familiar to us all :—

> "Was ever Knight for lady's sake,
> So tost in love as I, Sir Guy?"

which goes on to degrade the name of Guy's bride, Felice, into Phillis, fit appellative only for clownish Corydon's rustic sweetheart. Yet we find this ballad in the year 1590, entered in the registers of the Stationers' Company as "A *pleasant* song of the valiant deeds of chivalry of Guy of Warwick." The legend was next reduced to prose, and appeared in successive chap-books. Several of these I have seen—one in black letter, printed at the Sun and Bible in Pie-corner, London, was anciently procurable for the reasonable sum of threepence. Another was on sale at "The Sign of the Red Lion on London Bridge," apparently for an equally modest charge as its predecessor of Pie-corner. From these accounts of our county hero—good, bad, and indifferent—I have tried to piece together a mosaic exhibiting Guy's life as it was known to our forefathers.

In the reign of good King Athelstan, there was an Earl of Warwick named Rohand, who was lord also of Oxford and Buckingham. His steward was Siward, Lord of Wallingford. The steward had an only son, Guy; his master an only daughter, Felicia or Felice—not Phillis.

> "White she was, as a field flower,
> Her visage of a fair colour;
> Fair her forehead, fair her hair,
> Such a maid was never there,

> So fair shapen and well dight
> Joy it was to see the sight." *

So says the author of the Cambridge MS., and summing her up in a phrase which has since become a vulgarism, he calls her a "sweet thing." Now it fell on a day at Whitsuntide that the Earl made a great feast. Knights and earls, and bold barons, and ladies, and "maidens fair and free,"came thither from town and country, and the Earl sent Guy to serve his daughter with the wine cup. Thirty maidens in the hall fell in love with Guy at first sight, as he ministered to his master's daughter; but Guy had eyes for Felice alone, and went home stricken with love for her. Soon after he feels his love too strong to hide, and he goes to his mistress and falls upon his knees before her, with the simple words, " For thy love I soon must die."

> " But the maiden looked on Guy full grim,
> And wrathfully she answered him,
> Art thou not Guy the steward's son?
> Who made thee so foolhardy an one
> As to talk to me of love?
> By Jesu who sitteth enthroned above,
> If I to my father this should say
> For his word he thee will slay,
> Men shall come and shall thee draw,
> And hang thee on gallows, and that is law.
> Wend thee hence out of my sight,
> Or thou shalt die : my word is plight."

It is at first surprising that Guy's humble avowal should have provoked such a storm, but on turning to one of the chap-books I find the proposal worded thus : " Fairest of all the curious works of nature, whose equal never breathed in common air; more wonderful than any earth can yield; the bright idea of celestial beauty; eternal honour wait upon thy name. The suit I have to thee is much like that which once Leander came to Hero with; the present which I bring is a heart filled with love, and love alone can satisfy my soul. Incline then, madam, to my humble motion. Compassionate the griefs that I endure, and let that life that rests at your devotion be regarded. With pity take my dying heart in care, and let it not expire in groaning torments, nor burst with grief, because too well it loves thee. I know dear Phillis [this perversion of her name was an insult in itself] that great princes love thee, and deeds of honour for thy sake have done, but neither king nor prince can love thee more, no, nor so much as I, though but the son of thy great father's

---

* The poetic quotations in this paper are modernised throughout, by the omission of obsolete words, &c.

steward, for so inestimable is my love that whatsoever all others shall pretend can never countervail it." No wonder the lady thought hanging a fit punishment for a lover who could talk like that.

All the light died out of Guy's young life through longing for Felice. The once light-hearted boy became moody, silent, sad. His only wish was to die. At last, with the boldness of despair, he goes once more to the tower in which Felice lives, and falling at her feet in a swoon, tells her his love once more, and finally Felice relents :—

> "When thou hast been dubbed a knight,
> And proven well in every fight,
> Then forsooth I promise thee,
> Thou shalt have the love of me."

From this answer of Felice, we may infer that Guy's language was not on this occasion as the chap-book has it : "Beautiful, though severe, creature, I have once more presumed to throw myself at your feet, desiring you to look upon my bleeding wounds with eyes of compassion, and put an end to all my sufferings by giving me hopes of living happy in thy love." Guy's life is once more all gladness, the hopes of youth are high within him, and the future seems to stretch before his eyes a shimmering vista of golden haze. He determines, if hard work will win him his coveted bride, she shall be won, for he will go to foreign lands—to the world's end if need be—and win name and fame. He took three companions with him, and

> "They drew sail and the wind was good,
> They rode upon the briny flood :
> They sailed forth with never an oar,
> And lost the sight of England's shore."

They land in Normandy, and look out for adventures. Rumour soon brings them news of a great tournament to be held in honour of the German Emperor's daughter, Blanchflower. The successful knight, as the Cambridge MS. quaintly has it, .

> "Was to have the love of that young thing,
> Unless he had another darling,"

—a commendable instance of consideration for vested interests. I have no time to dwell on the details of the day. It is enough to say that Guy was invincible and won the prize, but he would not claim her, because he could not satisfy the conditions. This victory was the first of a series of successes in every town on the Continent, until a year was over, when Guy returns to England and to Felice. But the Earl's daughter now sets him a harder task—

> "My lover thou shalt not be hight
> Until thou be the boldest knight
> That may be found in any land
> For doughtiness and strength of hand."

Guy turns away in despair. The joys he had pictured to himself, it may be during the awful pause before a bloody fight, it may be in many a lonely vigil by flickering camp fires under the quiet stars, have vanished and gone :—

> "The best I can never be,
> In all the lands of Christian'ty,
> I will wend to some far strand
> More of battle will I find,
> From the death I will not flee,
> If I die, it is for thee."

He returns to the Continent, and becomes once more a wanderer. He is triumphant at every tourney and at every battle—triumphant alike over hostile warriors and over ravening monsters such as seemed more fitting denizens for the realms of fable than even for the wildernesses in which he found and fought them. Time would fail to tell the half of his deeds. But one adventure, in which his constancy as well as his courage was put to the test, I cannot forbear telling. The turbaned Saracens had long pressed the Greek Emperor hard, and oftentimes had Guy's sword done good service against them. At last the Emperor resolved to stake all upon a single combat between one of his own soldiers and one of the Sultan's men. For some time men looked blank at hearing this, and none were found to take the imperial proposal to the Sultan, until Guy volunteered. While Guy was on the road we get a glimpse of the Sultan at home. He is discontented with the way in which the war is going on, and has quarrelled with his idols about it.

> "He bade his men before him stand
> All his three gods at his hand.
> 'Gods,' he said, 'ye are untrue,
> By your necks the Devil hang you ;
> I have done you many a good deed
> Evilly do you requite my meed.'
> He took a staff of apple tree
> And beat those gods, beat all the three :
> He brake each arm, he brake each leg,
> 'Ye did me never no good,' he said."

The Sultan's forehead is still studded with the beads of perspiration resulting from this goodly exercise, when Guy draws near :—

> " As he rode up and down
> He knew the Sultan's pavilion.
> An eagle of gold thereon was bright
> And a stone that gave great light,
> That men might see all through the night
> As it had been the sunshine bright."

Guy delivers his message to the panting potentate. The Sultan finds

out who he is and tries to secure him, but the Warwickshire man was
not to be caught.

> " He smote the Sultan with the sword,
> That the head came trundling down on the board,"

and ran for his life to Constantinople, flourishing in triumph the
grinning head which he had caught up as he ran out.   The Emperor
is overjoyed at the sight of the Sultan's head, and says that Guy shall
marry his own daughter.   The bridal morning dawned ; was Felice
forgotten ?   It seemed so.

> " On the morn Guy dight him nobly,
> And went to the church right merrily :
> And his fellows every one
> With him full merrily have gone ;
> And when to church door they had come,
> There Guy saw many a goodly man,
> King, and duke, and gentle baron,
> The best of all that region.
> The bishop came in splendour dressed,
> Rings he brought of gold the best ;
> When he saw the rings brought,
> On fair Felice ran Guy's thought.
> ' Felice,' he said, ' my lady bright,
> I have loved thee with all my might.
> Shall I for riches now forsake thee ?
> Not so shall it ever be—
> Thy bare body is dearer to me
> Than all the gold of Christian'ty.' "

The strong man fell swooning on the paved floor, and when he rose
he went in silence from the church, and never again looked upon
the imperial lady who had so nearly been his bride.

Then came fresh adventures succeeding one another in an endless
chain of victories, until Guy returns once more to England.   In all
the pride of conscious triumph he makes his way to Warwick, and
pleads once more with Felice, and he does not this time plead in
vain.   They are wedded, and spend fifty glad days together.   But
no happy wedded life was to be theirs.   Guy's youth had passed
away, and the sober, sombre thoughts of manhood had come upon
him.   Happy though it was to be with Felice, there was, he felt, a
higher, holier happiness within his reach, if he would but stretch out
his hand for it.   Full of these thoughts, Guy stood one night upon
the parapet of his castle.   He looked up to the sky, graven with
silver hieroglyphics of unfathomable mystery ; he looked down to
earth, hushed in the solemn sleep of night, and a something not of
this world seemed to enter into him, and to show him the emptiness
of his past life.   He formed a high resolve.   He would leave the
earthly idol in whose service he had spent his youth, and consecrate

himself to his Heavenly Father, and go to the Holy Land in penance for having forgotten his God. We can imagine the last night spent together by the pair. We can almost hear Felice's soft tones sweetly pleading and talking of earthly happiness, and Guy's deep voice gently soothing her, and trying to inspire her with his own holy zeal, feeling himself all the more determined not to flinch, as his wife's pleading brings more acutely home to him the intensity of the sacrifice. The morning comes at last. Guy puts on a Palmer's attire, receives from his wife of fifty days a kiss to wear on his lips and a ring to wear next his heart, and starts for Palestine with an unearthly fire burning within him.

(*To be continued.*)

Our Old Country Towns.

No. III.—CAERLEON-UPON-USK.

I DO not know a pleasanter pilgrimage than that which I made recently to Caerleon-upon-Usk, or, as the natives call it, Carleen, the "Isca Silurum" of the Romans, and their chief station in the far West eighteen centuries ago. But it has sad memories; its grand and historic past offers the strongest and strangest of all possible contrasts to the Caerleon of to-day. The city in which the second Roman legion had for several years its summer and its winter quarters,—the city in which King Arthur was crowned as King of the Britons, and which shared his love with Tintagel, where he was born, and with Glastonbury, where he lies buried,—the city in which Dubritius sat as Archbishop in the earliest days of British Christianity, and where he numbered St. David among his pupils,—this city of old renown is now a tiny village, lying off the highway of traffic and of pleasure, forgotten by the world, and rarely visited even by the ubiquitous tourist and artist. In fact, its motto may be comprised in one Latin word, *fuit*. It has once lived; it has had its day. But on this very account it is dear to the historian and the antiquary who delights in the task of revisiting scenes of past glories, and waking them up into life again. Unlike the common herd of tourists, he sees at a glance the Roman road, and bridge, and walls, and towers, and amphitheatre; he traces in the green turf the outlines of the Christian temple to which those buildings gave place; and the dry bones of history live once more before his eyes.

Caerleon lies upon the west or further bank of the River Usk, and is distant some three miles from its present mouth at Newport, a name which tells its own tale, showing clearly that the original " port" and mouth of the river was further inland. The sea must, indeed, have receded very far from Caerleon, and at a very early date, for at Newport there is a castle, parts of which date from the days of the Edwards. The village occupies a gentle slope rising from the water-side, and is surrounded on almost every side by lofty hills. The pilgrim nowadays is set down at Caerleon by a branch line of railway leading from Newport up to Usk; but there are not many houses in sight. He must walk some three or four hundred yards south, and then turn to the right, when he will find himself at one end of a triangular village green, which could probably tell some stories of old days, of fairs and rural sports, if its grassy turf " had language." At the other end of this green he must turn sharp to the left, and make his way towards the village church, grouped around which he will find the parish school, the squire's mansion, the old village inn, and the local museum, about which I shall have more to say presently. There is still a market place; but the market and the market house are both gone. The church of Caerleon is really a Norman structure, but its Norman character is very much disguised externally by additions in later styles. It is dedicated to St. Cadoc, and it is the only survivor of some seven other churches and chapels which once reared their towers towards heaven in Caerleon. The church has been recently embellished by a sculptured marble reredos, of artistic merit, representing the Lord's Supper; but in other respects there is little to remark about it.

Beyond the church is the village inn, the " Hanbury Arms," which must be one of the oldest hostelries in England, if it has been, as it appears, an hostelry from the first. It stands at a corner commanding three approaches, and its low-browed windows, with their thick stone mullions and square hooded dripstones above, tell us, as plainly as words could do, that its walls were built in the fourteenth or fifteenth century. Here, I was told, Alfred Tennyson lodged one summer, some thirty years ago, when he was seeking from the *genius loci* inspiration for those Arthurian Legends, the " Idylls of the Kings," to which he has given a new and immortal life.

On the same side of the way is another private house, the Priory, the stone mullions of whose windows carry us back to the days of the early Tudors at the least, if not to the Plantagenets. On the opposite side is " The Bell," another old inn, which formerly was an appendage to the prior's residence, and was doubtless frequented by pilgrims on their way to St. David's shrine. We walk on down the winding village street, noticing as we pass along how the cottage walls are built out of the remains of hoar antiquity. In the Priory grounds these relics are most numerous. At the back of the "Hanbury Arms" inn is still to be seen part of one of the towers of its castle; and near it are the remains of what was once a lofty artificial mound called the Castle Tump.

At the end of the street we see before us a quaint narrow stone bridge over the Usk; the few scattered houses which form a hamlet beyond are called, we are told, Caerleon *ultra pontem*, as they were in the days of Hadrian—a strange survival of the Latin tongue. Until the end of the last century there was at this spot a wooden bridge, remarkable for being constructed of beams of wood which were moveable, like that thrown by Julius Cæsar across the Rhine, and described by him in his "Commentaries."

Part of the Roman wall of Caerleon is visible in the meadows to the right, about 300 yards from the bridge, and connected with it by a lane called the Broadway; but it is only a fragment, though fairly perfect so far as it goes. The wall is about 12 ft. high. The eye of the merest tyro can read in it the selfsame handiwork which is to be seen in the massive walls of Pevensey in Sussex, and of Richborough in Kent, to say nothing of the walls of old London near the Minories and the Tower.

In a meadow within the Priory grounds, to the west of this wall, now known as "King Arthur's Field," the grass rises in "many a mouldering heap," but not so irregularly as to prevent the eye from seeing that, whatever ruined walls it once covered, they were circular in form. The local belief identifies this field with King Arthur's Round Table. It is clear, however, to the discerning eye that here once stood the Roman Amphitheatre, in which wild beasts and slaves fought on a blood-stained arena, as recorded in the pages of Juvenal and Martial. Here stood the *retiarius*, ready to catch his antagonist in the folds of his net; there stood the *mirmillo* on the defensive, whilst fair Roman ladies looked on from the seats that rose on every side around, as they now look on at the bull-fights in Madrid, and possibly cried out "*Christianos ad leones!*"

The history of Caerleon after the departure of the Romans reads like a romance. It is said that in the Anglo-Saxon days it gained a higher rank and importance than it had held under the victorious eagles of the Roman Emperors. Indeed, it is gravely said that it became the metropolis of the kingdom of Britain, and the favourite residence of King Arthur and of the Knights of his Round Table. Even the present inhabitants of what is now a plain country village most firmly believe in these ancient glories of Caerleon, and hold that the exploits of this mythical hero are matters of history. They point to the circle of green hillocks which certainly conceal the relics of a Roman amphitheatre, as being the site of the Round Table, and suppose that here, in the middle of the field, was founded a military order which first raised the spirit of chivalry in Europe, producing first the twelve peers and the *table ronde* of Charlemagne, and ultimately giving birth to the Order of the Garter. It is almost a pity to shake the local belief in so poetical a tale, but in the interests of history the truth must be stated; and happily nothing that I can say or write will serve to disabuse the good people of Caerleon of this fond delusion. "Within the precincts of this area," writes Archdeacon Coxe, in his "Tour in Monmouthshire," "Arthur and his knights are recorded to have held their feasts, seated at a round table for the purpose of promoting social intercourse and superseding the distinctions of State. But this legend has no foundation in history, and the articles of the Order, which have been gravely quoted as authentic, display internal evidences of forgery; for they contain notions of chivalry, honour, and gallantry which did not prevail in that age in any country of Europe."

The Roman station of Isca Silurum was in all probability founded by Julius Frontinus, about A.D. 70, and the various monuments found here from time to time prove that it was for many years the head-quarters of the second Augustan Legion. Its modern name of Caerleon, the "City of the Legion," there can be little doubt, is derived from this fact. As the capital of the province of Britannia Secunda, it was certainly a place of great importance in its day; yet we must not be led away by the exaggerated descriptions of its extent and splendour given to us by the writers of the Middle Ages. Its area within the walls was about fifty acres; and, if so, it could not well have contained more than six or seven thousand inhabitants. The public buildings, though time has so ruthlessly blotted them out of existence, were, doubtless, handsome and well-built; yet, when Giraldus Cambrensis, writing of its remains as existing even in his time, mentions "immense palaces ornamented with gilded roofs," we may well doubt whether any roof of Roman construction, to say nothing of its ornamentation, could have lasted through the seven centuries which had then passed since the last of the Roman eagles was seen in Britain. Henry of Huntingdon, who wrote a century before Giraldus, gives a very different, and probably a far more truthful, account of the place ; for he tells us that though it had been the seat of an archbishop, the walls of the city were even then scarcely visible.

The local history of Caerleon during the Roman occupation, in spite of its importance, is a complete blank, with the exception of the tradition that here was the court of Caractacus or Caradoc, and that St. Julius and St. Aaron were martyred here in the persecution under Diocletian in the fourth century. Very little also that can be depended upon is recorded while it was under the dominion of the Welsh or British chieftains who subsequently governed the country. Under the designation of Kings of Glamorgan and Gwent, these princes appear to have interfered but little in the endless quarrels of their countrymen in other parts of the Principality, and, after the sixth century, to have lived, generally speaking, on good terms with their Saxon neighbours of Mercia. Some time in the latter half of the ninth century they voluntarily placed themselves under the protection of King Alfred, and paid homage to him and his successors down to the Norman Conquest.

Being almost the only stronghold on the coast below Cardiff and Chepstow, the possession of Caerleon was frequently a matter of severe struggle between the English and the old British inhabitants. It was seized by Henry II. in 1171, on his way to Ireland, and three years later the town and castle were taken by the Normans, when Rhys ap Griffith, Prince of South Wales, did homage to the English King at Gloucester.

It is said that Caerleon was the seat of a Christian bishop or archbishop as early as A.D. 182 ; but little is known of the city as a See before the time of Dubritius, who is said to have founded here schools of philosophy and science in the fifth century. Not a trace can be found of the site of the bishop's cathedral, nor of the three fine churches, with convents attached to them, which Giraldus Cambrensis tells us once rose within its walls ; and the scholars, as well as the schools, have all vanished for many a long century. And yet it is said that Caerleon was the capital of fifteen important Roman stations in Siluria, covering with its suburbs a tract of land nine miles in circumference, the residence of the Prætor, who here had his Domus Palatina, the place where the eagles were deposited, where justice was dealt out in the name of the Emperor of far-distant Rome, and where the Imperial edicts were proclaimed.

It would be impossible, within the compass of this paper, to

describe the contents of the local museum which has been established
at Caerleon, thanks to Mr. Charles Morgan, F.S.A., and other local
antiquaries. Its contents have not been "far to seek." Mosaic
pavements, altars, columns, statues, friezes, sarcophagi, fibulæ,
intaglios, rings, seals, vases, brass and silver coins, fragments of
lamps, and of crosses, pins, and personal ornaments have been discovered in every corner of the deserted city; and such as have not
been carried off to enrich the collections of private owners, have
found their final and, it is to be hoped, their abiding home within its
walls. Some of the *objets de luxe* found at Caerleon came from
Italy or from Flanders, so that its military inhabitants had evidently
a taste for foreign luxuries.

Readers of the "Idylls of the King" will not need to be reminded
in minute detail of the legend which makes this desolate village the
headquarters of King Arthur and his chiefs in arms :—

> " For Arthur on the Whitsuntide before
> Held court at old Caerleon-upon-Usk."

And every pilgrim who has visited the place will recall the remains
of the fort on the other side of the bridge, which was doubtless
erected at once to protect the passage where the river was fordable and
to guard against the incursions of the Welsh from the mountains. It
is probably to this fort, or else to an artificial eminence still to be
seen in the Priory grounds—from either of which the Severn and
the coast of Somerset beyond may be seen—that Tennyson alludes
in the often-quoted lines :—

> " Now thrice that morning Guinevere had climb'd
> The giant tower, from whose high crest, they say,
> Men saw the goodly hills of Somerset,
> And white sails flying on the yellow sea ;
> But not to goodly hill or yellow sea
> Look'd the fair Queen, but up the vale of Usk
> By the flat meadow, till she saw them come ;
> And then, descending, met them at the gates,
> Embraced her with all welcome as a friend,
> And did her honour as the Prince's bride,
> And clothed her for her bridals like the sun ;
> And all that week was old Caerleon gay,
> For by the hands of Dubric, the high saint,
> They twain were wedded with all ceremony."

It is to be feared that, the sea having so far receded from the town
whose walls it once all but washed, there is little or no prospect of
Caerleon ever regaining its old importance; but it may be safely
asserted that no single spot in England, or in Wales either, is richer
in historic memories, or more worthy of a visit from the British
pilgrim who loves the study of the past. E. WALFORD.

Easter Eggs.

MANY of the popular observances connected with Easter are doubtless of Pagan origin. The goddess Ostara or Eastre appears to have been the personification of the opening year or spring. The Anglo-Saxon name of April was Ostermoneth. The worship of this deity was brought into England by the Saxons; and it continued to be celebrated in many parts in the north of Germany down to the beginning of the present century, by the kindling of bonfires and other religious rites. The bonfires can be traced in the great "Paschal tapers," sometimes weighing as much as 300 lbs., with which churches were lighted on Easter Eve. In the ancient church disbursements of St. Mary-at-Hill, in the city of London, is an entry "for a quarter of coles for the hallowed fire on Easter Eve, 6d."

But the most characteristic Easter rite, and the one most widely diffused, is the use of Paschal (or Easter) eggs. "These," observes a writer in "Chambers' Encyclopædia," "are usually stained of various colours with dye-woods or herbs, and people mutually make presents of them; sometimes they are kept as amulets, sometimes eaten; games are also played by striking them against one another. In some moorland parts of Scotland it used to be the custom for young people to go out early on 'Pasch Sunday' and to search for wild-fowls' eggs for breakfast, and it was thought lucky to find them. There can be little doubt," continues the writer, "that the use of eggs at this season was originally symbolical of the revivification of nature—the springing forth of new life in spring. The practice is not confined to Christians; the Jews used eggs in their feast of the Passover; and we are told that the Persians, when they keep the festival of the solar year (in March) mutually present each other with coloured eggs."

The origin of popular customs generally is a subject hard to unravel; but the subject of "Easter eggs" appears to be less so than most. Some authorities content themselves by supposing that in the infancy of Christianity, the old pagan emblem, and the proceedings by which expression was given to it, were adapted to symbolise and commemorate the Resurrection and the new life. What Easter Eggs were really intended to typify in Christian festivals is clearly shown by the words of the benediction for these eggs, which was sanctioned by Pope Paul V.—namely, that they were used to signalise the belief in the Resurrection.

Dr. Brewer, in his "Dictionary of Phrase and Fable," remarks that "the practice of presenting eggs to our friends at Easter is Magian or Persian, and bears allusion to the mundane egg, for which Ormuzd and Ahriman were to contend till the consummation of all things. It prevailed not only with the Persians but also among the Jews, Egyptians, and Hindus. Christians adopted the custom to symbolise the Resurrection, and they colour the eggs red in allusion to the blood of their redemption. There is a tradition, also, that the world was 'hatched' or created at Eastertide."

Let us glance at the practice observed in different countries of distributing eggs, and at the various artistic imitations of eggs, at this Easter season. There can be little doubt that the mere act of making presents at this time of the year throughout the Christian world is traceable to the offerings (or, in ecclesiastical parlance, the "customary dues") which were, and are still made to the Church at Easter, by all sorts and conditions of the Catholic laity. The practice of interchanging eggs was popular in Persia more than a century and a half ago. Le Brun states that on the 20th of March, 1704, the Persians celebrated, during several days, the festival of their solar new year; and that, *inter alia*, the people made presents to one another of coloured eggs—eggs, it may be assumed, which presented that rich brilliancy of colour and variety of ornamentation which is conspicuous in the decorative works of Eastern nations. Travellers who stop at Smyrna at Easter time are unmercifully pestered by boys who crowd around them with strings of eggs, streaked, dotted, striped and chequered in all sorts of gaudy colours. In Greece the inhabitants have some pretty ceremonies illustrative of the season, orange and citron buds and jasmine flowers being introduced; the presents consisting of coloured eggs and cakes of Easter bread. In Russia, Easter is celebrated in a manner different to any other country. Hakluyt, who wrote his "Voyages and Discoveries" about the middle of the sixteenth century, has given some account of the proceeding, the substance of which is as follows: As the day approaches the people dye a great number of eggs red, using Brazil wood for the purpose. Some of these are presented on Easter morn to the parish priest. The people carry some of the eggs about with them, not only on Easter Day, but for three or four days afterwards. To quote his own continuation of the report of the festival: "The gentlemen and gentlewomen have eggs gilded, which they carry in like manner. They use it, as they say, for 'a great love,' and in token of the Resurrection, whereof they rejoice. For when two friends meet during the Easter holidays (after the salutations of the day have been passed between them) they kiss and exchange their eggs, both men and women continuing in kissing four days together." "An eye-witness," in describing the "Feast of Pâque" as kept at Moscow on the 5th of April, 1702, says that the bells were rung during all the night which preceded the *fête*, and likewise during the gala day, and the morrow. The eggs were distributed for fifteen days, the practice prevailing among the rich and the poor, the young and the old. The shops were filled on all sides with tinted eggs, many of which were inscribed with the sentence "Christ is risen." Persons of distinction kept their eggs within doors, and made gifts of them to visitors, ejaculating as they did so the words given above, which were reiterated by the visitors with emphasis. The ordinary people gave their eggs in the streets. Domestics offered them to their masters and mistresses, and received presents in return.

In Germany the Easter egg is a very popular gift. Among the middle classes in Naples, the merry-making at Easter includes presents of eggs arrayed in baskets or trays of *pasta legera casatiello;* whilst among the wealthy inhabitants the Easter eggs belong either to the class *confetti*, or to the toy magazine. In Vienna the natural egg has been almost entirely superseded by the artificial one—at any rate among the well-to-do residents. Gold, silver, bronze, and other metals are used in its manufacture, as well as various other materials, such as mother-of-pearl, ivory, and scarce woods; and the interior is handsomely fitted up and furnished with toys, jewellery, and other articles of infinite variety. Paris has now become the rival of Vienna in the fabrication and display of the Easter egg.

In England the custom of distributing Easter Eggs was once general, and it still survives in some parts. It can be traced back with certainty to the thirteenth century, and there are doubtless records of the practice at an earlier period. An entry in the roll of the household expenses of Edward I. is to the effect that 18d. were disbursed for 400 eggs at Easter—for the seasonable gifts, of course. Tradescant, the Dutch gardener to Charles I., had in the museum which he established at Lambeth, specimens of the "Easter eggs of the Patriarchs of Jerusalem." The custom of holding festivals in honour of the Pasque, Pasch, Pace, or Paste egg (as it has been variously called in this country) seems to have been most prevalent in the northern counties, such as Northumberland, Cumberland, West-moreland, Yorkshire, Lancashire, and Cheshire. From the records of these observances the eggs appear to have been dyed or stained and painted in different colours, and sometimes gilded. The exterior was frequently ornamented with tracery; and the interior frequently divided into compartments, which were filled up agreeably to the taste and skill of the designer.

Mr. Cremer, of Regent-street, the vendor of modern Easter Eggs, has published a small *brochure* in which he gives an interesting account of the customs connected with them, and to this account we are largely indebted for the materials of this sketch. He tells us that on " Paste Egg Day," as it is called in Cheshire, children go round the village and beg eggs for the Easter dinner. They repeat a doggrel, addressed to the farmer's dame, asking for an egg, bacon, cheese, or an apple, or " any good thing that will make us merry." It concludes thus : " And I pray you, good dame, an Easter egg."

The Terminations " Hope " and " Thorpe ; "

WITH SOME REMARKS ON MR. COLE'S "SCANDINAVIAN PLACE NAMES."

THE publication of a treatise on place names by a scholar of such admitted attainments as the Rev. E. M. Cole, M.A., justifies its being placed in the crucible of criticism; but it may seem daring for one almost unknown to venture to dispute a point with so high an authority. Mr. Cole has undoubtedly done good service to an interesting study by the publication of his " Scandinavian Place Names in the East Riding of Yorkshire," a field, we are assured, rich and ripe for investigation in this and other aspects of historic interest; but both in his pamphlet, and in subsequent communications to the Press, he has made some remarks which deserve consideration before they are admitted to the region of accepted facts.

Mr. Cole, so far as I can learn from his pamphlet, lays no claim to Old Norse or Icelandic scholarship; therefore it will not be thought uncharitable if I point out where I think he has erred in judgment as well as in knowledge. He has personally referred to Cleasby and Vigfusson's "Icelandic Dictionary," and his knowledge of words and quotations appears to be solely based upon that important work. At page 6 of his pamphlet he avails himself of this authority in treating of the word "thorp," to which, however, he appends a few original remarks. " The word ' thorp,' " he writes, "was originally applied to the cottages of the poorer peasantry crowded together in a hamlet, instead of each house standing in its own enclosure. Hence we should not expect to find it in a mountainous country, where, as a rule, cottages do not lie close together. Nor, in fact, do we. It is rare in Norway; still rarer in Iceland. There are no instances in Cumberland; very few in Westmoreland. But, on the other hand, it is very common in Denmark." And then Mr. Cole repeats the "ups," and "rups," and "trups," so frequently occurring as terminals in Denmark.

Now in claiming the "hopes" of Northumberland and Durham as belonging to the family of "thorp," Mr. Cole evidently bases his deductions on the elision of the *th* sound as displayed in modern Danish names. But Mr. Cole seems to be unaware that such elision is a strong factor in the genius of the Danish language, while its retention is an equally strong factor in the genius of the English, and, indeed, speaking dialectically, the sound of *th* is very improperly multiplied among us. Had these "hopes" ever been "thorps," the evidence is in favour of their remaining "thorps" as long as the English tongue is spoken. But facts, as well as arguments, are strongly against Mr. Cole's theory. Many of these "hopes" occur in places such as Mr. Cole has himself defined as unsuited for them, if, as he says, they were first established as "thorps."

It may seem daring in me, but I am prepared to hazard the opprobrium of differing, not only from Mr. Cole, but also from Vigfusson, in the definition of the word "thorp," or, perhaps it were better said, in adding somewhat to it. Mr. Cole, as already stated, has copied the definition, but he has not observed the hesitating "we think" with which Vigfusson has prefaced his remarks. It is one thing to find a word bearing a certain signification in circumstances which have grown up since its first application; it is another to learn how, or why, and to what, it was *originally* applied. Saxon and Norse scholars will understand what I mean when I refer to the word "tún," or "tón," the variations of which it is comparatively easy to track as time has worked its changes around the spot to which it was first applied in its primary and restricted sense. The word "thorp" it is more difficult to trace through the same system of change; but I have no doubt it has been affected quite as materially, and in much the same way. Its primary signification I believe to have been *farm*, as opposed to "garð," and its application has subsequently embraced the cottages which increased in number upon the "thorp" as the extension of agriculture made them necessary. It is more than probable that it defined not only the lands allotted to agriculture, but also the conditions under which they were cultivated, as, for example, their occupancy by rent, or their cultivation on behalf of a non-resident proprietor. There is some evidence produceable in support of this view : (1) All places whose names have the final "thorp" are found in localities cultivated even so long ago as the time of the Danelagh ; (2) Their absence in mountainous countries is a more satisfactory solution under this view than under that suggested by Mr. Cole and Vigfusson ; and (3) The former component of at least some place names would entirely lose its significance if applied only to "a collection of cottages for the poor."

We know that great part of the Yorkshire Wolds, and much of the North Riding, where this final is but thinly scattered, have been brought under cultivation only within comparatively modern times ; and the frequent occurrence of this final (though corrupted) in Denmark, and its conspicuous absence in Norway and Iceland, are accounted for by the relative merits and demerits of those respective countries in an agricultural sense. It must be borne in mind also that the earliest examples of Old Norse or Icelandic literature are long posterior to the "original" application of this and other words, and also that the conditions of such application did not exist in that northern island, and amidst that ancient republic, whence this literature has almost wholly sprung. Still, I take it, the terms "thorpari" and "thorp-karl" definitely denoted the ancient tillers of the soil—the rustics of that far-off age—in contradistinction to other classes of the commonalty defined according to their occupations by other terms which I need not here repeat. In Sweden—where, without question, more of the primitive meaning of ancient words has been retained than in either Denmark or Norway—the word "torp" signifies to-day, not a collection of cottages, but a dwelling to which some land is attached for cultivation—in reality a *small farm ;* and when Mr. Cole visits Skåne (as I have done) he will meet with many an out-of-the-way "torp," and be enabled to enjoy the society (*om han talar språket*) of little but interesting groups of "torpkarlar."

Whether the learned will accept this view of the "original" application of "thorp," or not, I do not know ; but I think both facts and arguments weigh heavily against Mr. Cole's theory of its assimilation with the termination "hope."

There is one termination with which Mr. Cole is evidently puzzled, and which he has given up in absolute despair. For this he is not much to blame, for it certainly seems to be unique. On page 22 of his pamphlet he treats us to a little essay on "Kirby Grindalyth." He says: "The word Kirby, or Kirkby, is essentially Danish, and needs no explanation; but what is Grindalyth?" Then he describes the locality very accurately, and with the help of Vigfusson comes very near to clearing up the difficulty. He gets us to "*grynnir dalinn*—the dale became shallow, less deep;" and then he might have asked, "What about the *lyth?*" Truly, a little knowledge sometimes is a dangerous thing. Mr. Cole seems to be just reaching out his hand when the golden fruit tantalisingly disappears. Yet with this same Vigfusson's dictionary the whole matter would have been easily cleared up—at least by a Norse scholar of even small attainments. Only Mr. Cole does not think of the proper initial. Had he read more of Icelandic literature, his mind would have been directed to the expressive "Hlíðskálf" (the seat of Odin); he would have remembered something about the famous Gunnar of "Hlíðarenda," and "Fljótshlíð," both situated in Iceland, and frequently occurring in "Njaals Saga;" and would have known that "Hlíðandisnes" was the ancient name of Lindesnæs, the south-western point of Norway. He would also have known how in all these cases the "hlíð" denoted the sloping extremity to which they were severally applied. WILLIAM PORTER.

A Bundle of Old Letters.

No. I.—*A JOURNEY FROM POOLE TO BRIGHTON IN* 1760.

THE Editor possesses a very large collection of old letters, many curiously illustrative of ages, manners, customs, places, and things which are now almost past and forgotten. Selections from these, which are mostly unpublished, will appear from time to time in the pages of THE ANTIQUARIAN MAGAZINE AND BIBLIOGRAPHER. The first of them, endorsed by the receiver as "an historical letter," will be found to present in the "Brighthelmstone" of 1760 a strange contrast to the "Brighton" of 1885. The sketches of Southampton, Arundel, and Bramber, will interest those who know the Sussex of to-day. The writer, Sir Peter Thompson, was a City merchant, then residing in the pleasant and rural suburb of Bermondsey; he had been M.P. for St. Albans in 1747. The orthography of the original is preserved.

BRIGHTHELMSTON, FFRYDAY, 26 *Sepr.* 1760.

DEAR SIR'S,—

I wrote from Wickham that we came from Poole on Tuesday morn, and that the Land waters made us take a round about way to Southampton—that notwithstanding all precaution we were pester'd with waters —— but I hope we got no cold.

Southampton is much changed for the worse, full of Idlers and Gamesters; only one Small Snow and a Brigantine in the River and a few fisher boats —— and the only goods we saw on the Key was two Waggons Laded with Hay. They Import a little wine, and that is all their present Trade,—— In my time they had 8 or 10 Ships to Newfoundland —— the D—ke of Y—k, I am told, has done some real good things there to discourage the covetous practice of Gaming—particularly when some were laying high betts at Bragg. He bet only six-pences, wch put the Sharpers out of Countenance; they have not appear'd since in the public Rooms.

Mr. Damans undertakes to get Rowclift's money, for wch I have promised to procure for him a barrel of good Porter. The Cask he is to send by one of their Coasters.

Wednesday at noon we left Southampton, after seeing the rooms and Baths. We got to the Black bear at Havant (a very good Inn and civil people), a good road. Lodged there.

Thursday morn^g at Breakfast we got to Chichester, saw the Cathedral, and viewd the great nusance, the Fine Gothic Cross in the middle of the street, built in 1478, wch ought to be presented by the Grand jury. Got to Arundell to dinner—it was Fair day, and abundance of Hoggs for Sale, of all sizes. The road so farr pretty good. From Arundell we took a Guide for Bramber, the most miserable Borough I ever saw. The road hilly and winding, difficult beyond all conception for a Stranger to find out, for we went on all points of the compass—a very disagreeable way. We got to Bramber before dark, and Lodged, that is, was Shelter'd from Boisterous Gales and rain at the Lion. Bramber had anciently a very large Castle—the ruins are still visible in many places. The Duke of Norfolk is Lord of the Manor, and appoints the Constable, who is returning Officier. They vote by Scot and Lot, the most eligible way of any, but most shamefully perverted in this little Borough, wch consists of 35 stragling houses built *Scripture-wise,* for they don't join together—money'd men have bought those vile Hutts at extravagant Sums—Sir Harry Gough has got 20—the Late Lord Windsor's Father purchased 10—and 5 still remain —— Independant Voters formerly they were all so. Sr H. G. having the Majority, he brings in two Members such as he thinks proper— His Tenants always Vote as he pleases—they never pay any rent— and once in 7 years, that is at every Election, they have £30, £40, or £50 each given them—not for their Votes to be sure; but to repair their Hovels—one of them told me this tale, and said they

were never Sworn —— Lord Windsor's Tenants are not on so good
a footing, they never pay any rent—but then they never have any
money for their Votes, so his Ldsps' cottages are a tumbling, in
a Condition not to be described—one of them told me they had not
heard from his Ldsp' for 30 years past. —— Upon the whole 'tis
a shocking Borough—quite miserable—poverty stares out at every
Cottage—a reproach to this happy Constitution that such slaves
shou'd be deem'd Scot and Lot men—a comprehensive word—
meaning such as pay to Church and poor, &c.

This ffryday morn, with the assistance of a Guide, we got to this
place, amid a deal of wind & rain—we pop'd in unawares just as
Mas^{rs} Sharp was siting down to Breakfast, & surprised them not
a little—after Breakfast we went to view the Boisterous sea, w^{ch}
beat very high waves & has wash'd away the Eastermost Grine—
& put some in great ffright least the Houses to the Eastward of
the Battery shou'd undergo the same fate; it was full Sea and
Spring Tides, & the water uncommonly high, so that it flowd
plentifully into the Battery wch must go, unless skelter'd by Grines;
ano^r thing its only built with mortar, when it ought to have been
built with Tarris —— A large piece of the ruinated Castle fell into
the Sea this morn. When I was here in 1718 the Castle was
intire & some distance from devouring Neptune—I really think since
that period Neptune's encroachment at the Castle must be about
30 yards—I venture to prophesy that the Sea God will not be
satisfied with less than the whole Toun——Stone Grines laid in
Tarris, similar to what is now doing at Ramsgate, is the thing—but
how they will raise money to raise such a work the Inhabitants are
to consider who mean to keep their Freeholds—my Barber Skinner
tells me stone will not stand—I say let them try before they give an
Opinion.

The Distance from Poole to this place the way we came, as
follows :—

Poole to Southampton thro Lymington, &c.	Miles 44.
to Havant thro Botley, Wickham & Southwick	23.
to Bramber thro Chichester & Arundell, &c.	33.
to Brighthelmston	11.

Miles. 111.

Saturday 27th: y^r kind letter by Mrs Jones with y^e *Public
Advertiser* came to hand last night—the wind continues in the
Southerly quarter, quite stormy with much rain.   Dr Russell's
Garden I hear has been much lessen'd by the impetuous Waves
last night—the poor fishermen were bussied all night in taking care
of their boats—this Wind will blow the Gentry to the Northwards—
Mr. Dineley sat out this morn., Mrs Randal of Rotherhith to morrow
—when we intend to set of, with Mrs Holloway & Mas^r Sharps

for Lewis & Dine there—they return in the evening—we go on
to Grinsted—this is our scheme—so that no School time will be
lost—we hope to get to Bermondsey before Dark on Monday next
—please to give my Love to Mrs Haselden, and desire her to
order a Bed for Capt Bayly. I observe the Dutch Mail brought
no letters—the Letters sent me to Poole will be return'd to
London.

Mrs Churchill continues very well, her Dear Love to her Babes.
Hally and Jacky present their Duty to their Pappa and Mamma.

I am Affectionately Y^{rs},

PETER THOMPSON.

Notes on Words and their Origins.—I.

(1) LUNCHEON, OR NUNCHING.

IN Risdon's "History of Devon," p. 53, mention is made of
"*nunching*, or *noon-ching*, *i.e.*, *noon-meal*, sometimes called
"bever" or "beverage," sometimes "drinking." It is often
thought that "luncheon" is only an altered form of the same word,
but Mr. Ford, in his "Handbook for Spain," derives luncheon from
las once, the "eleven o'clock" (meal). Those who prefer this
etymology to the English one are, of course, at liberty to adopt it.
Lastly, we have in "Hudibras," Part I. cant. i. line 346:—

> "They took their breakfasts or their nuncheons."

The word "lunch," of course, is only a popular abbreviation of
"luncheon."

(2) ALBUM.

Johnson, in his Dictionary, defines it as "A book in which
foreigners have been accustomed to insert the autographs of
celebrated people." But this is certainly an inadequate account.
An album is a book with blank pages, *albis paginis*, ready to
receive the names, mottos, or devices of all kind of respectable
travellers. Such books lie open at most places of public resort,
in universities, colleges, libraries, museums, country seats, &c., in
England, as well as on the Continent.

It was in the Album of the "Grande Chartreuse," the head convent
of the Carthusian monks, that, finding himself in a mood congenial to
the melancholy aspect of that most romantic place, our poet, Gray,
extemporized his justly admired Latin lines upon that religious

establishment. And in the Album of the University of Copenhagen, Algernon Sidney wrote the following effusion of his patriotic soul :—

> " Manus hæc inimica tyrannis
> Ense petit placidam sub libertate quietem. "

> "A foe to tyranny, this armed hand
> Seeks for repose where peace and freedom bless the land."

Reviews.

The Genealogist (New Series). By WALFORD D. SELBY. Vol. i. Bell & Sons. 1884.

MR. SELBY, whose labours in the Public Record Office are not unknown to most of our readers, is to be heartily congratulated on the completion of the volume now before us, in which, by means of the literary assistance which he has been able to command, he has reached even a higher standard of excellence than the *Genealogist* had previously held. Among the articles of special interest in the present volume may be mentioned " The Chiefs of Grant," " Sir Francis Knollys," " The Family of Le Fauconer," " The Ormonde Attainders," " Queen Elizabeth at Helmingham," and " The Scutage and Marshal's Rolls." An important feature in the present series of the work is the addition of thirty-two pages to each number, devoted to a " New Peerage," which includes all the *extinct* and *dormant*, as well as the *extant* peerages. This Peerage is compiled on a plan similar to the well-known " Synopsis of the Peerage," edited by the late Sir Harris Nicolas. " The Genealogist," it may be added, embraces within its scope original articles of an antiquarian and topographical character ; and, as the Editor tells us in his preface, it "is intended to be, not a mere temporary vehicle of amusement, but a permanent storehouse of authentic information, to which reference may hereafter confidently be made."

Calendar of State Papers, Domestic. 1657-1658. Rolls Series, published by the authority of the Master of the Rolls. Edited by MARY A. E. GREEN. Longman & Co. 1884.

MRS. GREEN'S new volume of Commonwealth State Papers embraces a short but eventful period of eleven months. Once more we find the central object of interest in the colossal figure of the Protector still struggling with the hopeless task of establishing a form of government on a strictly constitutional basis, short of monarchy. We have learnt already to regard the parliamentary policy of the great Protector as something more than a virtual failure, but Mrs. Green initiates us here into several obscure and most instructive causes of that disastrous experiment of an impossible ideal of good government. The temper of a legislative body which murmured that "there was no need of a House of Lords without a king, and if they *must* have a king they would have the right one," is deeply significant. We are naturally prepared for inconsistencies on the part of irresponsible patriots who have found too late the burthen of good government beyond their strength ; but the strangest of them all is contained in this surly threat of factious malcontents that the constitutional powers with which they had but just now endowed their idol were to be postponed to a later caprice on pain of a counter-revolution. How differently would the Commons of James I. or Charles I. have treated such treasonable agitators against "the Cause."

The House of Lords—or rather Senate—which was the main cause of the parliamentary squabbles treated of in the present volume, is here described in detail. The truth of the saying that the English-speaking race dearly love a lord was never, perhaps, better illustrated than in the case of the hearty ridicule and contempt amidst which the sturdy plebeian heroes of 1645 proceeded to assume their unaccustomed state as a quasi-hereditary assembly of the notables.

Considerable legislative activity was displayed within the short compass of this last Parliament of the Commonwealth, the results of which are shown in these papers. But the most interesting part of the volume must undoubtedly be held to consist of the glimpses of foreign politics revealed in the preparations for the campaigns in Flanders and the papers relating to the Navy. The Spanish prisoners in this country, we read, complained bitterly of their usage, and especially of the scantiness of their prison fare. The discreditable severities thus inflicted certainly contrast with the humane treatment of the survivors of the Armada under Elizabeth.

The miscellaneous subjects of interest touched on in this volume are many, and peculiarly attractive to the student of social history, who always looks for a specially ample allowance of information under this head at the hands of Mrs. Green.

One special feature is the list of attendances of the Protector's Council of State from June, 1657, to April, 1658. Walter Strickland is credited with the largest number, namely 107 out of a full number of 114, the average attendance of the majority being far below that figure. It is worthy of notice, too, that the present volume is the first result of a new experience in cheese-paring at the Stationery Office, being bound in half-boards and in a style that is by no means to the credit of a literary Government.

The Edburton Parish Registers, 1558—1673. By the Rev. C. H. WILKIE, M.A. Brighton: J. G. Bishop, *Herald* office. 1884.

WE have much pleasure in directing attention to the little *brochure* now before us, which gives, in the space of some 68 octavo pages, what purports to be as literal and as exact a copy as possible of the early Register Book of the parish of Edburton. The preservation of parish registers is a subject which has always obtained our heartiest support and encouragement. For many years the subject has happily been growing and widely extending, in connection with that general regard to all national antiquities and historic records which distinguished the present century. The printing of these old registers preserves for future use the entries which they contain, besides having the advantage of making them more popular. The register before us contains a large number of baptisms, marriages, and burials, and also a list of "Collections" for charitable purposes which have at different times been made in the parish.

The Tolhouse at Great Yarmouth (J. Buckle, Great Yarmouth, 1884) is the subject of a *brochure* by Mr. F. Danby Palmer, compiled and published "in the hope of assisting the effort now being made to preserve an ancient building, for many ages connected with the history of his native town." Having already given in these pages some account of the history and chief architectural features of the old Tolhouse, and of the discoveries made in the progress of the work now being carried on with the view to its preservation (see vol. vi. pp. 3—5, and p. 111 *ante*), it only remains for us to state that Mr. Palmer has dived deep into the past history of this interesting building, and has probably told us all that there is to be said upon the subject. It is to be hoped that sufficient funds for its preservation will flow in, so that the structure may eventually be utilised for the benefit of the inhabitants of the borough, probably as a town museum.

Aidan, the Apostle of the North, by Dr. A. C. FRYER (Partridge & Co., 1885) is a short but picturesque biography of the great saint to whom the North of England owes its conversion to Christianity. In his efforts on behalf of the Cross, St. Aidan was largely helped by the personal friendship of Oswald, king and martyr; but this fact does not detract from his own merits. His saintly manners had about them as grand a charm as belongs to none of the other British saints, if the sketch of his life and labours which has come down to us from the pen of Bede is to be accepted as true. Dr, Fryer, perhaps, might have drawn out in greater detail the peculiar similarity of Lindisfarne to the Island of Iona, in the far west of Scotland, from which its founders came to evangelise the natives of Deira and Bernicia; for the likeness is one that cannot fail to strike the travelled visitor who makes a pilgrimage to both places; but he could not well have improved his account of Aidan, the man and bishop, whose character he has illustrated most truthfully. Dr. Fryer is already known to the student of history by his work on "St. Cuthbert, of Lindisfarne," a companion volume to that now before us. We cannot well call it a 'sequel,' because St. Aidan belonged to the generation which was passing away just as Cuthbert grew to man's estate. It may be added that Dr. Fryer has related the story of the variations between some of the ceremonies and observances of the Roman missionaries in the south, and of their Celtic brethren in the north, with great fairness from first to last.

UNDER the careful editorship of Mr. ERNEST C. THOMAS, late librarian of the Oxford Union, the *Transactions and Proceedings of the Fourth and Fifth Annual Meetings of the Library Association of the United Kingdom*, held in London in September, 1881, and at Cambridge in September, 1882, have been recently published. The Transactions and Proceedings of the Cambridge meeting occupy by far the larger portion of the volume, for, besides the opening address of the President, no less than fourteen of the papers read are here printed, together with an Appendix giving "Some Account of the Organisation of the Cambridge University Library," "Local Libraries considered as Museums of Local Authorship and Printing," and other kindred subjects; whereas, besides the opening address, only eight papers were read at the London meeting. Notwithstanding the delay in its publication, the volume will be heartily welcomed by the members of the Library Association, and more especially by those who were unable to be present at the annual meetings. The papers contained in the volume are of great interest and usefulness, as may be judged from the following list of some of the principal : "Legislation for Free Public Libraries," "Suggestions as to Public Library Buildings," "The Libraries of the Inns of Court," "Outline of a Plan for the Preparation of a Catalogue of (British) Periodical Literature," "Some Account of the Early Book Fairs," "The Printing of the British Museum Catalogue," "On Some Recent Schemes of Classification," "Thoughts on the Cataloguing of Journals and Transactions," &c.

THE March number of *English Etchings* (D. Bogue, 27, King William-street, Strand), contains, *inter alia*, an admirable example of the etcher's art in "Bramber Castle," by Mr. W. Holmes May. The plate is powerfully executed, full of light and shade, and highly effective. The old historic ruins of Bramber Castle form a picturesque study.

MR. EDMUND GOLDSMID, F.R.H.S., some of whose publications have been already noticed in these pages (see vol. v. p. 86), has sent us another instalment of the series of "curious out-of-the-way books" which he is issuing under the title of *Bibliotheca Curiosa*. The series contains many extremely rare volumes, those before us comprising Caxton's "Reynard the Fox," and Grotius' "Dissertation on the Origin of the Native Races of America," to which is added Peter Albinus' "Treatise on Foreign Languages and Unknown Islands:" the two latter works are translated from the original Latin, and enriched with biographical notes and illustrations by Mr. Goldsmid. The printing of these curious volumes is excellent, the type being the same as that used in the "Parchment Library." We have also received "Kempe's Nine Daies' Wonder, performed in a journey from London to Norwich," edited by Mr. Goldsmid from the original MS., together with *fac-similes* of "The Celebrated Forged Letter from General Monk (afterwards Duke of Albemarle) to Charles II., which was circulated all over the country in January, 1660, and is said to have been the immediate cause of the King's Restoration ;" "No Blinde Guides," a pamphlet printed in 1663 "in answer to a seditious pamphlet of J. Milton's intituled ' Brief Notes upon a late Sermon, Titl'd, the Fear of God and the King ; Preach'd, and since Publish'd, by Matthew Griffith, D.D., and Chaplain to the late King,' addressed to the author ;" and also "Colchester's Teares," a curious tract, published in 1648, giving some account of the misery brought upon the inhabitants by the siege of Colchester.

The Manx Note-book (Douglas : G. H. Johnson), a quarterly journal devoted to matters of the past and present connected with the Isle of Man, of which the first number is before us, bids fair to attain a high position among antiquarian literature. Both in appearance and in the subject matter of its contents, the new magazine is all that could be desired, and reflects the highest credit upon the Isle of Man, where it is printed and published. We wish it every success.

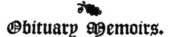

Obituary Memoirs.

"Emori nolo ; sed me esse mortuum nihil æstimo."—*Epicharmus.*

MR. HODDER M. WESTROPP, the well-known archæologist, died in February, at his residence, St. Maur, Ventnor, in his 64th year. Mr. Westropp was educated at the University of Dublin, and developed early a strong taste for antiquarian and archæological studies. Under the auspices of the British and American Archæological Society he delivered a course of lectures in Rome on the Dædalean period, the Æginetan age, the Phidian age, the age of Praxiteles, and the age of Decline. A second course of lectures was delivered in Rome in connection with the same society in February, 1882, the subject being "The Wall of Servius Tullius," "The Temples of Rome," "Oriental Deities," "Ancient Painting," "Ancient Marbles," and "The Catacombs." In April last Mr. Westropp delivered a course of three lectures at the Royal Institution, Albemarle-street, on "Recent Discoveries in Roman Archæology," embracing the investigations of the Colosseum, the Forum, and the Palatine hill. Besides translating several works from the French and Italian, Mr. Westropp was the author of "Epochs of Painted Vases," "A Manual of Precious Stones and Antique Gems," "The Handbook of Archæology," "Pottery and

Porcelain," "Homeric Doubts," "The Cycle of Development," and "Imperial Rome."

Mr. John F. Campbell, of Islay, Argyllshire, who died on the 17th of February, at Cannes, was well known as the collector from his fellow-countrymen of tales of ancient folk-lore, having passed much of his time by the fireside of Highland crofters and peasants, collecting stories told in the Gaelic language. He took an active part in the Ossian controversy, and his intimate knowledge of Gaelic entitled him to be an authority on all such subjects, even if many of his fellow-countrymen could not agree with his decisions on the much-vexed question.

Father Anselm Baker, a monk of the Cistercian order, and an heraldic draughtsman of rare abilities, died on the 11th of February, at Mount St. Bernard's Abbey, in Charnwood Forest, Leicestershire, in his 52nd year. His work was eagerly sought for by all able to appreciate the true beauty of mediæval blazonry. About two-thirds of the coats-of-arms in "Foster's Peerage" were executed by him, as were also the mural paintings in the Chapel of St. Scholastica's Priory at Atherstone ; at St. Winifred's, Sheepshed ; and in the temple in Garendon Park, the seat of Mr. Phillipps-De-Lisle, in Leicestershire. The "Hortus Animæ" and "Horæ Diurnæ," brought out by Philp, and several elaborate works published at Mechlin and Tournay both for his own and other religious orders, bear witness to his inventive genius. "Liber Vitæ," a record of the benefactors of St. Bernard's Abbey, is perhaps a unique production of this century, magnificently illustrated with the arms and patron Saints of the benefactors. Mr. Everard Green, F.S.A., was present at the funeral of the deceased, as representing the Society of Antiquaries.

Meetings of Learned Societies.

METROPOLITAN.

Society of Antiquaries.—*Feb.* 12, Dr. E. Freshfield, V.P., in the chair. The Rev. R. C. Jenkins communicated some particulars about a recent discovery of Saxon remains at Lyminge, Kent. A number of human bones, swords, spear-heads, three bosses of shields, two fibulæ, and a thin ornament for a necklet were among the most important objects found. Mr. T. F. Kirby exhibited, by permission of the Mayor of Winchester, some of the recently discovered charters of that city. Down to March last year the earliest charter of Winchester known to be in existence was that of Elizabeth, whereas now a hoard of charters from Henry II. to Henry VIII. inclusive have been found in a garret over a solicitor's office in Winchester. The charters, &c., exhibited this evening were the following : the first and second charters of Henry II. ; the charter of Richard I. ; a photograph of the charter of Henry III. ; a deed of gift by Philip and Mary to the city ; an indenture between the prior and convent of St. Swithun and Simon (le Draper), Mayor of Winchester ; and an indenture between Joan, Queen of England, and John Veel, Mayor of Winchester.—*Feb.* 19, Dr. J. Evans, V.P., and afterwards Dr. E. Freshfield, V.P., in the chair. Dr. Evans exhibited a complete set of twelve roundels or fruit trenchers of the year 1625 in their original case. Six of them bore the name of Roger Simpson and six of Mary Simpson. The inscription on the box recorded that they were the gift—presumably the wedding gift—of Thomas Martin, Vicar of Stone in Oxney, Kent. Through this clue Dr. Evans was able to identify the actual parties to whom the trenchers were thus given. The devices on these trenchers consisted of representations of fruits and flowers with tablets and scroll-work round the compartments, on which were the couplets and quatrains always found on these roundels. The couplet in each case referred to the particular fruit delineated; the quatrains consisted of the usual style of posies, not always adapted *virginibus puerisque*. Professor Ferguson exhibited two volumes which had been procured by him from the sales of the Hamilton and Syston Park libraries respectively. The former was a copy of a work by Albertus Magnus, "De Secretis Mulierum." The latter, which the colophon showed to have been one of the products of the printing press of Machlinia, was also a work of Albertus Magnus, "De Secretis Naturæ." This book bore the autograph of William Herbert, the editor of Ames. It is admitted that at one time Herbert had in his possession both these works under one and the same cover. Professor Ferguson holds that, either by Herbert himself or some subsequent possessor, the two works were separated, and after this divorce the work "De Secretis Mulierum" lost some leaves, and was no longer in the perfect state in which Herbert found it. Professor Ferguson was considered to have made good his theory. Thanks were voted to Mr. Telfer for his "Life of Chevalier d'Eon," and to other donors of books.—*Feb*. 26. Mr. E. Freshfield, V.P., in the chair. By permission of the Governors of St. John's House, Sherborne, Dorset, an interesting triptych was exhibited which formerly served as an altarpiece in the chapel of the hospital. The triptych when open measured about six feet in width by three feet three inches in height. In the centre piece was the miracle of the raising of Lazarus. In the dexter panel were two miracles, viz., the healing of the man with the deaf and dumb spirit (St. Mark ix.), and the healing of the man who was blind from his birth (St. John v.). On the sinister panel were the raising to life of the son of the widow of Nain and that of the daughter of Jairus. On the backs of these wings were the figures, in *grisaille*, of St. Paul, St. James, St. Peter, and St. Thomas. The composition of this picture was not without very considerable merit, but the execution was decidedly coarse. This may have been due to its having been retouched and repainted by successive restorers. Mr. W. H. St. John Hope exhibited a collection of sixty-three impressions of the seals of the University and of the colleges of Cambridge, which he accompanied by copious remarks illustrating the interesting features in each example.— *March* 5, Dr. E. Freshfield, V.P., in the chair. At the ballot for fellows the following gentlemen were elected: the Revs. Messrs. Calverley and F. Sutton, Messrs. Phillips, Green, Vinon, and Hazlewood. This being a business meeting, no papers were read.

BRITISH ARCHÆOLOGICAL ASSOCIATION.—*Feb*. 18, Mr. Thomas Morgan, F.S.A., in the chair. It was announced that Mr. Carew, of Crowcombe, to whom the Association, at its late Congress, reported the unsafe condition of the ruins of Carew Castle, Pembrokeshire, had arranged to have the necessary repairs executed at his own cost. These repairs will be strictly limited to the upholding of the building, to prevent injury by frost or tempest, and nothing will be done to alter the present appearance of the building. Mr. Loftus Brock, F.S.A., reported the existence of a large portion of old London Wall, now visible in the street of the same name at Moorgate, just to the west of Allhallows Church.

It is now revealed by recent excavations for buildings, having been buried by the accumulated earth of centuries. The Rev. Prebendary Scarth exhibited a drawing of a Roman pocket sundial, found at Herculaneum. Mr. Howlett exhibited a fine lamp, adorned with Christian symbols, found in the Roman Catacombs. A paper on " The Roman Baths of Bath " was then read by the Chairman. After referring to Mr. Irvine's conjectural restoration, which appears to be well supported by more recent discoveries, the lecturer proceeded to describe in detail the whole of the building now revealed, tracing the portions uncovered from their first discovery. It is already proved that the size of the structure was very great, and that it must have possessed great architectural beauty. The cold water was brought from the well known in mediæval times as St. Winifred's, while the hot water rises on the site. Probably only about one half of the vast building has been traced. The inscription, found on a leaden plate, has been the subject of various readings, but the lecturer made out its import to be that Cetus Minianus, with Vilvia and a little sister, with others, took the waters, the ladies having taken four, and the gentlemen five baths a piece. In the discussion, which followed, Mr. J. W. Grover, F.S.A., referred to Julius Solinus, who speaks of the hot springs of Britain, by which he believes those at Bath were meant. Mr. Previte, Mr. E. Walford, and several others took part in the discussion. The paper was illustrated by several paintings and drawings prepared by the Misses Morgan. Another portion was then read of the paper prepared by the Rev. G. F. Browne, on the remarkable cross in Leeds Church. The shaft is covered with remarkable figure subjects, having reference to old Norwegian or Scandinavian myths unique in England.— *March* 4, Mr. Thomas Morgan, F.S.A., in the chair. The Rev. Sir Talbot Baker exhibited a beautiful comb of large size, elaborately carved, the figures being supposed by Mr. Rylands and other speakers to represent some incidents in the Myth of St. Ursula and her supposed 11,000 Virgins. Mr. Irvine sent a large collection of drawings of antiquarian objects recently exhibited at Peterborough, and found either in the city or in the locality. Mr. Romilly Allen described a hitherto inedited stone at Colsterworth Church, near Grantham. It has been part of the shaft of a Saxon cross, and is covered with interlaced patterns. Mr. Earle Way exhibited some curious Roman silver coins, and Mr. E. Walford an old engraving of the Carfax, Oxford, showing the position of the old conduit erected in 1610, but now removed. The Rev. Prebendary Scarth described a carved stone pedestal, of which a drawing by Mr. Thompson Watkin was produced. It was found in a Roman hypocaust at Chester, and it is carved with some curious and very unusual patterns, one of the ornaments being very similar to the *fleur de lys* of mediæval times. Mr. G. R. Wright, F.S.A., exhibited a leaden bulla of Pope Gregory XI., found at Snitterley, Norfolk, in the ruined wall of a conventual building, some notes of the history of the latter, prepared by Mr. Proctor Burroughes, were read. Mr. A. Cope described an early cross at Dunblane, carved on a massive monolith, probably of earlier date than the cross. The concluding portion of the Rev. G. F. Browne's paper on the cross in Leeds Church was then read, the author pointing out that the various sculptured panels on the shaft represent events recorded in the ancient mythology of Scandinavia, unique in England, and that probably the cross was erected to some descendant of the heroes represented. He believed that the cross was set up on the grave of King Olaf Godfreyson, and that the stone, upon which is a runic inscription, was erected at the foot of the grave. A paper by Mr. E. J. L. Scott, M.A., on original documents relating to the south part of Pembroke, was then read by Mr. de Grey Birch, F.S.A., in the author's absence. Many valuable references were made in the documents to places visited during the recent congress. The proceedings were brought to a close by a paper on the old signs of the shops in Paternoster-row, by Mr. H. Syer Cuming, F.S.A., Scot., read by Mr. Loftus Brock, F.S.A. The rise and progress of many bookselling houses was traced, and reference given to books published and tokens issued in "the Row." A discussion followed, in which Messrs. Rylands and E. Walford took part, who remarked that nearly all the streets about St. Paul's were named from parts of the ancient services of the church— such as "Creed" Lane, "Amen" Corner, and "Ave Maria" Lane—and that "Paternoster Row" simply followed the rule. Mr. Walford remarked on the predominance of *Black* Swans, *Black* Crows, *Black* Boys, &c., among the names of old publishers' signs, but thought that still blacker signs were needed for sundry modern publishers in "the Row."

ROYAL ARCHÆOLOGICAL INSTITUTE.—*March* 5, Lord Percy, M.P., President, in the chair. The following papers were read : "Roman Inscriptions discovered in Britain in 1884," by Mr. W. T. Watkin, and "Church Bells," by Mr. J. L. Stahlschmidt. Among the objects exhibited were rubbings and casts of bell inscriptions, by Mr. Stahlschimdt ; a copy of a wall painting in the church of Notre Dame du Câstel, Guernsey, drawing of a sculptured stone coffin, from Guernsey, and drawings of flint and bronze implements, by Mr. J. J. Carey ; and also the Corporation maces of Maidstone, by Mr. W. H. St. John Hope.

ROYAL HISTORICAL SOCIETY.—*Feb.* 19, Annual general meeting, Mr. J. Heywood, F.R.S., in the chair. The report, which was adopted, showed that eleven papers had been read during the session of 1883-4, and that the number of Fellows on the roll at the close of the year was 621. Mr. C. A. Fyffe and Mr. W. E. H. Lecky were elected as the new Vice-Presidents, and the Rev. W. Cunningham, Mr. J. Bass Mullinger, Mr. F. K. J. Shenton, and the Rev. R. Thornton as members of the Council, in the place of the four retiring members.

ST. PAUL'S ECCLESIOLOGICAL SOCIETY.—*Feb.* 24, Mr. Charles Browne in the chair. Mr. Arthur Taylor read a paper on the "History of Stained Glass." He commenced with a general description of the material used in the production of stained or painted glass in different ages and of various styles, and afterwards treated the subject historically, illustrating his remarks by the exhibition of several examples.—*March* 10, Major Heales in the chair. A paper on the "Ecclesiology of the Roman Catacombs" was read by Mr. Charles Browne, who, with the aid of drawings and diagrams, gave a graphic description of these famous and remarkable excavations.

HELLENIC SOCIETY.—*March* 12, Mr. C. T. Newton in the chair. Professor William Ramsay read a paper on "Painted Vases from Asia Minor."

NUMISMATIC.—*Feb.* 19, Dr. J. Evans, President, in the chair. Dr. Wright exhibited a silver stater of Azbaal, King of Citium, in Cyprus, *circa* B.C. 410—387. Mr. Copp exhibited a gold octadrachm of Arsinoë, the wife of Ptolemy Philadelphus, in very fine preservation. Mr. T. Bliss exhibited a British gold coin said to have been found in Bedfordshire, and a British silver coin attributed to the Icini similar to Evans, "Ancient British

Coins," pl. xv. 4 ; also two silver coins of Constantius II., lately found in an earthern vase under the foundations of Sion College, London Wall. Mr. H. Montague exhibited a very rare shilling and sixpence of George III., struck in 1786, of which only three specimens are known. Mr. Evans exhibited a *méreau de présence* of the Dyers' Company, having on one side three woolpacks and on the other a large D. Canon Greenwell communicated a paper on some rare or inedited Greek coins in his own and other collections. Among them the most remarkable were a silver octadrachm of Ichnæ, in Macedon, and a very fine tetadrachm of Camarina, in Sicily, in his own cabinet, and a magnificent gold stater of Lampsacus, bearing on the obverse a figure of Nike sacrificing a ram, in the cabinet of Dr. H. Weber. Mr. B. V. Head read a paper by Dr. A. Smith, " On Nummi Pelliculati, or Plated Groats, of David II. and Robert II. of Scotland."

NEW SHAKSPERE.—*Feb.* 13, Mr. F. J. Furnivall in the chair. Miss G. Latham read a paper " On the Dramatic Meaning of the Construction of Shakespeare's Verse, with Special Reference to the Use of the Run-on Line and Extra Syllable." Miss Latham said that Shakespeare, writing not to be read, but to be heard, constructed his verse, with all its irregularities, with a view to the expression by sound of the ideas and passions of the *dramatis personæ*. In illustration she quoted from " Midsummer Night's Dream" and "Richard III." as early plays, and from "Coriolanus" as a later one.

PHILOLOGICAL.—*Feb.* 6, Rev. Prof. Skeat, President, in the chair. Mr. H. Sweet read a paper on "Old English Contributions : 1. *reck* was from A.-S. *reccean*, not *recan*, by confusion with *reccean*, to rule, govern, to recount, tell ; 2, *bilewit* (L. *innocens*), white of bill, applied first to young birds, then to innocent persons (like *blanc-bec*, *béjaune*, Ger. *gelb-schnabel*) ; 3, the Mid. Eng. suffix -*ild*, in *fostrild*, foster-nurse, &c., from A.-S. name suffix *hild*, meaning war, also seen in *begeneld*, a female beggar (Wedgwood), Matilda, &c. ; 4, on palatal mutation, *heah* to *heh*, the absorption of the *a* being due to the guttural *h ;* 5, on the development of *y* (*u*) for *i* in late West Saxon in unaccented words ; *hire* is *hure* in Robert of Gloster ; 6, tar, A.-S. *teoru ; eo* becomes *ea*, and then *a* is dropped (*em*, I am, becomes *eom*, *eam*, *am*) ; *teoru* goes to *tearu*, and then *taru ;* 7, *viking*, not Norse, but *wig-ing*, warrior, which occurs in a Kentish charter of the ninth century, *Wigingaham.—Athenæum.*

ANTHROPOLOGICAL INSTITUTE.—*March* 10, Mr. Francis Galton, F.R.S., President, in the chair. Mr. James G. Fraser read a paper " On Certain Burial Customs, as illustrative of the Primitive Theory of the Soul." The Romans had a custom that when a man who had been reported to have died abroad returned home alive, he should enter his house not by the door but over the roof. This custom (which is still observed in Persia) owed its origin to certain primitive beliefs and customs with regard to the dead. The ghost of an unburied man was supposed to haunt and molest the living, especially his relatives. Hence the importance attached to the burial of the dead—and various precautions were taken that the ghost should not return. When the body of a dead man could not be found he was buried in effigy, and this fictitious burial was held to be sufficient to lay the wandering ghost, for it is a principle of primitive thought that what is done to the effigy of a man is done to the man himself. The Director read a paper by Admiral F. S. Tremlett, on "The Sculptured Dolmens of the Morbihan." About eighty sculptures had been found, invariably on the interior surfaces of the capstones and their supports. It is remarkable that they are confined within a distance of about twelve miles, and are all situated near the sea coast, beyond which, although the megaliths are numerous, there is a complete absence of sculptures. The sculptures vary in intricacy from simple wave lines and cup markings to some that have been compared to the tattooing of the New Zealanders.

SOCIETY OF BIBLICAL ARCHÆOLOGY.—*March* 3, Dr. S. Birch, President, in the chair. The following communications were read : " On the Inscription of the Destruction of Mankind in the Tomb of Rameses III., by M. E. Naville, " Notes on the Martyrdom of the Coptic Martyr Isaac of Tiphre," by Mr. E. A. W. Budge, and "The Weasel and the Cat in Ancient Times," by the Rev. Dr. Placzek, translated by the Rev. A. Löwy.

PROVINCIAL.

CAMBRIDGE ANTIQUARIAN SOCIETY.—*Feb.* 9, Mr. J. W. Clark, M.A., President, in the chair. Mr. H. F. Wilson read a paper "On an Inscription in Ashwell Church, Herts, relating to the Black Death." After criticising the interpretation of it put forward in Cussan's " History of Hertfordshire," he stated his belief that it referred to both the visitations of the pestilence, namely, in 1348-9 and 1361. Besides a rubbing of the inscription, and a copy containing his emendations of it, Mr. Wilson exhibited a rubbing from an incised picture (believed to be of Westminster Abbey), which is to be seen on the north wall of the church-tower at Ashwell. Mr. Pell exhibited several objects dug up in or near Wilburton, including a specimen of gold ring-money, a silver spoon, apparently of the sixteenth or seventeenth century, a Celtic urn, bones of animals, &c. Mr. Pell afterwards commented at some length upon the terms "hide," " carucata," " virgata," &c., in the Domesday Book, Professor Birkbeck and Dr. Bryan Walker taking part in the discussion which followed.— *Feb.* 23, Mr. J. W. Clark, M.A., President, in the chair. Professor Hughes exhibited the results of several excavations in the neighbourhood of Newmarket, including a fine bronze leaf-shaped sword, belonging to Mr. Tharp, of Chippenham Hall. He then described an interment which had been discovered in cuttting a drain in Chippenham Park. The pit contained five skeletons, but no relics of any kind were found with them. The contents of the tumulus known as Nine-Score Hill, on the Newmarket race-course, which had been recently removed in order to level the ground, were next exhibited and described. Professor E. C. Clark read a paper upon the inscribed stone from Brough-under-Stanemore, now in the Fitzwilliam Museum. After commenting on the importance of the document as a palæographic record, Professor Clark proceeded to state that this was an epitaph, in Greek hexameters, on a youth bearing the name of the god Hermes, and coming from the northern part of Syria, Commagene. Mr. Browne, Canon Taylor, and Mr. Sandys joined in the discussion which followed. The Rev. Precentor Venables exhibited a photograph and drawings of a sculptured stone, lately discovered in digging the foundations of a new school at Lincoln. The stone, which bears no inscription, was probably a sepulchral memorial. Not far from the stone were discovered two coarse funeral urns, one containing burnt bones.

ESSEX ARCHÆOLOGICAL SOCIETY.—*Feb.* 7, Mr. G. A. Lowndes, President, in the chair. Mr. Laver having made a report of the discovery of a Roman villa at Alresford, which is probably extensive, a committee was appointed, the consent of the owner and the occupier of the land being obtained, to superintend the exploration of the site, and authorised to expend, if necessary, an amount not exceeding £50 upon the work. A grant of £50 was made towards the expenses of alterations and repairs in the Colchester Museum. The annual general meeting of the Society was appointed to be held in Tendring Hundred on Tuesday, August 11.

ISLE OF MAN NATURAL HISTORY AND ANTIQUARIAN SOCIETY.—*Dec.* 16. A paper on "The Monumental Crosses of Man" was read by Mr. P. M. C. Kermode, and a letter by Mr. F. Swinnerton on some "Flints" found by him at Port St. Mary was also read; specimens of the flints were exhibited.

Antiquarian News & Notes.

A FREE library has been opened at Gateshead, at a cost of £8000.

A MONUMENT is about to be erected at Rome to Cardinal Mezzofanti, the great linguist. It will stand near that of Tasso.

A NEW edition of Mr. E. Walford's "Greater London" is already called for, though the work has not been published a year.

THE coins recently stolen from the Cardiff Museum have been returned by post anonymously.

A BUST of Robert Burns, lately placed in Poet's Corner, Westminster Abbey, has been unveiled by the Dean.

MESSRS. LONGMANS announce the publication of "The Cyclades; or, Life among the Insular Greeks," by Mr. J. Theodore Bent, B.A.

MR. REDWAY is about to publish "Hints to Collectors of Original Editions of the Works of Charles Dickens."

MR. T. TYLER, M.A., has been delivering at the British Museum a course of three lectures on "The Hittites and their Monuments."

THE 400th anniversary of the foundation of Reading School will be celebrated in July.

MESSRS. MACMILLAN announce a history of the University of Oxford, from the earliest times to the revival of learning, by Mr. H. C. Maxwell Lyte, author of a "History of Eton."

PROFESSOR C. F. RICHARDSON, of Dartmouth College, New Hampshire, author of "A Primer of American Literature," has nearly ready the first volume of his projected "History of American Literature."

ON Sunday, March 1, a service was held at the Temple Church in commemoration of the 700th anniversary of its consecration by Heraclius, Patriarch of Jerusalem.

THE attendances at the Guildhall Library, Reading-room, and Museum during the year 1884 were 384,864, being an increase of 2,805 over the previous year.

MR. JUSTIN SIMPSON, of Stamford, is compiling a history of the Grammar School of that town, its Masters and Scholars. Mr. Simpson invites communications.

THE important collection of pictures formed by the late Mr. Christopher Beckett Denison, chiefly from the Hamilton Palace sale, is announced for sale in June.

THE Richmond Theatre, on the boards of which Edmund Kean trod so often, has lately been pulled down, thus bringing to light one of the octagonal towers of the garden wall which surrounded the old palace of Sheen.

MR. H. R. TEDDER, librarian of the Athenæum Club, and Mr. Ernest C. Thomas, Hon. Secretary of the Library Association, have announced the "Library Handbook," containing matter of value to librarians, bibliographers, and book-lovers.

A PETITION has been presented to the Court of Common Council of London, by the Society for the Protection of Ancient Buildings, praying the Court to adopt measures for the preservation of the ancient buildings of Staple Inn, now in danger of demolition.

MR. F. J. FURNIVALL, on the occasion of his sixtieth birthday, in February, received from the Philosophical Faculty of the University of Berlin the degree of Doctor of Philosophy, for his labours in the cause of Early English literature.

THE Public Library of Hampstead, after fifty years of existence, was reopened in its new quarters, Stanfield House, High-street, on February 25. This old institution had among its earliest supporters Samuel Rogers, Joanna Baillie, Constable and Linnell, and others.

MR. W. J. HARDY, of the Public Record Office, has been occupied in calendaring the unbound documents relating to the mediæval guild in the possession of the Corporation of Stratford-on-Avon; the calendar is being published week by week in the *Stratford-on-Avon Herald*.

MR. STANLEY LANE POOLE has undertaken to prepare for the Clarendon Press a *corpus* of Mohammedan coin-inscriptions, to be entitled "Fasti Arabici: the History of the Mohammedan Empire as established by Coins."

EFFORTS are being made to obtain for the National Portrait Gallery a fine picture, painted by Hickel, a German artist, representing Pitt addressing the House of Commons in 1794, which is at present in the Galleries of the Belvedere at Vienna.

PROFESSOR JULIUS VON PFLUGK-HARTTUNG has just brought out the second part of his "Iter Italicum," published by Kohlammer, of Stuttgart; and also the first part of the second volume of his "Acta Pontificum Romanorum Inedita," published by Fues, of Tübingen.

MR. THOMAS MASON, librarian of Stirling's and Glasgow Public Library, Glasgow, has in preparation a work of great bibliographical interest on the "Public and Private Libraries of Glasgow." It will be devoted to matters relating to rare and valuable books, and will contain full descriptions of sixteen of the principal libraries of the city.

MR. H. E. SMITH, author of "Reliquiæ Isurianæ," proposes to publish by subscription a monograph on Conisborough Castle. Mr. G. T. Clark's essay upon the remains of the castle will be reprinted in it, by permission of the Council of the Yorkshire Archæological and Topographical Association, from its *Journal*.

UNDER the will of the late Lord Stafford, the family pictures, the picture by Maynard of James II. and Mary of Modena, the silver staff formerly belonging to the Lord High Constable of England, Stafford, Duke of Buckingham, and some other articles are made heirlooms to go with the hall and estate of Costessey.

THE Edinburgh Town Council have resolved to place memorial tablets on all spots of historic interest in the city, beginning with the site in Chambers-street (formerly College Wynd) of the house where Sir Walter Scott was born. A memorial stone is also to be erected over the grave of the novelist's father, in Greyfriars Churchyard.

THE *Weekly Register* states that the Benedictine congregation of England, which was founded, A.D. 596, by St. Augustine, numbers 250 members, divided in four monasteries. In their colleges the Benedictines educate 300 students. They have built seventy parish churches, and are now constructing one of the finest monastic churches erected since the Reformation.

THE Essex Field Club has resolved to attempt a thorough investigation of the Deneholes, in Hangman's Wood, Little Thurrock, and those existing at East Tilbury and near Purfleet, and in other parts of Essex, in the hope of determining, as far as possible, the age and purposes of these interesting excavations.

AN historical work, it is said, will shortly be published by Capt. R. E. Temple. It is a record of the events from the accession of Runjeet Singh in 1805 down to the annexation of the Punjab in 1849. The record was kept by a vakeel of the Court of Runjeet Singh, and it extends to upwards of 7,000 MS. pages.

MR. ROBINSON ELLIS will contribute to the Classical Series of the "Anecdota Oxoniensia" (1) a collation of Cod. Harl. 2610, a MS. of the tenth century containing i.—iii. 622 of Ovid's "Metamorphoses"; (2) twenty-four Latin epigrams from MSS. in the Bodleian or elsewhere; (3) Latin glosses on Apollinaris Sidonius from a MS. of the twelfth century.

THE cornelian ring with Pope's head, which was given by the poet to Bishop Warburton, was sold for seven guineas at the recent sale at Trentham Vicarage. One of the glasses blown for Prince Charles Edward at Derby, and intended to be used at a banquet at Windsor on the triumph of the Jacobite cause, was bought by Her Majesty for £17 10s.

SOME articles of Roman pottery have lately been found during excavations in a field at Donnington, near Newbury. They consist of two broken, jar-shaped vessels, 4½ and 6 inches in height, unornamented and without handles; the handle of an amphora, or wine jar of the Romans and numerous portions of other Roman fictilia. Bones of animals also were found in the neighbourhood of the pottery.

A FINE bronze statue of Hercules, in fair preservation, excepting a fracture across the legs, has been discovered in the course of the works connected with the building of a new theatre in the Via Nazionale, near the Gardens of the Colonna Palace, Rome. It is, therefore, probable that it belonged either to the Baths of Constantine or to Hadrian's Temple of the Sun, which stood near each other at that corner of the Quirinal Hill. The statue measures upwards of six feet in height.

LORD BRABAZON writes that the old York House Water-gate, the work of Inigo Jones, at the bottom of Buckingham-street, Strand, is in danger of removal, through the proposed new street from St. Martin's-place to the Victoria Embankment. He suggests that some means should be found to rescue this old relic, not only from threatened destruction by railway companies, but from neglect and decay.

MR. RICHARD JACKSON, of Leeds, announces the early re-publication, by subscription, of "The Costume of Yorkshire," showing the manners, customs, dress, and industries of Yorkshire, at the beginning of the present century. The work, which was originally published in 1814, is illustrated with *fac-similes* of original drawings in colours, with descriptions in English and French, by the late Mr. George Walker, of Killingbeck Hall, Leeds.

MR. ROWLAND STRONG has commenced the publication of a series o reprints of old plays by English dramatists, including Otway's "Venice Preserved," Drummond's "Cypress Grove," Congreve's "Double-Dealer," Ben Jonson's "Bartholomew Fair," Dryden's "Don Sebastian," and

Webster's "Duchess of Malfi." The editor's object is to reproduce accurately the first, or best editions ; and an analysis of the plot is prefixed to each play.

THE collection of pictures, miniatures, enamels, and other objects of art belonging to the late Mr. Henry G. Bohn, was sold by Messrs. Christie & Co. on the 19th of March and eight following days. The sale included examples of the early French, Italian, Dutch, Flemish, and German schools ; illuminations from ancient missals ; and also pictures by Gainsborough, Holbein, Janet, Kneller, Lely, Zucchero, and other masters.

SOME interesting facts respecting William Gray, author of the "Chorographia," the earliest history of Newcastle-on-Tyne, have recently come to light. A copy of his will, dated 1656, has been found in the archives at Durham, and it is now known that he was connected by marriage with the Ellisons of Newcastle and Hebburn. Lord Northbourne, the present representative of the Ellison family, possesses an interlined copy of the "Chorographia," prepared by the author for a second edition.

THE Council of the Harleian Society has issued the first volume of the "Christenings at St. James's, Clerkenwell," from 1551 to 1700. The continuation up to 1754 will form vol. ii., and is nearly all in the press. The Visitations of Bedfordshire in 1566, 1582, and 1634 are also being issued, and that of Dorsetshire in 1623 is nearly completed. It is proposed to print the weddings which have taken place at St. George's, Hanover-square, from the commencement of the registers, and Mr. G. Leveson Gower, F.S.A., will edit the volume. The registers of Christ Church, Newgate-street, are transcribed, and will shortly be put in the press.

THE old Jamaica Coffee-house in St. Michael's-alley, Cornhill, is to be rebuilt. This coffee-house was for many years the headquarters of those who represented the shipping interest. The old lockers still remain which were used by the City magnates of a past age. In the new building which is to be erected on the site, a record of the past will be kept by painted windows representing old scenes which have taken place within its walls and the arms of the old City merchants. The rooms will be furnished with the old mahogany tables and chairs on which have sat Sir Thomas Gresham and other celebrities of past ages.

MR. W. ST. CHAD BOSCAWEN commenced, on Wednesday, February 25, the delivery of a second course of afternoon lectures on the monuments and inscriptions of the ancient Assyrian and Babylonian empires. With a view to rendering the lectures suitable to all classes of students, Mr. Boscawen selected for his subjects—The Chaldean Temple, its Construction and Services ; the Palace, its Architecture and Ornament ; the Libraries of Chaldea and Assyria ; to be followed by three lectures on the Legends of the Creation, the Deluge, and War in Heaven.

A DISCOVERY just made at the Acropolis of Athens is a valuable addition to the history of Greek art. In the course of the excavations being carried on around the Acropolis the foundations of the Propylæa have been laid bare. Among them have been discovered a number of sheds or verandahs (γεῖσα) built of tufa (πῶρος), which were evidently existing on the spot when the Propylæa were being erected, about 430 B.C., and were built into the foundations. Some of them are in a state of perfect preservation, and retain still quite fresh the paintings with which they were originally decorated. The colours employed were blue, red, and yellow.

THE Delegates of the Clarendon Press announce " The Plays performed by the Crafts or Mysteries of York on Corpus Christi Day in the 14th, 15th, and 16th Centuries," edited from Lord Ashburnham's MS. by Miss Toulmin Smith. The text consists of forty-eight plays, and a full glossary is appended. *Fac-similes* are given of the music accompanying one of the plays, which has been edited by Mr. W. H. Cummings. The introduction contains extracts from the municipal records of York relating to the plays, including Burton's list of A.D. 1415 ; notices of other early religious plays performed at York ; a comparative table of the cycles of English plays ; and a list of all known plays or cycles, and places where they have been performed in Great Britain.

THE collection of water-colour drawings of the early English school, drawings by Blake, with some etchings and engravings belonging to the late Mr. Alfred Aspland, of St. Helen's Field, Dukinfield, Cheshire, lately sold by Messrs. Sotheby, Wilkinson & Hodge, contained many examples that were good as artistic work of the time, and more especially interesting as representing the feeling and style of William Blake. The collection included twelve illustrations to " Paradise Lost," the set of eight illustrations to the " Comus," with several other separate drawings and sketches, most of which are comprised in the numbered list given by Mr. Gilchrist in his life and works of Blake. The 267 lots realised close upon £670.

A PARLIAMENTARY calendar lately issued gives a list of the Cecil MSS., the property of the Marquis of Salisbury, preserved in the library of Hatfield House. As stated in the introduction, these manuscripts, although forming a private collection, may be justly regarded in the light of a national treasure, contributing as they do to one of the most remarkable epochs in English history—the memorable administration of Sir William Cecil, afterwards Lord Burghley, and of his son, the first Earl of Salisbury. The collection consists of upwards of 30,000 documents, including State papers of various reigns, from Edward I., numerous illuminated manuscripts, theological treatises, rolls of genealogy, plans, charts, and voluminous correspondence between illustrious personages.

THE sale of two very interesting collections of autograph letters of Byron and Keats took place on Monday, March 2, at the rooms of Messrs. Sotheby. The letters of Byron, twenty-two in number, were written to his intimate friend, Francis Hodgson, between 1808 and 1821 ; there were also five from Lady Byron, and twenty-eight from Mrs. Augusta Leigh, the sister of the poet, with others from Moore and Rogers, all of which have remained in the possession of the Hodgson family, and have now been sold by the Rev. Canon Hodgson. The Byron letters were sold in one lot for £106, to Mr. Bain, the bookseller of the Haymarket ; the letters from Lord Byron's sister realised £70. The Keats letters (thirty-five in number) were all love letters to Miss Fanny Brawne, written in 1819-20, and obtained high prices throughout, the total of the sale amounting to £544.

THE opening of the Vatican archives to historical research has been followed by the institution, within the Palace itself, of a School of Paleography, in which the Sovereign Pontiff takes extreme interest and pleasure. Here students will be trained in the science of historical study, the first course of lectures being entrusted to Canon Carini, of Palermo, chosen for his eminent attainments in this branch of science. The Canon will give instructions, in the first place, in the science of MSS., Semitic, Greek, Italian, Latin, and Mediæval, with a special study of mediæval Latin work. With this will be a study of ciphers and of the accessory signs of MS. Then will follow instructions on the material of ancient books and the instruments of writings. The formulæ, seals, nomenclature, titles, and signatures of Papal archives are a study in themselves, and will be passed under exhaustive examination.—*Weekly Register.*

A PARLIAMENTARY return has been issued showing the sums expended by the trustees of the National Gallery in each year from 1860 to 1884 inclusive in the purchase of pictures from moneys provided by Parliament. The total sum so expended during that period has been £250,100. Apart from the years 1871-2 and 1872-3, the returns for which are *nil*, the smallest amount expended in any one year was £350 (1877-8), and the largest £76,500 (1870-1.) This is by a long way the largest sum spent in any year embraced in the return, the nearest approach to it being £25,299 in 1882-3. The figures for other years vary from £2,819 to £16,678. During the period mentioned no single picture was purchased for a sum of or exceeding £10,000, but the following prices above that amount have been paid for groups of pictures purchased at the same time out of one collection : £75,000 for 77 pictures and 18 drawings purchased from Sir Robert Peel's collection in 1870-1, £10,395 for 13 pictures from the Barker collection in 1874-5, and £21,042 for 10 pictures from the Duke of Hamilton's collection in 1882-3.

THE first part of the second series of the Palæographical Society's fac-similes, just issued to subscribers, contains two plates of Greek *ostraka* from Egypt, on which are written tax-gatherers' receipts for imposts levied under the Roman dominion, A.D. 39—163, and specimens of the Curetonian palimpsest Homer of the sixth century ; the Bodleian Greek Psalter of about A.D. 950, the Greek Gospels, Codex Γ, of the tenth century, and other Greek MSS. There are also plates from the Ancient Latin Psalter of the fifth century, and other early MSS. of Lord Ashburnham's library ; Pope Gregory's "Moralia," in Merovingian writing of the seventh century ; the Berne Virgil, with Tironian glosses of the ninth century ; the earliest Pipe Roll, A.D. 1130 ; English charters of the twelfth century ; and illuminations in the Bodleian Cædmon, the Hyde Register, the Ashburnham Life of Christ, and the Medici Horæ lately purchased by the Italian Government.

MR. JOHN T. GILBERT, F.S.A., late Secretary of the Public Record Office of Ireland, has recently completed, in five volumes, "Fac-similes of National Manuscripts of Ireland, from the earliest extant specimens to A.D. 1719." The work furnishes characteristic specimens of the documents which have come down from each of the classes which, in past ages, formed the principal elements in the population of Ireland, or exercised an influence in her affairs. It embraces the earliest roll of Chancery in Ireland, the Chartulary of the Priory of St. John of Jerusalem ; the Declaration of the Anglo-Irish against sending Representatives to England ; the Magna Charta Hibernie ; Irish Genealogies ; the Psalter of Christ Church, Dublin, with miniatures, &c. ; the Plantation of Ulster, with map of Ulster lands granted to London Companies in 1622 ; Examination "taken at the rack," and the Cromwellian Roll of Account for Ireland, A.D. 1649-56 ; and a large amount of other interesting information affecting the sister kingdom. The first of the five volumes is already out of print.

THE *Times* of March 12 states that litigation has arisen in France respecting a chalice presented by James I. of England in 1604 to Frias de Velasco, Constable of Spain and Ambassador to London. The chalice is a work of the thirteenth or fourteenth century, and is of great value. The recipient presented it to the Convent of Medina de Pomar, with reversion, in case of the convent being dissolved or being indisposed to keep it, to Burgos Cathedral. It remained in the convent till 1883, when the Abbess, on account of pecuniary straits and fear of robbery, entrusted it to a priest for sale. A French collector, Baron Pichon, bought it for £6,500, but the convent received only £4,500. The Duc de Frias and the Burgos Chapter now claim it. The Spaniard who sold it to Baron Pichon told him it had belonged to the Duc de Frias, and the Baron accordingly wrote to the Duc to inquire as to its history. The latter then wrote to the Abbess, and she admitted the sale, but pleaded that the convent records did not show the origin of the chalice, which tradition connected with a Turkish Sovereign. The chalice, however, bears a Latin inscription, showing when and by whom it was given.

THE following articles, more or less of an antiquarian character, appear among the contents of the reviews and magazines for March : *Cornhill*, "Recollections of Buddhist Monasteries," and "And a Very Old Master ;" *Chambers' Journal*, "Kerry Legends," "City Companies," and "Roman Remains in Lincoln ;" *Fortnightly Review*, "Tasso ;" *Blackwood*, "The Hero of Lepanto and his Times ;" *National Review*, "Nature in Folk-Songs ;" *Argosy*, "Among the Welsh ;" *Macmillan*, "Blackstone," and "Old Mythology in New Apparel;" *Cassell's Magazine*, "France in 1685 ;" *Sunday at Home*, "An Excommunication in the Thirteenth Century ;" *Red Dragon*, "Orinda, a Literary Heroine of the Restoration ;" *Time*, "A Mahdi of the Last Century;" *Merry England*, "Holbein and the Age of Portrait Painting; "*Harper's Magazine*, "The House of Orange ;" *Magazine of Art*, "The Older London Churches ;" *Contemporary Review*, "Native Faiths in the Himalayah ; " *Art Journal*, "Silver Plate at the Bethnal Green Museum ;" *Nineteenth Century*, "The Eton Tutorial System;" *English Illustrated Magazine*, "Pilgrimages."

AN interesting collection of old Japanese "kakemonos" (the painted strips, fastened on rollers, of which the cheap modern examples are so familiar) is on view at the new premises of the Japanese Fine Art Association, in King-street, St. James's. They extend from the fourteenth to the end of the eighteenth century, and bear all the great names from Chodensu to the famous Hokusai. From the hand of the latter, who is regarded as the reformer of Japanese pictorial art and the founder of the modern school, are two very characteristic and beautiful examples ; but they must yield in interest to the work of the older masters, to the "Tahunder-god" of Chodensu, and to the Botticelli-like "Goddess of Mercy" from the hand of Kogen, an artist of the fifteenth century. The collection was formed by the archæologist Wakai, of Tokio, the "art adviser" to the Mikado. He has also sent over some six-fold screens, of unusual brilliancy and splendour, painted by Sanrei, Ippo, and the other eighteenth-century artists, as well as some "vieux lac" of high merit.

CATALOGUES of rare and curious books, most of which contain the names of works of antiquarian interest, have reached us from Mr. E. Parsons, 45, Brompton-road ; Mr. F. Edwards, 83, High-street, Marylebone ; Messrs. Robson & Kerslake, 23, Coventry-street, Haymarket (including the "Nuremburg Chronicle," &c.) ; Messrs. J. Poole & Co, 39, Book-sellers-row, W.C. ; Mr. G. Harding, 6, Sardinia-street, Lincoln's-inn-fields, W.C.; Mr. W. J. Smith, 141, North-street, Brighton (including works from the library of the late Rev. Robert A. Willmott) ; Mr. G. P. Johnston, George-street, Edinburgh (including a selection of scarce and valuable works from the library of the late Sir Henry Seton-Steuart, of Allanton) ; Mr. J. Aston, 49B, Lincoln's-inn-fields, W.C. (including Sale Catalogues of the Beckford, Towneley, Comerford, and Sunderland Libraries, and also index volumes of 1st, 2nd, and 4th series of " Notes and Queries ") ; Mr. H. Gray, Cathedral-yard, Manchester ; Mr. A. Iredale, Torquay (including portraits of the Court of Henry VIII., engraved by Bartolozzi and Cooper) ; Messrs. Reeves & Turner, 196, The Strand ; Von Albert Cohn, Berlin (containing various autographs and historic documents) ; and M. Clouzot, of Niort, France.

AN important discovery has been made in digging the foundations of a new house to the south of the Acropolis at Athens, between the Temple of Jupiter Olympius and the new Military Hospital. This plain, now almost wholly unoccupied, was the site of the city of Athens before Themistocles moved it further away from Phalerum in favour of the Piræus. The discovery consists of an inscription, which is entire, belonging to the beginning of the fifth century, B.C., ordering an enclosure to be made around the Temple of Codrus, and some two hundred olive trees to be planted therein. Our interest in this inscription lies in the fact that no one knew before that there was a temple dedicated to Codrus in Athens. The stone has been purchased by the Greek Archæological Society, and will be shortly published in their *Journal*. A sister society has been founded in Athens for the study of Christian archæology, with the object of examining and preserving whatever remains of Christian antiquity are found in Greece. To most lovers of art it will be undoubtedly a matter of regret that this Association was not founded sooner. How many mosaics and other Byzantine remains in Greece are now lost or ruined beyond hope of repair ! The head of the new society is Alexander Barouchas, and the Secretary I. M. Dambergis, the director of the museum being T. Bisbizes.— *Athenæum.*

THE Rev. Mandell Creighton, Dixie Professor of Ecclesiastical History at Cambridge, has received the degree of M.A., *honoris causâ*, of that University. The Public Orator (Mr. J. E. Sandys), in presenting Mr. Creighton on the occasion, referred to the Professor's volume on " The Age of Elizabeth," and also to his important work on " The History of the Papacy during the Period of the Reformation," the first two volumes of which had already been published. In these volumes, he observed, a large space was devoted to the life and times of Pope Pius II. (Æneas Silvius), some striking scenes from whose career were depicted by the art of Pinturicchio in the Piccolomini Library at Siena. Great, indeed, he continued, would have been the surprise of Æneas Silvius, who once visited England and Scotland, and, while passing through Northumberland, met with some remarkable adventures among a rude and uncivilised people, if he could have foreseen that a day would come when an accomplished scholar in that very county would minutely study his " Commentarii " and trace his chequered career with the faithful pen of an impartial historian. In allusion to one of the aphorisms of that Pope, "dignitatibus viros dandos, non dignitates hominibus," the Orator concluded as follows : " Orator ille si hodie adesse et Professoris nostri merita omnia percensere potuisset, sui proverbii memor non immerito dixisset, hodie non homini cuilibet dignitatem esse datam, sed virum dignum dignitati."

IN the *Globe* of January 31 a correspondent writes respecting the discovery of St. Clement's Well, in the Strand : " This interesting relic of 'Old London' was laid bare during the process of removing the rubbish from the western side of the Royal Courts of Justice. The Percies, in their 'History of London,' vol. ii. p. 167, state that St. Clement's Inn, whose history dates back as early as 1478, took its name from St. Clement's Spring or Well. Under this name it had been known from time immemorial. In Ethelred's reign and afterwards penitents and pilgrims visited this as a holy spot, as well as for rest and refreshment, and the sick for healing, and it was customary for the newly-baptized to assemble here at Ascensiontide and Whitsuntide clad in white robes. Fitzstephen, who wrote in the reign of Henry II., speaks of certain excellent springs whose waters are sweet, salubrious, and clear. Among these Holywell, Clerkenwell, and St. Clement's Well are the principal, as being much the most frequented, both by the scholars from the school (Westminster) and the youth from the City when on a summer's evening they are disposed for an airing. Mr. Nightingale, in 'The Beauties of England and Wales,' published in 1815, says a pump now covers St. Clement's Well ; and in 1841 it is stated that it flowed as steadily and freshly as ever. The well is said to have been originally 300 feet deep. It is now being rapidly filled up with earth. As it does not appear likely that the spot will ever be built upon, an ornamental fountain would be a fitting memorial to mark the spot where once existed St. Clement's Well, as well as to perpetuate its usefulness."

MR. THOMAS BOND, of Tyneham, the editor of Hutchins's "History of Dorset," sends the following to the *Dorset County Chronicle :* "An act of Vandalism has recently been perpetrated in this county which, in an age when ancient monuments are almost daily attracting more and more interest and receiving more and more care from all but the most ignorant and uneducated, seems hardly credible. It is the less justifiable because it cannot plead utility as an excuse. In the church of Lytchet Maltravers there is—alas ! I fear I must almost say there *was*—a sepulchral monument of very great artistic, heraldic, and historical interest. It consisted of a grey marble slab, measuring 9 ft. 10 in. by 3 ft. 6 in., round the verge of which was inlaid a strip of brass containing an inscription in Norman-French, which recorded the death of the deceased interred underneath it and asked for prayers for his soul. Extending throughout the intermediate space was an inlaid brass *frette*, as in heraldic language it would be described. When Hutchins first wrote the 'History of Dorset,' a fragment of this inscription still remained, but before the third edition of his work was published the whole had been removed, and nothing but the matrix remained. There is no difficulty, however, in identifying the monument as commemorating one of the family of Maltravers, who were lords of this manor from the Norman Conquest, a *frette* constituting their armorial bearings. Hutchins considered it clear that the monument was placed here in memory of Sir John Maltravers, Lord Maltravers, who was buried in this church. He was some time constable of Corfe Castle, and one of the principal actors in the barbarous and revolting murder of Edward II. at Berkeley Castle. The character of the man (if, indeed, this is his monument) need not lessen—but, on the contrary, it should rather heighten—the interest attaching to his tomb, which was a remarkable example of monumental art. Such being the case, I feel sure it will be a subject of universal regret that the 'Lord of the Manor,' in laying down an encaustic pavement in the church, has thought fit to use this monument as a base, covering it with a coat of cement, in which the tiles have been embedded, thus concealing it for ever from view and utterly defacing the sculpture. The rector of the parish has, I understand, emphatically remonstrated against this act of pure and wanton mischief, but his remonstrances have been disregarded. The Lord of the Manor claims some individual rights in the aisle in which the tomb was placed, but whether such claim is well founded or not is quite immaterial as regards the present subject, for it is perfectly clear he has acted illegally in injuring and concealing a monument over which he has no legal right of control. The legal right over sepulchral monuments belongs to the representatives of the deceased whom they commemorate, and no one else has any power to deal with them. I believe the Duke of Norfolk is the heir and representative of the family of Maltravers, and he reckons the Barony of Maltravers amongst his other ancient titles. Can nothing be done to rescue this unique and interesting relic of antiquity? If public opinion is invoked I feel sure that so useless and wanton an act of Vandalism will meet with universal condemnation."

Antiquarian Correspondence.

Sin scire labores,
Quære, age : quærenti pagina nostra patet.

All communications must be accompanied by the name and address of the sender, not necessarily for publication.

CURIOSITIES OF TUDOR NOMENCLATURE AND THE IRISH CALENDAR.

(See vol. iv. pp. 118, 222.)

SIR,—Mr. Round contends that when *filius* is followed by a Christian name we may render it Fitz, "and continue it with that name as a sur-name." According to this, " filius Thome " should be " Fitz-Thomas," and " Johannes filius Thome " should be " John Fitz-Thomas "—one person. To this definition I object that, surnames being of very doubtful significance in early times, *filius* followed by a Christian name should never be trans-lated from Records of this date other than " son of." Thus " Johannes filius Thome " should be read " John, son of Thomas "—Thomas himself being further credited, or not, with any nickname we please : so long as we are careful to remember that John is here one person and Thomas another, and that the former is own son to the latter. Otherwise in a period when people were styled by their true titles, and identified only familiarly by their nicknames, there was danger of serious confusion, as I conclusively showed from a case in the Year Books 11-12 Edward III. Here a co-deforciant appealed in Aid-Prayer by his own side is objected to by the demandant's counsel as being a bastard. The rejoinder ensues that, as the person in question is styled in the writ itself " son of Thomas," *ergo, he must be Thomas' son.* The ingenious suggestion is then hazarded by the other side that "son of Thomas "—*i.e.*, " *filius* followed by a Christian name," may be rendered Fitz and be combined with that name " as a surname" (to quote Mr. Round's own definition), and therefore that the demandant's name is John Fitz-Thomas. Now, on Mr. Round's own showing, this is a valid objection, because (as in the case of the Fitz-

Alans, &c., quoted by him) John may here have taken his surname from a remote ancestor, and not from a father called Thomas, and may thus, in truth, have been a bastard.

But, on the other hand, if this had been the case, John would have been styled in the *Latin* writ, according to the correct usage, "Johannes Fitz-Thomas," and not "Johannes filius Thome." The Judge, well versed in a legal formula (the entire ignorance of which has been the cause of Mr. Round's disastrous philological speculations) is down upon the attorney with the reproof, "It will never be adjudged a surname, because you have called him, *in Latin*, 'son of Thomas.'"

If only the wording of this writ had read "Fitz-Thomas" the whole aspect of the case might have been altered, for "Fitz-Thomas," as I have said, may mean anything, whereas "filius Thome" can only mean one thing—and that, "son of Thomas." I must further complain of the disingenuous attempt made by Mr. Round to pervert the sense of my instance by his parentheses. "De G." is not once used in direct connection with John's father, though it is no matter whether we understand it or no. Not otherwise, certainly, should we get an example of Mr. Round's own definition of "*filius* followed by a Christian name," if we persisted in understanding a surname after it in parenthesis.

But if Mr. Round is not satisfied with my present instance, I will find him another—a dozen more, I warrant you, if needed—which does not afford the support of a last straw such as the "sorry quibble" of a parenthesis.

A certain Richard, named after his father Fitz-Steven, grants to I. the manor of W. for term of her life ; and after, Richard's son Gilbert, who calls himself Gilbert Fitz-Steven, grants the reversion to one J. de C. The latter sues a writ of *Quid juris clamat* against the existing life-tenant. The case is argued, and it is objected for I. that J. de C.'s cognizor is incorrectly described in the writ as "Gilbertus, filius Stevani," whereas he is no such person, being "son of Richard son of Stephen." The other side retort that it is notorious that the cognizor's name is "Gilbert Fitz-Steven," and this has only been *Latinised* as "filius Stevani."

Nevertheless the Court holds that "filius Stevani" does not properly describe the grandson of Steven, being a definite statement that he is the latter's very son, and therefore the writ is abated by reason of a misnomer which prevents any "Fine" being made in the case.

Now, this case is conclusive as against Mr. Round. It is really he, as well as the "Editor," who confuses "filius" and "Fitz." "Filius Stevani" is one thing, and "le fitz Estevyn" (I am sorry to observe that Mr. Round would Gallicise it "fils de Estevyn"—"queer Norman-French, you'll say") is quite another. The loose use of fitz as a Norman patronymic is well enough, but filius in Record Latin can never be safely rendered Fitz, according to Mr. Round's definition. By the way, I would add that the false quotation for which Mr. Round takes me to task is very clearly a misprint. I may allege this with some degree of confidence, as the passage in question at p. 183, from which we both quote, was originally written there by myself.　　　　　　　　HUBERT HALL.

A "BOOKE OF THE NOBILITY."

SIR,—I have lately been possessed of an old parchment-bound manuscript book, 7½ by 4¼ inches in size, and of a date somewhere, I presume, between 1623 and 1632. The first page is thus inscribed: "This Booke of the Nobility hath bine Continued from the first yeare of the raigne

Kinge James, to the *Second yeare of the* raigne of Kinge Charles." The words which I have here italicised were subsequently erased in the original, and they seem to indicate the year in which the record was commenced. The next three pages contain the order of "Placeing the Great Officers in the Parliament Chamber according to a Statute 31 Hen. 8;" but in this "order" there is an insertion by a later hand, "Lord vicegerent to take place above yᵉ Archbishops." Then follow 204 artistically illuminated shields of arms of Dukes, Marquesses, Earls, Viscounts, and Barons, with accompanying legends. The first is "Azure, 3 fleurs de lys, or; on a bordure, gules, 8 buckles of the second."——"Loudowick Steward, Duke of Richmond [21 Jac] first created Baron of Settrington, and Earle of Richmond 11 Jacobus." The latest record is that of "Weston, Earle of Portland, and Lord Treasorer 8 Cha," with his shield, "Or, an eagle displayed sable, membered gules."

There is no definite record of the compiler, but the first page has the signature of "Joh. Steward," with this note, "given to me by my owld friend and fellow [word torn off] Mʳ Steward on his death bed." To the cover of the book was once attached a sheet of paper, now torn off, but on a scrap which remains is the date "14 Novembr. 1633." I should be glad to learn anything concerning the probable compiler, and to know whether the roll is of any real interest and value, or worthy a place in your columns.   HENRY NORRIS.
Tamworth.

TO CORRESPONDENTS.

THE Editor declines to pledge himself for the safety or return of MSS. voluntarily tendered to him by strangers.

HERALDICUS.— You are quite right; in our review of Mr. Creeny's book of Foreign Brasses (p. 136, *ante*) mention ought certainly to have been made of the elaborate and standard work of Mr. J. G. Waller and his brother, "A Series of Monumental Brasses." The oversight was quite unintentional.

Books Received.

1. The Monuments at Athens. By P. G. Kastromenos. Translated by Agnes Smith. E. Stanford. 1884.
2. The Chevalier D'Eon. By Capt. J. B. Telfer, R.N., F.S.A. Longmans & Co. 1885.
3. The Abbeys of Arbroath, Balmerino, and Lindores. By G. S. Aitken, F.S.A. (Scot.) Dundee: J. Leng & Co. 1884.
4. Elfrica, an Historical Romance of the 12th Century. By Mrs. E. Boger. 3 vols. W. Swan Sonnenschein & Co. 1885.
5. Western Antiquary. Part 9. Plymouth: W. H. Luke. February, 1885.
6. Parodies. Collected by Walter Hamilton. Part 16. Reeves & Turner. March, 1885.
7. English Etchings. Part xlvi. D. Bogue, 27, King William-street, W.C.
8. Cuthbert of Lindisfarne.—Aidan, the Apostle of the North. By Dr. Alfred C. Fryer. Partridge & Co. 1885.
9. Chronicles of the Abbey of Elstow. By the Rev. S. R. Wigram, M.A. Parker & Co. 1885.
10. Northamptonshire Notes and Queries. Part v. Northampton Taylor & Son.

11. Miscellanea Genealogica et Heraldica. No. 15. Hamilton, Adams & Co. March, 1885.

12. Manx Note-Book. No. 1. Douglas: G. H. Johnson.

13. Bouquet. By Wm. Bayley. Bayley & Co., Cockspur-street. 1885.

14. Shropshire Folk-lore. Edited by Charlottte S. Burne. Part ii. Trübner & Co. 1885.

15. Notes on Wanswell Court —The Berkeley Manuscripts, and their Author, John Smyth.—The Shipwreck of Sir Cloudesley Shovell on the Scilly Islands in 1707.—The Last Hours of Count Solms. By James H Cooke, F.S.A. Gloucester: J. Bellows.

16. The Library Chronicle. Published for the Library Association at 137, Long-acre.

17. Exeter during the Religious Persecutions and Rebellions. By T. J. Northy. Plymouth: *Western Antiquary* Office. 1884.

18. The Dutch Church Registers. Edited by W. J. C. Moens. Privately printed. Lymington: 1884.

19. Gundrada de Warrenne. By Robt. E. Chester Waters, B.A. Exeter: W. Pollard. 1884.

20. The Cries of London. (Second Edition.) By Charles Hindley. London: C. Hindley, Booksellers-row.

21. List of Contributions to " Notes and Queries " written by the Rev. J. Pickford. Bale & Sons, 87, Great Titchfield-street, W. 1885.

22. Hints to Collectors of Thackeray's Works. By C. P. Johnson. G. Redway. 1885.

23. Le Livre. Nos. 62 and 63. Paris: 7, Rue St. Benoit. Feb. 1885.

24. Electricity. By W. E. Steavenson, M.D. Churchill. 1884.

25. Harrow School and its Surroundings. By Percy M. Thornton. Allen & Co. 1885.

Books, &c., for Sale.

Works of Hogarth (set of original Engravings, elephant folio, without text), bound. Apply by letter to W. D., 56, Paragon-road, Hackney, N.E

Original water-colour portrait of Jeremy Bentham, price 2 guineas. Apply to the Editor of this Magazine.

A large collection of Franks, Peers and Commoners'. Apply to E. Walford, 2, Hyde Park Mansions, N.W.

Notes on Poems and Reviews. By A. C. Swinburne. Address, E. Walford, 2, Hyde Park Mansions, N.W.

Books, &c., Wanted to Purchase.

Antiquarian Magazine and Bibliographer, several copies of No. 2 (February, 1882) are wanted, in order to complete sets. Copies of the current number will be given in exchange at the office.

Dodd's Church History, 8vo., vols. i. ii. and v.; Waagen's Art and Artists in England, vol. i.; East Anglian, vol. i., Nos. 26 and 29. The Family Topographer, by Samuel Tymms, vol. iii.; Notes and Queries, the third Index. Johnson's Lives of the Poets (Ingram and Cooke's edition), vol. iii. Chambers' Cyclopædia of English Literature, vol. i. Address, E. Walford, 2, Hyde Park Mansions, Edgeware-road, N.W.

A Frank of Francis Atterbury, Bishop of Rochester between 1713 and 1723, and other Bishops' franks of the 18th century. Apply to J. D.

Archæologia, vols. xxii., xxiii., xxiv.; vol. xxxviii. part i.; vols. xxxix. xl., xli. part i.; vol. xlvii. part ii. A. G. H., 47, Belsize-avenue, N.W.

R

MARY & ELISA CHULKHURST

IN A
1100 34

BIDDENDEN

THE "BIDDENDEN MAIDS."

(*See p.* 223.)

W. Dampier, *del.*

The

Antiquarian Magazine
& Bibliographer.

The Playhouses at Bankside in the Time of Shakespeare.

PART I.

By W. RENDLE, F.R.C.S.

VEN now, after so much research and discussion, the topography and identity of these places are by no means clear, and this chiefly because scarcely any inquirer seems to think it necessary to know the Bankside, and to study it with the maps before him; surely it would be very useful and pleasurable to know the locality as it was, and to be somewhat clear about these renowned playhouses. We are well supplied with maps; there are those of Aggas, and Norden,. and Faithorne; and to bring these in harmony with more modern times, while yet many of the old names remained, there is the map by Rocque of 1746—1751.

Our best writers who touch upon the subject,* always excepting Mr. Halliwell-Phillipps, are far from clear. All my friend's stores have been freely opened to me, and I have studied and lived at hand in Southwark some sixty years or more; I may, therefore,

---

* One authority says: "I have sometimes doubted if the Hope were not identified with Paris Garden." The two were, in fact, in different manors, and the Hope was built about fifteen years after the other. In the last edition of Collier, the vignette which had represented the Swan now represents the Fortune. Cunningham's Hand-book of London notes the Swan, but his "Swan" was· ar from here, near to London-bridge.

without arrogance, attempt a better and more certain narrative than has yet been given of this interesting place and time.

I had intended to make a complete work of it, and may yet do so, in a second edition of " Old Southwark and its People." But time goes on, and I am become one of its old people; this hints to me that I may not be able to complete this desire of my later life, albeit the work is well-nigh done.

No one will, I think, deny that this knowledge will help us to a much better estimate of the Bankside, its people, and their doings. It will be needful, first, to glance at the houses erected for sports, bear-gardens, and the like, built, as some of them were, for

SMITH'S ARMS, BANKSIDE.

a double purpose. The bear-master and his rough creatures had their days; and anon, the stage placed and the scene shifted, the great productions of Marlowe, Massinger, Fletcher, and their fellows, are presented within the same walls.

Let me then land at Paris Garden Stairs, and as I go, portray as well as I can, what I see—with the mind's eye—of the place during that hundred years or so of the reigns of Elizabeth and James.

Here, then, exactly opposite Bridewell, are Paris Garden-lane and Stairs. As we land we may look about us, and even cast an eye forward in time, a hundred years it may be. We see by the signs of the houses about, the kind of enjoyment provided. The Orange Tree-inn, at the corner next the river, The Windmill, Five Pints,

Hot Water-inn; near at hand the Next Boat, Beggars' Bush, and Holland's Leaguer; Noah's Ark is there; and opposite, close to Cardinal Cap Alley, is the Smith's Arms, which looks in the illustration opposite * as if the bear people, the players, and the poets had refreshed themselves within it long ago. At hand, too, is the Falcon, dating from before 1540, its stairs, and the ferry which long ago went to and fro on the river at this spot. The houses noted were places of diverse refreshment, some of them tea-gardens by the riverside to the beginning of the last century.

We see in the map of 1627 † plots of ground, and small houses beginning to multiply upon them, and sparsely here and there are Rents and Alleys, named after owners, whose names appear in the map and in the token-books. These small plots of ground, extending from Upper Ground, the highway parallel with the river, to the river margin, are interesting, showing in what way the copyholders began to cover the ground with houses.

The oldest view in Aggas's map is, I suppose, precise enough as to the locality, and rudely shows the stairs, lane, houses, and boats; the streams from St. George's Fields, one of the ancient crosses erected every here and there in the public ways. We see in Rocque's map old names identifying the locality, and hinting at the old uses; for not until after this, in our time of railways, did the Bankside advance beyond all recognition.

Passing up Paris Garden-lane, a little to the left over Mill-bridge, and then on again south, we come to the "Old Playhouse" of the 1627 map. Paris Garden Playhouse, that is, the Swan, what is left of it, no doubt in bad condition by this time,

MANOR MAP, 1627.

is, in fact, the "Old Playhouse." The Swan is some six poles due south from the landing-place at Paris Garden Stairs. "The Swan took its name from a house so called," says an authority; this is scarcely possible. The Swan, that is, the *house*, not the *playhouse*,

---

* The gift of my friend Mr. Jarvis, a Shakesperean author. (See p. 208.)
† My friend Mr. Marsland's old map of the manor of Paris Garden is now in the Guildhall Library; à small portion of it is given above.

the signe of the Swanne, "now built, 1606, is in the occupation of Alexander Walshe, a fruiterer." *

Usually playhouses are first; and the house of refreshment at hand is named after it. The Swan playhouse was built about 1598, and the house about 1606.

Cunningham is wrong. The first notice I find of this theatre is 1594. " The Lord Mayor, writing to the Lord High Treasurer," says that " Francis Langley, one of the Alnagers, for sealing cloth, intends to erect a new stage, or theatre, on the Bankside," and prays that the same may be prevented.†

1598. "It is ordered by the Vestry‡ that Mr. Langley's new buildings shall be viewed, and that he and others shall be moved for money for the poor in regard to the playhouses and for tithes."

In 1600, we identify the house. In a letter to the Justices of Surrey, 1600, Peter Bromville is recommended from the Court to their favour; he is known to the French King for his great skill in feats of activities ; " he has exhibited the same before the Queen," and wishing to appear in some public place, "*has chosen the Swann, in Old Paris Garden, being the house of Francis Langley.*" §

1602. We have Ben Jonson playing *Zulziman*, at Paris Garden, that is, the Swan.

1603. "England's Joy," an apotheosis of Queen Elizabeth, is played here.

> "Poor old Vennor, that plain dealing man,
> Who acted England's Joy first at the Swan."||

1604. At a contest for a prize at the Swan, one Turner is thrust in the eye and killed.

1611. Moll, the roaring drab, is told how a Knight, seeing the last new play at the Swan, lost his purse with seven angels ¶ in it.

Among others, Middleton's play of "A Chaste Maid in Cheapside" was performed at the Swan.

1613. The Globe is now destroyed by fire, the Swan, no doubt, supplying some of the lack during the time of the rebuilding, the chief use being, no doubt, at the Blackfriars.

---

* State Papers, Dom., James I., vol. xix., No. 100, Suit for lands concealed.
† City Remembrancia, p. 354 : 1579—1664.
‡ Minutes St. Saviour's Vestry.
§ This valuable note was with his perennial generosity handed to me by Mr. Halliwell-Phillipps.
|| Taylor, the Water Poet.
¶ A gold coin, with the figure of an angel on it, worth about ten shillings.

1613. Gilbert Katheren's contract to pull down the Old Bear Garden-house, on the northern square courtilage of the lane called the Bear Garden. He rebuilds a bear-garden, now named the Hope; and "the Hope is to be in compass, form, wideness, like the play-house called the Swan in the lib'tie of Paris Garden;" but of this more hereafter, in another paper.

1623. Licence for T. B. and three assistants to make shows of Italian motion, at the Princes Arms, or the Swan. About this time prize-fights are at the Swan, which are noticed by Malone.

1627. The date of the map of the Manor of Paris Garden, in which is the "Old Playhouse," otherwise the Swan; this map will well reward a close study; it is, as I have said, at the Guildhall Library, and has been copied for the New Shakespeare Society.

1632. Is a picturesque passage,* touching the three playhouses. The lady of Holland's Leaguer is recommending her house and the neighbourhood; "there are," she says, "pleasant walks, and a con-course of strangers; three famous amphitheatres can be seen from the turret, one, the continent of the world (meaning the Globe), to which half the year (summer) a world of beauties and of brave spirits resort—a building of excellent hope (The Hope) for players, wild beasts, and gladiators—and one other, that the lady of the leaguer, or fortress, could almost shake hands with, now (1632) fallen to decay, and, like a dying swanne (The Swan) hangs her head and sings her own dirge." As the Leaguer says, it had now fallen to decay, and was probably out of all practical use by 1633.

We have books, known as Token-books, most interesting to us, both as to what we find and what we have lost. These rough, chandler-shop-like books are annals in possession of St. Saviour's Vestry; and from their ragged, neglected look, they reflect no credit upon the richer and chiefer people of the parish; indeed, but for the care of the Registrar, they would probably have been wholly in rags and tatters long ago. An account of them by myself is to be found in *Notes and Queries*, August, 1878, and in *The Genealogist*, January, 1884. These books comprise a list of places, courts, &c., and of all people of age to take the Sacrament in all the years, say from 1587 to 1646; it will be seen presently how valuable they are.

Unhappily the books for the palmiest years of Shakespeare's and Alleyn's doings are, the best of them, missing. A tale of crime appears to be involved; it may be concerning people of some

---

* Holland's Leaguer, 1632.

literary position now passed away—suspected, indeed known, but not brought home. Some extracts from these token-books, pertinent to the Swan, will at least imply the serious loss we have sustained. They contain, as will be seen, stray notes and entries over and above the regular business of the book :—

1596. Mayster Pope has four new built houses in Mayster Langley's ground.

Thomas Pope is in the list of principal actors in Shakespeare's Plays, in the Edition of 1623.

1602. Mr. Langley's New Rents near the playhouse.

Many such entries.

1621. Near the Playhouse, Paris Garden. John Lowen, et Ux.

Joane Lowen.

Servants.

Lowen, a Shakespearean actor in the same list.

1623. Near the Playhouse. Mr. Doctor Gilbourne.

Mistres Leake.

John Lowen.

Leake is of the great brewer family. A Samuel Gilburne is in the list of players. In the margin, by these names, is "Mill-Bridge, close to the Swan."

1627. Near the Playhouse. Robert Nashe.

Peter Hemynges.

Mr. John Lowen.

Widowe Phillipps.

Mr. Leake.

These people are all of playhouse or other known associations.

1629. Copt Hall, near the Playhouse, as the map shows.

1630. Pigsnie Lane—street side from the Swan upward. &c. &c.

At least some seventeen to twenty names, all of known actors of the time, appear in the books, and in them also are clues to questions of historical, religious, and dramatic moment; the points are clear to students of that great period.

(*To be continued.*)

THE ARCHBISHOP OF CANTERBURY has conferred the degree of D.C.L. on the Rev. John Charles Cox, of Enville, Staffordshire, in recognition of his labours in arranging and tabulating the muniments and archives of Lichfield Cathedral.

Banquo and Fleance.

By James A. Smith.

CHAPTER I.

A'S most genealogists are doubtless aware, the able and laborious George Chalmers, author of " Caledonia," following the lead of Lord Hailes, has attacked the Banquo and Fleance tradition of the origin of the Royal House of Stuart, and claims to have refuted it as a piece of historical fiction—taking credit to himself at the same time for having first discovered and pointed out the true progenitor of this dynasty in the person of " Alan, the son of Flaald," progenitor of the Fitz Alans, Earls of Arundel in England. Chalmers points to the unchallengeable fact that Walter, the first High Steward, is uniformly designated " Walter, son of Alan," in every charter of his time in which his paternity is referred to, and never as Walter, son of Fleance, and that the mystery who Alan was had puzzled every genealogist until his own successful discovery.

According all due credit to Chalmers for this discovery and its results, as far as they go, I feel bound, on grounds of historical integrity, to call attention to a somewhat remarkable set of facts, beyond the range to which he carried the inquiry, and which fairly challenge the logical accuracy of his somewhat too confident *ergo*, that the Banquo and Fleance tradition was wholly a fiction. Accepting the fact he claims to have established, that Walter, the young Welshman, was not the son of Fleance, but the son of Alan, and grandson of Flaald, the question still remains as puzzling as ever, though one generation more remote than the range of Chalmers' inquiry, viz., Who was this Flaald, the father of Alan ? To give point to the question, and direction to the investigation before us—was he, in fact, any other than the son of Banquo ? The means of following out this inquiry are almost exclusively English, and after going into them so far, I found that I had been in a great measure anticipated by the Rev. R. W. Eyton, the learned author of the " Antiquities of Shropshire," who, in vol. vii. of that work (pp. 211-23 *et seq.*), retraverses the whole subject with an accession of facts which Chalmers never had before him, and, while submitting the entire subject to further consideration, does not hesitate to place on record his own conclusion, *ad interim*, as follows (p. 277) : " My belief, then, is that the son of Fleance was named Alan, not Walter, and that he whom the English called Alan Fitz Flaald was the person in question. The change from Flaucus to Flaaldus is not very great, when we compare it with other instances where a foreign name had to be accommodated to an English ear. We must remember, too, how a Norfolk jury, wishing evidently to designate the father of Alan Fitz Flaald, called him Flaucus, though this probable approach to etymological correctness was adulterated with a great historical inaccuracy."

While Mr. Eyton thus substantially arrives at the precise conclusion at which we are now to aim, it is necessary, as matter of accuracy, to point out that he does so by very inadequate and incorrect means, which do not, on investigation, support his deductions. Thus his conclusion obviously, but inaccurately, presupposes that the true name of Banquo's son was *Fleance*, and that the Norfolk jury in naming him *Flaucus* made an approach to etymological correctness from *Flaald* toward *Fleance*. He also assumes that there was some earlier Scottish tradition than that current in England, and that in this Scottish tradition *Fleance* was the recorded name. But of such an earlier Scottish tradition there is not the slightest evidence, and Mr. Eyton, as we shall presently see, was by these two assumptions completely misled in basing his conclusion.

The tradition, from its recording the fate of Fleance in Wales, clearly suggests that it travelled, in its completed form, from the South to the North, and probably not before the Stuarts, through their progenitor Walter, son of Alan, and his immediate descendants, had grown to national importance in Scotland; perhaps not till the accession to the throne of Robert II. That is really the logical aspect of the question, and there is, and was before Mr. Eyton in his own pages, much better evidence in support of the tradition, had he not been misled by his assumptions before mentioned, than that on which he has chosen to found his conclusion above quoted. The *Flaald* and *Flathald* versions of the name are authentic forms of it, but the version *Fleance* is not. We have the name varying Flaaldi, Flahaldi, Fladaldi, and Flathaldi in the charters and citations of them as used by Alan, and it is not necessary to suppose that he made any mistake in thus recording the name of his father, or in designating himself, by part of his own signature, when subscribing a public document. If, therefore, Alan was the grandson of Banquo, that was the true name of his father and of Banquo's son, and not Flaucus nor Fleance, as traditionally handed down. The Flaucus and Fleance versions of the name must have come into existence and use after the death of Alan, and otherwise than through him, and it remains to be considered how they were originated. Mr. Eyton himself shows that the Flaucus version arose with a Norfolk jury in 1275, which then, more than 150 years after Alan's death, made a report on the tenure of a considerable fief held by the Fitz Alans in Norfolk-shire. Quoting the incident he says: "These jurors said that Melam (Mileham) with its appurtenances was in the hand of William the Bastard at the Conquest, and the said King gave the said manor to a certain knight who was called *Flaucus*, who came with the said King into England, and afterwards the said manor (descended) from heir to heir till (it came) to John Fitz Alan, now (1275) in the Kings' custody.[24] [To this Mr. Eyton adds the following foot-note: "[24] Rot. Hundred, i. 434. The jurors made a mistake as to the name of the minor then in custody. It was certainly Richard (*i.e.*, Richard Fitz Alan, not John Fitz Alan). There was, therefore, a Norfolk tradition, the counterpart of that current in Shropshire, except that it made Flaucus or Flaald the feofee of the Conqueror and not his son Alan." This is the "great historical inaccuracy" referred to by Mr. Eyton in the first quotation from him *supra*.] (Antiquities of Shropshire, vol. vii. p. 213.) Mr. Eyton, as we have said, assumes *Flaucus* to be the Norfolk jury's version of Fleance, and Fleance to be the Scottish version of the name. It now remains therefore to discover, if possible, how the Fleance version arose, and, having no separate Scottish tradition to refer to before that of Hector Boece, we are driven to search for earlier English authority than the Norfolk Flaucus of 1275. In pursuing that search we come upon the "Fitz Warin Chronicle," composed mostly about 1241, *i.e.*, thirty-four years earlier, and chiefly derived from the songs of the Trouvères of, so far as the matter in question is concerned, the preceding century. This chronicle, edited for the Warton Club by T. Wright, Esq., and printed in 1855, professing, *inter alia*, to give an account of William the Conqueror's visit to Wales, incidentally mentions the name of Alan as "Alan Fitz Flaeu." This new version of the name we may therefore presume was transcribed from a trou-badour song of the twelfth century. But the significance of it is, that in it we have very plainly the original germ of the name Fleance, for we have only to suppose it to be, as it certainly would be in some of the early transcriptions, converted into a Latin nominative by the addition of the letter s when mentioning Flaald alone, and we have the name written *Flaeus*, which, in the writing of that period, would with equal propriety sound *Flaeus* or *Flaens* according to the taste or discretion of the reader, while *Flaens* in the unsettled spelling of these times would be the exact equivalent of *Fleance*—both being

obviously identical in sound. The introduction of the Fleance version is thus distinctly traceable, and the period of its introduction
identified ; and I venture to think that, beyond this, the name Fleance
never had any real existence or authority. Mr. Eyton. had the
passage of the Fitz Warin chronicle before him in which the name
as " Alan· Fitz Flaeu " occurs—in fact he quotes it ; but, for reasons
already explained, completely fails to note its significance in furnish-
ing the above remarkable explanation and indissoluble *nexus* with the
tradition. He believed that "Fleance" stood recorded in some
early Scottish history or legend. But there was no such thing, and
Chalmers (Caledonia, vol. i. p. 411, foot-note *f.*) tells us : " Even
the names of Banquo and Fleance seem to be fictitious, as they are
not Gaelic." As to the name Fleance, we quite agree with Chalmers
for the reasons above stated, but must reserve consideration of this
objection till we see if we cannot turn his argument against himself.

But there is another point of considerable interest and importance
on the very surface of the case which Mr. Eyton has very strangely
overlooked altogether, *i.e.*, How came the Norman prefix *Fitz* to be
adopted by Alan and his descendants ? We know this to be a distinctive surname given by the Normans and their descendants to the
illegitimate sons of kings and princes of the blood. This, as a general
rule, is what it signifies, and what it must be held to signify here.
Of Flaald we find no authentic English mention whatever, save simply
in connection with the name of his son, who is certainly called Alan
Fitz Flaald. What claim, then, could Alan have to the surname Fitz
through Flaald his father? On this subject history is absolutely
silent and genealogy a blank, unless the tradition as to Banquo and
his son be referred to. But turning to it we at once find the missing
explanation, for the tradition tells us that when Fleance fled from
Scotland to escape Macbeth's emissaries, he found refuge at the
Court of Gryffith-ap-Llewellyn (eighteenth king of North Wales)
where, being possessed of winning and agreeable manners and an
attractive person, he succeeded in becoming the paramour of the
Princess Nesta, or Mary, Gryffith's daughter, and was slain by King
Gryffith for the offence. If, then, Alan were the fruit of Fleance and
Nesta's amour, we have at once a ground for his adopting the surname
Fitz at the Court of the early Norman kings at which he lived.
Banquo was also, according to the tradition, a grandson of Grimus,
King of Scotland, and, therefore, a prince of the blood, and Fleance
was, by his mother, said to be descended from an earlier Scottish
king, so that Alan, as the son of Nesta and Fleance, had a right to

the surname Fitz through both his father and mother. If these be not the reasons for his adopting this prefix, history certainly presents us with no other, though the unquestionable fact still remains that Alan was called Fitz Flaald, and that his lawful children and their English descendants were called Fitz Alan, as a proof that Flathald, Flaens, or Fleance, was not a person of mean rank.

Then there is another circumstance, the significance of which Mr. Eyton has failed to perceive, though he establishes the fact itself completely enough, viz., that Alan Fitz Flaald held the lordship of Mileham in Norfolkshire among, if not as, the first of his English possessions, and before he acquired any of his Shropshire lands. Mr. Eyton cannot perceive any connection which Alan could possibly have on the ground of descent or otherwise with Norfolkshire, even keeping the tradition in view. But the tradition does give to Alan a very positive connection with Norfolkshire, not *per expressum* certainly, but by implication ; for Nesta's mother, the wife of Gryffith-ap-Llewellyn, was Algitha, or Editha, daughter of Algar Earl of Mercia, the son of Earl Leofric and the celebrated Lady Godiva, and Mr. Eyton, though mentioning this fact, strangely overlooks the connected circumstance that Algar was also, as history testifies, Earl of Norfolk, and that he may have quite probably dowered his daughter Algitha with the lordship of Mileham and other lands from his Norfolk earldom on her marriage with the King of North Wales. A presumption of some strength in favour of the relationship of Alan to Nesta and her mother is therefore created at this point by his first acquisition being the Norfolk lordship of Mileham. According to the tradition, Algar, Earl of Mercia and Norfolk, would be great-grandfather to Alan, and undoubtedly, according to history, Algar got the Earldom of Norfolk from Edward the Confessor by the forfeiture of Harold, Edward's brother-in-law, during a rebellion in which Harold joined his turbulent father Earl Godwin. Algar restored the Earldom of Norfolk to Harold on his reconciliation with Edward in 1052, and Harold, on the death of Godwin, his father, gave it back to Algar for his generosity ; after which, Algar being in exile for some of his numerous offences, the Earldom came again to the King, who, at Harold's intercession, pardoned and restored Algar, so that he continued to enjoy this earldom till his death.

The tradition tells us that the offspring of Fleance and Nesta was " reared in the country," *i.e.*, not at the Court of North Wales, and that, on growing up, some one ventured to reproach him with the circumstances of his birth, when the fiery boy slew his insulter and had to fly. . . . As the probabilities seem to point to not later than the year 1050 as the period of Alan's birth, and as Gryffith-ap-Llewellyn was slain by some of his own inmates in 1063, hired, it is said, by Harold, who certainly married Gryffith's widow Algitha, the mother of Nesta, Alan may have been about fifteen when he fled from Wales, and it is quite probable that, on doing so, he would fly to Algitha and Harold her new husband, who being King of England from the death of Edward in January, 1066, to October of that year, when he fell at the battle of Hastings, would be also again in possession of his deceased father-in-law Algar's Earldom of Norfolk, for it was in the Crown at the death of the Confessor, and also at the Conquest. We know that Algar's sons Morcar, Earl of Northumberland, and Edwin, Earl of Chester, who would then be brothers of King Harold's Queen, took part with Harold against the Normans, but that after Harold's death they deserted the citizens of London on Edgar Atheling being brought forward, and rendered homage to William, who took them to Normandy with him in March, 1067; and, on the hypothesis of the tradition, it is quite within ordinary probability that so promising a youth, as Alan's subsequent career implies he must then have been, may have gone in the train of these, his kinsmen, and by some early feat of daring won the notice and favour of the Conqueror, to whose liberality the bend sinister on Alan's escutcheon would form no bar. Thus, and in no other connected way, can we account for Alan Fitz Flaald acquiring the lordship of Mileham, out of which, as shown by charters, he made donations to the Cathedral Priory of Norfolk, and also, in conjunction with his wife Adelina, to the Priory of Castle Acre. Alan, therefore, certainly did acquire that lordship, and was in great favour with the Norman kings. I reject altogether Mr. Eyton's suggestion that he first fled to Scotland, and only came to England with the Princess Matilda on her marriage with Henry I. His adoption of the surname Fitz could not have been made in Scotland, in which no such usage prevailed, but implies an early contact with the Norman Court and customs.

(To be continued.)

Forecastings of Nostradamus.

By C. A. WARD.

PART VII.

(Continued from p. 58.)

THE French used always to engage in a battle willingly on St. Louis' Day, April 11, and the English on St. George's Day, April 23. But September 3, St. Mansuetus Day, was ruinous to the Royalists and prosperous to Cromwell. He won the Battle of Dunbar on September 3, 1650, and the Battle of Worcester on September 3, 1651.

With all this Nostradamus tells Prince Charles to hope on, for—

CENTURY X. QUATRAIN 4 (p. 38).

" Sur la minuit conducteur de l'armée
Se sauvera, subit esvanouy,
Sept ans après sa fame non blasmée,
A son retour ne dira-t-on qu'ouy."

" Upon the stroke of midnight the leader of the army shall save himself and pass away suddenly. Seven years later, his fame no longer clouded, he shall return, and no one say anything but *yes*."

At this point one of those curious incidents in history is noted by D. D. The Battle of Worcester, so decisive in its consequences, commenced at three o'clock in the afternoon on September 3, 1651, as before noted, and at three o'clock in the afternoon on September 3, 1658, Cromwell died, on what is called his *Fortunate Day*. "Nature herself," says his last chronicler, in the ninth edition of the "Encyclopædia Britannica," " seeming to prophesy, in the voice of the great tempest that swept over England, that a great power had passed away." It was a tremendous tempest, no doubt, and men at the time said the Devil had run away with *Old Noll*. He certainly died broken-hearted, when the last Parliament convened by him in January, 1658, refused to acknowledge his House of Peers. So great a burden " drank up his spirits," says Maidston.

We get a further prediction at—

CENTURY X. QUATRAIN 22 (p. 39).

" Pour ne vouloir consenter au divorce,
Qui puis après sera cogneu indigne,
Le Roy des isles sera chassé par force,
Mis á son lieu qui de Roy n'aura signe."

" The King will not agree to the divorce of his crown, which would be afterwards thought unworthy, so will be driven from home by force, and a thing put in his place with no sign of kingship."

The Republicans murdered the King and gave the rule to Cromwell, driving the future Charles II. into France.

CENTURY VIII. QUATRAINS 41—57—76.

(41) "Eleu sera Renard, ne sonnant mot,
    Faisant le Saint public, vivant pain d'orge,
    Tyrannizer après tant à un cop,
    Mettant à pied les plus grands sur la gorge."

(57) "De soldat simple parviendra en Empire,
    De robbe courte parviendra à la longue :
    Vaillant aux armes en Eglise ou plus pyre,
    Vexer les prestres comme l'eau fait l'esponge."

(76) "Plus macelin que Roy en Angleterre,
    Lieu obscur nay par force aura l'Empire ;
    Lasche sans foy sans loy saignera terre,
    Son temps s'approche si pres que je souspire."

" A fox shall be elected, who personates the simple ; playing saint in public and living on barley bread. He will tyrannise at once, and set his foot on the necks of the greatest."

The next verse stands both for Cromwell and Bonaparte.

" From a simple soldier he shall advance to Empire. From the military short robe he will reach the flowing purple. Valiant in arms, but in the Church degraded, he will treat the priests as water does the sponge.
"More butcher than a king of England, obscurely born, he will seize the reins of government. A coward, faithless, lawless, he will bleed the land, and his period is so near at hand that I draw my breath affrighted."

Cromwell was a great Chiliast, or Fifth Monarchy man. He was moderate in diet, and much more given to ambition than to pleasure, as is the case with men of his saturnine complexion. "His fortunate star, Mars," so says our learned D. D., had rendered him "the glory of a valiant hero and general" (p. 43).

Here follows D. D.'s notion of a "*Wig*, or *Trimmer*, that is, a wavering man or hypocrite, from the original words to '*wag* and to *trim* a boat" (p. 48). Of course, we know that his etymology is not worth much.

CENTURY II. QUATRAINS 51, 52, 53.

" Le sang du juste à Londres fera faute,
    Brulez par foudres de vingt trois les six ;
    La dame antique cherra de place haute,
    De mesme secte plusieurs seront occis."

" Dans plusieurs nuits la terre tremblera ;
    Sur le printemps deux effors suite ;
    Corinthe, Ephese aux deux mers nagera,
    Guerre s'esmeut par deux vaillans de luite."

" La grande peste de cité maritime,
    Ne cessera que mort ne soit vengée
    Du juste sang par pris danné sans crime,
    De la grande dame par feincte n'outragée."

Here we have a most remarkable prophecy of the Fire of London :—

"Bruslé par foudres vingt-trois les six" (1666).
"De mesme secte plusieurs seront occis."

A great many of one and the same sect shall be killed. A bloody sea-war took place in 1665, 1666, and 1667 between England and the seven united provinces of the Netherlands, cruising in the narrow seas, which he likens to Corinth and Ephesus, and he describes them as they really were, commencing with each ensuing spring—*sur le printemps.* D. D. also remarks that they were so obstinately contested, all these fights, that they would last for days on a stretch, or, as Nostradamus says, *nights. Plusieurs nuits la terre tremblera,* according to the English custom of reckoning by a *fortnight* and not fourteen days. Now, the French reckon the fortnight as a *quizaine,* that is, up to the 15th day, which, of course, contains only 14 nights; and you might say *la terre tremblera,* for the cannon re-echoing between the cliffs shook them sensibly. *La grande peste* is the plague, and *la grande dame* is the great city, London, metropolis, mother-city—a kind of Eastern way of speaking. D. D., in his learned way, says here: "The great fire has only metamorphosed the city, *ex Ligneâ in Lateritiam,*" converting it from wood to brick.

CENTURY III. QUATRAIN 80.

"Du regne Anglois le digne dechassé,
Le conseiller par ire mis à feu
Ses adherans iront si bas tracer,
Que le bastard sera demy receu."

"From the kingdom of England when the unworthy one is driven away; his councillor shall angrily be cast into the furnace; and his adherents shall take to courses so unworthy that the nation shall be half inclined to receive the Bastard."

King James II. is of course to be taken here as the unworthy one; but some of the English editions read "worthy," and the scansion of the verse will admit both. "The King," says D. D., "was likewise both in relation to the different judgments formed about it. To a Papist he was very worthy; to a Protestant, looking with other eyes, he would appear utterly unworthy."

King Charles had, when in exile, an illegitimate son, the Duke of Monmouth, whom he had named James. The bastard pretended legitimacy, and landed in the West of England with a small army in 1685. But he was routed in the first encounter, brought to the Tower, and beheaded on that hill of death adjacent to it. The people now turned to William, Prince of Orange, who could claim the British Crown by a twofold title. His mother, Mary, was the daughter of Charles I., whom we see as a child in Vandyke's canvas, and his wife was Mary, the daughter of James II. himself.

As the fleet that bore him coasted westerly, courier after courier came galloping over London Bridge, so that the citizens crowded thither to learn the news, and, hearing that the Dutch forces were large, concluded that if they refused their trained bands when called for by the King, he would soon be rendered powerless to withstand his son-in-law. The King fled, and Parliament, declaring his flight to be abdication, elected the Prince of Orange, 13th February, 1689.

The bastard was half received, as Nostradamus says, and the unworthy King *dechassé*.

(To be continued.)

Nooks and Corners of Old England.

NO. IV.—BIDDENDEN, KENT.

FAR away from the busy haunts of men, located upon the high ground overlooking the Wealden district of Kent, lies the peaceful and secluded village of Biddenden, a spot which has become famous among Kentish men by reason of an Eastertide custom which has prevailed there for several centuries. The village is situated about six miles eastward from the market-town of Cranbrook, and four miles from Headcorn, where there is a station on the South-Eastern Railway. The church, which is of some interest, is a large handsome structure, with portions ranging in date from the Early-English to the Late-Perpendicular periods. It consists of a nave and side aisles, chancel with aisles or chapels, and a lofty embattled and pinnacled tower. The south chancel aisle is ceiled with wainscoat in panels, the corners of which are carved and painted with different devices and armorial bearings, among which are those of the See of Canterbury. In 1643 some land in this parish was left by Alice Bedlynston to make a new window on the south side of the church; and in the beginning of the reign of Henry VIII. a new aisle was built by the aid of several legacies left to this church. The east window, of four lights, is filled with stained glass, and in the chancel are the usual piscina and sedilia, and also an aumbry or cupboard, with a shouldered arch. The tower is open to the body of the nave, and near it is an Early-English font of Bethersden marble. The church contains several interesting monuments and brasses; among them is an altar tomb, of Bethersden marble, for Sir John Mayne and Margaretta his wife, date 1566. The brasses, some of which are very curious, commemorate William Randolph and Elizabeth his wife, daughter of John Curtis (1641); Barnard Randolph, and Jane his wife (1685); Sir William Boddenden and his wife with their six children (1579); and John Everenden (1598); Sir Edward Henden, Baron of the Exchequer in 1662, lies buried in a chamber or vault on the north side of the great chancel.

Among the various charities in this parish is one which has acquired some little celebrity. On the afternoon of Easter Sunday a quantity of small flat cakes, made only of flour and water and impressed with figures of two women, united at the sides after the fashion of the Siamese twins, are distributed in the church porch to all comers. Bread and cheese, to a considerable amount, are given at the same time to the poorer parishioners. This, says tradition, was the legacy of twin sisters, called the Biddenden Maids, who lived for many years united in their bodies after the manner represented in the cakes,* and then died within a few hours of each other. There is also given to the recipients of the cakes a printed paper bearing upon it a representation of the impression on the cakes, and purporting to contain "a short and concise account of the lives of Elisa and Mary Chulkhurst, who were born joined together by the hips and shoulders, in the year of our Lord 1100, at Biddenden, in the county of Kent, commonly called the 'Biddenden Maids.'" It then proceeds : " The reader will observe by the plate of them, that they lived together in the above state thirty-four years, at the expiration of which time one of them was taken ill and in a short time died. The surviving one was advised to be separated from the body of her deceased sister by dissection, but she absolutely refused the separation, by saying these words : 'As we came together we will also go together;' and in the space of about six hours after her sister's decease she was taken ill and died also." By their will, they bequeathed to the church-warden of the parish of Biddenden, and his successors, churchwardens, for ever, certain pieces or parcels of land in the parish of Biddenden, containing twenty acres, more or less, which now let at 40 guineas per annum. There are usually made in commemoration of these won-derful phenomena of nature about 1,000 rolls, with their impressions printed on them, and given away to all strangers on Easter Sunday after divine service in the afternoon ; also about 500 quartern loaves and cheese in proportion, to all the poor inhabitants of the said parish.

It may be added that a similar distribution takes place on the

---

* See illustration on p. 206.

Tuesday following. Hasted, the historian of Kent, with many others, considers the story fabulous; he states that the print is of modern origin, and that the land was given by two maiden sisters, of the name of Preston, for a distribution of bread and cheese on Easter Sunday, twenty acres of land having been left by them to the parish for this purpose. W. DAMPIER.

Guy of Warwick.

By THE REV. F. CONWAY, M.A.,
Member of the Royal Asiatic Society.
PART II.
(Continued from p. 166, ante.)

I CANNOT follow Guy through all his travels. Everywhere he is the champion of the oppressed, battling to right the wronged. After one of these fights, in a German town, Guy is surprised while asleep in his bed by some of his adversary's hirelings, and thrown into the sea :—

> " Guy awakened at the last
> And his head up he cast,
> He saw the stars bright shining,
> On no side saw he land,
> But broad water all about,
> Therefore he was in fear and doubt.
> ' God,' he said, ' who with Thine hand
> Didst 'stablish the water and the land,
> Who hath done to me this deed ?
> Lord, award to him his meed.'
>   *   *   *   *   *
> With that came a fisher
> In a boat Guy full near,
> What he was he bade him say,
> And if he believed in God or nay."

Guy tells him that he is a Christian man, and describes what has befallen him.

> " ' I am,' quoth he, ' the pilgrim
> That fought the fight till yestereen,
> We were parted yesternight,
> We could no longer see to fight.
> Into a chamber was I brought,
> Of no treason had I thought,
> Into bed I climbed anon,
> I was weary, and slept soon,
> Now I am here, I know not how,
> O, my dear friend, help me now.' "

The fisher takes him to land, and Guy appears in the lists next day, to the dismay of his antagonist.

Many adventures, as stirring as this one, befell our Warwick hero. Many times is he called upon to fight the good fight of faith; to assert the honour of the Cross against the blaspheming bands of the Crescent. At last he returns to England once more. Here there is work waiting for some one to do. The Danes are again in the land. Athelstan is cooped up in Winchester, and the Danish king says he must either yield or find a champion to fight with the Danish giant Colbrand. England's heart stood still.

> " They have sent through all the land,
> To young and old, I understand,
> That they must fast for days full three,
> And night and day in prayer must be,
> That God may send them such a man
> That will, and dare, and may, and can,
> Through help of God Almighty,
> For England's sake in battle stand
> With the giant hight Colbrand."

And none is more sick at heart than the King himself. But a dream comforts him :—

> " The King at night to bed was brought,
> In cloth of gold, full richly wrought ;
> And all that night he lay and waked,
> And to our Lord his prayer he maked,
> And God forgat him nothing,
> As he was a-sleeping
> An angel He sent to him from heaven
> To comfort him with blessed vision ;
> ' King,' said the angel, ' sleepest thou ?
> I bring thee words from King Jesu :
> To-morrow, when that it is day,
> Take thou the readiest way
> And go unto the Northern Gate,
> And look whom thou dost find thereat—
> A pilgrim wight thou there shalt meet,
> On God's behalf do thou him greet,
> And thou shalt take him on with thee,
> And pray him for his charity,
> That he the battle undertake,
> In Jesu's name, for Jesu's sake.' "

The King rose in the morning and did as he was bidden, and found a wild and haggard figure in pilgrim's clothing leaning on a pilgrim's staff. It was Guy mourning for his sins, but the King knew not that it was Guy. No need to dwell on the details of their meeting—how the Palmer agreed to fight; how his leap upon his horse recalled to all the leap of the lost Sir Guy; how the Danish giant, for all his boast that he would crown his master " king of little England for ever and for aye," was slain with his own axe by the Saxon, and the kingdom was saved from the pillage of the Pagans.

But all this time men had been asking each other, "Who can this mysterious stranger be?" None could say, not even Athelstan himself. Long did the King importune the Palmer to tell his name. Long did the Palmer keep his secret. At last they two went with none other to a lonely cross, and there, where King and wanderer could meet as man with man, where nothing but the grave forest trees and gay forest flowers could hear the avowal, Guy revealed himself to the King under oath of secrecy, received the royal blessing, and went on his way alone. A new life now opened to Guy. He felt that Heaven in its mercy had crowned his career as a warrior with a final triumph in his country's cause; and that the rest of his life might be peace. Although he felt that the sweet wifely companionship of Felice was a lure to make him love the things of this world above heavenly things, yet he could see no sin in living near her, in seeing her pass and repass, in gathering and treasuring a wayside flower that haply had been trodden under her heedless foot. He went to a hermitage near Warwick, and lived there a life of prayer and fasting. So husband and wife dwelt, seemingly severed but by a mile; severed in reality by the distance of heaven from earth. And Guy is at peace; and often he sees his wife, unconscious of her husband's presence, intent upon good deeds, with that look of chastened sorrow on her beautiful face, and he feels that a peace has fallen upon her, and a happiness which no husband's love could have brought.

And at last came the time for Guy to die.

> " On one night asleep he lay
> And God's angel stood him by.
> ' Son Guy, son Guy, sleep'st thou now?'
> ' Nay,' said Guy, ' but who art thou?'
> ' I am Christ's own messenger,
> Saint Michael, that thou seest here :
> From the Lord Jesus I come to thee,
> Who sends thee blessed words by me.
> Shrive thee, Guy ! for as I thee say,
> Eight days from this day thou shalt die.' "

And now at last the husband triumphs over the saint. The ring— her own ring which she had given him at parting—is sent to Felice and she comes to the cave, but Guy is too near death to speak.

> " Head to head lay wife and lover,
> Sweetly either kissed the other,
> But one word Guy never spake,
> And the ghost soon from him brake."

From that day the cave became Felice's home; she said she would never leave it as long as she lived.

" Forty days there lived that lady
Till she died like good Sir Guy,
In one pit they lie together now,
Jesu keep their souls from woe."

But I am sorry to say that no substratum of fact underlies this romantic tale. In spite of names made up by monkish sycophants, to square with the traditions of families that patronised them, it is very doubtful if there ever was a Rohand of Warwick. Anyhow, a Saxon would never have named a daughter " Felice," or a son " Guy." These are Norman names, and must have been introduced into the tale after the Norman conquest, probably in compliment to contemporary Warwick worthies. To carry conjecture further still, a certain Turkill de Warwick, who is mentioned in Domesday Book, actually had a grand-daughter named Felicia, who must have been living about the time that the French romance of Guy was written, and what more likely than that the courtly poet named the heroine after her? Guy's final renunciation of his wife from religious scruples could hardly have formed a part of the legend in Saxon times. Morbid asceticism was alien to Saxon feeling, and nothing was so honourable in Saxon eyes as the position of house-father, or paterfamilias. This part of the tale bears the impress of the thirteenth century mint. The thirteenth century witnessed a tremendous religious revival. Worldly torpor was suddenly succeeded by a fierce religious enthusiasm, insisting on the abnegation of all pleasures, insisting on the repudiation of all earthly ties, substituting the frozen isolation of monasticism for the warm sympathies of active piety. Every preacher of the time called upon his hearers to renounce the world by walking out of it into a hermitage, and every writer strove with his pen to help on the good work. I am in my own mind convinced that some enthusiast for monasticism found in our legend a case of wife-desertion ready to his hand, and shaped it to suit his purpose, by introducing religious motives which were never contained in the original story. As to the single combat at Winchester, it certainly never took place. It is true that, in Athelstan's time, the Danes were in the land, but they never got to Winchester, or anywhere near it. It is true that Dane and Scot and Northumbrian and Welchman rose in arms with one accord to defy the Saxon ; but Dane and Northumbrian, Welchman and Scot, together, could do nothing against the terrible Athelstan. This glorious Prince of Saxon England, a warrior, a law-giver, and a singer ; this Prince, with the bar sinister upon his birth, but not a blot upon the white page of his deeds ; this Athelstan, with the stature of a Colossus, the great yellow beard of a Viking, and the dreamy blue eyes of a poet, met his enemies far away northward, at Brunanburgh, in Northumbria, and there gave the Danes such a lesson as even Alfred never gave them. But it was a battle of host against host, not a duel between Colbrand and Guy. It is enough to quote the contemporary Saxon Chronicle : " In this year King Athelstan and Edmund his brother led a force to Brunanburgh, and there fought against Olaf, and, Christ aiding, had victory ; and they there slew five kings and seven jarls." There is nothing about Guy here, or in any other early account of Athelstan's reign. But it is no wonder that a tale of Saxon triumph should be assigned by the poet to the reign of Athelstan, for the glories of this reign were the favourite theme of Saxon glee-men, and all floating tales would gravitate and cluster round it.

(*To be continued.*)

The History of Gilds.

BY CORNELIUS WALFORD, F.S.S., *Barrister-at-Law*.

PART IV.

(*Continued from p.* 131.)

CHAPTER XL.—*Gilds of Oxfordshire.*

I DO not find that the Gilds of the various towns in this county, other than those of Oxford itself, call for special comment.

Oxford City.—This ancient seat of learning boasted at quite an early period of a Gild Merchant, which, in process of time, assumed the civil government of the City, and controlled with an arbitrary will the other leading Companies, or Craft Gilds, therein. This assumption of control probably was not generally recognised until after 1388 ; for the returns made to the writ of that year embraced three Gilds, none of them presenting features of special interest. The point I think most worthy of elucidation now is the manifestation of control, as shown in the records of the City.

It is interesting to note that the founders of the University itself constituted themselves into a Gild, of whom the head was the " Rector Scholarum." This was at least not later than Henry I., or early in the twelfth century. " They created a Brotherhood for the good of their profession and the advantage of the public." (Annals of Oxfordshire (Jeaffreson), i. 65.)

In an Ordinance of the City, under date October 23, 1534, there was contained the following :—

... " Also it ys enacted and agreed by the same Mair, Aldermen, Bazlyffs, and Comynalte of the seid Toune, that no person ne persons shall use eny maner of marchauntdyse, or marchauntdysyng, nor use and exercise eny vytelyng, bying or sellyng, or eny handy craft or ocupacon wythyn the seid Town or subbarbs of the same, except he or they be free of the guyld of the seid Mair and Comminaltie wythyn the seyd toun and subbarbs of the same, under the payn of every person and persons offendyng contrary to this present ordinaunce after monycyon gevyn unto hym or them by the Mair and Chamberlyns of the seid Toun for the tyme beyng, xls., for every tyme so doyng or offendyng, the oon half to our sovereyng lord the kyng, and thother half to the Mair and Commonalte of the same town. . . ."

At Burford there was a Merchant Gild formed on the model of Oxford City.

Bakers.—There was a Craft or mystery of Bakers in this City at an early date, of which I cannot find any precise details ; but on September 30, 1538, the following order was made by the Council of the City :—

At a Counsell holden the xx day of September, in the xxx[th] yere of the reigne of King Henry the viij[th], it is condyssented, establyshed, and enacted for ever by the hole assent of the Mayre, Alderman, Bayllyffs, Burgeses, and Comminaltye of the Towne of Oxford, that from this day forwarde ther shall noe Alderman thought to be elected and chossyn to the office of a Alderman, or that he be admytted to the rome of a Alderman, shall not be sworne to the same office, nor were his cloke vntyll suche tyme as he be bounden to the Mayre, Bayllyffs, Bourgeses, and Comminaltye of the same towne, and to ther successors in a obligacion of c[li] w[t] ij sufficient surties wth hym to be p[d] to thusse of the same Towne under the condicion foloing, that ys to saye, that he shall not usse ij occupacions of vytlelyng crafts, that ys to say a baker and a brewer, a bocher and a brewer, a brewer a inholder, a brewer and a fyshemonger, nither baker and fyshemonger, nor noe other dobyll vytlelyng craftes, but to leve one of the same vytlelyng crafts, uppon payne of forfayture of the sayd c[li] to thusse aforesayd. And further it is enacted from this day forward that ther shall never noe baker hereafter be chossen to the office of the mayraltye of this Toune excepte he leve the occupation, crafte, or mystery of bakers for the tyme that he shalbe Mayre. And he to be bounde in a obligacion of c^{li} w^t ij sufficient surtyes w^t hym to the Baylliffes, Burges, and Comminaltye of the Toune of Oxford, and to ther successors."

It will not probably require much reading between the lines to discover that this harsh treatment of the victuallers in general, and of the Bakers in particular, really arose out of the claims of the University (as against the City) to have exclusive control of the Victualling trades, under its title to the Assize of Bread and Ale. To this same cause may be attributed the following Order :—

" At a Counsaill holden the viij day of January 1559, it was agreed by the Mayre, Aldermen, and Counsaill of the Citie that as well the Bakers as the towne dwellers shall grynde all there breade corne at the Castell mylls, according to an old custome, uppon forfeyture of there corne that shall grynde else where, to be taken by the Bayles for the tyme beyng, thone moytie of every forfeyture to be to the use and profytt of the body of the Towne, and thother moytie to the said Bayles."

In 1570-1 it was agreed at the City Council that the White-bakers should be incorporated,

On Sept. 2, 1580, the following entry was made in the City record :—

" Hit ys also agreed at this Counsell that the bakers of this Cytie shall and may use theire Learned Counsell, towchinge some orders to be made emongest them, for calling theire companye together, and for expellinge suche fforreners as bringe breade and put hit to sale at this markett being not free nor inhabytaunts of this Cytie, so that suche orders as they shall devise be first sene and allowed by this howsse."

Butchers' Company.—The Charter of this Company recorded in Archives of the City, under date 1536. It recites their petition to the Judges of Assize to oversee and examine their orders made by the Master Wardens of the said Craft of bochers, and approved by the Mayor and two Aldermen of the City ; and also the approbation of the said Judges.

Then follow the orders, among which it is first " ordeyned that the election day of their must be allways uppon Monday next after the feast of St Luke ye Evangelist." Another of their orders is that " no bocher shall serve or sell any flesh to any manciple, coke, or any other newe comer to him to be retayled, tyll he have very knowledge y^t ye sayde manciple, or coke, or any other person standeth clerely out of danger for fleshe wth ye person of whom the said manciple, coke, or other person, is so indebted before, or else y[t] it be openly and evidently understood that a full agreement and accorde is made for the contentation of all such debt or debts for fleshe wth y[e] person of whom y[e] sayd manciple, coke, or other person or persons is so indebted before, except that they pay ready money for such flesh as they shall buy, upon payne of . . . at every time, to be employed to the use aforesayde." · Another order is that "y[e] M[r.] and Wardens of the bochers shall have the serch of all fleshe that shalbe slayne or killed w[th]in y[e] Towne and suburbs of Oxford, or franchises thereof, to be sold in grosse or by retayle, and if they finde any flesh not wholesome, then to seaze uppon it as forefayted, and the party offending to be punished by y[e] Mayor and y[e] Justices for the time beinge. And y[t] any bocher bringinge fleshe to the Towne to be sold, shall also brynge the hyde or skin and tallow of the same flesh to be sold there, under payne of forfeyture."

This may be the commencement of the corporate powers of the Craft. As early as 1532-3 "at a Counsell holden the xxj day January, in the xxiiij yere of King Henry viij, it is agreed by the more part of the Council [of the City] the bochers of the Towne of Oxford shall every Sonday in the yere sell flesshe in theyr shoppys."

In 1535 it had been "condyssented and agreed by the more part of the Counsell, that the bochers of the Towne and suburbys of the same shall sell ther talloe to the chandlers of the Towne, and to noe other persons, dwelling out of the Towne, under the payne to forfayte at every tym that doe the contrarye to the usse of the Chamber of the Town xx[s.], and the talloe that ys soe takyn to be to the usse of the Chamber." In the same year the butchers had been voted the use of a piece of "voyde grounde wythowte South Bridge," to make "sklautter housse apon paying yerly therfore a compotent rent." They were to kill no more in their old slaughter-houses after a day named.

On the 28th of August, 1556, it was ordered that all the butchers of the City, being freemen, should occupy and keep their standings in the new shambles by seniority, and they were to be "dyschargyd of the fiftene for there bochers shoppes, and of there wekely pence."

Brewers' Company.—The Ordinances of this Company were enrolled upon the City records under date February 4, 1570-1. These consisted of a supplication of the Brewers to the City for their establishment, tendered February 4, 13 Queen Elizabeth, and of 17 Articles, a few of which will be now noticed :—

" Art. 1. The master and wardens of this craft or mistery of brewers, is to be chosen the Sunday next after the Nativitie of St. Mary the Virgin, accordinge to the grants of the progenitors of our Soveraigne Lady the Queen that now is, &c.

" Art. 5. No man must entice away one anothers customers, under the payne of x*s*.

" Art. 6. No brewer to serve any typler or hucster with bere or ale unless he is suer that y*e* sayde typler or hucster standeth clerely out of danger for ale or bere with y*e* person he is indetted to, ar at the least hath compounded for it ; nor unless the said typler have entered into recognisance for kepinge good rule in his house, &c., under payne of forfeyture of xx*s*. for every such offence.

" Art. 7. No customer, typler, or hucster may lend, sell, breke, or cutt any brewers vessell, or put therein any oth'er ale or beare then of y*e* owners of the same vessell, under the payne of 3s. 4d. to the fellowship of brewers.

" Art. 8. None but freemen may brewe ale or bere, under peyne of forfeyture of the drink to the Baylives and 40s. to the Company.

" Art. 15. Journeymen out of service, or ale bearers, must by 6 of the cloke in the morning present himselfe at St. Peter's church dore in the Bayley, there to be hired," &c.

Here there is reference to the fraternity as having exercised earlier privileges from the Crown ; and I find a reference dating back to 1513 (4 Henry VIII.) to the effect that any brewer discontinuing the exercise of his craft in the city " by the space of a hole yere," or in " time of derth of malte doe refuse and will not brew, and afterward in time of good cheap malt will take uppon him to bryw againe," such person should pay such fine as the occupation of bruers " should determine, or pay 40s. for such subsequent brewing.

The solution of this apparent complication will probably be found in the fact that the Craft of Brewers was originally under the regulation of the University, as distinguished from the City. Here is a decree directly in point :—

" *Concerning Bruers.*—Memorand. y*t* y*e* xij*th* day of July in y*e* yeare of our Lord God 1525, y*e* 8 (*sic*) yere of y*e* reigne of Kinge Henry y*e* 8, it was inacted and established for evermore by the consent and assent of my Lorde Chancellor of y*e* University of Oxon, the Commissary, Doctors, and other the hedds and governors of y*e* sayd Universitie, at y*e* instant labour, sute, petition of all the brewers of Oxford for that time beinge, y*t* where the sayd brewers, not only by y*e* reason of the high price of malt and other thinges, but also by y*e* reason of the great number of brewers being occupied and continue-ing the sayd craft be now decayed and in a manner undone, that fro henceforth these brewers that now be occupieinge and usinge the sayd craft continually shall use and occupy the same crafte during their lives, or as long as they shall be contented to continue in the same craft, provided allway that when and as often as it shall happen any of the sayde brewers that now occupyinge and usinge the sayd occupacion to depart out of this world, or doe refuse and leave of ye same crafte of bruinge, that then no brewer to occupy ye sayde occupation wthin ye Town of Oxford or suburbe of the same be admitted, neither by ye sayde Chancellor, Commissary, Doctors, and other hedds or governours of the same University, ne by ye sayde brewers for ye time beinge, unto ye time that ye sayde bruers come to the number of 16 brewers only, and then the same number of 16 so to continue for ever, and no more to be taken in. And if it shall happen any person or persons hereafter to be taken uppon them to brewe wthin ye sayde Towne or suburbes over and above ye said numbre of 16 brewers, neither be not admitted on of ye same 16, that then ye same person or persons so brewinge and usinge ye same craft contrary to the form of this act and statute to forfeit for every time so doeinge, uppon a sufficient proffe there uppon made, x^{li}, to be applied in manner and form followinge, that is to say, to ye Commissary of ye sayde University for ye time being 40s.; to ye common chest of ye sayde University for ye time being 40s.; and to the Master, Wardens, and Fellowship of the sayde occupation for the time, other 40s.: provided alway that if any brewer depart out of this worlde, and his wife over live him, then she to brue, if she will, as long as she is sole and widowe, and no longer; and if any brewer have a son liable to occupy the sayd occupation, and will occupy the same, that then he to be preferred before any other forreyner comminge into the same occupation."

In the preceding decree the Master, Wardens, and Fellowship of the Company of Brewers is fully recognised; and hence the earlier independent existence of the Gild seems to be established.

As early as 1534 the City had proposed to grant an Ordinance to the Brewers and to the Bakers. In 1561 they were "forbidden to carry ale or bere within the city with iron-bound carts, upon payne of the forfeiture of their wheels."

Finally, in 1575, "the citie's pretented Corporation of Brewers" was abrogated by the University, on the plea that as well by the Charter of 21 Edward III., as by Act of Parliament 12 Edward IV., the Chancellor of the University had and ought to have wholly and solely the custody of the assize of bread, ale, and wine, together with the punishment and correction of all offenders, " and the fynes, yssues, and commodities thereuppon risinge."   And further, that the Chancellor, by assent of the Convocation, had authoritie to make societies or corporations, " namlie, touching victellers and sundrie others, as appeared by ye Charter of King Henrie ye 8th."   The new book of Laws and Ordinances of the Brewers' Company was therefore ordered to be " brought and cancelled before the Chancellor, or his Commissarie, with^t delaie."

The Company therefore reverted to its earlier position, whatever that may have been.

Weavers and Fullers.—The Mystery of the Weavers and Fullers was incorporated by the Corporation of the City by order dated February 14, 1571-2, approved by the Judges of Assize ; but whether upon the lines of any former foundation does not seem clear.   Most probably it was so.

They were to have a circuit of five miles allotted to them about the city and suburbs, " wthin which bounds no man must worke in ye misterie of weavers and fullers unlesse he be of their fellowship."

They were to choose two wardens every year, the one a weaver the other a fuller, upon the feast of the " Exaltation of the Crosse," being the 14th day of September, " uppon which day they all goe to church togeather to heare some prayer or homilie red there to them, &c.; that beinge done, then they are to goe to ye choice of their two wardens and four bedells or warners."

Those two wardens were to make search at times convenient after any kind of weavers or fullers' work not well and competently done, and to see that every weaver have in his house or shop " from the summe of 16 bores to the summe of 700 harneyses and slayes, 3 beares between every harnys ; and y^t every fuller have eleven corse of handells and 2 payre of sheres at ye least, &c., under ye payne of 2s. 6d., and no fuller within the sayd circuite may kepe or occupy in their houses journeymen, otherwise called cardes, upon payne of 6s.," &c.

They might keep their Courts upon the four usual quarter-days every year, fourteen to be sworne of ye jury to inquire if the orders be well kept.

Mercers and Woollen Drapers.—In the records of the City, under date September 9, 1572, it was agreed that the mercers and woollen drapers should be incorporated in one incorporation ; and on the 12th day of the same month " Kewars (*sic*) of the Ordinances of the Mercers and Woollen Drapers " were appointed to " have the comyssion and be comythies of the boke of ordinances for the incorporacion of mercers and drapers, and to certifie this howse of theyer proceedings therein at the next Counsell."

On June 5, 1573, it is recorded " Hyt ys agreed at thys Counsell that the booke of the corporacion of mercers and wollen drapers shalbe engrossed and sealed, wth the proviso for the suffycyent auctorytye of the Mayor for the tyme beinge to order and reforme all complaynts and contencyons, and that the Town Clarke for the tyme being be theire steward, and have a reasonable ffee for the same."

No further details, except that in 1569 it had been agreed that the " occupacion of mersers and haberdashers shall have a corporacion, and also that the taylors and woollen drapers wthin y^{is} citye shall have a corporacion "—combinations of trades not finally adopted.

(*To be continued.*)

Autograph Letters.

No. VI.

BARONETS AND THEIR FEES.

THE following curious letter, apparently original and not to the Editor's knowledge published, has a place in his private collection of autographs. It is given here *literatim*. The letter has no superscription or address :—

S^R,

My Lord Treasurer hath directed Processe to be issued against all the Bar^{ts} of England that are not already discharged of the 1095 *lb* that they were to pay in consideration of that Dignity ; & this morning finding your name in ye list of those against whom Processe already issued, I give you notice of it, y^t you may apply yourselfe to my Lord Treasurer to have a Warrant for stoping Processe, & to gett a discharge as all other are doing of ye summe. If you thinke I can serve you in this matter, you may freely dispose of

S^r
your most humble Servant
20th March 168⅔. Wm SHAW.

Reviews.

Harrow School and its Surroundings. By PERCY THORNTON. Allen & Co. 1885.

MR. THORNTON has evidently been undertaking a labour of love in becoming the biographer of his old school ; and although the early annals of Harrow are not connected like those of Eton, Winchester, and Westminster with any abbey or religious foundation, yet he has contrived—thanks to sundry charters lately found in the School chest—to claim a respectable antiquity for John Lyon's work. The part of his book which deals with the more ancient history of the School is very carefully and exhaustively written ; and others, beside old Harrovians, will be glad to learn more than outsiders generally know of the precise aim of the far-sighted founder of the School, as well as of its connection, in more recent times, with the honoured names of Sumner, Drury, Thackeray, and Butler. Mr. Thornton gives a most interesting account of the old annual custom of shooting at the Butts for a silver arrow, a custom which continued till about a century ago, and of which we gave our readers an illustration not long ago.* The volume contains engravings of the brasses of John Lyon and his wife in Harrow Church and a plan of the original School, all of which will commend themselves to the antiquarian reader.

Catalogue of the Medals of Scotland from the Earliest Period to the Present Time. Arranged by R. W. COCHRAN PATRICK, M.P. Edinburgh : D. Douglas. 1884.

THIS is a work which will gladden the hearts not only of numismatists, but of all scholarly antiquarians. Though its author very modestly states in his preface that it "has no claim to be considered exhaustive," yet, so far as it goes back, it seems to us fairly complete. The first chapter gives a minute description of those of the Scottish kings from *their* James the First ; the second is devoted to the medals which record the members of the House of Stuart other than the actual Sovereigns, commencing with the famous Albany Medal, struck by the Regent Albany, nephew of James the Third. Next follow medals which record events in Scottish history ; medals struck in honour of distinguished persons, mostly those born north of the Tweed, *e.g.*, Lord Lynedoch, the Duke of Lauderdale, John, Duke of Argyll and Greenwich, David Hume, Lord Mansfield, Lord Heathfield, Lord Duncan, Sir Ralph Abercromby, Sir John Moore, James Watt, Sir Walter Scott, Robert Burns, Sir Charles Napier, Dugald Stewart, Thomas Carlyle. The later chapters treat of "Local" and "Miscellaneous" medals, particularising those relating to Edinburgh, Glasgow, St. Andrew's, Aberdeen, Moffat, Glenalmond, Ardrossan, &c., to the various regiments of Scottish volunteers, and to the national games of Curling and of Golf. The plates, which occupy more than half of this handsome and well-printed volume, are executed in a manner and style which is almost above praise. The impression, we should add, is limited to 350 copies.

The Dutch Church Registers. Edited by WILLIAM J. C. MOENS. Privately printed. 1884.

IN a quarto volume of some 200 pages Mr. Moens has preserved for easy reference the Registers of Marriages, Baptisms, and Burials between the

---

* See vol. v. p. 53.

years 1571 and 1874, together with copies of the monumental inscriptions, in the Dutch Reformed Church, Austin Friars, London. In Holland a society has been formed for the purpose of collecting together all the matter connected with the history of the Walloon churches in that kingdom ; and, as we learn from the volume before us, in the most spirited way possible has copied and arranged in one vast collection all the Registers of the numerous French and Walloon churches in the various towns of Holland, where the refugees from Belgium and France, during the sixteenth, seventeenth, and eighteenth centuries, and their descendants, assembled together for divine worship conducted in the French tongue, according to the tenets of the Reformed religion. " It is much to be desired," adds Mr. Moens, "that the eighty-nine Registers of the French and Walloon churches · established at London, Canterbury, Norwich, Plymouth, Southampton, and Thorpe-le-Soken, dating from 1567 to the present day, and now in the custody of the Registrar-General at Somerset House, London, should be treated in a similar manner by some existing society, or by one formed for the special purpose." Mr. Moens has prefixed to his copy of the Registers an historical account of the Dutch settlers in England, from which much interesting information may be gleaned.

Shropshire Folk-lore : a Sheaf of Gleanings. Edited by CHARLOTTE SOPHIA BURNE. Part ii. Trübner & Co., 1885.

THIS work, the first part of which was noticed by us at the time of its publication in 1883 (see vol. iv. p. 96), has been edited from the collections of Miss Georgina F. Jackson. The long delay that has occurred in the publication of the present instalment has enabled Miss Burne to incorporate in it much new and interesting information which otherwise would have been excluded. The "gleanings" in the part before us embrace a rich variety of subjects, including charming and divination ; superstitious cures ; superstitions concerning animals, birds, insects, and plants ; superstitions concerning the moon, the week, numbers, and dreams ; luck and unluck in daily life ; customs and superstitions concerning birth, marriage, and death ; customs and superstitions concerning days and seasons. It has been found impossible to compress the materials at the editor's command into two parts, as originally intended ; a third part will therefore be issued as soon as completed, and may be expected to appear before the close of the present year.

The Municipal Corporations' Companion, Diary, Directory and Yearbook of Statistics, and *The County Companion, Diary, and Magisteriat and Official Directory for* 1885 (Waterlow & Sons), compiled and edited by Mr. J. R. Somers Vine, F.S.S., are two very useful works in their way, and contain, beside a vast amount of information compressed into a limited space, a quantity of historical notes on the several counties and towns of England and Wales. These comprise descriptive and concise histories of the several castles, cromlechs, and other antiquities to be met with in different parts of the country. These Directories merit our heartiest commendation.

Bouquet, by William Bayley (Bayley & Co., Cockspur-street), is the fanciful name given to a small volume of poems gathered like a veritable *sertum* of flowers from various sources, ancient, mediæval, and modern. Those from the old Classics and from Tasso are graceful and charming ; and the little book, printed on hand-wove paper, comes to hand in a dress so pleasing to the man of antiquarian tastes that it cannot help being welcome to our readers.

———

THE April number of *English Etchings* (D. Bogue, King William-street, Strand) contains, *inter alia*, a pleasing example of the etcher's art, showing the tower of an old church on the river Wey, near Guildford.

UNDER the title of *The Reference Catalogue of Current Literature*, 1885, Mr. J. Whitaker, of Warwick-lane, has just published in an elephant 8vo. volume, the full or selected lists of 128 publishers, embracing the current works in every department of literature. The great value of the work, of course, lies in the fulness of its index ; this extends to over 300 pages, and contains about 53,800.

Obituary Memoirs.

" Emori nolo ; sed me esse mortuum nihil æstimo."—*Epicharmus.*

DR. CHRISTOPHER WORDSWORTH, late Bishop of Lincoln, who died in March last, deserves notice here as the author, *inter alia*, of several works of an antiquarian character, and as having taken great interest in archæological matters. In 1837 he published his " Inedited Ancient Writings from the Walls of Pompeii." His " Athens and Attica," and his " Illustrated History of Greece," have each passed through several editions. He was also the author of " St. Hippolytus and the Church of Rome in the Third Century, from the newly-discovered ' Philosophumena,'" " The History of the Church of Ireland," and " Memoirs of William Wordsworth ;" and he edited the " Correspondence of Richard Bentley, D.D., Master of Trinity College, Cambridge."

MR. HERBERT THOMAS FRY, who died at Upper Tooting, Surrey, on the 17th of March, was born at Haverfordwest in 1831, and educated at the grammar-school there. As a literary worker of long standing, we can record that he was the author of our " Schools and Colleges," published in 1867 ; the " Road to Paris," illustrated by Mr. Prior, father of Melton Prior ; " The Guide to Normandy," written for Messrs. Bradshaw, and re-issued annually. Mr. Fry was also well known by his having edited the " Royal Guide to the London Charities," a work brought out under his direction for twenty-three years successively. In antiquarian literature may be named his annual " Guide to London," in which he described the past as well as the present of the great city. He was the founder of the Pall Mall Club in conjunction with Lord Townshend, and Honorary Secretary to the National Education League. Mr. Fry was a member of the British Archæological Association, and of the London and Middlesex Archæological Society.

ON Saturday, May 30 and June 6, the Rev. C. Taylor, D.D., Master of St. John's College, Cambridge, will deliver two lectures at the Royal Institution, in Albemarle-street, on a lately discovered document, possibly of the first century, entitled, " The Teaching of the Twelve Apostles," with illustrations from the Talmud.

Meetings of Learned Societies.

METROPOLITAN.

SOCIETY OF ANTIQUARIES. — *March* 12, Dr. E. Freshfield, V.P., in the chair. Mr. W. H. St. John Hope, F.S.A., contributed the second part of his paper on the "Seals of the University and Colleges of Cambridge," which he illustrated by the exhibition of several impressions. The colleges referred to were those founded after the year 1400. Mr. A. White, by permission of the Vicar of West Drayton, exhibited a chalice and paten, parcel gilt, still in use in that parish, and bearing the year mark for 1507. Lord Hatherton also exhibited a chalice and paten which had been gilt and repaired within recent years, and which was stated to have been found behind the wainscot at Pilaton Hall in the year 1750. On both these exhibitions remarks were made by Mr. St. John Hope, who at the same time exhibited numerous photographs of mediæval chalices and patens, and produced a list of forty-three examples. A letter was read from the Rev. W. Iago, local secretary of Cornwall, stating that in that capacity he had addressed a remonstrance to the Ordnance Survey against the practice of their surveyors of placing their bench marks on the stones and crosses of Cornwall. The remonstrance had been most courteously received, and an expression of regret that such a thing had occurred had been accompanied by the assurance that strict orders had been given that it should not occur again. It was announced that in consequence of a meeting having been held at York, in February last, under the presidency of the Archbishop, at which it was decided to follow the example of London with regard to the demolition of several of the old City churches, the Council of the Society had directed their local secretary to watch the proceedings at York, and from time to time to report accordingly.—*March* 19, Dr. E. Freshfield, V.P., in the chair. Mr. George Wardle read a paper on "The Gate-house Chapel at Croxden, Staffordshire," a building lately removed for the purpose of widening the road between Rocester and Cheadle. A discussion followed the reading of the paper. — *March* 26, Dr. E. Freshfield, V.P., in the chair. Mr. C. D. E. Fortnum read a paper on "A Greek Head of Terra-Cotta, found upon the Esquiline Hill, at Rome." A discussion followed, in which Professor Percy Gardner and Mr. C. S. Murray took part. Mr. A. J. Jewers, F.S.A., read a paper on "The Parish Registers of Sheviock, Cornwall," and he also exhibited one of the volumes of the register in a very torn and dilapidated condition.—*April* 16, Dr. E. Freshfield, V.P., in the chair. The balance-sheet and the auditors' report for the past year were read. Lord Carnarvon's Presidentship being about to expire, the Council propose Dr. John Evans, F.R.S., as President in his place. Several objects were exhibited, including some beautifully-illustrated heraldic and devotional works from the pen of the late Father Anselm Baker, of the Cistercian Monastery, in Charnwood Forest. Mr. R. S. Ferguson reported the discovery of some ancient gold and silver coins, near Carlisle. These, in accordance with the present law of "Treasure Trove," were sent to London to the authorities of the Treasury, who graciously (but not very liberally) allowed the local museum to purchase a few specimens for 15 shillings! This procedure elicited strong expressions of dissatisfaction with the existing law. Dr. E. Freshfield then read a paper "On Variations in the Apostles' Creed in the Book of Common Prayer." The paper treated of the divergence between the Creed as it stands in the Daily Service, and in the Occasional Services in the Book of Common Prayer, the expression in the former with regard to the ascension of our Lord being "He sitteth *on*," and in the latter "He sitteth *at* the right hand of God the Father," and he showed that the latter was part of the new element introduced by the foreign reformers in the Second Book of Edward VI.

BRITISH ARCHÆOLOGICAL ASSOCIATION. — *March* 18, the Rev. S. M. Mayhew in the chair. Mr. E. Walford exhibited an old engraving, the masterpiece of Theodore Maes, of the Battle of the Boyne. It showed the whole of the local surroundings, having been drawn on the spot at the time. King James' army is shown flying "like a flock of sheep," thus illustrating Lord Macaulay's description of the scene. The engraving, when it came into Mr. Walford's possession, was in a soiled and sadly mutilated condition, but it has been restored by Mr. Grisbrook, of Panton-street, and in such a manner as to elicit the admiration of the members present. Mr. Loftus Brock, F.S.A., described a beautiful example of Etruscan fictile ware. Mr. Cecil Brent, F.S.A., exhibited some Arabic inscriptions on cornelian and sard, and Capt. Mascie Taylor a small dial ring found at Corwen. The Rev. S. M. Mayhew produced a large collection of ancient objects, mostly found in the City in some recent excavations. Among these the following may be specially mentioned : a wine vessel of peculiar form, found in Abchurch-lane ; some bone pins from a Roman cemetery at Spitalfields, one having an iron point, and another being formed of a porcupine's quill ; a Roman cock, of bronze, enamelled, of great beauty, found near Throgmorton-avenue. The first paper, by the Rev. John Edking, D.D., of Pekin, read in his absence by Mr. W. H. Rylands, F.S.A., was on "Ancient Navigation in the Indian Ocean." The paper treated upon the references to the early intercourse between China and the Ancient World mentioned in the little known Chinese writers, and the introduction of foreign plants by traders. Jessamine was thus introduced before the Christian era. Henna was imported 1,400 years ago, and African plants were also well known, there having been an Arab colony then in Canton. The uncle of Mahomet lived there, and after paying a visit to Asia after the death of the Prophet, returned there to die. There were relations between the Kings of Babylon and the Emperors of China many hundred years before Christ. The divisions of the stars into constellations was known in China in the seventh and eighth centuries B.C., and the earth was known to be round 700 years B.C. An animated discussion followed, in which Messrs. Morgan, Rylands, Wright, and Walford took part. Mr. J. T. Irvine read a description of the opening of a barrow at Croyland, Lincolnshire, in which were found some Roman remains and also some prehistoric flint implements. With these were a great many objects of hard baked clay similar to the teeth of a harrow, and the opinion was expressed that they had been used for a similar purpose. Similar articles have been found near Peterborough.— *April* 1, Mr. Thos. Morgan, F.S.A., in the chair. Mr. Sheraton reported the discovery of the foundations of a small Norman chapel in a field near Ludlow, which had been called Chapel Field from time immemorial, although there was no record whatever of any such building having stood there. The foundations show that it consisted of a simple nave ending in a semicircular eastern apse. A few encaustic tiles were found. Among the objects exhibited were several of the singular objects manufactured many years ago by the Whitechapel firm of " Billy " and " Charley," whose forged antiquities were exposed at the time by Mr. Syer Cuming, F.S.A.

(Scot.), and some other members of the Association, but so many of the articles are still current in old curiosity shops that in the interests of this generation of young collectors the selection exhibited had been brought together by Colonel Adams, F.S.A. Mr. Loftus Brock, F.S.A., exhibited a curious bronze mounting of an old English cabinet, probably a relic of the Great Fire of London. An elaborate paper was then read on Domesday Book by Mr. W. de Grey Birch, F.S.A. The author treated at length upon the origin of the survey and of the mode of its completion, pointing out that it did not include the extreme northern counties, probably on account of their disturbed condition. The three books of Domesday were fully described, and the peculiarities in these pointed out, attention being drawn to the long misunderstood test of the Cambridgeshire portion in the British Museum. The importance of collating the various manuscripts was dwelt upon, and it was suggested that this would afford abundant and useful work for a new "Domesday Society." A discussion which followed the reading of this paper elicited a strong feeling in favour of Mr. Birch's suggestion. A paper by Dr. Alfred Fryer on ancient glass had to be "taken as read," owing to the lateness of the hour.

ST. PAUL'S ECCLESIOLOGICAL SOCIETY.—*March* 24, Mr. G. H. Birch in the chair. Mr. Somers Clarke, F.S.A., read a paper on "Some Churches in North Germany," in which he described the architectural peculiarities and general appearance of several interesting ecclesiastical buildings in that part of the continent, more especially those of Lubeck, Limeburg, Oldenburg, Munich, &c. Mr. Clarke illustrated his remarks by the exhibition of diagrams, drawings, and photographs, and the reading of his paper was followed by a discussion. A letter from the Rector of the church of St. Bartholomew-the-Great, Smithfield, was read by the Chairman, asking for help to rescue and preserve some of the older portions of that interesting structure.

NEW SHAKSPERE.—*March* 13, Dr. C. K. Watson in the chair. Mr. S. L. Lee read a paper "On an Elizabethan Learned Society." Mr. Lee spoke strongly on the mistaken estimate of the character of the Elizabethan age as being one of tumultuous, ill-directed passion. That there was another side to it was shown by the birth of the old Society of Antiquaries, founded in 1572. Outside the universities such learned organisations had not hitherto existed in England, though flourishing abroad. The dissolution of the monasteries had caused a complete cessation of historiography ; Henry VIII., indeed, sent one man, Leland, where fifty would not have sufficed, throughout the country to search monasteries and other religious foundations for historical matter. Mr. Lee then described three great antiquaries—Archbishop Parker, William Cecil, and Nicholas Bacon—as having a better right to be considered representative men of the age than Greene, Marlowe, &c. The great need of antiquarian study was secular development ; it is therefore especially interesting to note the large proportion of laymen in the society. The list includes men of every class—nobles, statesmen, and scholars such as Camden and Cotton, together with merchants and small tradesmen, like Stowe the tailor. It was noticeable that English was employed in their disquisitions, not Latin, in spite of Camden's preference for it. We find these antiquaries on the best of terms with the ordinary men of letters, as seen in the case of Jonson and Stowe, the help given by Selden to Drayton, &c. This may account for the small mention of them in the contemporary drama, as they could hardly be introduced except in a burlesque or travesty of them, which their friendly relations with the stage put out of the question. Mr. Lee then sketched the decline of the society through the suppression of private meetings owing to a fear of conspiracy ; the failure, owing to the death of James I., of their schemes for a great literary academy endowment of research, &c. ; and concluded by insisting that any true interpretation of the age must include these men.—*Athenæum.*

LONDON AND MIDDLESEX ARCHÆOLOGICAL SOCIETY. — *March* 24, Mr. J. G. Waller in the chair. Mr. G. L. Gomme, F.S.A., read "Some Notes on the Westminster Folk Moot," after which Mr. John E. Price, F.S.A., the secretary, described some Roman and other pottery, coins, and various other objects of interest found during recent excavations in the City. Mr. Price referred to the proposed restoration of the Church of St. Bartholomew-the-Great, West Smithfield. A discussion followed, in which the Rev. W. Panckridge, rector of the parish, Mr. Alfred White, F.S.A., and others, took part. Mr. Price further announced that the Society had been in correspondence with the Chief Commissioner of Works in reference to the proposed restoration of Westminster Hall, and read a letter which the Council had addressed to him, stating that they had appointed a committee, consisting of Mr. C. B. Thurston, F.S.A., Mr. A. White, F.S.A., Mr. E.W. Brabrook, F.S.A., the President, Treasurer, and Secretary, to represent its views to the Parliamentary Committee, if desired.

ANTHROPOLOGICAL INSTITUTE.—*March* 24, Mr. Francis Galton, F.R.S., President, in the chair. A paper was read by Mr. A. J. Duffield on "The Inhabitants of New Ireland and its Archipelago." The author first dealt with the assumption that the inhabitants of these islands are the descendants of remote but superior races, that they retain inherited powers which have become weak by lack of use, and that these moral and intellectual powers could be easily restored. Mr. R. Brudenell Carter and Mr. C. Roberts read papers on "Vision Testing."

ARCHITECTURAL ASSOCIATION. — *March* 28, a visit was paid to Fishmongers' Hall. Mr. Towse, the Clerk of the Company, escorted the members through the apartments, and described the various objects of interest belonging to the Company. The Fishmongers are the fourth on the list of the twelve great City Companies, and their hall was erected in 1831, on the site of the old hall, built after the Great Fire by Mr. E. Jarman, the City Surveyor. The earliest extant charter of the Company is a patent of 37 Edward III. Having inspected the several rooms, the members proceeded to the Merchant Taylor's Hall, in Threadneedle-street, where a paper was read by Mr. W. H. Nash, giving a short description and history of it. This Company was incorporated in 1466. The hall is the largest of the Companies' halls, and was, like the Fishmongers and Drapers' halls, rebuilt after the Great Fire, by Mr. Jarman. The members inspected the premises, from the very interesting crypt to the several chambers of the new buildings, including the strong room, containing the ancient silver "yard stick," formerly used at Cloth Fair, and the several "loving cups," &c.

NATIONAL SOCIETY FOR PRESERVING THE MEMORIALS OF THE DEAD.—*March* 27, Mr. Vaughan in the chair. Reports as to the work of the society were submitted and approved. These included the Deanes monuments in Great Maplestead Church, the Poll monument in Snarford Church, the Barnewall monument at Luck, Ireland ; the Pedlar's Window, Lambeth, which has been very satisfactorily replaced by the Vicar ; the

Corfield and other monuments in Deuxhill Church ; the Fewtrell monument at Easthope ; Matthews' tomb in Llandaff Cathedral ; the Kirton monument at Thorpe Mandeville ; the monuments in Chiswick and Sprowston Churches ; brasses at Radwell, Newenham, St. Alban's (St. Michael's), Fryerning, Northleach, and Bishop Auckland (St. Andrew's), many of which are about to be restored by different individuals and members of the Society at their own cost ; tombs at Carshalton and Fladbury Churches ; a slab at Lytchett Maltravers ; Henry VII.'s tomb, Westminster Abbey ; coffins at Wytham ; and inscriptions at Upton-upon-Severn.

PHILOLOGICAL.—*March* 7, Rev. Prof. Skeat, President, in the chair. —Dr. Furnivall read a paper, by the late Mr. C. B. Cayley, "On the Conditions of Onomatopoiia." Mr. B. Dawson read a paper on the Revised Version of the New Testament, dealing chiefly with Acts xvii. He commended the accuracy of the revisers, but condemned their "transverbation" of the Greek ; they had lost the old free spirit of translation, of English poetic feeling which had turned the foreign "*seventy* years" into the household "threescore years and ten."

HISTORICAL.—*March* 19, Mr. Alderman Hurst in the chair. Mr. J. F. Palmer read a paper "On the Development of the Fine Arts under the Puritans," in which he endeavoured to show that the influence of Puritanism upon the fine arts was really beneficial. Not only the drama, he contended, but also poetry, painting, and architecture entered upon a new era during the sixteenth and seventeenth centuries, and this at a time when the Puritan idea was rapidly becoming the leading mental feature throughout the country. All the advanced Puritans of the independent types showed a far more liberal spirit towards the arts than did the Presbyterian section, who alone were responsible for all acts of iconoclasm. Cromwell himself saved from destruction the cartoons of Raffaelle, appointed a committee to established a college of music, and permitted Sir W. Davenant to commence a series of dramatic performances.

NUMISMATIC.—*March* 20, Dr. J. Evans, President, in the chair. Mr. H. Symonds exhibited a baronial coin of the Earl of Warwick struck at London. Dr. W. Frazer sent for exhibition a silver medal of Suleyman I., the son of Abbas II., of Persia, A.D. 1666-1694, similar to a specimen first described by Mr. E. Leggett, of Kurrachee, in the *Numismatic Chronicle*, 1884, part iii. Mr. H. Montagu exhibited a variety of the groat of Henry VIII.'s fifth coinage, issued in the thirty-seventh year of his reign, reading REDD. CVIQ' Q' SVVM EST. The Ven. Archdeacon Pownall exhibited, by permission of the Ven. Archdeacon Thicknesse, a bronze medal by Christophorus Hierimia, of Mantua, struck in honour of Alfonso V., King of Aragon, Naples, and Sicily (1416—1458), surnamed "the Magnificent," similar to one described in Armand, "Médailleurs Italiens," vol. i. pp. 30-31 : obverse, ALFONSVS REX REGIBVS IMPERANS ET BELLORVM VICTOR ; reverse, CORONANT VICTOREM REGNI MARS ET BELLONA. Mr. A. E. Copp exhibited a Hamburgh century-medal in gold, dated 1801. Mr. B. V. Head read a paper, by Mr. T. W. Greene, on "The Medals of the Hanna family by Leone Leoni," and exhibited specimens of the medals of Martin, Daniel, John, and Paul Hanna, all apparently cast about the middle of the sixteenth century. Dr. Evans read a paper on a find of Anglo-Saxon coins in Meath.

PROVINCIAL.

CAMBRIDGE ANTIQUARIAN SOCIETY.—*March* 9, Mr. J. W. Clark, M.A., President, in the chair. The President exhibited a skeleton of a red stag (*Cervus elaphus*), lately added to the Museum of Zoology and Comparative Anatomy. The bones were found in Burwell Fen last summer. A skeleton of an adult stag from Scotland was also exhibited, in order to show how much the species had degenerated in size in recent times. The Rev. W. Graham F. Pigott exhibited, among other curiosities recently found in the coprolite-excavations at Abington Pigotts : (1) An *aureus* (probably unique) of Cunobelin, *obv.* Horse, wheel underneath, CVNO, *rev.* Ear of barley, CAMV. *i.e.*, the mint of *Camalodunum*, now Colchester ; it was ploughed up in 1875. (2) A *denarius* of Nero Drusus (plated antique), *rev.* Equestrian statue of Drusus on a triumphal arch, DE GERMANIS, dug up in October, 1884 ; and a *third brass* of Constans and of Gratian. Mr. H. F. Wilson read a short paper descriptive of some objects of antiquarian interest discovered by him in an attic in the Great Court of Trinity College. The "find" consisted of bones, broken bottle-glass, a key of antique pattern, and other " rubbish," among which were several scraps of manuscript of various ages from the sixteenth to the present century, and some fragments of printed books. The bottle-glass probably had figured at a supper party, held by persons *in statu pupillari* under the old régime ; it was of an old-fashioned type, such as was common in the seventeenth century. Mr. Wilson then gave some account of the printed and manuscript scraps, which comprised : (*a*) a page from an undergraduate's common-place book or collection of Latin passages of about 1550 ; (*b*) a few sentences from a Latin essay of the same period ; (*c*) portions of a congratulatory address to some dignitary of Trinity College, probably of the seventeenth century ; (*d*) a fragment of a poem in English ; (*e*) a worm-eaten leaf from an old play, which has not yet been identified : the dramatis personæ engaged in the dialogue being given as Warh. and Dorc. respectively.

EDINBURGH ARCHITECTURAL ASSOCIATION.—*March* 21, a visit was paid to Granton Castle, Royston, and neighbourhood. Mr. Thomas Ross said that in Granton they had a type of building designed to resist attack, perched on the summit of a rocky knoll overlooking the Firth of Forth, with enclosing walls loopholed for guns, and a walk behind for the defenders. Much of this castellated character had, however, disappeared, owing to alterations which had taken place between 1544 and 1696. On the other hand, they had in Royston a stately house, built for the entertainment of guests, but with little or no thought of defence ; yet, like Granton, extremely characteristic of the Scottish architecture of its period, and further interesting from the alteration it underwent in 1696, when its south front was transformed from the homely Scottish style. At Granton they had a building of the familiar " L " plan, with a circular staircase and entrance at the re-entering angle. The kitchen appears to have been in the north wing, and is now the only vaulted part of the main building. Perhaps the most interesting features of Granton are the surrounding walls, which follow angle-wise the outline of its rocky site, and the skilful way in which the entrance has been chosen so as to be enfiladed by a return in the wall at a point where the rock is highest and steepest.

ROYAL IRISH ACADEMY.—*March* 16, Sir S. Ferguson in the chair. The annual report, which was adopted, stated that the museum had been enriched with some valuable donations during the past year, and there had been purchased various implements of flint and bronze, together with two fine lunulæ of gold, recently found in the North of Ireland. The attention of the Council having been called to the sale of the Fountaine collections of antiquities, they drew up a memorial which they forwarded to His Excellency the Lord-Lieutenant, pointing out the desirability of securing for Ireland one of the most valuable objects in this Art collection—viz., the bronze reliquary of St. Lachten, and of depositing it in the museum of the Academy, where it might take its place along with other similar objects. Through the representations of the Council, the Government gave instructions for the Reliquary to be sent from the South Kensington Museum to the Academy, where it is deposited in the museum.

HAILEYBURY COLLEGE ANTIQUARIAN SOCIETY.—*November* 24, the Rev. G. E. Jeans, President, in the chair. The Rev. C. W. Barclay read a paper on the Antiquities of Western Palestine. The remains of antiquity to be found in Palestine, unlike those of Egypt, Greece, &c., require to be sought for and need excavation, especially in Jerusalem, where the Palestine Exploration Fund has done good service in throwing much light on the remains of the old bridge from Mount Moriah to Mount Zion ; they have also explored many ancient aqueducts and underground passages hitherto unknown, including that to the Pool of Siloam.— *December* 2, the Rev. L. S. Milford read a paper on "Saints and their Symbols."—*February* 9. Mr. A. F. Chilver gave a short account of the ruins of Cowdray House, near Midhurst, mentioning a curse supposed to be attached to the estate, which was once Church property. Mr. S. F. Williams described a house at Purleigh, in Essex, date about 1500, which was a refuge for Protestants in the Roman Catholic persecutions, and *vice versâ*. Mr. J. S. Liddell gave an account of a visit to the Palace of Versailles. Mr. A. D. Carlisle gave a short description of the Alban Hills, near Rome. They are of volcanic origin. Mount Algidus and Tusculum stood on parts of the wall of a great extinct crater. The lakes of Nemi and Albanus also occupy old craters, their regular oval shape being very distinct. At Tusculum many old remains exist, notably a theatre, an amphitheatre, foundations of the citadel, and a perfectly preserved road, paved with basaltic blocks, leading down to the old Via Latina. The site of Alba Longa is uncertain ; an ancient well, of peculiar shape, like another discovered on the Palatine Hill, affords some evidence that the town stood on a ridge on the N.E. side of the Alban Lake. The Chronicler (Rev. L. S. Milford) spoke of Parma and its connection with Correggio, and gave a short description of its cathedral. In speaking of Bologna, he mentioned the west front of the cathedral and the church of St. Stefano, which in reality consists of seven churches, all of different dates. Passing on to Rome, he described the "preaching of the children " and other ceremonies on the Feast of the Epiphany. He also spoke briefly of the discoveries in the Forum, and the House of the Vestal Virgins, of which he passed round several photographs. The President (Rev. G. E. Jeans) described the four great churches—Christ Church, Wimborne, Malmesbury, and Tewkesbury—which he had seen in the holidays, thus completing the series of all the great churches in England. He called special attention to the parochial tower and high-raised choir of Christ Church ; the two towers in line with one another, of Wimborne ; the massive round pillars combined with pointed arches, of Malmesbury ; and the high Norman nave and beautiful Decorated choir, of Tewkesbury. He also mentioned the Market Cross at Malmesbury, the famous Saxon church of Bradford-on-Avon, one of the oldest in England, having been built as far back as 780 A.D.; and the very interesting churches of Bosham, near Chichester, and Deerhurst, near Tewkesbury.

PENZANCE NATURAL HISTORY AND ANTIQUARIAN SOCIETY.—*March* 13, the Rev. W. S. Lach-Szyrma, President, in the chair. Most of the papers read were in the Natural History section, especially one from New Zealand, contributed by the Rev. W. S. Colenso, and others by Messrs. Bailey, Ralfs, &c. An interesting account of the antiquities of the parish of Godolphin, near Helston, was read by Rev. S. Rundle, and the President closed the session with a paper on "Tidal Folk-Lore."

SUFFOLK INSTITUTE OF ARCHÆOLOGY AND NATURAL HISTORY.— *March* 27, annual general meeting, Lord John Hervey, President, in the chair. The annual report was received and adopted. After the transaction of some other business, a conversation took place with reference to the preservation of the old ruin at Bury St. Edmund's, which formed part of St. Saviour's Hospital; and it was decided that a sub-committee, consisting of the President, the two Hon. Secretaries, Mr. Beckford Bevan and Mr. Prigg, should take the matter into consideration, with power to act. It would appear that there are no funds belonging to the Institute available for the preservation of national monuments. The Rev. Evelyn White, Hon. Secretary, suggested that there should be two excursions during the present year, one in May or June, and that the society should take the neighbourhood of Lowestoft, and, if possible, visit Burgh Castle; and one either in September or October, to be held at Sudbury.

Antiquarian News & Notes.

THE ninety-sixth anniversary dinner of the corporation of the Royal Literary Fund will take place at Willis's Rooms on May 6.

CAPTAIN BURTON expects soon to bring out five volumes of his translation of "The Arabian Nights."

THE Rev. Sir Philip Perring has in preparation a volume entitled "Hard Knots in Shakespeare."

MR. GLADSTONE has offered to restore the old Town Cross of Edinburgh, in memory of his connection with Midlothian.

THE City of Dublin has been robbed of about 40 cwt. of its public records, which have been actually sold as old parchment.

THE suggestion that Lancaster Castle should be used solely as a military prison has been opposed by the county justices.

THE old Grammar School at Shrewsbury has been converted into a Free Library and Museum.

THE ancient church of St. Michael, Farnley, Yorkshire, is being rebuilt.

MR. SEDDING has been appointed architect for the restoration of the great screen in Winchester Cathedral.

A NUMBER of oil-paintings by old masters have been lent to the South Kensington Museum by Lord Kilmorey.

THE third and fourth volumes of the Duc d'Aumale's "Histoire des Princes de Condé" are announced for early qualification.

THE Public Orator of Cambridge, Mr. Sandys, has nearly completed a critical and explanatory edition of the "Orator" of Cicero.

THE "Stercorarium" of the ancient Temple of Vesta, in the Forum at Rome, has just been brought to light by Professor H. Jordan.

Two experienced clerks in the Foreign Office are engaged on a history of British diplomacy.

THE Welsh National Eisteddfod, to be held at Aberdare in August, will be under the patronage of Her Majesty.

THE sermons lately preached at the Temple Church on the occasion of its seventh centenary will be published in a volume by Messrs. Macmillan.

IT appears that the Church of S. Clemente at Rome was spared from confiscation by the Italian Government at the intercession of the Prince of Wales.

SOME Roman relics, consisting of swords, spears, and other warlike implements, have been discovered by some men whilst quarrying at Harbledown, near Canterbury.

MR. J. H. POLLEN has lately delivered before the Society of Arts the four Cantor Lectures, taking as his subject "Ancient Carving of Furniture."

THE buildings in St. Paul's Churchyard formerly occupied as St. Paul's School were put up to auction lately, but the reserved price was not bid.

THE fine old church of All Saints, Great Driffield, recently restored at at a cost of £12,000, is now nearly clear of debt ; the vicar, the Rev. Canon Newton, contributed £3,000 towards the cost.

THE Norman church of St. Oswald, at Oswaldkirk, Yorkshire, is about to be restored. In this building Archbishop Tillotson preached his first sermon.

HELEN, Lady Ruthven, last year presented her collection of Greek antiquities, which she had gathered in earlier life, to the Antiquarian Museum in Edinburgh.

IT is proposed to restore the chancel and east window of St. Bride's Church, Fleet-street, one of Sir C. Wren's best specimens.

THE old chained Bible long carefully preserved in the Cathedral Library has been replaced in Canterbury Cathedral.

TEMPLE BAR, the stones of which have been carefully stowed away, is shortly to be rebuilt in King's Bench-walk, almost within a stone's throw of its old site.

A FACULTY has been obtained from the Bishop's Court, at Worcester, for the restoration of the parish church of Stratford-on-Avon, in which Shakespeare lies buried.

M. LUCIEN PEREY and M. Gaston Maugras have in preparation a work on the private life of Voltaire at Les Delices and Ferney (1754-78), drawn from unpublished documents.

THE MS. of two unpublished tales, by Perrault, has just been discovered. The titles are "La Fée des Perles" and "Le Petit Homme de Bois." The MS. will be offered to the Bibliothèque Nationale.

THE Lords of the Treasury have sent to the Mitchell Library, Glasgow, a collection of the works which have appeared under the direction of the Master of the Rolls. It comprises over 200 volumes.

THE parclose screen at Aveton Giffard, South Devon, which had been long put aside as "past restoration," has been lately restored by Mr. H. Hems, of Exeter. It is said that the work is of the reign of Richard II.

LADY BRASSEY has published, through Messrs. Bryce-Wright, of 204, Regent-street, a description of a collection of gold ornaments formed by her from ancient graves in Central America.

HER Majesty has been pleased to accept from Master Edwin Beresford Chancellor (aged 17), the eldest son of Mr. Chancellor, of Richmond, a copy of his new work, entitled "Historical Richmond."

THE thousandth anniversary of the martyrdoms of St. Methodius and St. Cyril, the great Sclav apostles, is being celebrated through the present and next months by a succession of pilgrimages to their graves at Welchred, in Moravia.

MR. JOHN EVANS, LL.D., F.R.S., has been elected President of the Society of Antiquaries in the place of Lord Carnarvon, whose term of office has expired. The approaching retirement of Mr. C. Knight Watson, the Secretary, is announced.

MISS GARNETT'S Greek Folk Songs, the publication of which has been delayed by her publisher for more than a year, has at last made its appearance—a proof, it is to be hoped, that the author has "held her own."

MR. W. ST. CHAD BOSCAWEN delivered, on April 1, the concluding lecture of his second series of British Museum lectures on the History and Antiquities of Assyria and Babylonia. Mr. Boscawen announced that the six lectures comprised in this series will be published shortly.

ON Thursday in Holy Week Her Majesty's "Maundy" was distributed by the Lord High Almoner at Whitehall Chapel. At Vienna the Emperor observed the annual custom of washing the feet of twelve poor men between 88 and 93 years of age.

MR. JOHN MACKAY, of Heddlesdale, is preparing for publication a chronicle of the exploits of "Mackay's Regiment," from its formation in 1626 to the Battle of Nordlingen in 1634; and of its subsequent incorporation with the corps now known as the Royal Scots, or 1st Regiment.

MR. JOSEPH CRAWHALL, of Newcastle-upon-Tyne, will, says the *Athenæum*, shortly publish, jointly with Messrs. Field and Tuer and Messrs. Sampson Low & Co., under the title of "Izaak Walton, His Wallet Booke," a collection of the songs and poesies contained in the "Compleat Angler." The numerous quaint illustrations are designed and cut by Mr. Crawhall himself.

MR. JAMES FERGUSSON writes to the *Times* condemning the models of the proposed additions to the west front of Westminster Hall as unworthy of being carried into execution; he contends that the Hall, being a one-storied building, should be architecturally treated as such in dealing with its façade.

ACCORDING to the *Academy*, Messrs. Bell will shortly publish the first four books of the "Iliad," in English hexameters, by Mr. H. Smith Wright. The translator, formerly a scholar of Trinity College, Cambridge, is the son of the late Mr. I. C. Wright, who is also known as a translator of Homer and Dante.

PROFESSOR JULIUS WELLHAUSEN'S "Prolegomena to the History of Israel" have been translated into English under the author's supervision, and, with the addition of an amplified reprint of his article "Israel" in the "Encyclopædia Britannica," will be published by Messrs. Black. The preface is by Professor W. Robertson Smith.

MR. DAVID DOUGLAS, of Edinburgh, has lately published for the University Press of that city, a volume entitled "Quasi Cursores," consisting of portraits of the chief officers and professors of that University at its recent Tercentenary Festival, drawn and etched by Mr. William Hole, F.R.S.A.

MR. SWINBURNE'S new tragedy, *Marino Faliero*, is dedicated to Aurelio Saffi, the Italian patriot. This will indicate that the striking chapter of

Venetian history upon which the drama is based has been treated in some measure politically. The chronicle, however, has been faithfully followed as to incidents.

THROUGH the liberality of the Duc d'Aumale, the Hungarian National Gallery has acquired, by exchange, two valuable pictures, a Girolamo da Libri and a Rembrandt. The former is a large Apotheosis of the Blessed Virgin, and the latter shows an angel awaking the Holy Family and ordering them to flee into Egypt.

AT a sale at Messrs. Sotheby & Wilkinson's, on April 18, "Tam o' Shanter" and another poem in the autograph of Robert Burns fetched £152, and fifteen letters of Dean Swift were knocked down for £160. Other lots fetched equally high prices. The greater part was bought by Mr. Waller, of Artesian-road, and by ¦Mr. Barker, of Brook-green, Hammersmith.

ON Good Friday, two ancient customs in the City were carried out. Sixty of the youngest boys of Christ's Hospital each received a new penny and a bag of raisins, at the Church of Allhallows, Lombard-street ; and in the churchyard of St. Bartholomew-the-Great, West Smithfield, twenty-one new sixpences were placed on a tombstone, and picked up by twenty-one aged widows.

DURING her sojourn at Aix-les-Bains, Her Majesty has visited, among other places of historic interest, the Abbey of Hautecombe, which was the burial-place of the Princes of the House of Savoy ; the old castle of Chambéry, the former capital of the dukedom of Savoy, and which dates from the 13th century ; and the Château de Bourdeau, an old shooting-box of the same princes.

THE Archbishop of Canterbury, acting as arbitrator in the matter of the dispute as to the plan upon which the central tower of Peterborough Cathedral shall be rebuilt, recommends the replacement of the pointed arches of A.D. 1380 with provision for a future superstructure, and that the recovered fragments of the Norman time should be fitted together and retained to illustrate the antiquities of the cathedral.

A GENEALOGICAL family manuscript book, which has been lately found among the treasures of a collector at Berlin, contains 150 miniatures in oils, painted for the most part on thin plates of gold or silver, by Lessnipp, Henr. Schmidt, Wittjequast, and other long-forgotten artists. The book dates from the sixteenth century. It is intended to reproduce it in fac-simile.

THE Rev. F. W. Weaver, M.A., of Milton, Evercreech, Bath, is preparing for publication " The Visitations of Somerset in 1531 and 1573." The work will comprise many notes and references to Collinson's " Somerset," Hoare's " Wilts," Hutchins' " Dorset," Westcote's " Devon," and to the Visitations of those counties, and also some pedigrees from Sir Thomas Phillipps' " Visitation of Somerset," a very scarce book.

A PORTION of the library of Mr. Alexander Ireland, of Bowden, Cheshire, was sold by Messrs. Sotheby & Co. on the 13th of March and three following days. It included specimens of early printing—1473-92 ; early English poetry and the drama ; early Scottish poetry and ballads ; Literary Miscellanies and Collections ; histories, biographies, correspondence, journals, &c.

THE total realised by the sale of Mr. Bohn's art treasures (see *ante*, p. 195) is about £50,000, the sum at which they were roughly valued by their late owner. Some of the lots, which he had originally bought very cheap, fetched high prices ; but with many other lots the reverse was the case.

The miniatures, most of them very small, sold well ; among them were included six early portraits of Edward VI., Queen Elizabeth, Charles I., Henry VIII., Queen Mary, and James I.

MESSRS. MARCUS WARD & CO. will publish, in the autumn, an illustrated volume, entitled " Echoes of Hellas ; The Tale of Troy, and the Story of Orestes." The " Tale of Troy," comprising scenes from the " Iliad " and " Odyssey " of Homer, translated by Professor Warr, was performed at Cromwell House in 1883; and the " Story of Orestes," from the Orestean Trilogy of Æschylus, is to be performed during the ensuing season at King's College, London.

THE commission entrusted with the publication of the correspondence of Peter the Great has collected 8,000 letters and other documents, among which are the copy-books used by the Emperor when a child, and one letter written to his mother in 1688 from Pereyslavl, giving her an account of the work of rigging the ships then in course of construction on the lake of that name. These documents will be printed with as little delay as possible.

THE old colours of the Scots Brigade and 90th Regiment (Perthshire Volunteers) have been deposited in St. Giles's Cathedral, Edinburgh. The colours of the Scots Brigade, presented by Lord Reay, were formerly in the possession of the Dutch Government, the brigade having been in the Dutch service from 1572 to 1782. Those of the 90th Regiment, which have been presented by Mr. Maxtone-Graham, of Cultoquhey, Perthshire, were carried in the Egyptian campaign of 1801, under Sir Ralph Abercrombie.

THE *Athenæum* of 21st February contained two columns chronicling the most important features of Mr. James Greenstreet's recent discovery at the Public Record Office of two original documents illustrating the history of the stage in the time of Shakespeare, and the origin of Drury Lane Theatre. We are pleased to learn that Dr. Furnivall, recognising the great value of the information afforded by these documents, has decided to print the entire text of both of them in the *Transactions of the New Shakespeare Society.*

LIEUTENANT-GENERAL PITT-RIVERS, Her Majesty's Inspector of Ancient Monuments under Sir John Lubbock's Act of 1882, recently inspected the Kentish monument known as Kit's Coty House, and as a result of his report, the monument, which has of late years been greatly damaged, has now, with the consent of the owner, Mr. H. A. Brassey, M.P., been placed under the guardianship of Her Majesty's Commissioners of Works, who are taking the requisite steps to prevent further mutilation of the monument.

IN the course of recent excavations in the lobby of the French Huguenot Church in the crypt of Canterbury Cathedral, a finely-chiselled head and fragments of stone, many of which are richly gilded, and in one of which a pearl remains, have been exhumed. They are evidently portions of the shrine of St. Dunstan. At the Reformation the shrine was broken up, and it is supposed that the pieces were subsequently collected as rubbish and thrown into the Black Prince's Chantry (now the site of the French Church), where St. Dunstan himself is said to have been interred.

IN the *Archivio Storico*, published at Trieste, will shortly be published a collection of documents, recently discovered, which relate to the life of Panfilo Custaldi, for whom the honour of the invention of printing has been claimed by patriotic Italians. It is not stated that these documents give any support to this claim, but it appears that Custaldi, who was a physician in Capo d'Istria, was already practising the art of printing with movable types as early as 1461, in partnership with two other residents in the same town.

THIS year being the bicentenary of the Revocation of the Edict of Nantes, several gentlemen, descendants of the Huguenots, propose to establish a Huguenot Society in London. The object of the association is to form a bond of fellowship among those who inherit or admire the characteristic Huguenot virtues, and the interchange and publication of knowledge relating to the history, settlements, genealogy, heraldry, and registers of the Huguenots. The opening meeting was held at the Criterion, Piccadilly, on April 15. Sir A. H. Layard is its president.

MR. MURRAY'S April list of publications contains, *inter alia*, the Marquis de Nadaillac's " Pre-Historic America ;" " The Correspondence and Diaries of John Wilson Croker ;" Smith's " Student's History of the Christian Church" (1003-1614); Professor Brewer's " Reign of Henry VIII. ;" Wordsworth's " Historical Account of Greece ;" Dr. Schliemann's works ; and Murray's " History of Greek Sculpture." The list of forthcoming works includes Schliemann's " Pre-historic Palace of the Kings of Tiryns ;" Miss Twining's " Symbols and Emblems of Christian Art ;" the concluding volume of " The Life and Times of Raphael ;" and a revised edition of Cunningham's " London."

THE existence of a most interesting Masonic relic has been communicated to the London Freemasons by Mr. Lamb Smith, of Worcester. It is a most curiously engraved and embellished tobacco-box, made of brass, which was given by the Duke of Perth at the defeat of Prince Charles Edward in 1746 to the great-grandmother of the present owner, as the box of the Hon. John Drummond, who in 1685 became Earl of Melfort. The Earl was the only member of the Perth family who had a right to heraldic bearings coupled with an esquire's helmet. The lid bears the Masonic insignia, and the armorial bearings are on the bottom of the box. Over the latter is the crest, a dog, with the well-known motto of the Drummonds, " Gang warily " : " J. D. 1670."

IN the excavations now being made for Waterlow & Co.'s new premises in London-wall a large portion of the ancient wall of the City has been unearthed. It is probably part of the original work ordered by Constantine the Great, being built, after the Roman manner, of stones with layers of Roman bricks. The upper part of the wall is of later date. Very few relics have been found except some coarse Roman pottery, a few bones, and a skull, black with age. This may be accounted for from the ground being outside the wall. On the site of the new Stock Exchange vast quantities of Roman remains were discovered last year, including fine specimens of Samian ware, but nothing remarkable as regards pavement or metal.

A CORRESPONDENT writes to the *Weekly Register:* "At Godstowe, about two miles from Oxford, some men are employed in widening the river, and in their excavations of the ground, which is close to the old Godstowe Nunnery, they have come across some stone coffins in almost perfect condition, containing the bones of some of the nuns. Several of the coffins have been broken up, and the bones taken out, given away or stolen, and I even heard that a skull was offered for sale for a shilling. On Sunday I saw some boys playing with the few remaining bones, and one whistling a tune and beating on a skull with a stick by way of accompaniment." Such indecent and disgraceful conduct should be stopped.

MESSRS. SOTHEBY, WILKINSON & HODGE sold on Friday, the 20th of March, and following day, the Clandon Library, with which was included the collection of books formed by the Right Hon. Arthur Onslow, some years speaker of the House of Commons, many of them enriched with his autograph notes. Among the works offered for sale were " Milton's Collection of Original Letters and Papers of State addressed by Oliver Cromwell," edited by J. Nickolls ; the first edition of " Paradise Regain'd " and " Samson Agonistes "; a folio edition of " Shakespeare's Comedies, Histories, and Tragedies," and Wren's " Parentalia." The library was " sold with all faults " in consequence of many of the portraits and plates having been cut out of the various volumes to form the collections of engravings included in this sale.

THE following articles, more or less of an antiquarian character, appear among the contents of the reviews and magazines for April :—*The Century*, " A Florentine Mosaic ; " *Chambers's Journal*, " Church Ales ; " *All the Year Round*, " Chronicles of English Counties ; " *Art Journal*, " The Early Madonnas of Raphael," " The Mammoth Hunter," and " London Club-Land ; " *Nineteenth Century*, " The Eastern Pediment of the Parthenon ; " *Cassell's Family Magazine*, " A Pilgrimage to Buddha's Tooth," and " Shakespeare's Birthday ; " *Magazine of Art*, " The Art of Periclean Athens," " Profiles from the French Renaissance—Le Primatrice," and " Peg Woffington ; " *Atlantic Monthly*, " George Frederick Handel ; " *Belgravia*, " Babylon ; " *Contemporary Review*, " The Women of Shakespeare ; " *The Quarterly Review*, " Recent Discoveries in Greece," and " Early Britain."

AN important discovery has, says the *Athenæum*, been made in digging the foundations of a new house to the south of the Acropolis at Athens, near the Temple of Jupiter Olympius. This plain was the site of the city of Athens before Themistocles moved it from Phalerum towards the Piræus. The discovery consists of an inscription, belonging to the beginning of the fifth century B.C., ordering an enclosure to be made around the Temple of Codrus, and some two hundred olive trees to be planted therein. The stone has been purchased by the Greek Archæological Society. A sister society has been founded in Athens for the study of Christian archæology, with the object of examining and preserving whatever remains of Christian antiquity are found in Greece. To most lovers of art it will be undoubtedly a matter of regret that this Association was not founded sooner. How many mosaics and other Byzantine remains in Greece are now lost or ruined beyond hope of repair ?

AN appeal has been made by the Vicar of St. Bartholomew's-the-Great, West Smithfield, for funds wherewith to free that grand old Norman fabric from certain structural encumbrances which have long disfigured it. The church is crowded on all sides by secular buildings, some of which encroach singularly upon it, and occupy what were once parts of the church itself. A smith's shop stands where the north transept once did ; the old Lady-chapel, desecrated probably ever since the suppression of the college, is now part of a fringe factory, which also extends itself above the eastern part of the aisles ; and the triforium over the north aisle is now used as a school. It is to be hoped that the necessary funds for the preservation of the church will be forthcoming, and that whatever is done in the way of " restoration " will be judiciously executed. If a few thousand pounds are subscribed towards the fund before the middle of May, there will be a possibility of the work being effectively carried out.

AN important discovery has been made in connection with the topography of the Roman Forum. In dressing and carrying back as far as
possible the escarpment of the accumulation on the unexcavated portions
of the north-east site, between the Temple of Antoninus and Faustina and
the Church of St. Adriano, a part of the pavement of the ancient street
connecting the Forum with the Suburra has been uncovered. It lies some
eighteen inches below the flagged area of the Forum, which is that of the
seventh century at the earliest. The street extends along the south-east
side of that part of the Curia which is now the church of St. Adriano. The
pavement is in fine preservation, and on one side of the street stands a
large pedestal, probably of a statue dedicated, as the inscription shows, to
Constantinus II. by Memmius Vitrasius Orfitus, who was Præfectus Urbis
from 355 to 359. The point at which the end of this street touches the
area of the Forum is still covered with masses of marble, such as pedestals
of columns, pieces of cornice, and other fragments, found beneath the
accumulation removed on the carrying back of the escarpment some ten
to twelve feet. Among these remains is a large portion of the shaft of a
fluted column, cut from a beautiful coloured marble.—*St. James's Gazette*,
April 1.

THE Court of Aurillac will shortly have to pronounce upon a curious
claim which has just been set forth in a pamphlet published at Marseilles. The claimant and author of this pamphlet is Antoine Dujol, an
employé in a manufactory of chemicals at Russuen, where he at present
earns about £5 a month. He maintains that he is the heir of no less a
house than the Valois, and he has already had his cards printed :
" Comte d'Usson d'Auvergne, duc d'Alençon, Prince de Valois." He
makes out his genealogy thus : Francis, Duc d'Alençon, fourth son of
Henri II., did not die childless, as has been stated, but married in 1575
a Duchess de Medina Cœli, and had issue a son named Henri d'Usson
d'Auvergne, who perpetuated the race. In 1757, Louis XV., in order to
forestall any contention which might arise from the claims, or be supported by documents of this family, caused its head to be confined in
the Bastille. The son of the captive was, however, in the meantime
confided to a farmer named Guinet-Dujol, and was reared by his wife.
This couple had no children of their own, and their fosterling came in
time to be known by the name of Guillaume Dujol. The two knotty
points which may be expected to tax the wisdom of the Aurillac tribunal
are the alleged marriage of the Duc d'Alençon, and the asserted identity
of Guillaume Dujol with the Prince de Valois, entrusted in 1757 to the
Cantal farmer Dujol.

CATALOGUES of rare and curious books, most of which contain the
names of works of antiquarian interest, have reached us from Mr. C.
Golding, Colchester ; Mr. J. Buchanan, 49, Great Queen-street, W.C. ;
Mr. T. Gladwell, 101, Goswell-road, E.C. ; Mr. G. Redway, 15, York-
street, Covent - garden, W.C. (including a large number of works
illustrated by Bewick) ; Mr. J. Salkeld, 314, Clapham-road, S.W., including an extraordinary collection of cuttings from English and
American newspapers, mounted in 118 volumes) ; Mr. E. Daniell, 53,
Mortimer-street, W. (comprising a large collection of topographical
works, privately-printed pedigrees, &c.) ; Mr. Grose, 322, Kennington
Park-road ; Mr. J. Salisbury, 4, Paternoster-row, E.C. ; Messrs. Meehan,
32, Gay-street, Bath (including a valuable and unique collection of
original editions of Dickens' works); Messrs. Jarvis & Son, 28, King
William-street ; Mr. G. P. Johnston, 33, George-street, Edinburgh ; Mr.

E. W. Stibbs, 32, Museum-street, W.C. (comprising selections from the library of the late Rev. J. A. Giles, D.D., dramatic works, Italian literature, British topography, and Bewickiana).

In the collection of relics belonging to the late Mr. W. Terry, of Peterborough House, Fulham, lately sold at the rooms of Mr. J. C. Stevens, in King-street, Covent-garden, was a wax taper said to be the identical one carried in penance by Henry II. to the shrine of Thomas à Becket in Canterbury Cathedral. It was found in the year 1773 in the shrine, and by some means was obtained by Dr. Menish, of Chelmsford, in whose museum it remained for many years until it passed into the hands of the late owner. Whether it is the identical taper may be a question, but it is remarkable that it should bear the arms of England embossed upon it. Matthew Paris relates that the King did penance to expiate his participation in the murder of the Archbishop, bearing a taper and laying it upon the shrine, and that afterwards he was scourged on the bare back by many clergy assembled for the purpose. It was sold for £6. The other antiquities of interest were a fine square bell of bronze with a stone clapper, found at Kilgort, county Tyrone, in 1839, which sold for £3 10s.; and an ancient Syrian talisman of bronze, engraved with figures and characters, originally gilt, described by Mr. Lindsay, of Cork, and other writers. It was brought from Syria by Sir T. Tobin, and is supposed to be Chaldean work. It sold for £4 4s. Two Babylonian tablets, incised, of the date of the 6th century B.C., sold for £7 10s.

Antiquarian Correspondence.

Sin scire labores,
Quære, age: quærenti pagina nostra patet.

All communications must be accompanied by the name and address of the sender, not necessarily for publication.

MORE CURIOSITIES OF OFFICIAL SCHOLARSHIP.
(See *ante*, p. 201.)

Sir,—Your readers were, probably, no less surprised than myself at the vehement letter in your April number, in which Mr. Hall suddenly renews a controversy long forgotten.*

It would seem, however, that this singular delay, in the case of a simple issue of fact, which, even to an antiquary of ordinary ability, should present no difficulty, has brought forth but sorry results :—

"Parturiunt montes; nascetur ridiculus mus."

The vials, however, of Mr. Hall's wrath have for fifteen months, we must remember, been filling, and in their discharge on my devoted head we have the all too familiar substitute for those proofs which his protracted labours have failed to produce.

Experience has shown me that, as in the notorious case of Mr. Cordy Jeaffreson and "the Leicester Inquests," vehemence of denunciation, in

---

* The delay is not to be set down to Mr. Hall's score. His paper has been held over, month after month, for want of space.—ED. *A. M. & B.*

officials as in others, is in inverse ratio to the strength of their case. I
am, therefore, in no way surprised that Mr. Hall should accuse me of
"entire ignorance," for, when officials have no other resource, "it is their
nature to," as Dr. Watts would say. Indeed, from Mr. Hall it is more
especially to be expected. For no less an authority than Mr. Elton
observes, when reviewing Mr. Hall's recent work :—

"We hear a little too much of 'grievous mistakes' and 'glaring errors.'" *

We do, indeed. Mr. Hall will remember that when I once crossed
swords with him anent his criticisms on Dr. Stubbs, he was eventually
compelled to write : "I admit I tried to prove too much." On this, Mr.
Elton, with fine irony, thus tersely comments :—

"Mr. Hall confesses to having started an erroneous hypothesis in the course of
castigating Bishop Stubbs, and it seems to be a further grievance that the
historian, after 'tacitly accepting' the lesson, never noticed the author's subsequent acceptance of a correction of his own correction."†

The question at issue between Mr. Hall and myself is short and
simple enough. I had pointed out in the first instance (*ante*, iv. 179),
that by the erroneous rendering, in a Government Calendar, of a record
relating to Irish history, both its interest and its meaning had been
obscured. In so doing, I had specially drawn attention to the loose
rendering of the word *filius*, which, even where its meaning was the
same in the original, was indiscriminately rendered by the editor "Fitz"
in one place, and "the son of" in another (*Ibid.* p. 180). This Mr. Hall
has not attempted to defend. But I went further, and suggested a rule,
by the application of which, in the case of such Records, we should
always in practice be able to secure a correct rendering of *filius*.

"The rule to be observed is, I take it, as follows : When *filius* is followed by a
Christian name, we may render it 'Fitz,' and combine it with that name as a
surname. But where *filius* is followed by a surname as well, we must then
render it 'the son of.'" (*Ante*, iv. 179.)

I proceeded to show that, by the application of this rule, we obtained
an absolutely correct rendering of this Record, so erroneously interpreted by its neglect.

This rule, which I hoped might be found to be of use, was reluctantly
admitted by Mr. Hall to be "substantially correct" (iv. 279). He
endeavoured, however, to object to it "technically," on the plea that in
a lawsuit, the word *filius*, when followed only by a Christian name, had,
by one of those quibbles so dear to the heart of the mediæval lawyer,
been held not to form part of a surname, but to mean absolutely "the
son of." Of this case I not only disposed in full detail (*ante*, v. 50), but
also showed that Mr. Hall's theory would involve a *reductio ad
absurdum* :—

"Every member, for instance, of the great house of Fitz Alan, for two hundred
years before this date, must, according to Mr. Hall, as a '*Filius Alani*,' have
been in the eyes of the law the son of a man called Alan. Surely no wilder
proposition ever emanated from an antiquary's brain." (*Ibid.*) .

Mr. Hall, unable, of course, to meet this crushing objection, flees for
refuge to a last remaining quibble. He boldly asserts that when "Fitz"
formed part of a surname, it was never Latinised as *filius*, which term
was strictly reserved for "the son of." He rashly adds that my "entire

---

* Academy, March 7, 1885. † *Ibid.*

ignorance" of this (alleged) fact is the cause of my "disastrous philological speculations, and assures us that : "—

"If only the wording of this writ had read ' Fitz-Thomas,' the whole aspect of the case might have been altered, for ' Fitz-Thomas,' as I have said, may mean anything, whereas *filius Thomæ* can only mean one thing—and that, ' son of Thomas.' . . . ' Filius Stevani' is one thing, and ' le fitz Estevyn' is quite another. The loose use of fitz as a Norman patronymic is well enough, but *Filius in Record Latin can never be safely rendered Fitz*, according to Mr. Round's definition." (*Ante*, p. 202.)

Can it not? Let us see. I am willing to pass over the fact that in the original Record in dispute, *filius* both could and should bear that meaning, as Mr. Hall does not attempt to deny. I will meet him on his chosen ground, a writ of the reign of Edward III. I will take the well-known surname of Fitz-Warine. What then do we find? We have William Fitz Warine recorded in Latin writs quite indifferently, as "Willielmus *le fitz* W'aryn," * or "Willielmo *filio* Warini," † where *filius* is not only the equivalent of "le fitz," but does precisely *not* mean what Mr. Hall says it " can only mean," since William was *not* the son of "Warine," who was his remote ancestor. Nay, further, we have on the same page, by the very side of "Wilielmus *le fitz* Waryn," the forms "Fulco *filius* Warini," and "Johannes *filius* Fulconis *filii* Warini,"‡ where *we have only strictly to apply my rule to obtain at once the correct renderings*—"Fulk *Fitz* Warine" and "John *son of* Fulk *Fitz* Warine," while no quibble on earth can conceal the fact that if we applied Mr. Hall's rule that *filius* " can only mean " what he says it does, we should make as pretty a mess of this Record as has been made of that which I originally corrected. Let Mr. Hall keep to the point, and disprove this assertion *if he can*.

Let me advise Mr. Hall to hesitate, after this, before he again commits himself, or accuses me of "entire ignorance." That my "speculations" are "disastrous" to him, I can indeed well believe. But he has not only himself to consider. Will he not pause before he does for the Record Office what Mr. Lindsay has done for the College of Arms, or Mr. Jeaffreson for the Commission on Historical MSS.? Will no one stop him from adding further to my list, already too long, of the " Curiosities of Official Scholarship" ? J. H. ROUND.
Brighton.

TOWN AND BOROUGH CHARTERS : A WARNING.

SIR,—The borough charters of Pembroke were sent up to London at the time of the great Exhibition of 1851 ; but they were never returned to their lawful owners. Can any of your readers assist in throwing light on their fate ? MUS RUSTICUS.

THE FAMILY OF SHAW.

SIR,—I should be glad if any of your readers can assist me with any information bearing upon the personal history of the Shaws of Ayrshire and Greenock. JAMES SHANKS.

Ballyfounder, Portaferry, co. Down.

---

* Lords' Reports on the Dignity of a Peer (1827), iv. 434. † *Ibid.*, p. 538.
‡ *Ibid.* 434. Cf. " Fulconi Fitz Waryn " (*Ibid.*, p. 428).

SALDEN HOUSE, BUCKS,

SIR,—The Rev. William Cole, the Cambridge Antiquary, states, in a MS. volume of his collections, at the British Museum (Add. MS. 5840, p. 412), that he obtained from the executors of Mr. Browne Willis *three drawings* of this mansion—made "by no injudicious hand"—at Mr. Willis's request, before it was pulled down in 1738. Mr. Cole further states that he presented the drawings, in 1778, to Sir Sampson Gideon, Bart., who had purchased the estate. I should be glad to receive information as to their present place of deposit.   RICHARD SIMS.
British Museum.

THE "ANTIQUARY'S" LATIN.

SIR,—I thank you for your bold and honest protest against the "bad Latin and worse Greek"* which marks the pages of your rival. Your scholarly readers must be amused at finding in a recent number of Stock's magazine mention of "the patrician family of Sixinius (!) Crassus." But even in English names the editor blunders terribly ; for instance, Whittlesey, Archbishop of Canterbury, is styled by him "Whittesley." Is he not aware that some surnames are local, and that there is a Whittlesey or Whittlesea in Cambridgeshire ?   MUS RUSTICUS.

♦♦♦♦♦♦♦♦♦♦♦♦
TO CORRESPONDENTS.

THE Editor declines to pledge himself for the safety or return of MSS. voluntarily tendered to him by strangers.

ENQUIRER is informed that the registers of St. Mary's, Colchester, are beautifully and neatly written, especially the portion executed during Morant's time, and very accurate, as far as can be judged. An account of Morant will be found in THE ANTIQUARIAN MAGAZINE, vol. i. pp. 73—8.

CLIFTON, BT.—Katherine, daughter and sole heir of Sir Gervaise Clifton, married in 1607 Lord D'Aubigny. This connection with the Stewarts procured advancement for her father in the following year, when he was created Baron Clifton, of Leighton Bromswold, Northamptonshire. (See Ben Jonson, "The Forest," xiii.)

Wanted communications relative to the genealogy of the HODNETT family, members of which migrated from Shropshire to Ireland.—Replies to H., care of Editor.

MR. MAXWELL V. WOODHULL, of 2033 G. Street, Washington, United States, head of the American Branch of Wodhull or Woodhull, offers a reward of £21 for legal proof of the exact relationship between Richard Woodhull, of Long Island, U.S., and Thomas, second Lord Crewe, of Stene ; and also a reward of £5 5s. for a certified extract from a parish register of the birth or baptism of the said Richard Woodhull.

♦♦♦♦♦♦♦♦
Books Received.

1. History of the Copingers, or Coppingers. Edited by Walter A. Copinger, M.A. (New Edit.) Sotheran & Co. 1884.

2. Who Spoils our New English Books ? By Henry Stevens. London : H. N. Stevens. 1884.

3. Churches of West Cornwall. By J. T. Blight. (Second Edit.) Parker & Co. 1885.

4. Cornish Ballads. By Rev. R. S. Hawker. (Second Edit.) Parker & Co. 1885.

---

* See *ante*, p. 98.

5. Osborne Gordon : a Memoir. Edited by the Rev. Geo. Marshall, M.A. Parker & Co. 1885.

6. The Rights, Duties, Obligations, and Advantages of Hospitality. By Cornelius Walford, F.I.A., F.S.S. Privately printed. 1885.

7. Reference Catalogue of Current Literature. J. Whitaker. 1885.

8. City of London Directory. Collingridge, *City Press* Office. 1885.

9. English Etchings. Part xlvii. D. Bogue, 27, King William-street. April, 1885.

10. Hamilton's Parodies. Part xvii. Reeves & Turner.

11. Johns Hopkins' University Studies. Baltimore : March, 1885.

12. History of Aylesbury. By R. Gibbs. Part xiii. Aylesbury : R. Gibbs. March, 1885.

13. Leicester Castle, Kirby Muxloe Castle, and Trinity Hospital. By Wm. Jackson. Leicester : Clarke & Hodgson. 1885.

14. Lancashire and Cheshire Antiquarian Notes. Vol. ii. Part v. Leigh : *Chronicle* Office.

15. Miscellanea Genealogica. No. 16. Hamilton & Co. April, 1885.

16. The Genealogist. No. 6. Bell & Sons. April, 1885.

17. East Anglian. (New Series.) Parts ii., iii., iv. Ipswich : Pawsey & Hayes.

18. Le Livre. No. 64. Paris : 7, Rue St. Benoit. April, 1885.

Books, &c., for Sale.

Notes on Poems and Reviews, by A. C. Swinburne. Cassell's History of England, 9 vols. ; Beauties of England and Wales, 6 vols., half calf, uniform : Cumberland, Derbyshire, Devon, Dorset, Hants, Herefordshire, Lancashire, Leicestershire, Lincoln, Middlesex, Somerset, Staffordshire, and Isle of Man. (May be had separately.)—Address, E. Walford, 2, Hyde Park Mansions, N.W.

Lord Chesterfield's travelling box (large size).—Offers to Alice Parkinson, 39, Regent-street, Blackburn.

Original water-colour portrait of Jeremy Bentham, price 2 guineas. Also a large collection of Franks, Peers and Commoners'.—Apply to E. Walford, 2, Hyde Park Mansions, N.W.

Books, &c., Wanted to Purchase.

Dodd's Church History, 8vo., vols. i. ii. and v. ; Waagen's Art and Artists in England, vol. i. ; East Anglian, vol. i., Nos. 26 and 29. Notes and Queries, the third Index.—E. Walford, 2, Hyde Park Mansions, N.W.

Patterson's "Families of Ayrshire."—Address J. Shanks, Ballyfounder, Portaferry, co. Down.

Antiquarian Magazine and Bibliographer, several copies of No. 2 (February, 1882) are wanted, in order to complete sets. Copies of the current number will be given in exchange at the office.

A Frank of Francis Atterbury, Bishop of Rochester between 1713 and 1723, and other Bishops' franks of the 18th century.—Apply to J. D.

Archæologia, vols. xxii., xxiii., xxiv.; vol. xxxviii. part i. ; vols. xxxix., xl., xli. part i. ; vol. xlvii. part ii.—A. G. H., 47, Belsize-avenue, N.W.

"Tour of the Isle of Wight," vol. i. illustrated, 8vo. Hookham, 1790." —Address, G. Unwin, 71a, Ludgate-hill, E.C.

GREAT FLOOD IN MONMOUTHSHIRE, 1607.

From "The Pictorial Press."

The
Antiquarian Magazine
& Bibliographer.

The Pictorial Press.*

 N an octavo volume of some 360 pages, bearing the above title, Mr. Jackson has laid before the reader a vast amount of curious and interesting information concerning the subject of pictorial representation as applied to the newspaper Press from its earliest stages. "The inherent love of pictorial representation in all races of men and in every age," writes Mr. Jackson, "is manifest by the frequent attempts made to depict natural objects under the most unfavourable circumstances and with the slenderest means. The rude drawing scratched on the smooth bone of an animal by the cave-dweller of prehistoric times, the painted rocks of the Mexican forests, and the cave-paintings of the bushmen, are all evidences of this deeply-rooted passion." In the words of Horace—

> " Segniùs irritant animum demissa per aures,
> Quam quæ sunt oculis subjecta fidelibus."

Indeed, ocular demonstration of an event, however rudely represented by pictorial aid, has at all times and in all places been recognised as making more impression on the mind of the general reader than mere descriptive writing. True it has often happened that the pen was none the better for the fellowship ; nevertheless, the public taste in the early days of news illustration was not fastidious, and the work

---

* "The Pictorial Press, its Origin and Progress." By MASON JACKSON. Hurst & Blackett. 1885.

sufficed for the occasion. When the printing press came into use
this love of pictures had a wide field for development. Some of the
first books printed in England were illustrated with woodcuts; and
many of the tracts, or "news-books," which preceded regular newspapers, were adorned with rude engravings. The idea of "illustrated
journalism," our author tells us, may be traced from the earliest
years of the seventeenth century down to 1842, the date of the first
number of the *Illustrated London News*. The art of wood engraving
had fallen very low in the seventeenth century, and the illustrations
to be found in early newspapers are mostly of a very rude description.
A great fire—a remarkable murder—a fatal balloon accident—an
alarming flood—these were the subjects seized upon at the moment
to satisfy the public craving for illustrated news. Our author gives
numerous examples of the engravings of different periods, one of
which, by the courtesy of the publishers, we are enabled to reproduce :
it represents the "Great Flood in Monmouthshire, in 1607," and,
but for its title, might easily be mistaken for the work of a Japanese
artist. This woodcut, the author tells us, is the earliest instance he
had met with of an attempt to illustrate the news of the day. It was
printed on the title-page of a small tract, or "news-book," entitled
"Wofull Newes from Wales, or the lamentable loss of divers Villages
and Parishes (by a strange and wonderful Floud) within the Countye
of Monmouth in Wales : which happened in January last past, 1607,
whereby a great number of his Majesties subjects inhabiting in these
parts are utterly undone." Before, and for a long time after, the use
of newspapers became general, illustrated broadsides were published
relating to particular events, or satirising the vices and follies of the
period. The *Weekly News*, which was started in 1622, appeared
with an illustration in 1638, but it seems doubtful if the experiment
was successful, as it does not appear to have been repeated. Events
in the Irish Rebellion of 1641, and also in the Civil War in England,
were frequently seized upon as subjects for illustrated pamphlets and
newspapers. The *Welsh Post*, of 1643, is a curious illustrated
pamphlet, which relates to the news of the Civil War. The *Mercurius
Civicus, London's Intelligencer*, which was commenced in the same
year, frequently gave illustrations, and it is, therefore, as our author
remarks, entitled to be ranked as the first illustrated newspaper.
The early part of the eighteenth century saw the introduction of
several illustrated periodicals, such as *The Postman*, *The Grub Street
Journal*, *The Weekly Journal and British Gazetteer*, and the *Daily Post*.
Heathcote's Intelligencer, another paper of the reign of Queen Anne,

had occasional illustrations of eclipses and other events of the period. The eighteenth century, in fact, was remarkable for a class of publication that possessed many of the characteristics of illustrated journalism, without exactly belonging to the newspaper category. This kind of journal is represented by the *Gentleman's Magazine*, which was started by Edward Cave in 1731. *The Observer*, of which the first number was published December 4, 1791, appears to have been the first regular newspaper that availed itself of the restored art of wood-engraving, which Berwick's numerous pupils had so largely helped to bring about. In the early years of the present century *The Times* occasionally appeared with an illustration, as also did the *Morning Chronicle* and the *Sunday Times*. *Bell's Life in London*, *The Weekly Chronicle*, and *Observer*, appear to have been the main supporters of the pictorial spirit until it culminated in the *Illustrated London News*, of which the first number appeared on May 14, 1842, and from that time down to the present great strides have been made, not only in the quality of the workmanship, but also in the rapidity with which events of public interest, both at home and abroad, are portrayed. For full and complete details of the *Illustrated London News* and other illustrated journals, for particulars of artists who have assisted in founding the pictorial press, and for information concerning the production of an illustrated newspaper, we must refer the reader to the book itself, which will amply repay perusal.

UNDER the title of the Leland Club, a society of wandering archæologists has grown out of the bosom of the British Archæological Association; it has been founded by Mr. George R. Wright, F.S.A., for the purpose of making, at certain times and seasons of the year, excursions on the Continent and elsewhere, "at home and abroad," with a view to the examination and elucidation at the places visited of cathedrals, churches, abbeys, castles, or chateaux, and other buildings, together with any further objects of antiquarian research connected with prehistoric, Roman, or mediæval times. The first excursion, or "trial trip," of the Leland Club, was lately carried out by a party of ladies and gentlemen in Normandy. It is intended to issue an account of each expedition, and the account of the Society's doings in Normandy is now in progress. Amongst the contributors to it may be mentioned the names of Sir James A. Picton, F.S.A., and Mr. John Reynolds, who by their papers, &c., added largely to the success of the excursion. Among the places visited were Rouen, the chateau and remains of the monastery of St. Wandrille (formerly called Fontanelle), the abbey of Bonport, Pont de l'Arche, Boscherville, Candeber, Louriers, Caen, Lisieux, and the Chateau of Lasson, &c.

Professor Freeman on his Defence.

By J. H. Round, M.A.

" Once more, in all these enquiries, our one object is truth—truth to be sought after at all hazards, at whatever sacrifice of preconceived opinions."—FREEMAN'S *Historical Essays*, i. 38.

WITH characteristic confidence, in his Colchester Address to the members of the Royal Archæological Institute, Mr. Freeman proclaimed that Colchester Keep was " clearly the work of Eudo,"* that is of Eudes de Rie. Such, indeed, was the accepted story, handed down, as yet without question, from one authority to another. It was, however, pointed out by a troublesome critic, a few years later, that for this legend there was absolutely no historic evidence whatever, and that, against it, there was not only the negative evidence of its being ignored in the history of Eudes compiled by the monks of his Foundation, but also an overwhelming presumption, arising from the facts of the case, that this " the vastest of Norman donjons,"† was the work of the Conqueror himself.‡ Mr. Freeman, thereupon, reluctantly confessed that there was " perhaps something in this." Unwilling, however, to admit that he had been betrayed into the acceptance of a baseless legend, he contended that " it is perhaps safest to leave the matter open," though at the same time, inconsequently enough, determining to repeat his own story— " I have left what I wrote," he tells us, "attributing the Castle to Eudo."§

I propose here, not to repeat the arguments against Eudes having built the Keep,—as that ground appears to have been sufficiently traversed,—but simply to examine the pleadings of Mr. Freeman when thus placed " on his defence." And I would ask that it should be carefully borne in mind that what I am about to criticise is not his original error,—for from errors no one is free,—but his determination to adhere to that error, sooner than admit that he can have been mistaken.

I need scarcely add that Mr. Freeman enjoys every advantage in the controversy, the whole of which is comprised within his own special period, covered by his works in the fullest detail.

---

* Arch. Journ. xxxiv. ; Macmillan's Magazine, 1876.
† Norm. Conq. (1879), ii. 250.
‡ History and Antiquities of Colchester Castle (1882), pp. 27—29.
§ English Towns and Districts (1883), pp. 416, 417.

Let us notice, in the first place, that Mr. Freeman, when thus brought to task, is unable to produce one scrap of evidence for his assertion that the Keep was "clearly" (or even probably) "the work of Eudo." If I may be allowed to quote from his own words, when questioning a similar story—

"The story is perfectly possible ; we only ask for the proof . . . then we will believe. Without such a proof we will not believe."[*]

But it is just "such a proof" that Mr. Freeman himself is here unable to produce. Nay, we may go further still. We may point out that this story of his is not "perfectly possible," that, indeed, from all we know of the case, it is as improbable as it well can be. The presumption, as he himself, though reluctantly, admits, is against the Keep being "the work of Eudo." On Mr. Freeman, therefore, the *onus probandi* rests with even greater weight. Unable, however, to produce evidence where no evidence exists, Mr. Freeman falls back on two arguments directed against the evidence adduced to prove that the keep was *not* "the work of Eudo." Even if successful in this (which, as we shall see, he is not), he would still, obviously, be no nearer to proving that the Keep *was* his work, the point which he is forced to evade.

The two points which Mr. Freeman has selected for that counter-attack which, like a skilled strategist, he boldly substitutes for defence, are the evidence of a certain Charter and the evidence of Domesday itself. He questions the evidence of the Charter that Eudes did not build the Keep, and he appeals to the evidence of Domesday against the suggestion that the Conqueror did. I shall first deal with the Charter.

Far be it from me to contend that any Charter should be accepted without question. But when Mr. Freeman speaks of "a suspicious ring" in this Charter, he is bound to produce the grounds for his suspicion. This he does not do. The Charter in question is taken from a "cartulary," which Mr. Freeman, apparently unaware of the fact, assures us, in a prominent place, is among the "things that want printing." In that opinion I most cordially concur. For this Charter will then be given to the world, and Mr. Freeman, whose predilection for printed authorities is matter of common knowledge, will then be able to refer to it without the trouble of consulting a MS. Meanwhile I may explain that the Charter purports to grant, *inter alia*, to "Eudo" the castle of Colchester, a grant which it is

---

[*] Contemporary Review, June, 1877, p. 22.

contended is incompatible with the Castle being of his own building and in his own possession from the first. The obvious date of the Charter, as Mr. Freeman has clearly shown, must be Christmas, 1101. This, therefore, is the date at which "Eudo" is first brought into connection with the Castle, and then only as its grantee. But the masonry of the Keep, the building in dispute, is admittedly of the previous century :—

"Of this [*i.e.* military] masonry, there is but little which can be referred to the reign of either the Conqueror or William Rufus—that is, to the eleventh century. Of that period are certainly London and Malling, . . Colchester, &c. &c."[*]

Indeed, Mr. Freeman speaks of it as "a work dating from the days of the second William."[†] Consequently, if the Charter is to hold good, it follows that the Keep, so far from being "clearly the work of Eudo," was built and standing some time before it passed into his hands, indeed in the preceding reign and in the previous century.

Mr. Freeman's simplest resource is, therefore, to impugn the Charter. But, in so doing, he plunges into a worse difficulty. For even assuming the Charter to be a forgery (of which there is no proof), it would follow, in the first place, that even a forger did not venture, any more than did the monks, to claim the Castle as "a work of Eudo," and, in the second, that in abandoning the Charter we should abandon absolutely the only evidence that Eudes was ever in possession of the Castle.[‡]

Mr. Freeman, it would seem, must have perceived this, for at the same time he hazards the contention that it may be even possible to accept the Charter, and yet to reject the deduction drawn from it. He puts his argument thus :—

"If Eudo had anything to do with the treasons of that year [1101], a fresh grant of the Castle might well be needful, whether the Castle was his own building or not."[§]

On this I would observe : (1) that the King says, in this Charter, "me dedisse *benignè et ad amorem* concessisse Eudoni." Now, at this time, we know, "the Lion of Justice" was rather intent on punishing and ruining those who had "had anything to do with the treasons of that year" than on rewarding them "benignè" or "ad amorem." Indeed, as Mr. Freeman himself reminds us of this eventful winter: "No enemy escaped him, no traitor avoided forfeiture

---

[*] Clark's Mediæval Military Architecture, i. 40.
[†] English Towns and Districts, p. 411.
[‡] His grant of the tithes of the Castle Chapel may be held to suggest it as an inference, but is not evidence of the fact.
[§] English Towns and Districts, p. 417.

or heavy fines." * (2) We find Eudes, so far as we can tell, a supporter and favourite of the king throughout his reign. Consequently this Charter, if to a valued supporter, is in singular accordance with Mr. Freeman's own remark that Henry, at this period, " rewarded bountifully all who served him faithfully.† (3) Mr. Freeman's suggestion that the Charter was " a fresh grant," is (besides the improbability of the "treason" hypothesis) obviously opposed to the word "dedisse," which, as has been observed more than once, is scarcely compatible with previous possession. But, lest Mr. Freeman should question this, I hasten to add that in the same cartulary there appears by the side of this Charter another one, distinct from it, re-granting to Eudes all that he had possessed under the previous reigns, and that here the formula runs, as we should expect—" me *reddi*disse et benignè ad amorem concessisse." Therefore, whether Eudes had been concerned or not " with the treasons of that year " (for this can only, at present, be matter of hypothesis and conjecture), we see from the language of the two grants that the rights and properties which he had previously possessed were carefully distinguished from the Castle which he had not. (4) Lastly, the reference in the respective Charters to the previous tenure, in each case, is equally conclusive in the matter :—

| " Sicut pater meus et frater et ego eam melius habuimus unquam." | " Sicut ipse unquam illa melius tenuit." |

The former, we see, describes the Castle as having been continuously in the possession of the Crown up to the very time of this grant to " Eudo."‡

It must, then, be admitted that if we accept the Charter, no other deduction can possibly be drawn from it than that it placed "Eudo" for the first time in possession of this Royal fortress. Nothing, therefore, remains for Mr. Freeman but to abandon his untenable compromise, and to prove that the Charter is a forgery. Should he succeed, however, in so doing, he will still, we must remember, be no nearer to producing any evidence for his confident assertion that the Keep was " clearly the work of Eudo."

I propose in the second part of this Paper to deal with the witness of Domesday, Mr. Freeman's arguments with regard to which will suggest some interesting reflections.

(*To be continued.*)

---

* William Rufus, ii. 417.   † Ibid.
‡ See, on these two Charters, *Notes and Queries*, 6th Ser. v. 82 (Feb. 4, 1882).

Curll's Miscellanies, 1727.

THE influence which Edmund Curll had on the works of the great Scriblerus Club, Pope, Swift, Arbuthnot, and others, whether for good or evil, was great, and forms a very interesting chapter in the literary history of the early part of the eighteenth century. There is at present no bibliographical catalogue of the works which he printed or published which has any pretensions to completeness or accuracy. Looking to the large number of readers who are now studying the subject and making notes, more or less with a view to future publication, it is probable that ere long we shall see a systematic list of Curll's publications, with explanatory notes.

In considering any of Curll's Miscellanies, or compound volumes, it is necessary to bear in mind the especial manner in which he conducted his business. Now, the first thing to be observed is, that whenever Curll got hold of anything which he deemed likely to attract the public, or, in other words, to "sell," he printed it at once. Right or wrong, correct or incorrect, decent or indecent, he printed it forthwith, and sold as many copies as he could. In those days it was not always so easy to get rid of back stock, and tracts, poems, and lampoons, when their day was passed, hung heavy on hand. This did not suit Curll, and he ever sought by some ingenious device or other to put a new face upon his old wares, and give a new title to the publications of a previous year. His first step always was to procure a copy of something new, smart, or smutty, which would attract controversy; and as a general rule he cared nothing about the presumed rights of authors, or the jealous prejudices of their publishers. He had two great leading principles of action, which might be expressed by two old sayings—" The early bird gets the worm," and "First come first served." These were the lines on which he traded, and he well understood—in accordance with the taste of the times—that nothing was so attractive as scandal, either direct or implied ; and indecent stories, either open and told with unblushing impudence, or delicately wrapt up so as to please at the same time both the rakes and the prudes.

As an illustration of how he thus acted in early times, let us take the case of Swift's " Broom Stick." Curll got hold of this pretty early, and he forthwith had it printed, and published it under the title, " A Meditation upon a Broom Stick, and somewhat beside ; of the same Author's. Utile dulci. London. Printed for E. Curll, at the Dial and Bible, against St. Dunstan's Church in Fleet-street; and sold by J. Harding at the Post Office in St. Martin's Lane." 1710, 8vo. pp. 1—29, price sixpence. Curll added at the end a notable " advertisement." " Speedily will be published, some other pieces relating to the last subject herein mention'd, and what has hitherto been printed of any of these, were from very Faulty and incorrect Copies."

The following year Curll printed the Key to the " Tale of a Tub," but he had still on hand many copies of the " Meditation upon a Broom Stick," so he joined the two together, and printed a new title-page :—

" Miscellanies, by Dr. Jonathan Swift.— [This included six tracts, namely, (1) The Broom Stick; (2) Baucis and Philemon; (3) To Their Excellencies; (4) To Mrs. Biddy Floyd; (5) History of Vanburgh's House; (6) Key to the Tale of a Tub.]—London : Printed for E. Curll, at the Dial and Bible, against St. Dunstan's Church, in Fleet-street, 1711," pp. 1—36 and 1—29.

In consequence of this mode of proceeding, it becomes necessary in dealing with Curll's publications, to be doubly careful in ascertaining whether the date on the title-page is the real year of publication, and also whether the volume under consideration is perfect and complete in itself, or whether it is not made up of previous issues, with a new or modified title-page and date. I am led to make these remarks in reference to Mr. Roberts' note on "Swiftiana" in a former number, p. 157; and now pass on at once from Curll's proceedings in 1711 to what he did in 1727. In that year Pope and Swift published their " Miscellanies in Prose and Verse," in three volumes octavo, and Curll determined not to be set aside, even by the authors themselves. He therefore brought out his " Miscellanea " in five volumes, 12mo. Mr. Roberts has described the two first of these ; but it will not do to be very exact as to the contents of these two volumes ; they were in great part made up of old stock, and therefore wrong. I have three copies, two agreeing in all respects with the description as given by Mr. Roberts ; but the other having an important difference. In it the second volume is the same up to page 99, which in all copies has at foot " Finis." The one issue, then, has " Laus Ululæ, the Praise of Owls," pp. 1—101, which is clearly a piece of booksellers' " padding." The other has the well-known "Court Poems," pp. 1—24, followed by two independent small collections of " Poems on Several Occasions," pp. 1—42 and 1—33, ending with a list of books lately published on an Elzevir

Letter, in a neat pocket volume. Printed for E. Curll. These two collections are clearly made up of old stock, and include little of interest; perhaps the most remarkable amongst them is the stupid and malignant attack on Steele for printing " This incomparable Elegy on the Death of Queen Mary, Publish'd eighteen years after it was written." This was, of course, founded on an error, for Steele published the poem entitled the " Procession " in 1695, though without his name, and only first printed it with his name in his " Poetical Miscellanies " in 1714. This shows that Curll's little collection, though thus used in 1727, must have been printed about twelve years earlier.

The third volume of Curll's " Miscellanies " was entitled " Whartoniana; or, Miscellanies in Verse and Prose, by the Wharton family and several other persons of distinction." London : Printed in the year 1727 (Price 5s.) Dedication i. to vii., signed E. Curll, pp. 1—85, page 1, and the succeeding first page of each following sheet bears at foot vol. iii. In this volume there are several poems which may be fairly designated " Swiftiana," such as—

(5) Prologue to a Greek Play. By Dean Swift.

(11) Wood's Half-pence. By Dean Swift.

(21) Upon Rover. By Dean Swift.

(26) An Excellent New Song. By Honest Jo., i.e., Dean Swift.

It is characteristic of his modesty, and amusing to note, that amongst these "poems by persons of distinction," there is at p. 146 an epigram " by E. Curll, late Bookseller."

The fourth volume of " Miscellanies " was also published in 1727, and is of a very miscellaneous character. It contains letters to Lady Wharton, letters from Mr. Norris to Corinna, St. John's " Almahide," Mrs. Wharton's " Lamentations," novels by Mrs. Plantin, letters by Lord Rochester, &c., pp. 1—168, after which is added, to make up the volume, Observations on Jamaica, a few more short poems, and Pylades to Corinna; pp. 1—33. There seems to have been some arrangement between Curll and W. Warner, of Dryden's Head, next the Rose Tavern, without Temple Bar; fresh title-pages were printed with his name, and half the edition of vols. ii. and iii., therefore, bear on the title-page the name of the real original publisher, E. Curll, the other half that of W. Warner. In this fourth volume there was no " Swiftiana."

The fifth volume of " Miscellanies " was entitled :

" Atterburyana; being Miscellanies. By the late Bishop of Rochester, &c., with a Collection of Original Letters. The Virgin

Seducer, a true History. The Batchelor Keeper. By Philaretus. London : Printed in the year 1727, price 2s. 6d." The dedication is to Dr. Towne ; it is signed E. Curll ; and in it he says, " Let me place this fifth volume of ' Miscellanies ' on the same shelf with the four preceding ones, it being the pin-basket of my collections for the year seventeen hundred and twenty-six."

Like the preceding four volumes, this last miscellany is made up ; it commences with a postscript, entitled, " Just arrived from Twickenham (as I am assured), Mr. Pope's Receipt to make Soup. For the use of Dr. Swift." This is the well-known little poem, commencing—

> " Take a knuckle of veal,
>   You may buy it or steal ;'
>   In a few pieces cut it,
>   In a stew-pan put it."

Then follows " Miscellanea," vol. v. : " Pylades to Corinna," &c., pp. 1—153, after which follows " Court Secrets ; or, The Lady's Chronicle, Historical, and Gallant, from the year 1671 to 1690. Extracted from the letters of Madam de Sevigné, which have been suppressed at Paris. London : Printed in the year 1727," pp. 1—41. The volume concludes with a list of books " printed for Mr. Curll, in the Strand." This was, of course, done for a purpose, and on the face of it is false, for the list includes such books as the " Count de Gabalis," and the " Patch Work Screen," both of which bear on the title-page : " Printed for E. Curll, over against Catherine-street, in the Strand." In 1727 Curll was in daily fear of criminal proceedings and public punishment, and he thought it prudent to transfer, as far as he could, some part of his business and stock to his son Henry, who already had an independent shop in Henrietta-street. Curll's " Miscellanies," in five volumes, 12mo., 1727, is not a common book, though single volumes of it are often to be met with.

To return to the part of the second volume entitled " Swiftiana," the title-page states that it is by Dean Swift and several of his friends. There are twelve articles, and seven of these are clearly said not to be by the Dean ; five are attributed to him, though it may well be doubted whether any one of them was really by Swift. The " Broken Mug," as Mr. Roberts has pointed out, was written by Laurence Whyte, and is found entire in his little volume entitled " Poems on Various Subjects. Dublin : Printed by S. Powell," 12mo. i.—xx. and 1—236. In the preface, the history of the " Broken Mug " is thus given :—

" The Broken Mug, I must own, was a Task imposed on me in the year 1720 by a deceased friend, Mr. Robert Steele, an eminent Teacher of Mathematicks, and a very facetious and agreeable companion, at which time, by his importunity, I writ two Cantos on that important subject : the first was handed about and printed here without my knowledge or direction, 'twas in some time after printed in London, and bound-up there in a collection of Poems supposed to be written by a celebrated Author in this Kingdom, much like some of our countrymen, who, being despised at home, had the good fortune by crossing the seas to fall into good company and meet with honour and Preferment abroad."

It is right that Whyte, and not Swift, should be known as the writer of this poem ; and Whyte's account is interesting as showing how, during Swift's life, this was printed as " written by Dean Swift," and then many years subsequently, but still in Swift's lifetime, publicly claimed by the true writer. Laurence Whyte had a high admiration of and respect for Swift, and in his volume of poems there is one on the publication of the new edition of Swift's works by Faulkner, in 1735, which commences—

> " Pardon, great Swift, the Freedom of a Bard !
> Who writes for neither Interest or Reward."

The lines are highly complimentary, and fairly entitle the little volume to a place amongst " Swiftiana."

With regard to the second poem, " The Reply to the Rebus," by Miss Van Homrigh [Vanessa], I do not know of any distinct evidence as to the writer, like that which we have in the case of the " Broken Mug ; " and without that it was, perhaps, fair for Curll to say it may have been written by Swift. It is very improbable that the rebus was written by Vanessa, but there is nothing in the reply, with one exception, which might not have been written by Swift ; the ideas are good, and very like what we may presume he would have written to her about the time he went to live at Letcombe, in 1714. With half an eye the answer to the rebus could be seen, and in a few minutes the reply could be scribbled down. It begins with an exaggerated compliment, practically treating her as a little child, who would not perceive the gentle sarcasm ; and then going on to bewail and depreciate himself.

I have said there is one thing which I think could not have come from the pen of Swift, and that occurs in the very first line :—

> " The Nymph who wrote this in an Amorous Fit."

Now, there is nothing at all amorous in the rebus, and the use of that word renders the whole reply absurd and improbable. I have seen early copies of the poem commencing :—

> " The Nymph who wrote this in a Humorous Fit."

If, as some may think possible, the lines are by Swift, then I have very little doubt that he wrote humorous, and not amorous. This will agree with what follows :—

> " For mean's her design, on a subject so mean,
> The first but a rebus, the last but a Dean,
> A Dean's but a Parson, and what is a rebus,
> A thing never known to the Muses or Phœbus.
> The corruption of verse, for when all is done,
> It is but a Paraphrase made on a Pun."

The writer then proceeds to praise her " great wit," and says :—

> " So the wit that is lavishly thrown away here
> Might furnish a second-rate Poet a year."

The subsequent lines are what anyone might have written, but they seem to express with force and accuracy Swift's real feelings at a time of mental depression :—

> " Her fine panegyricks are quite out of Season,
> And what she describes to be merit is Treason,
> The changes which Faction has made in the State
> Have put the Dean's Politicks quite out of date.
> Now no one regards what he utters with Freedom,
> And should he write Pamphlets no great Man would read em."

There is all throughout from " only a dean," to the final statement that his occupation as writer of political pamphlets is at an end, a great deal which reminds us of Swift, and seems to favour the belief that he wrote the " Reply." Perhaps Curll's issue of them in 1727 was not the first, but I am unable to produce an earlier edition, or to substantiate my suggestion that the word as originally written was " humorous." I presume the poem was not made public till " Cadenus and Vanessa " was printed, that is, till after the death of Miss Van Homrigh, and that then the four last words of the first line " who his mistress deny'd," may have suggested a change in the reply from humorous to amorous, throwing an apparent meaning into it which the original did not really warrant. On the whole, I am led to the conviction that the rebus was not written by Vanessa, and that the reply was not the work of Swift ; it is a clever imitation of his style by some one who knew him well, but had no great love for him.

EDWARD SOLLY.

The Playhouses at Bankside in the Time of Shakespeare.

By W. Rendle, F.R.C.S.

PART II.

(Continued from page 212.)

THE study of Paris Garden and the "Bancke" in the time of the sport and play-houses will prove more useful, and far more interesting, if we see, as it were, the social conditions and scenery of the spot and time. The finest description that could be given out of one's educated imagination would not avail; my labour in so limited a sphere is to narrate concerning the past with complete fidelity. The historical antiquary especially is of no use unless he does this, the novelist would otherwise be more in place.* Happily, here, this can be easily done; State papers of more or less importance are at hand, kindly people have the care of them, and the arrangements of the Public Record Office are more than liberal. We have official documents, trials at law, confidential correspondence, leases and the like, none of them intended to describe social conditions or scenery, and therefore the more likely when thus incidentally and faithfully given to disclose the actual truth; and as they are of the time we are studying, they are as near as possible to the very sources of truth. Here is one which enables us to see Paris Garden in the year 1578 † much as the people themselves then living saw it. The scene laid is in the time of conspiracies; the Protestant Queen had enemies everywhere. Paris Garden was a favourite place of resort for those who would plot; we see why, it was covered with trees, full of hiding-places, river-side landings, and near to the lodgings of Court disturbers over the river. Fleetwood writes: "The French Ambassador lying in Sackville-street meets in the summer with confederates, on the Thames side behind Paris Garden toward Lambeth, in the fields. This place was the continual haunt of the Bishop of Ross, and here was he taken giving instructions to my Lord of Southampton. In the aforesaid fields between ten and eleven o'clock last night, behind Paris Garden, the French Ambassador held secret conferences for about an hour with Sir Warham St. Leger and Sir

---

* This indispensable qualification I learned from my friend before quoted, to whom I am much indebted.

† Fleetwood, Recorder of London, to Burleigh, 13th July, 1578. See State Papers: Domestic Calendars.

William Morland, until the watch came and did examine what they were. Sir Warham St. Leger and Mr. Morgan did use themselves courteously and mildly. The French Ambassador caused three of his men to stand at the lane end with naked swords drawn, to foresee who drew near and to use lustie bragges against the Queen's watch; the knights used fair words, but the Ambassador swore great othes that he wolde do many thinges, and that he was a privileged person; he used himself like a monarke, but the wache said unto him that they knew not his dignitie nor yet his authoritie; but they told him plainly that he sholde not in the night time use any conference in that place with any of her Majesty's subjects without license, and they said to him that forasmuch as he and his men had broken the peax and were night walkers contrary to the law, that if he wolde not quietly get them home to his house and depart immediately they wolde carry him over into the city to the Recorder : and then in great rage with many othes he departed, every one in a several boate." "Sir Warham lives at the Bell in the Strand." Afterwards, "I got a skuller to Paris Garden, but the place was dark and shadowed with trees, that one man cannot see another unless they have lynceos oculos or els cattes eys, shewing how admirable a place it was for such doings. The place is that boowre of conspiracies, it is the college of male counsell." "There be certain virgulta (twigs or young trees) or eightes of willows set by the Thames near that place ; they grow now exceeding thick, and are a notable covert for confederates to shrowd in ; a milkmade lately did see the French Ambassador land in that virgulta." Fleetwood, to pursue it further, "took a light horseman of five oars, the master who was the sternsman, was Watson of Battlebridge."

Gerard's Herbal was published in 1597. We learn from him of the wild plants that grew here about : the hedgehog or harrie grasse, from Paris Garden bridge to St. George's Fields ; the great water burre or burre reed, by the ditches in St. George's Fields ; the narrow-leaved arrow-head was here, the crow-foot, and in nearly every pool the frog-bit : the botanist would be able to see what manner of place it was by the known habits of the plants. Again, as to the character of the locality. In a suit, 1625, it is recited of the manor of *Parish* Garden, *alias* Paris Garden, that there is a house within le Mote, two gardens abutting on a marsh, a Gatehouse, le Pond-yard, le Coney Garth *alias* Coney-gree, Chapel Howe Hawe or Hall, and Walnuttes; pastures of willows and the like, all giving a vivid notion what kind of place the now parish of Christchurch was then.

It may be profitable here to give one more State paper, this one the date 1657, but which puts before us a picture of the past, pertinent to the subject of this essay. It is altogether an interesting State paper, and has much to do with the history and progress of the locality :*—

"To His Highness the Lord Protector, &c.

The humble petition of the tennants, copyhold^rs, inhabitants of the manor of old Paris Garden, in the parish of St. Saviours, Southwark, in the county of Surrey, and the parte thereunto adjacent. That whereas for the space of 220 years last past, the copyholders inhabitants of the said manor have quietly enjoyed a waste ground and highway in common lying within the said manor leading from the ffalcon on the Bankside to St. George's Fields, and from the said ffalcon to the parish of Lambeth, in Surrey, and other places as a right belonging to your petitioners, both in the late Earl of Arundel's time and others who have been Lords of ye Demeans : And whereas one William Angell hath lately purchased the demeans, and hath erected and built several cottages and houses and intendeth to erect very many more upon the same waste ground, hath dammed up the common shores, and will bring into the liberty many poor people to inhabit therein to the utter undoing of the ancient inhabitants and copyholders of said liberty, who are not able to keep their own poor. Besides the said erections will be dangerous to bring infection by their stopping up and taking away the Ayre from the now petitioners' houses and stopping up the highway which belongeth to your petitioners, and barred your petitioners from all liberty of taking water, either for their necessary uses about their household affairs or in case of danger from fire for quenching the same, all the means for having water for these purposes being by his excessive building utterly obstructed and taken away from your petitioners to their utter ruine." Among other signatures are those of James Austin, James How, and Richard Arthur, very noted people then, who pray His Highness to stay the building. It is endorsed Oliver P. in his own hand, with this remark : "We refer the petition to the consideration of our Councell, desiringe the petitioners may be speedilye heard thereupon. May 22, 1657." The Hows were rising people; Sir Richard was member for Southwark thrice, in 1678 and after, and he was captain of the train bands. The tenor of the petition, considering the quantity of uncovered ground, and the

---

* State Papers, Dom. Inter. vol. clv.

sparseness of houses, is almost ludicrous. In 1670, when the Act was passed constituting the parish of Christchurch, three-fourths of it consisted of fields: the population—a thousand or so—has become at the present time 13,000.

Further as to the aspect of the locality; before this, from time immemorial there was right of common and pasture. In early maps cattle are shown feeding; a sewers presentment of 1618 declares that "those who keep cattle at Pond End of Maid Lane, next St. George's Fields, ought to repair the banks broken down by the cattle."

The generally received opinion of the origin of the name seems to be taken from Blount,* who says Paris Garden, anciently so called from Robert de Paris, who had a house *and garden* there in Richard II.'s time, who by proclamation ordained that butchers of London should buy that garden for receipt of their garbage and entrails of beasts, to the end that the City might not be annoyed thereby. As yet there could have been no bear sports on the Bankside, else the butchers' garbage, cut up and carefully conveyed to midstream of the Thames, would have found a more ready and effectual ending. Blount cites the Close Roll, 15 Rich. II., 1391 or 3. In the original cited there is no mention of a garden; the garbage was to be conveyed "juxta domum Roberti de Parys." Blount seems to have superadded the garden.

Taylor, the water poet, before Blount, says in his sportive way—

> "How it the name of Paris Garden gained—
> The name it was from a Royall Boy,
> Brave Ilion's firebrand . . . . . .
> From Paris, Paris Garden hath the name."

In the earliest records of the name that I have seen, 1420, it is Parish Garden; in 1434, "Molendina de Wideflete cum Gardino, &c., vocato Parish gardin." Early this place was a local parish or chapelry belonging to the Temple on the opposite side of the river. Upon the whole, I am inclined to think that the manor may have been first known as Parish or Parysh Garden, becoming at length about the time of Henry VIII. and Edward VI. Paris Garden, or indifferently as it was spelt Paris or Parish. Taylor would hardly have said even sportively, what he did as to Paris of Troy, had he known of Robert de Parys.

I have by good hap and friendly favour come across a rare pictorial

---

* Glossographia, 1681, p. 473.

illustration (which is here carefully represented) of the famous passage
from Holland's "Leaguer," p. 211.   That it does refer to the Swan
and the Leaguer, "the turret, and the shaking hands with the dying
Swan," which at the period the sketch was no doubt taken was so to
speak dying, is in the highest degree possible : the apparent incongruity of the relative position is so very slight, that I do not hesitate
in commending it at least as a study to students of the period, taken
some years probably before the publication in 1649.*   Holland's
"Leaguer," familiarly Nobs Island, has a small history of its own,
sufficiently given in Wilkinson's "Londina."†   In the Roxburghe
Collection of Ballads, among others is one entitled "The Map of
Mockbeggar Hall, with his situation in the spacious Countrey called

THE SWAN.   HOLLAND'S LEAGUER.

BANKSIDE, 1649.

Anywhere."   In a note Mr. Halliwell-Phillipps says of the elaborate
woodcut accompanying the ballad, that it represents a notorious
brothel in Southwark, kept by a Mrs. Holland in the reign of
Charles I.   The present Holland-street is *said* to derive its name
from this woman, and runs over the site of the house.   In Domestic
Calendars, Charles I., 1630, a "Susan Holland states that she is per-
secuted, her goods kept from her, and she charged as an incontinent
woman by Sir Thomas Whorwood, Knt."   1631, State Papers, vol.
ccv., 33, "showeth that petitioners Hunt and Rogers of late bought a
lease of house with divers goods wherein a Mrs. Holland lately dwelt :"
the bad character of the house is stated.   The presence of the train

* Gotofredi, Archontologia Cosmica, fol. 1649.   In the British Museum is an
edition of 1638.
† Holland's Leaguer, Bankside.

bands is desired, as the 'prentices threaten to demolish the houses. But this as part of the larger subject of the Stews on the Bankside has been given by the present writer in the ANTIQUARIAN MAGAZINE, August, 1882.*

(To be continued.)

Guy of Warwick.

BY THE REV. F. CONWAY, M.A.,
Member of the Royal Asiatic Society.

PART III.
(Continued from p. 228, ante.)

BUT though the legend is to be banished from the sober annals of history, yet it must, like everything else, have had a beginning—a why and a wherefore. I will try to find the beginning now. The first noticeable thing in the tale is its threefold form—its three absences, its three journeys ; and I am sure that the first step to be taken in its analysis is the mathematical one of extracting the cube root. Guy's three journeys are merely three different accounts of one and the same journey. The tale was afloat amongst the people long before it was written down ; and as it passed from mouth to mouth, from generation to generation, it became modified into more or less different versions. When, in a literary age, Guy was made the subject of an elaborate written romance, these varying versions, each with its own distinct episodes, were made into three distinct journeys. If, then, my view is right, the early form of the tale must have been something like this : " Once upon a time "—even in the days of the Saxons stories always begin with "once upon a time "—" there was a warrior, braver and mightier than all other warriors, who wedded a fair and gentle girl, but straightway left her and lived a life of toil, to be reunited with his wife only in the hour of death." And this is a story which is found among the legends of many widely-severed nations. It is the tale of Ulysses fighting for ten years far away from the patient Penelope ; in peril of shipwreck, in peril of cannibals : sorely tempted by Calypso, sorely tempted by Circe, sorely tempted by the Lotus Eaters, till all his trials are over and his work is done at last, and husband and wife are re-united before they

---

* See vol. ii. pp. 70—77.

cross the river of eternity. It is the tale of Ariadne left forlorn on the lonely island, to make her moan to the winds. It is the tale of Mariana in the moated grange. It is the tale of the labours of Hercules. It is the Hindoo tale of Nala wandering in the wilderness, severed from his wife, Damayanti, of the slender waist. I could multiply instances indefinitely, but it is enough to say that the Greek and Roman forms of the legend were so numerous that the Roman poet, Ovid, wrote a whole series of fictitious epistles, purporting to be penned by each deserted fair one to her truant lover. Here is the legend in a Greek form, as told by Sir G. Cox, in his "Tales of Ancient Greece": "Œnone was a water nymph, who loved Paris of Troy. Many a time he sat with the maiden by the side of the stream, and the sound of their voices was mingled with the soft murmur of the waters. He talked to her of love, and Œnone looked up with a wondrous joy into his beautiful face, when the morning dew glistened white upon the grass, and when the evening star looked out upon the pale sky. So was Paris wedded to Œnone, and the heart of the maiden was full of happiness, for none was braver or more gentle, none so stout of heart, so lithe of limb, so tender and loving, as Paris. Thus passed the days away in a swift dream of joy, and Œnone thought not of the change that was coming. But the change came. Paris went far away over the sea, and returned with another man's wife, and the vengeful husband followed with all the chivalry of Greece, and there was war in the land for ten years, until, in the final struggle, a fatal arrow struck Paris down. But as he fell the forsaken Œnone stood before him, fair and beautiful as in the days that were past. And she laid her hand upon him and said gently, 'Dost thou know me, Paris?' and Paris said, 'I have wronged thee, Œnone, fairest and sweetest, and what may atone for the wrong? My head reels and mine eye is dim; look but upon me once, that I may fall asleep and die.' And Œnone knelt by the side of Paris, and saw the wound which the arrow had made; and she knew that the end had come. And she cried as she knelt, 'O Paris, we have loved and suffered, but I never did thee wrong, and now I follow thee to the dark land of Hades.'"

Here we have the same main features as those of the Guy legend. A great hero deserts his loving bride, and lives a life of storm until, in the hour of death, she comes to him again. This story of the truant husband is one of a bundle of tales which form the common literary heritage of the Indo-German races. The bundle contains also the Sleeping Beauty, whose enchanted slumber none but the one chosen hero can break ; the story—so familiar to us all in its Arabian dress—of the fisherman and the bottle that held the Jin, and the story of Cinderella and the crystal slipper. They have all run down the stream of time from a hoary antiquity. Once upon a time—long before any history was written or any inscription cut— the ancestors of German and Greek, Roman, Kelt, and Hindoo, English and French, formed one people, dwelling—somewhere. I am sorry that I cannot define, even approximately, the original habitat of this nation. Had you, ten years ago, asked me to tell you where the original home of the Aryans was, I should have answered " in the high lands of Central Asia." But so intolerant is the age of any fixed belief in anything whatsoever, that even this out-of-the-way subject has not escaped the general doubt, and while one Dr. Dry-as-dust insists upon the claims of Scandinavia, and another upon those of Southern Russia, and literary conserva-tives still remain to adhere to Asia, I feel I must make no definite statement on this point, for fear of misdirecting travellers. But you must not from this be led to suppose that the *existence* of this primi-tive people is a matter of doubt. Though no written record exists to tell us when or how or where, yet the languages that live around us have a tale to tell to those who ask aright ; and language tells us that the existence of this people is as strictly a historic fact as the battle of Waterloo, and maps out its wanderings as surely as the modern historian maps out the campaigns of Napoleon. At this pre-historic period, mankind collectively was in its infancy, and had the feelings such as characterise individual children nowadays. You have all probably seen a child, when it has struck itself against a chair, retaliate against the piece of furniture, and call it " Naughty chair." This it does because its mind is not yet developed to con-ceive anything except what is human and animate like itself. Just so man, in the infancy of the world, endowed all his surroundings with human feelings, human hopes and fears. He had life, so all things had life ; birth and marriage and death were the great chapters in *his* existence, so birth and marriage and death must be common to everything in nature. Through grunts and groans and growls and grimaces—the original apparatus with which he was equipped for the purpose of exchanging ideas with his fellows—he had gradually evolved a limited number of words ; but this language could, of course, express only his own feelings—was capable only of describing things by investing them with human garb. Let us now try to put ourselves into the position of a being with this limited range of ideas and this limited power of expression. I must remind you that at the epoch I am describing there were no speculators in electric lighting, no gas companies with their Christmas bills; lamps were things of the future, and no one had yet dreamed of the humble tallow candle. It was, indeed, a dark age, especially at night, and our ancestor used to go to bed at sunset and get up again at daybreak, as systematically as if he knew the reward promised by the proverb to those who are early to bed and early to rise. Hence the first thing that met his wakening eyes was the flushing glow of the sky, that heralds the sun's appearance. The sun rises and the flush disappears, and right through the long day the sun toils on. As a favourite nursery lyric tell us :—

> " He never tires nor stops to rest,
> But round the world he shines."

At last evening comes, and then round the setting sun, whose toil is done at last—round the sun as he goes down to his resting-place in the west—appears again that soft and rosy flush, and for awhile lingers, as if lovingly, in the western sky, after the sun has set, until it, too, sinks to rest with him. It is a thoughtful saying that through the length and breadth of nature runs the law, that when a thing is struck it rings : and man is no exception to the rule. External phenomena awaken in him a response. This is the case now, and this was the case with the Aryans. The daily recurring panorama of the sun's life and death awakened a vague response, and the Aryan, in his childish, untaught, unreasoning way, tried to put this feeling into words, and told in his imperfect, anthropomorphic language of a mighty warrior, the sun, loved in youth by a fair bride, the fair flush of dawn. But a life of toil is the warrior's portion, and the fair bride is deserted, and all the warrior's life is spent in toiling and battling—toiling onward through the sky and battling with the storm clouds—until the struggle is over, and then, when the warrior is about to pass away, when the sun is about to set, his fair bride reappears in the flushing tints of heaven, and is with him once more. This tale the Aryan wanderers took with them in their migrations, along with their packs and cattle, and children, and wives, and carried it wherever they went, and bequeathed it as a heritage to their widely-scattered descendants, ourselves among them. As time passed on the meaning of the tale was lost, but the tale itself survived ; and the names of national heroes were gradually introduced into what had come to be regarded as a relic of veritable history.

But through what chain of accidents this tale became localised in Warwickshire instead of some other county it is useless to inquire. As well might we ask why, as we walk along some country lane, we find a spray of wild white convolvulus climbing the hedge on one side of us, and not growing on the other side of the way instead. Accident or circumstance, call it what you will, choose the spot for the seed to be sown and the flower to spring, and accident or circumstance determined the locality where the legend should take root and thrive.

If, then, any of my hearers wish to visit the shrine of our Warwickshire hero, let them not go to Guy's Cliffe and grope among clammy caves and damp, dreary dens, but let them look into the sky at evening, some evening when it is coloured with the same weird pencil that painted the sunsets of last year. Let them look upon the giant when he is down, when the last bountiful, vivifying ray has been lavished upon earth and upon us, and he is yielding at length, for all his might, to the powers of darkness—when his work is done and he is passing to his rest. Let them look, I say, upon this, and mark how the clouds, rosy, creamy, maiden-blush, clasp him in a last embrace before he sinks from the sky, and still hover—regretfully, wistfully, yearningly hover—round the place where he has died; and they will have seen a sight which threw its spell over our ancestors thousands of years ago, and though its voice speaks not to us as it spoke to them, yet some of us at least will find it not impossible to realise that, in the weary sun, dying in the embrace of the tender clouds, they see the true parting of husband and wife; the real death-bed of Guy of Warwick.

LORD ROSEBERY has introduced into the House of Lords a Bill for the restoration of the ancient dignity and Earldom of Mar to the noble lord from whom it seemed to be taken by a decision of the House ten years ago which adjudged an Earldom of Mar (dating from 1565) to Lord Kellie. This Bill, it is understood, is brought in by command of Her Majesty, who takes the deepest personal interest in all that relates to the antiquities of Scotland. If it should pass, there will be two Earls of Mar, just as there are two Lords Stafford, two Lords Talbot, and two Lords Stewart. The introduction of the Bill has been to a great extent brought about by the interest awakened in the subject by the late Lord Crawford's book on "The Earldom of Mar in Sunshine and in Shade," and possibly by the articles on the "Earldom of Mar," which have appeared in these pages. (See vols. i. 178; ii., 114, 231; iii., 51, 201; and iv. 52.)

Forecastings of Nostradamus.

By C. A. WARD.

PART VIII.

(Continued from p. 222.)

CENTURY IV. QUATRAIN 89.

" Trained de Londres secret conjureront,
　Contre leur Roy, sur le pont l'entreprise ;
　Les Satellites la mort desgoûteront,
　Un Roy esleut blonde, natif de Frize."

" Train-bands of London shall secretly conspire against their King.　Upon the bridge the plot shall be.　These Satellites shall taste of death.　A fair-haired King, born in Friesland, shall be elected."

" *Trente de* Londres " is the general reading of the passage, and is so in Garencières, so I cannot tell whence D.D. obtained it.　The *Quarterly Review*, however (vol. xl.), admits this as predicting with tolerable clearness the Revolution of 1688.

Friesland is part of Holland, but William III. was born at The Hague, which, though Dutch, is not in Friesland.

Here he mentions the *trained bands* that were not in existence in his day by an English word that had not at that period been so applied.　They form this resolve against the King, *sur le pont* (*de Londres*), and elect in his place a native of Friesland (?), with fair hair, for King.

D. D. is a little exercised to interpret here, so he says that perhaps he had fair hair in his youth., " or it might be an allusion upon his name, Guilliaume, *because* (*sic*) of *Cil*, signifying the *eyebrows*." Gentle reader, pray excuse this vermicular wriggle of our most excellent cleric.　If you have seen much of etymology you will be able to lay your hand in an hour on twenty origins quite as groundless, and perhaps less amusing.

CENTURY IV. QUATRAIN 91.

" Au Duc Gaulois contraint battre au duelle,
　La nef de Mole, Monech n'aprochera,
　Tort accusé, prison perpetuelle,
　Son fils regner avant mort taschera."

" A French Duke compelled to fight a duel, The ship of Mole shall not come near Munich, Wrongfully accused shall have perpetual prison, His son shall endeavour to reign before his death."

Here we get a very curious prophecy.　The Duke of Marlborough was very fortunate, now acting with the *High Allies* against the French in the Netherlands.　In 1704 his presence was required in

Germany, where the Elector of Bavaria, Maximilian Emanuel, had been induced to receive French troops into the Electorate, where they threatened to overrun Germany. Marlborough attacked the French and Bavarians at Schellenberg, and thoroughly defeated them ; in August, nearly six weeks later, routed them at Hochstadt so completely, that Marshal *de Tallard*, the French General, remained his prisoner on the field, and was carried by him to England, where he remained at Nottingham to the end of the war. His conduct had been misrepresented to the King, so that he would not redeem him.

The Elector says D. D. is here called *l'aîné*, because of his superiority amongst the secular Electors. It is a fact that the Elector could not for ten years approach *Monech*, or *Munich*, *i.e.*, till the war was over.

Prince Charles of Bavaria, the Elector's son, implored the Emperor, Charles VI., when returning from Spain to Germany, that his father's conduct might not be laid to his (the son's) charge, nor bar his hereditary right of succession. " Son fils regner avant mort taschera," The son will try to reign before his father's death. (P. 68.)

I must give the next century more for the interest attaching to the interpretation by D. D. than for any particular bearing that it has upon English history.

Century VI. Quatrain 53.

" Le grand prelat Celtique, à Roy suspect,
De nuict par cours sortira hors du regne :
Par Duc fertile a son grand Roy Bretagne,
Bisance à Cypres et Tunes insuspect. "

" The great French prelate, suspected by the French King, shall retire out of the kingdom by night-time, passing by Ipres and Bethune unsuspected, by help of the Duke fertile in conquests, to his great Kingdom of Great Britain."

It refers to the Cardinal de Bouillon, Great Almoner of France, who was misrepresented to the French King, so that he could not appear at Court. After years he threw up his charge, and determined to quit France. He was related to Prince Eugene, who was with Marlborough, near Arras. The Cardinal came over in the night to them under the protection of a good convoy for the allies to defend him from the scouts of Ypres and Bethune. When he reached Antwerp, he simply sent in his Riband of the order, and his resignation to the French Court. He is called " Prelat Celtique," as the Duchy of Bouillon is in Gallia Celtica. The " grand-roy Bretagne " is abbreviated, *Roy* standing for *Royaume*.

"But the allusion on the Duke of Marlborough is still prettier. Had his genius dictated unto him *Marnebourg*, he might have understood and written down without hesitation, for the English *Marl* and the French *Marne* are one and the same. The Dæmons speak all sorts of languages, but Nostradamus did not understand the English, whence it came that at the hearing of the name of Marlborough, he startled, and thought, *qu'est-ce que Marl?* Thereupon it was inspired to him, *C'est une terre fertile et graisse*, whereby he is ascribing to him both *Nomen* and *Omen* at once. 'The Duke, by whose indefatigable zeal and incomparable valour the Kingdom of Great Britain should be fertile in conquests.'"

CENTURY II. QUATRAIN 68.

" De l'Aquilon les efforts seront grands,
Sur l'Ocean sera la porte ouverte :
Le regne en l'Isle sera reintegrand,
Tremblera Londres par veille descouverte."*

"In the northern parts of England great efforts shall be made. On the sea coast there will be an open door. The Government in the island shall be redintegrated, and London in consternation at a fleet discovered."

On March 23, 1708, the Pretender cast anchor before Edinburgh, but nobody came out to him. He sailed away, narrowly escaping the English fleet. In consequence an Act of Parliament declared him a *rebel*, and set a reward for his head. From this time Nostradamus designates him always by the title of *Rebel*.

The affairs of Queen Anne, and the commencement of the reign of George I., are graphically touched upon in the following eight lines :—

CENTURY VI. QUATRAIN 63, 64.

"La Dame seule au regne demeurée :
L'unique esteint premier au lict d'honneur,
Sept ans sera de douleur epleurée,
Puis longue vie au regne par grand heur.

" On ne tiendra pache aucune arresté,
Tous recevans iront par tromperie :
De paix et trefue, et terre et mer protesté
Par Bacelone classe prinse d'industrie."

"The lady who alone was left to the Crown, Her only son extinct in the bed of honour [D. D. translates "the flower of his age"], Seven years later will endure a like misfortune. Yet she will continue longer to enjoy the kingdom, and her prosperity. No one will be longer kept in durance, Even such as have appropriated money by deception. By land and water peace and friendship is professed. Except Barcelona taken by a fleet, and the assiduity of the besiegers."

As to Queen Anne, on the death of William III. she ascended the throne April 23, 1702, being the only Protestant descendant of Charles I. Her only son, the Duke of Gloucester, had died in 1700, a youth of much promise (*au lict d'honneur*). Prince George

---

* It is to be noticed that T. Bouys, "Sur les Oracles," p. 91, interprets this of Napoleon's threatened descent on England.

of Denmark, her consort, died October 28, 1708, and about six years later she herself dies, August 1, 1714.

Then George I. is proclaimed King, and Nostradamus notifies that there shall then be a general liberation of all prisoners for debt. The Peace of Utrecht was concluded in 1713, and the peace between Germany and France at Radstadt followed in March, 1714. The war with France and Spain was over before King George ascended the throne—all but Barcelona, and that was taken by the French fleet and soldiers for the King of Spain on September 12, 1714. Honourable terms were conceded to the Catalonians in Barcelona at the earnest intercession of Great Britain, so that the mention of Barcelona by Nostradamus comes with singular felicity and appropriateness. We must recollect also that D. D. is writing only a year after the actual events, the publishing date of his pamphlet being 1715.

He says it is hoped that the approaching *Coronation Day* may empty most of the prisons.

He has an N.B. to the effect that the King of Sweden coming out of Turkey may not stand for a release of prisoners.

CENTURY II. QUATRAIN 87.

" Après viendra des extremes contrées,
  Prince Germain, dessus le throsne doré :
  La servitude et eaux rencontrées,
  La dame serve, son temps plus n'adoré."

"Afterwards there shall come from a distant land a German prince to mount the golden throne. The servitude in which the throne was placed shall come to an end. The Queen had submitted to the strong pressure of circumstances."

That is to say, that George I. should exercise a stronger personal control than it had been possible for Queen Anne to do.

CENTURY X. QUATRAIN 42.

" Le regne humain, d'Angelique geniture,
  Fera son regne paix union tenir :
  Captive guerre demy de sa closture,
  Longtemps la paix leur fera maintenir."

"The human throne, but of heavenly extraction, shall preserve a peaceful union in his kingdom. Prisoners of war are released from their confinement, and for a long stretch of time induce them to keep the peace."

D. D. then discovers that King George shall never want for an heir to his Royal house to the day of final judgment.

CENTURY III. QUATRAIN 57.

" Sept fois changer verrez Gent Britannique
  Taints en sang en deux cens nonante an,
  France non point par appuy Germanique,
  Aries double son pole Bastarnan."

"Seven times may you see the British nation change the strain of blood in 290 years. Not so France. This shall be accomplished by a German 'till the Gemini have finished their course from Aries to the double-poled colure.'"

At the Creation the Gemini (according to D. D.) stood in the house or sign now called Aries, near the equinoctial colure which has but its own one pole, but they are now in the fourth house called Cancer, near the Solstitial colure which has a double pole, viz., *mundi et eclipticæ*. *Basharion* is an Arabic word, and denotes *Humanus*. *Bashar* a substantive *caro*, hominis cutis, homo. In the three signs Aries, Taurus, Gemini, which have successively formed the Caput Zodiaci, none but Gemini is of human figure; that sign must be intended by the word Basharion. So that till the age of the world is 6,000 or 7,000 years old, *i.e.*, till the day of judgment, this will last. And now for the seven revolutions. From the time of the death of Charles I. :—

(1) 1649. The Commonwealth.

(2) 1660. The Restoration.

(3) 1685. King James II.

(4) 1689. King William III.

(5) 1711. The Whigs and Tories revived again most unexpectedly, the common credit fell, and ruined many foreign bankers.

(6) 1714. King George I. came to the throne.

(7) 1939, *i.e.*, 290 years from the death of Charles, the seventh and last revolution happens. Therefore, nothing remarkable is to happen in the 225 years that follow King George I.'s accession, and when the great day comes there will be found a direct descendant of that great king sitting on the English throne.

From the foregoing it will be quite evident to all that this pamphlet is one of amazing ingenuity, come what come may as to the realisations, and it is surprising that it should have passed into such utter oblivion as it has done. Its facts are conveyed in style somewhat cumbrous and difficult to understand, which may partly account for the neglect. To me, however, it seems far too curious to be allowed to lie hidden any longer, and this must be my excuse for setting it forth so elaborately.

AT the annual *conversazione* of the Royal Society, held at Burlington House on Wednesday, May 6, Professor H. N. Moseley exhibited a collection of Pueblo-Indian pottery, charms, prayer-sticks, &c., from Zûni, in North Mexico.

Reviews.

An Essay on the Genius of George Cruikshank. By WILIAM MAKE-
PEACE THACKERAY. London : George Redway.

DR. JOHNSON'S well-known definition of Genius as "Great powers
accidentally turned in one direction" never seems more true than when
we study and admire the marvellously wide genius of Thackeray. Great,
wonderfully great, with the pen, his fingers closed even more lovingly on
the pencil. But the elements of his character which secured his success
as a writer, the electric flashes of his wit, comprehensive observation and
profound reflection, were precisely those which kept him from gaining
his bread as an artist. He saw too much and too many things to be able
to elaborate painfully and carefully any one subject, and his energies
were in danger of being wasted, like scattered grains of gunpowder, in
little aimless pyrotechnic flashes of mirth and morality, had they not
fortunately been gathered into a charge for the great guns of his literary
essays and become powerful to demolish the fortresses of Humbug and
Snobbery.

But what an art critic he was ! How lovingly he lingers over some cut
of his favourite Cruikshank, noting every turn of the pencil, every subtle
drollery of expression which would escape the common observer as surely
as the print of a mocassin deceives all eyes but the Indian's. And when
we have him, as in this essay, at his best and brightest, who would not
wish to follow him as he turns over his portfolio, chattering his incomparable and inimitable chat, and giving his readers the help of his own
rose-coloured and yet clear-sighted spectacles ?

A word of special praise must be given to the concise and graphic
introductory article on "Thackeray as an Art Critic," by Mr. Church, and
to the excellent style of the printing and engraving of the book.

Robert Pocock, the Gravesend Naturalist. By GEORGE M. ARNOLD.
London : Sampson Low & Co.

THIS is an appreciative biography of one of those men of humble merit
who have dignified themselves by their unwearying love and pursuit of
knowledge for its own sake. The book consists partly of biography in
the third person, and partly of extracts from Robert Pocock's diary.
The life is exceedingly well written, and the book is a worthy memoir of
this enthusiast in science, who would recreate himself after the drudgery
of his printing-office by studying a rare plant or insect, and whose
holidays were spent in fossil gathering and antiquarian research in his
native Kent.

Records of St. Giles', Cripplegate. By the Rev. W. DENTON, M.A.
Bell & Sons.

THIS is a most valuable and carefully written history of one of the most
important of the London parish churches. We are told in the preface
that the volume is a collection of various articles written in a local newspaper; but certainly the work shows nothing of the disjointed character
that might have been expected from its composition. The book comprises an account of the church, a full history of the parish, with special
reference to the time of the great plague, and a description of the ancient
ceremony of "beating the bounds." Cripplegate was one of the parishes
most heavily visited by the plague on the two great occasions, 1503 and

1665. In fact, its sanitary condition never compared favourably with that of its not immaculate neighbours. Mr. Denton gives a vivid picture of that reign of terror which ensued when "the pestilence that walketh at noonday" set up its throne in the streets of the great city, and chronicles the names of some of its principal victims. Nor is there wanting an enumeration of the predecessors of the author in the vicarage, with short biographies of the more distinguished, such as Dr. Fuller, who was deprived and imprisoned for his opinions by the Long Parliament, in spite of his learning and eloquence, or the "noble and generous" John Dolben, afterwards Archbishop of York: The book is a monument of laborious research and polished style ; and we can heartily commend it to the notice of outsiders, as well as to those of the St. Giles' parishioners, who, to quote the words of the preface, "feel an interest in hearing of the early state of the place in which they live, and of its progress from the days when it was a waste outside the City gates."

Glimpses of our Ancestors in Sussex, and Gleanings in East and West Sussex. Second Series. By CHARLES FLEET. Lewes : Faracombe & Co.

IT is one result of this fast travelling age that the old "county" feeling is rapidly dying out, and with it many customs, traditions, and records of every class, which, to the future historian of the Victorian era, will soon be priceless. Were old Fuller now alive, he might find it difficult to collect materials for a new volume of "Worthies," if he assigned each to his native county. Men of Yorkshire and Sussex meet on the pavement of Pall Mall, and, except for the hunting season, their native county sees but little of them. We should therefore be inclined to look indulgently on the most faulty chronicler who endeavours to present us with a record of the past and present *notabilia* of his county. But no such indulgence is required in the present case ; such pieces of forcible and apt description as the chapter entitled "The Sussex Martyrs," prove a claim to great literary power as well as antiquarian learning. It would be difficult indeed to tell more vividly the story of brave Richard Woodman, pre-eminent though not singular among those who received the baptism of fire during the Marian persecution. Nor is our author wanting in gleams of sly humour, which effectively enliven his narrative of lighter subjects, as in the portions of a Sussex Diary, by a clergyman not entirely weaned from "pomps and vanities," among the entries in which is found : "25 Dec. I sent to Mr. Hely a ribspare and hoggspuddings, for which he returned me a box of pills and sermons." Our author modestly entitles his book of "Sketches and Gleanings," a name which scarcely applies to most of the chapters, which have nothing "sketchy" about them, in the worse sense of the word ; as for his gleanings, they are from a kinsman's field ; the sheaves are as full as those Ruth gathered in the corn-fields of Boaz.

Exeter during the Religious Persecutions and Rebellions. By T. J. NORTHY. Plymouth : W. H. Luke, *Western Antiquary* Office. 1884.

THIS was originally a lecture delivered by the author on two occasions in Exeter. Mr. Northy, who is an Exeter journalist, has in a brief compass given a carefully elaborated review of the religious and political associations of that ancient city during a period ranging from the rise of Wicliff, in the latter part of the reign of Edward III., to the accession of the Prince of Orange as William III.

The Book of the Sindibad, from the Persian and Arabic, by W. A. CLOUSTON, of Glasgow (privately printed), is the first attempt, in this country, to furnish a compendious account of the Eastern and Western groups of romances known respectively under their generic titles of "The Book of Sindibad" and "The Book of the Seven Wise Masters." The late Mr. Thomas Wright, F.S.A., wrote an introduction to his edition for the Percy Society of an Early-English Metrical version of the "Seven Sages," but the book was not without errors and faults, which Mr. Clouston has done his best to remedy.

THE May number of *English Etchings* (D. Bogue, 27, King William-street, Strand), contains, *inter alia*, an etching by Mr. S. H. Baker, of the Old and New Bridges at Dinas Mawddwy, Pembrokeshire. The subject is highly picturesque, and has been effectively treated.

The City of London Directory, 1885 (H. & L. Collingridge, Alders-gate-street), contains, besides the usual information concerning the trade and commerce of the City, a large amount of interesting historical informa-tion relating to the Livery Companies, including the history of the foundation of the several Companies, their armorial bearings, charters, charities, and privileges.

©bituary Memoirs.

"Emori nolo ; sed me esse mortuum nihil æstimo."—Epicharmus.

MR. RICHARD GRANT WHITE, the Shakesperian commentator, died recently at New York, in his 63rd year. In 1854 he published his "Shakespeare's Scholar," and in 1859 his "Essay on the Authorship of the Three Parts of *King Henry VI*." His critical edition of Shakespeare's works in twelve volumes, which appeared between 1857 and 1864, was followed by his "Life and Genius of Shakespeare." In 1853 Mr. White issued his "Handbook of Christian Art ;" and in 1863, an edition, with notes, of "The Book-hunter." His "Words and their Uses" (1870), and "Every-day English" (1880), were the subject of some controversy. Mr. White's "American View of the Copyright Question" was published in 1881, and his "England Without and Within" in the same year. The latter work fully showed the author's acquaintance with our literature, manners, politics, and society.

THE REV. FREDERICK FIELD, LL.D., the distinguished Greek and Hebrew scholar, died in April, at his residence at Norwich. Mr. Field was an honorary Fellow of Trinity College, Cambridge, and for many years Rector of Reepham, Norfolk ; but he resigned that living in 1863 with the view of devoting the autumn of his life to works bearing on the critical study of the Old Testament. Of his published labours in the cause of critical theology the earliest is his edition of Chrysostom's Homilies on St. Matthew, with a Greek text based on a fresh collation of MSS., followed by a similar edition of the same Father's Homilies on the Pauline Epistles. For the Society for Promoting Christian Knowledge he edited the text of the Septuagint based on Grabe's edition of the Codex Alexandrinus. His great work, by which he will be mainly known, was, however, his edition of the fragments of Origen's "Hexapla," which was printed at the Clarendon Press, and was published in parts from 1867 to 1874. Mr. Field was a member of the Old Testament Revision Company.

MR. ALFRED KINGSTON, one of the Assistant Keepers of the Public

Records, died on the 24th April, aged 55 years. Mr. Kingston, who was well known in literary and antiquarian circles, was appointed to the Public Record Office in 1844. He began his career at the old Record Office in the Tower, under the immediate superintendence of Sir Thomas Hardy, of whom he remained to the last the devoted friend and pupil. Besides holding an important position at the Record Office, Mr. Kingston had been for many years secretary of the Camden Society, having succeeded the late Mr. Timbs in that appointment.

MR. PHILIP SMITH, author of a "History of the Ancient World," &c., died at Putney, on May 12, at the age of sixty-eight. He was educated at the University of London (then University College). He contributed many articles to the Dictionaries of Greek and Roman Antiquities, Biography, and Geography, edited by his brother, Dr. William Smith. Besides the work above mentioned, Mr. Smith was the author of the students' manuals of "Old and New Testament History," of the "Ancient History of the East," and of "Ecclesiastical History," in two volumes, all published in Mr. Murray's series of students' manuals. He also wrote a "Smaller History of England," and completed the translation of Brugsch's "History of Egypt," which was begun by Mr. Danby Seymour. He likewise rendered valuable assistance to Dr. Schliemann in preparing his works for the press. Mr. Philip Smith was a constant contributor to the *Quarterly Review*, the April number of which contained an article from his pen on the "Early History of Britain."

Meetings of Learned Societies.

METROPOLITAN.

SOCIETY OF ANTIQUARIES.—*April* 23, anniversary meeting, the Earl of Carnarvon, the retiring president, in the chair. This was an anniversary of unusual importance. Not only did it see the completion of the period of seven years to which, under the revised statutes, the occupation of the presidential chair is now limited, but it was also the last anniversary at which Mr. C. Knight Watson, who has for twenty-five years filled the honourable post of secretary, sought re-election. The state of his health and other considerations have induced him to retire on the 25th of September next. These two circumstances furnished, as it were, the key-note of Lord Carnarvon's address. After calling attention to the most important names on the obituary, such as the Bishop of Lincoln and Mr. Coote, Lord Carnarvon passed under review the principal events which had marked his septenate, the various antiquarian undertakings and publications he had suggested, and the results which had followed. He dwelt at some length on the injury done to the Society by the delay in the appearance of the publications, and expressed a hope that the time might come again when the "Archæologia" for the current year might be laid upon the table at the anniversary of that year. He then passed on to a survey of the services rendered to the Society by Mr. Knight Watson. and not the least of these services was the new catalogue which Mr. Knight Watson had undertaken to complete. At the close of the address a resolution expressing regret at Lord Carnarvon's retirement was carried unanimously. A resolution was moved by Dr. E. Freshfield, seconded by Mr. G. Leveson-Gower, and carried unanimously, expressing the regret of the Society at Mr. Knight Watson's intended resignation. The following list was read from the chair of those who had been elected to fill the offices of President, Council, and Officers for the ensuing year : President, Dr. J. Evans ; Treasurer, C. S. Perceval ; Director, H. S. Milman ; other Members of Council, W. de Gray Birch, the Earl of Carnarvon, G. T. Clark, J. Clarke, C. M. Clode, the Hon. H. A. Dillon, Rev. J. W. Ebsworth, A. W. Franks, Dr. E. Freshfield, Prof. P. Gardner, A. C. King, General Sir J. H. Lefroy, C. T. Martin, E. Oldfield, G. Scharf, F. Seebohm, and Dr. W. Smith ; Secretary, C. Knight Watson. —*April* 30, Mr. J. Evans, president, in the chair. The following gentlemen were appointed Vice-Presidents : Dr. W. Smith, Dr. E. Freshfield, the Earl of Carnarvon, and Mr. A. W. Franks. Dr. C. S. Perceval exhibited some matrices of seals from Yorkshire. Sir J. S. Lumley communicated a paper on " Recent Discoveries at Cività la Vigna, the site of the ancient Lanuvium." This paper was illustrated by plans, photographs, and drawings, some of which were executed by Sir S. Lumley himself. The excavations are not yet complete, but sufficient has been found to show that the site is one of no ordinary interest.—*May* 7, Dr. J. Evans, President, in the chair. Dr. E. Freshfield exhibited a mediæval Greek baptismal badge, probably of the fourteenth century. The Rev. Canon Cooke exhibited a photograph of a wooden bench end from Cornelly Church, Cornwall, on which had been carved a figure, now much decayed, of an angel in alb and amice, holding a shield of the five wounds. Admiral Spratt made two communications : one on the Gulf of Symi, in continuation of a paper read last year on the Dorian Gulf; the other on a statue or torso (of which a photograph was exhibited) of the youthful Dionysius, recalling the style and execution of the school of Praxiteles. This torso is in a leaning attitude, 32½ inches in height from the nape of the neck to the lowest part of the right leg.

BRITISH ARCHÆOLOGICAL ASSOCIATION.—*April* 15, Mr. Thomas Morgan, F.S.A., in the chair. Three crucifixes of thirteenth century date were exhibited by Mr. W. H. Rylands. One of them was enamelled and set with turquoises and garnets, the others were enamelled with blue colourings similar to Limoges workmanship. A small representative collection of Persian art pottery was described by the Rev. S. M. Mayhew. Mr. F. Brent exhibited a bell of the time of Elizabeth, and among other objects, an ancient triptych, of Russian workmanship, from the Crimea, which was commented upon by Mr. Hodgetts. Mr. H. Watling sent a series of drawings of remarkable antiquarian objects, including a series of representations of St. Edmund, king and martyr, from churches in East Anglia, stained glass in Blythborough Church, and the curious pewter vessels of Puritan times, used in the Holy Communion at Irnham Church. Mr. J. Wilson described another of the Saxon crosses of which so many have been recently reported to the Association. It is in Hackthorne Church, and consists of a Latin cross incised on a large block of stone, the edges of the latter being ornamented with a cable moulding. Mr. Loftus Brock, F.S.A., exhibited some fragments of marble statues from Rome, including an arm of a Cupid of excellent workmanship. A paper was then read by Mr. Maunde Thompson, F.S.A., on a hitherto unnoticed vocabulary compiled by Abbot Ælfric. It occurs on the margin of a Latin manuscript in the British Museum, written in a French hand of the tenth century. The Saxon words are neatly written, and of these fully forty in number do not appear in Anglo-Saxon dictionaries. An animated discussion took place, in which Messrs. Rylands, De Gray Birch, Hodgetts, and others took part.

ROYAL ARCHÆOLOGICAL INSTITUTE.—*May* 7, Lord Percy, M.P., president, in the chair. The Rev. J. L. Fish read a paper on the "Ancient Records of the Parish of St. Margaret Pattens," which included some amusing extracts from the parish accounts of receipts and expenditures, and described the ancient church furniture, plate, vestments, &c., with which the church was richly supplied, prior to the Reformation. The records, which dated back to the fourteenth century, made mention of several bequests to the church and parish. The earliest MS. book, dated 1470, contained copies of deeds and wills, and references to the same; the earliest deed copied is dated 1305. The earliest inventory, in a perfect condition, is dated 1470. The inventories are continued on to 1549. The church-wardens' accounts begin in 1507, and are continued on to recent times. Mr. C. D. E. Fortnum read a paper on "Early Christian Gems," several specimens of which, engraved with sacred signs and symbols, he exhibited. Mr. R. S. Ferguson contributed a paper, which was read by the Secretary, entitled "Notes on a Ring-dial and on a Seal." Both the dial and the seal were exhibited: the former was an astronomical equinoctial ring-dial of brass, and the latter was engraved with an Oriental inscription. Among the other objects displayed were some Peruvian beads, shown by Mr. J. P. Harrison, and an MS. Mahabharata epic poem in the Telagu language, exhibited by Mr. T. H. Baylis, Q.C.

ANTHROPOLOGICAL INSTITUTE.—*April* 28, Mr. F. Galton, president, in the chair. Mr. A. L. Lewis read a paper "On the Past and Present Condition of certain Rude Stone Monuments in Westmoreland." A little to the south of the village of Shap are the remains of some extensive rude stone monuments, to which allusion was made by Camden in the sixteenth century, and by Dr. Stukeley in the middle of the last century; and a circle is said to have been destroyed when the railway was made. The most interesting monument in this neighbourhood is situated at a place called Gunnerskeld, two or three miles to the north of the village, and consists of two irregular, concentric, slightly oval rings, about 50 and 100 feet in diameter respectively, the longest diameters being from north to south. A paper by Admiral F. S. Tremlett, "On Quadrilateral Constructions near Carnac," was read, which described certain enclosures explored by the late Mr. J. Miln. A paper by M. J. L'Heureux, "On the Kekip-Sesoators, or Ancient Sacrificial Stone of the North-West Tribes of Canada," was read. The stone, which consists of a roughly hewn quartzose boulder, about fifteen inches high and fourteen in diameter, is placed on the summit of the pyramidal mound commanding an extensive view of both the Red Deer and Bow River valleys. In cases of public or private calamity, or when a special blessing is sought, a solitary warrior, after keeping vigil on the top of the mount from sunset till the rising of the morning star, lays a finger of his left hand on the top of the stone, and cuts it off. Amongst the Blackfeet these self-inflicted wounds ranked equal to those received in battle.

ARCHITECTURAL ASSOCIATION.—*April* 25, a visit was paid to the church of St. Bartholomew-the-Great, West Smithfield. The members were received by the Rev. W. Panckridge, the rector, and Mr. Aston Webb, the architect of the proposed restoration of the church. Mr. Panckridge detailed the history of the church and priory from its foundation in 1103, by Rahere, the founder of St. Bartholomew's Hospital close by, down to the years 1863 and 1866, when it was brought to its present condition by Professor Hayter Lewis. He also pointed out the chief architectural features of the church, monuments, &c. Mr. Webb next described some plans which were exhibited—one, which was drawn with the assistance of Mr. G. H. Birch, showed the exact condition of the church, with its cloisters, &c., as it existed in 1530. After perambulating the church the visitors departed, under the leadership of the Rev. Mr. Panckridge and Mr. Webb, on a visit of inspection to the Charterhouse, proceeding thither through Cloth Fair, and noticing by the way the old Whittington Inn, which owes its preservation to the intercession of the London and Middlesex Archæological Society.

ASIATIC.—*April* 20, Sir T. Wade in the chair. The Rev. Professor Beal contributed a paper "On the Age and Writings of Nâgârjuna Boddhisattva" (from the Chinese). From this paper it would seem that there were two writers called Nâgârjuna and Nagasena, though some authorities, differing in this particular from Professor Beal, have held that they were really one and the same person. The lives of both have been written. It appears that the former was an eminent Boddhisattva, residing in the south of India ; the latter merely a Bhikshu, or beggar, in North India. The former lived subsequently to the death of Kanishka, perhaps towards the end of the second century A.D. ; the latter flourished about 140 B.C. The characters of the two men differed greatly : the former was the founder of a new school, an ambitious innovator, and an adept in conjuration and magic ; the latter was a skilful disputant, but a loyal follower of the primitive doctrine of Buddha. Professor Beal then noticed two Chinese works, the "Sutra of the Bhikshu Nagasena," from the contents of which he derived his argument as to the date of Nagasena. He then proceeded to discuss in detail the information regarding Nâgârjuna, which is of a mixed character, and scattered through the Buddhist literature in China, the chief difficulty being to blend the scattered notices together so as to obtain a trustworthy whole.—*Athenæum.*

HISTORICAL.—*April* 16, Mr. Hyde Clark, V.P., in the chair. Mr. W. St. Chad Boscawen read a paper "On the Gizdhubar Legends, the Epic of Chaldea." A discussion followed, in which Mr. C. A. Fyffe, the Chairman, and others took part.

NEW SHAKSPERE.—*April* 10, Dr. F. J. Furnivall in the chair. Mr. F. A. Marshall read a paper "On the Tragedy of ' Richard II.'" (Egerton MS. 1994). The Egerton MS. contained fifteen plays, most of them written during the first forty years of the seventeenth century. The date of "Richard II.," however, was entirely a matter of conjecture ; but it was certainly neither the one seen by Dr. Forman nor the one played in connection with the Essex Rebellion. From the nature and quantity of the marginal notes, stage directions, &c., it seemed clear that the MS. had been used as a playhouse copy. Mr. Marshall held that the play was written by one with a large experience of the stage ; and also that it had probably been much "cut" by the actors themselves. Mr. Marshall read the opening scene to show the dramatic force and stir with which the play began, and passed on to the amusing scene between Woodstock and a "spruce courtier," interesting from its being an evident reminiscence of the "Osric" scene in "Hamlet." A study of the points of similarity in this play and Shakespeare's followed, with a summary of the metrical analysis, which yielded the following results :—Average of unstopped lines, one in nine ; of double endings, one in six; of rhymed lines, one in seven. Mr. Marshall held it to be certainly later in date than Shakespeare. In the discussion that followed the Chairman said that he had not the least doubt that the play was written after Shakespeare's time. The date was not earlier than 1620. The Rev. W. A. Harrison concurred as to the date, and supplemented Mr. Marshall's list of resemblances by many other parallelisms of ideas and in some cases of *ipsissima verba*. A paper " On Documents relating to the Players at the Red Bull, Clerkenwell, and the Cockpit in Drury Lane, in the Time of James I.," by Mr. J. Greenstreet, was taken as read.

INSTITUTE OF SHORTHAND WRITERS.—*April* 14, Mr. H. H. Tolcher, President, in the chair. A paper was read " On Shorthand, its History and its Prospects," by Mr. M. Levy. The author traced the connection of shorthand with the law courts, and referred to some celebrated trials, those of Lord Russell, Algernon Sydney, and Warren Hastings, raising the question how and by whom they were taken down.

ST. PAUL'S ECCLESIOLOGICAL SOCIETY.—*April* 15, Mr. C. Brown in the chair. Mr. E. P. Loftus Brock, F.S.A., read a paper entitled " Some Notes on the Churches of London," in which he gave a description of the group of churches within the walls of the City as it existed from the earliest times, and made some remarks on their dedication, with the view of showing that nearly all of them were founded before the Conquest. Mr. Brock referred to the large number of churches which the City contained, no less than 35 standing within a radius of a quarter of a mile of the statue of King William IV., near London Bridge, a number scarcely paralleled in any other city in the world, Rome not excepted. The paper was illustrated by the exhibition of a large number of drawings, many of them showing fragments of the old churches which still exist and have escaped the ravages of time, the devastation of fire, or the ruthless hand of the "restorer."—*April* 18. Under the guidance of Mr. G. H. Birch, the members paid a visit to the churches of St. Giles, Cripplegate, and St. Sepulchre, Snow Hill.—*May* 2. An excursion was made to Merton Abbey, where a paper on the Abbey was read by Mr. S. W. Kershaw, F.S.A. The members afterwards proceeded on a visit of inspection to the churches of Merton and Morden, where papers were read by Mr. Arthur J. Style.—*May* 7, the Rev. E. S. Dewick, F.G.S., in the chair. Mr. G. H. Birch read a paper on "The Ecclesiology of Paris," in which he described the various ecclesiastical edifices of the city.

PIPE ROLL SOCIETY.—*May* 1, committee meeting, Mr. W. C. Borlase, M.P., in the chair. Messrs. Walter C. Metcalf and J. H. Round were elected auditors. Much satisfaction was expressed at the success which has attended the scheme, it being the impression of the committee that the forthcoming "Key" would prove of the utmost value to the subscribers. Mr. W. J. Hardy, F.S.A., was elected a member of the committee in place of the late Mr. J. J. Bond, Assistant Keeper of the Public Records. The general meeting was fixed for the 22nd June. The hon. treasurer's accounts were passed, and it appeared that after the issue of the publications for 1883-4 and 1884-5, a balance of nearly £50 would remain.

CAMDEN SOCIETY.—*May* 4, a resolution was passed deploring the loss sustained by the Society in the death of Mr. Alfred Kingston, who had been secretary for thirteen years. The books which the Society proposes to issue for the years 1885-6 are:—(1) Proceedings in the Courts of the Star Chamber and High Commission in the Years 1631-2, to be edited by S. R. Gardiner, LL.D., director. (2) Custumals of Battle Abbey, *temp*. Edward I., from a MS. in the Public Record Office, to be edited by Samuel R. Bird, Esq., F.S.A. (3) Selections from the Lauderdale Papers, vol. iii., to be edited by Osmund Airy, Esq. In their last report the

Council announced their intention of printing an account of the war in Ireland after the Rebellion of 1642, from the pen of Colonel Plunket. Further inquiry has, however, shown that the amount of unpublished matter contained in the MS. was insufficient to justify its issue at the expense of the Society, and it has, therefore, been withdrawn.

SHORTHAND.—*May* 6, Mr. E. Pocknell, vice-president, in the chair. The "Shorthand Hymn-Book," written by the late J. Ward in the system of Holdsworth and Austin (1766), was exhibited, and arrangements were made by which, for the present, the book will become the property of some of the members of the Society, and be deposited in the library. Mr. J. B. Rundell read a paper "On Short Writing for English, French, and German," a system which is a modification of one which he published in 1876 under the title of "An Easy Way to Write English as Spoken." A discussion followed ; Mr. I. Pitman, Mr. A. J. Ellis, and others took part.

HELLENIC.—*May* 7, Mr. C. T. Newton in the chair. Mr. E. A. Gardner read a paper on a silver statuette in the British Museum, representing a boy with a goose. This was found near Alexandria, together with coins which fix the date of its burial at about 240 B.C. Miss J. Harrison read a paper on a hitherto unpublished vase now in the Campana collection of the Louvre, at Paris, a black-figured cylix of the potter Nicosthenes. In connection with this vase, the writer tried to show (1) that the art-form which the myth of Odysseus and the Sirens assumes on Greek vases has arisen from the juxtaposition, at first accidental, of two or more racing galleys, and the Assyrian bird-woman types already current in vase decoration ; (2) that the design appearing on the vase of Nicosthenes and some thirteen other Greek vases, namely, a succession of galleys apparently racing, is connected with nautical contests in honour of Dionysus.

SOCIETY OF BIBLICAL ARCHÆOLOGY.—*May* 5, Dr. S. Birch, President, in the chair. Some remarks were made by Mr. R. N. Cust on the excavations in progress or lately completed in Egypt. A paper by M. E. Revillout, entitled "Notes on some Demotic Documents in the British Museum," was read by the Secretary.

ROYAL ASIATIC.—*May* 18, annual meeting. Colonel Yule was elected President for the ensuing year, in the place of Sir Wm. Muir, retired

PROVINCIAL.

ROYAL HISTORICAL AND ARCHÆOLOGICAL ASSOCIATION OF IRELAND.—*April* 2, his Grace the Duke of Leinster, K.P., in the chair. The Rev. James Graves (hon. sec.) read the minutes of annual meeting, held in Kilkenny in January. Mr. James H. Owen, architect to the Board of Public Works, read a paper on Mellifont Abbey, co. Louth, the first foundation of the Cistercian Order. It was founded in 1140, and up to 1255 no less than forty monasteries had been erected for the Order. After it had passed out of the possession of the Cistercians, it became the residence of the Moores, lords of Mellifont and Drogheda. It was abandoned by them in favour of their residence at Monasterevan, and fell into ruin, but has since been taken into charge by the Board of Works. The Rev. James Graves said that the removal of the modern walls and *débris* left visible some specimens of magnificent mouldings. The architecture was of French type. Dr. Aquilla Smith read a paper "On some Ancient Irish Coins."

BIRMINGHAM ARCHITECTURAL ASSOCIATION.—At a meeting recently held at Queen's College, Birmingham, Mr. W. H. Kendrick, Vice-

President, in the chair, a paper was read by Mr. A. Reading on a "Comparison between English and Continental Renaissance Architecture." With the aid of a powerful lantern, Mr. Kendrick illustrated his remarks by views of some of the most important Renaissance buildings abroad and at home, and pointed out the successive waves of Renaissance expression, which differed very materially according to the country in which it was practised. The lecturer urged all admirers of this style to study and reproduce where possible the Early Italian Renaissance, as it was only to be found in that country in its simplicity and purity.

GLASGOW ARCHÆOLOGICAL SOCIETY.—*April* 16, Mr. Honeyman in the chair. Mr. J. Dalrymple Duncan, F.S.A. Scot., read a note regarding cinerary urns recently discovered at Uddingston, near Glasgow. Mr. Robert Munro, M.D., F.S.A. Scotland, contributed a paper on "The mportance attached to the Collection and Preservation of Prehistoric Antiquities by the various nationalities of Western Europe."

CAMBRIDGE ANTIQUARIAN SOCIETY.—*May* 4, Mr. J. Clarke, M.A., President, in the chair. Prof. Hughes having referred to the documentary evidence already laid before the Society, tracing the history of Horningsey to Norman times, drew the attention of members to a selection of objects —*palæolithic* weapons, *neolithic* implements—which carried the story of the occupation of the district back to the early stone period. Professor Hughes also exhibited the potter's bone modelling pins and lumps of clay kneaded into round masses ready for use, and other evidences of the Roman occupation of the district 1500 years ago. Mr. H. F. Wilson gave an address upon the Brandon flint trade, tracing its development from pre-historic times to the present day. He also gave an account of the famous neolithic workings known as "Grime's Graves,"—and one of which was explored with very interesting results by Canon Greenwell and others in 1870,—and suggested incidentally that the Society might carry on the investigation then commenced, as between two and three hundred of these remarkable pits still remain to be examined.

Antiquarian News & Notes.

MR. M. LENIHAN has received the thanks of the Prince of Wales for a copy of his "History and Antiquities of Limerick."

A ROMAN pavement has been discovered in the parish of Lancing, near Shoreham, Sussex.

LORD CARNARVON will preside over the Congress of the Archæological Institute at Derby in July or August.

SIR TATTON SYKES, Bart., has erected a handsome cross, sixteen feet high, in the churchyard at Kirby Grindalythe, East Yorkshire.

A SERIES of specimens from Rhages has been lent by South Kensington Museum to the exhibition of Persian art at the Burlington Fine Arts Club.

THE fund for restoring the church of St. Bartholomew-the-Great, Smithfield, has reached the sum of £5,000.

MR. J. A. SYMONDS has been for some time past engaged upon the sequel to his "Renaissance in Italy."

AN Historical Portrait Exhibition is open at Paris; it includes specimens of Sir J. Reynolds, Sir T. Lawrence, G. Romney, and other old masters of the English School.

MR. W. M. RAMSAY, the new Professor of Archæology at Oxford, is giving this term lectures on "Olympia," "The Arts and Antiquities of Athens," and on "Greek Vase-Painting in Attica" in the 5th century B.C.

THE foundation-stone of the new buildings for Sion College, which is to be removed from London Wall to the Victoria Embankment, was laid on April 21, with some ceremony.

THE Cambrian Archæological Society will hold its annual meeting at Newport, Monmouthshire, in August next. Lord Tredegar is to be the president, and Mr. T. D. Roberts the local secretary.

THE Council of the British Archæological Association have given up the intention of meeting this year at Oxford, but will hold their Congress at Brighton in August instead.

A SHAKESPEARE memorial window, which has been put in the chancel of Holy Trinity Church, Stratford-on-Avon, at the exclusive cost of American visitors to the poet's tomb, has been lately unveiled.

THE Prussian Government has purchased three paintings formerly belonging to the Blenheim collection—namely, the "St. Dorothea" of Del Piombo, and the "Andromeda" and the "Bacchante" of Rubens.

"EQUES," writing in *Notes and Queries*, suggests that the Pipe Roll Society should print and publish the abstract of some of the Rolls of the reign of Henry II., as the best substitute for the original Roll, which is lost.

THE tomb of Mr. John Nichols, many years the proprietor, printer, and editor of the *Gentleman's Magazine*, has been carefully and reverentially preserved in the churchyard of St. Mary's, Islington, which has just been given over to the public for the purposes of recreation.

THE MSS. journals of the Society for the Propagation of the Gospel, 1701-1800, illustrating the history of the English Church in America, Canada, and the West Indies, are to be published, if a sufficient number of subscribers can be obtained.

THE "Cock" Tavern, near Temple Bar, immortalised by Tennyson, and frequented by many generations of Templars, has been sold to the Bank of England, and is about to be pulled down, its site being wanted for building purposes.

A LOAN collection of mezzotints, illustrating the progress of the art from its invention by Louis de Siegen, was exhibited by Mr. Dunthorne during May. Mr. J. C. Smith, author of the "Catalogue of British Mezzotints," contributed an introduction to the catalogue.

THE forthcoming volumes in the series of "Early Britain," published by the Society for Promoting Christian Knowledge, will be "Scandinavian Britain," by Mr. F. York Powell; and "Post-Norman Foreign Influences," by Mr. H. G. Hewlett.

THE last number of Messrs. Kegan, Paul & Co.'s "Parchment Library" is "De Quincey's Confessions of an Opium Eater." It is edited by Dr. R. Garnett, of the British Museum, and enriched with extracts from the note-book of Mr. Richard Woodhouse, of the Temple, one of the contributors to the *London Magazine* more than sixty years ago.

THE collection of pictures of the early Italian, Flemish, and German schools formed many years ago by the late Rev. J. Fuller Russell, and also those belonging to the late Sir Edward Marwood-Elton, of Widworthy Court, Honiton, consisting of 61 pictures which belonged to the grandfather of the late baronet from 1770 to 1790, were lately sold by Messrs. Christie & Co.

THE Council of the Arundel Society have resolved to offer to all Associates enrolled prior to April last the option of at once becoming sub-scribers. Persons who now enter themselves sufficiently early as Associates, may become second subscribers in time to receive the second annual publications in 1886, and possibly in the present year.

A SOCIETY for the study of Teutonic and Romance philology has recently been founded in St. Petersburg. At its third meeting, lately held, "Beowulf" was the subject of the paper read by M. Th. A. Braun. M. Braun has prepared a close prose Russian translation from the text published by the Early English Text Society.

MESSRS. SOTHEBY, WILKINSON & HODGE recently sold by auction the collections of drawings and engravings formed by the late Mr. Edward Cheney, of Badger Hall, Shiffnal. Among the most important drawings were a Portrait of Sterne, by Carmontelle ; a Garden Scene with Figures, by Hogarth ; a View of Tivoli, by Claude Lorraine ; and a Portrait by Rubens. The total amount realised by the sale was £5,824.

MESSRS. SOTHEBY, WILKINSON & HODGE sold in April the following drawings by the old masters in the collection of the late Prof. August Grahl : The Minster at Aix-la-Chapelle ; a sheet of Dürer's "Travelling Sketch Book" (£290) ; View of Antwerp (£195) ; Anonymous German, St. Sebastian (£61) ; Lippi, Madonna and Child with four Saints, pen and ink (£76) ; total realised by the 355 lots, £1,813.

ACCORDING to the *Academy*, the Rev. George Edmundson has in pre-paration a volume entitled " Milton and Vondel," a curiosity of literature, in which he endeavours to show that Milton was largely indebted in the composition of his " Paradise Lost " to various poems of his Dutch con-temporary, Ioost van den Vondel ; and that " Samson Agonistes " also shows marks of having been suggested by a drama by Vondel on the same subject.

Mr. J. A. P. MACBRIDE, sculptor, delivered the second of his course of lectures at the British Museum on May 11, the subject being Assyrian Sculpture. The third lecture, on Early Greek and Etruscan Art, was delivered on the 18th, in one of the Greek Galleries. The lecturer interested his audience by his lucid explanations of these ancient bassi-relievi, which upwards of 2,500 years ago decorated the walls of the Palace of Sennacherib.

MR. WILLIAM BLADES has in preparation "An Account of the German morality-play, entitled 'Depositio Cornuti Typographici,' as performed in the seventeenth and eighteenth centuries, with a rythmical translation of the German version of 1648 ; also a literal reprint of the unique original version, written in Plattdeutsch by Paul de Wise, and printed in 1621." In its own land only seven copies of the book are known, and to most English readers and others versed in folk-lore the editor expects the book will come as a new piece of literature.

DR. INGLEBY is preparing "Shakespeare and the Welcombe Enclo-sures," a folio volume of autotypes of the extant pages of the private diary of Thomas Greene, Town Clerk of Stratford-upon-Avon during the later years of Shakespeare's life. They are accompanied by a transcript prepared by Mr. Edward Scott, of the British Museum, and an appendix, consisting of illustrative documents which, like the diary, are preserved at Stratford. To these Dr. Ingleby furnishes an introduction.

THE Rev. Henry J. Swallow, of Brancepeth, Durham, has announced a special offer of copies of his "History of the Nevills," post free, to clergymen, members of the Oxford and Cambridge Union, and members of any antiquarian society, on receipt of a postal order for 7s. 6d., *during June.* Orders should be sent to Mr. Reid, publisher, New-castle-on-Tyne. In the preparation of this work, Mr. Swallow has been able to collect a quantity of information relative to the Nevills not hitherto accessible to the general public, chiefly through the kindness of Lord Abergavenny and other members of the Nevill family.

AN exhibition of manuscripts relating to the history of music has been arranged in a series of cases in the Manuscript Department of the British Museum. This collection, of which the value from an educational point of view cannot be over-estimated, comprises early illuminations and drawings of musical instruments ; numerous specimens of the notation known as *neumata*, or *neumes*, of which the Museum possesses examples as old as the tenth century, and from almost every part of Europe ; manuscripts illustrating the notations written with two, three, four, five, and six lines ; choral books of imposing dimensions ; the early ballad and instrumental music of England ; and several specimens of autograph music by Handel and other masters of the art.

A CURIOUS ceremony was lately performed at Travancore. The Maharajah was weighed against a mass of pure gold, which is then dispensed in charity. This custom, called " Tulabhara," is one of great antiquity, and it is said to be traceable in Travancore to the fourth century. It is not unknown in other parts in India ; though of course gold is only used in the case of wealthy persons, the humbler sort being content to weigh themselves against spices or grain. On the present occasion the Maharajah weighed a little over nine stone. The Brahmins, it is said, wished to defer the ceremony, in the hope that the Maharajah might more nearly approach the weight of his father, who did not undergo the rite until 47 years old, when he weighed 14¾ stone.

THE latest additions to the Egerton Library of Manuscripts in the British Museum comprise : Original letters addressed to Mr. John Hanson, his solicitor, by Lord Byron, and members of his family and other persons, chiefly on business matters, 1795-1816, three vols. folio ; Diary of Lady Margaret Hoby, wife of Sir T. P. Hoby, 1599-1605 ; a miracle play of " Daniel," with musical notes, thirteenth century ; official letters of Napoleon Bonaparte, 1803-4 ; miscellaneous historical letters and papers, 1556-1753 ; original letters of Queen Henrietta Maria to Charles I., 1642-5 ; original letters of Oliver Cromwell, 1648-54; and correspondence and papers of Admiral Herbert, afterwards Earl of Torrington, chiefly relating to the Revolution of 1688.

MR. T. FISHER UNWIN has lately published for the Royal Society of Painters in Water Colours an illustrated catalogue to their summer exhibition. It comprises eighty-five *fac-similes* of sketches by the artists, among those of an antiquarian character being " Pembroke Castle at Low Tide," by Mary Foster-Lofthouse ; "Oystermouth Castle, South Wales," by Thomas Danby; " The Castle of Chilton," by W. Collingwood ; " La Boucherie, Old Antwerp," by S. J. Hodson ; " The Coliseum, Rome," by Arthur Glennie; "A Ruined City" and "The Claudian Aqueduct on the Campagna, Rome," by Collingwood Smith ; and "The Legendary Castle of Arran," by H. Clarence Whaite.

IN 1853 Sir George Grey, then Governor of New Zealand, published in the colony a copious collection of Maori songs and stories, under the title " Ko nga Motuatea," and two years later the same diligent scholar published in London (Murray) an English translation of the original Maori in a volume entitled " Polynesian Mythology and Ancient Traditional History of the New Zealand Race." Both these books having been long out of print, writes the *Athenæum*, the New Zealand Government has determined on their republication, and the reprinting is now proceeding in Auckland under the supervision of Sir George Grey.

LORD JERSEY'S Library at Osterley Park, Middlesex, sold last month by Messrs. Sotheby, Wilkinson & Hodge, realised a little over £13,000. It contained several specimens of Caxton's printing, the chief and most important lot being "The Historye of Troye," of which only three perfect copies are known to exist, and which was knocked down to Mr. B. Quaritch at £1,820. Two other fine Caxtons, the "Confessio Amantis," and "King Arthur" were sold to American purchasers for £810 and £1,950 respectively. It is worthy of note that the above-mentioned copy of the "Historye of Troye" was sold in 1756 for eight guineas !

THE following articles, more or less of an antiquarian character, appear among the contents of the reviews and magazines for May :— *Quarterly Review*, "Recent Discoveries in Greece," and "Early Britain ;" *Scottish Review*, "Stuart Pretenders ;" *Art Journal*, "The Gallery of Pictures by the Old Masters, formed by Francis Cook, Esq., of Richmond," "English Stall Work, Canopies, and Rood-screens of the Fifteenth Century," and "Babylon of Egypt ;" *The Atlantic Monthly*, "John Sebastian Bach—1685-1885 ;" *Chambers's Journal*, "Before the Invention of Printing ;" *Temple Bar*, "A Summer-day at Stratford-on-Avon ;" *English Illustrated Magazine*, "Legends of Toledo," and "In Canterbury Cathedral."

THE original design of Mr. Pearson for the restoration of Westminster Hall has been practically adopted by the Restoration Committee appointed by the House of Commons, with the exception of a proposal to re-construct the towers on the northern front of the Hall, facing New Palace-yard. The first object is the preservation of the existing Norman work, which the Committee propose to effect by erecting a two-storied building along the whole length of the Hall, with the exception of the two northernmost bays, similar to one that probably stood there in the time of Richard II., and by reproducing at the north-west end a building at right angles to it in the place of a building erected in the time of Henry III., and subsequently modified in Tudor times, the upper part of which was occupied by the Exchequer Court.

A MAGNIFICENT archiepiscopal cross, subscribed for by a number of the clergy and laity of the Southern Province, has been presented to the Archbishop of Canterbury. The cross, which surmounts a silver-gilt staff, over seven feet in length, is an exact copy of the crosses anciently carried before Dr. Benson's predecessors in the See of Canterbury, and is richly jewelled with sapphires, pearls, and diamonds. The design and ornamentation are of the most exquisite workmanship and finish, and a comparison with the accounts given of the ancient crosses in the registers preserved in the library shows that every detail has been copied with the utmost accuracy. The presentation took place in the library of Lambeth Palace, in the presence of a large and distinguished company.

THE *Bucks Advertiser and Aylesbury News* reports the discovery of coins at Long Crendon, near Aylesbury. The vessels containing them were beneath the wall of a stable which had fallen down. On making a new wall it was resolved to form a deeper foundation than before, and the vessels were found only a few inches below the base of the old wall, which had been erected since their interment. The coins—which numbered more than eight hundred—are mostly of the Elizabethan period but, as it transpires that there was among them a few of the reign of Charles I., it seems probable, after all, that the treasure was buried to protect it during the Civil War. According to the rules of the Treasury, a person with treasure trove is entitled to only bullion value, but it remains to be seen whether this stipulation will be strictly carried out. We hear that one gold coin, as a curiosity, being ancient, is of considerable value.

CATALOGUES of rare and curious books, most of which contain the names of works of antiquarian interest, have reached us from Mr. C. S. Palmer, 100, Southampton-row, W.C. (including a copy of " The Vinegar Bible," Foxe's Book of Martyrs, Poems and Plays by the Duchess of Newcastle, and a large number of works by or relating to William Prynne); Mr. U. Maggs, Church-street, Paddington-green (much space is occupied by works on America, Angling, Art, Heraldry, Old London, Scotland, Cruikshank, and publications of the Index Society); Mr. W. P. Bennett, Bult-street, Birmingham (among the rare works mentioned are Holinshed's Chronicles, Richardson's "Monastic Ruins of Yorkshire," and the Clandon Library Parliamentary MSS.); Messrs. Fawn & Son, Queen's-road, Bristol; Mr. James Thin, Lindsay-place, Edinburgh; Mr. H. Gray, Cathedral-yard, Manchester (including books relating to all the counties); Messrs. Reeves & Turner, 196, Strand, W.C. (including a finely-printed copy of the Salisbury Missal, 1555); Mr. George Harding, 6, Sardinia-street, Lincoln's-inn, W.C.; Mr. Walter Scott, 7, Bristo-place, Edinburgh; Mr. E. Spencer, 270, Holloway-road, N. (including copies of Hogarth's works); F. Muller & Co., Amsterdam; Mr. J. Thorpe, Ship-street, Brighton; Mr. J. Nield. Bath-street, Bristol (noted chiefly for county topography); Mr. J. E. Cornish, Piccadilly, Manchester; Mr. C. Herbert, 319, Goswell-road, E.C. (including Americana, Biography, Greek and Latin Classics, Topography, &c.); Mr. F. Edwards, 83, High-street, Marylebone; Mr. A. B. Osborne, 11, Red Lion-passage, W.C. (comprising several " curious and out-of-the-way books," and giving on the cover a further instalment of the "Account of Marylebone Bowling Green and Gardens"); Messrs. Jarvis & Son, 28, King William-street, W.C. (containing a large number of topographical and sporting works and old English literature); Mr. C. Lowe, Broad-street-corner, Birmingham; Mr. W. Downing, New-street, Birmingham (including a "Wicked" Bible and a "Treacle" Bible); Mr. W. Withers, Leicester; Mr. J. Commin, High-street, Exeter (including the Manx Society's publications and books illustrated by Blake, Bewick, and Cruikshank); Messrs. Taylor & Son, Northampton; Oswald Weigel, Leipsic (including works on the history, topography, art, &c., of Great Britain and Ireland).

Antiquarian Correspondence.

Sin scire labores,
Quære, age : quærenti pagina nostra patet.

All communications must be accompanied by the name and address of the sender, not necessarily for publication.

A SHAKESPEARIAN QUERY.

SIR,—Where can I find the probable original idea of a passage in "Othello," Act ii. sc. 1, 216?—"As, they say, base men being in love have then a nobility in their natures more than is native to them." I feel sure that it is to be found in one of the ancient Classics.

Athenæum Club, S.W. C. M. INGLEBY.

CURIOSITIES OF TUDOR NOMENCLATURE, AND THE IRISH CALENDAR.

SIR,—Mr. Round's letter in the May number of the *Antiquarian Magazine* is made up (1) of an insinuation as to the cause of my delayed rejoinder ; (2) of an attack on my official reputation, under an irrelevant change in the title of our controversy ; (3) of a personal animadversion on the character of a work published more than a year after my last letter was written, and in no way connected with the subject under discussion ; (4) of an *ex parte* review of our respective positions ; (5) of an amended answer to my original challenge.

As you have already exonerated me on the first score, Mr. Round's insinuation recoils upon himself. I will leave the good taste of Mr. Round's quotations from the *Academy* to the judgment of your readers ; and I pass by his allusions to my official position as beside the question, since, during the five years that it has been my great privilege to contribute to publications under your direction. I have studiously abstained from giving any indications of an official origin, and have been involved in no single controversy except with Mr. Round himself. It is, of course, open to all to discover, through the usual facilities, whether such an one is or is not an "official" ; but, as I have preferred to appear before your readers as a fellow-antiquary, with no pretensions to "official" knowledge, I object to being added to a fanciful list of victims of a crusade against official scholarship, which I am aware that all wise scholars regard with a hearty contempt as the outcome of a solitary vanity. Your readers will also be able to judge for themselves as to how far Mr. Round's *résumé* of the whole correspondence is a fair and impartial one ; therefore it only remains for me to reply to that part of his letter in which he attempts to deal with my former objection—one which will be found stated at p. 201 *ante*, ll. 1—14.

Mr. Round's real answer, then, begins at p. 256, l. 10 : " Can it not," &c., and to this I now reply that I never said " it couldn't."

Mr. Round, wholly unable to cope with a conclusive decision at law (which he feebly attempts to put aside as a "legal quibble," forgetting that "records" themselves are but the enrolments of the transactions of the law courts), attempts to fasten upon me some statement which he can safely disprove. He calls the reign of Edward III. my "chosen ground." Sir, I knew better than that, for I knew (which Mr. Round seemingly does not) that this is the very reign in which we find that the indiscriminate use of Filius and Fitz first obtains, and here I was able to show the attitude of the law courts successfully struggling to keep out this new abuse. If Mr. Round will refer more carefully to what I wrote, he will find that my words were (p. 201, ll. 6, 7 *ante*) : " Surnames being of very doubtful significance in early times, filius followed by a Christian name should never be translated from records *of this date* (*i.e.*, reign of John) other than son of." Moreover, I further observed (p. 202, l. 42) that " *the loose use of fitz* as a Norman patronymic *is well enough*, but filius in record Latin can never be *safely* rendered Fitz, according to Mr. Round's definition."

How *unsafe* it was, even as late as the reign of Edward III., for a suitor to commit himself to this *loose* rendering of filius as a surname, the result of the two great cases cited by me will sufficiently prove, whose evidence Mr. Round has never attempted to refute. Therefore it was not reserved for Mr. Round to discover that the same man was here and there styled in records of the reign of Edward III. both "filius Stevani" and "le fitz Estevan," since the *abuse*, which I have already shown to have been condemned by the highest possible authority, itself supposes the *use* in question. But, at least, I find in that irregular appellation no possible justification for Mr. Round's golden rule : That filius, followed by a Christian name, should always be rendered as a surname.

HUBERT HALL.

THE LOVAT PEERAGE.

SIR,—Some of your readers may remember a question lately put in the House of Commons, *àpropos* of the Lovat Peerage claim, concerning the alleged removal of coffin plates from the vault of the Fraser family in the parish churchyard at Kirkhill, in Scotland. The Lord Advocate replied that Lord Lovat had given permission to Sir William Fraser to visit the tomb, and that Sir William "and a gentleman who was supposed to be his secretary, along with a blacksmith, examined the coffins, one of which was that of Simon, the Lord Lovat of 1745."

It would be interesting to know what inscription, if indeed any, was found at Kirkhill by Sir William Fraser on the plate of what the Lord Advocate describes as the coffin of "Simon, the Lord Lovat of 1745." And for this reason : on the western wall of St. Peter's-ad-Vincula, in the Tower of London, are exhibited, or certainly were exhibited some 18 months since, the coffin-plates of the "rebel" Lords Balmerino, Kilmarnock, and Lovat, who suffered on Tower-hill for their share in the "'Forty-five." The plates were disinterred some years ago from their known places of burial beneath the gallery, now removed, of that church. It is stated, though, that no remains of their bodies or coffins were found also. I enclose for your information a sketch copy of Lord Lovat's coffin-plate, inscribed as follows :—Simon Dominus Fraser de Lovat Decollat Apr 9. 1747 Ætat Suee 80" It is oblong in shape, and being leaden is not so well preserved as those of his two compatriots, which are of pewter, and oval in form. I may add that the scaffold posts were lately dug up in the making of the Inner Circle Railway through Tower-hill, and that the site of the scaffold may be distinguished close to the shaft within the railing of Trinity-square garden. The block whereon was laid that aged if not very reverend head had not been used before, and was not used again. I have a fragment of the scaffold staging, and a silver tobacco or snuff box that Lord Lovat gave to his Prince, and which the latter gave to James Drummond, Duke of Perth, who commanded the second division at Culloden.

W. E. MILLIKEN.

TO CORRESPONDENTS.

THE Editor declines to pledge himself for the safety or return of MSS. voluntarily tendered to him by strangers.

MR. C. WALFORD'S paper on Gilds is unavoidably held over this month.

THE Index for Vol. vii. will be given with our next number.

Books Received.

1. De Nova Villa ; or, The House of Nevill in Sunshine and Shade. By Rev. H. J. Swallow, F.R.S.L. London : Griffith, Farran & Co. ; Newcastle-on-Tyne : Andrew Reid. 1885.

2. Le Livre. No. 65. Paris : 7, Rue St. Benoit.

3. Historical Richmond. By E. B. Chancellor. Bell & Sons. 1885.

4. Johns Hopkins University Studies. Third Series, IV. Baltimore : April, 1885.

5. Parodies. Part 18. Reeves & Turner. May, 1885.

6. Miscellanea Genealogica et Heraldica. Second Series. Vol. i. No. 17. Mitchell & Hughes. May, 1885.

7. York Plays. With Introduction and Glossary by Lucy Toulmin Smith. Oxford : Clarendon Press. 1885.

8. Northamptonshire Notes and Queries. Northampton : Taylor & Son. April, 1885.

9. Petition of Bishop White Kennett for Rebuilding the Church of Stoke Doyle. With Notes, &c., by the Rev. W. D. Sweeting. Northampton : Taylor & Son. 1885.

10. New England Historical and Genealogical Register. No. cliv. April, 1885.

11. Collections, Historical and Archæological, relating to Montgomeryshire and its Borders. Part xxxvi. Powys-land Club. April, 1885.

12. Shakespeare-Bibliographie, 1883 and 1884. Von Albert Cohn. Berlin : 1885.

13. English Etchings. May No. D. Bogue, 27, King William-st., W.C.

Books, &c., for Sale.

Notes on Poems and Reviews, by A. C. Swinburne. Cassell's History of England, 9 vols. ; Beauties of England and Wales, 6 vols., half calf, uniform : Cumberland, Derbyshire, Devon, Dorset, Hants, Herefordshire, Lancashire, Leicestershire, Lincoln, Middlesex, Somerset, Staffordshire, and Isle of Man. (May be had separately.)—Address, E. Walford, 2, Hyde Park Mansions, N.W.

Lord Chesterfield's travelling box (large size).—Offers to Alice Parkinson, 39, Regent-street, Blackburn.

Original water-colour portrait of Jeremy Bentham, price 2 guineas. Also a large collection of Franks, Peers and Commoners.—Apply to E. Walford, 2, Hyde Park Mansions, N.W.

Books, &c., Wanted to Purchase.

Dodd's Church History, 8vo., vols. i. ii. and v. ; Waagen's Art and Artists in England, vol. i. ; East Anglian, vol. i., Nos. 26 and 29. Notes and Queries, the third Index. Journal of British Archæological Association, March, 1877, and June, 1879.—E. Walford, 2, Hyde Park Mansions, N.W.

Patterson's "Families of Ayrshire."—Address J. Shanks, Ballyfounder, Portaferry, co. Down.

Antiquarian Magazine and Bibliographer, several copies of No. 2 (February, 1882) are wanted, in order to complete sets. Copies of the current number will be given in exchange at the office.

A Frank of Francis Atterbury, Bishop of Rochester between 1713 and 1723, and other Bishops' franks of the 18th century.—Apply to J. D., care of the Editor.

Archæologia, vols. xxii., xxiii., xxiv.; vol. xxxviii. part i. ; vols. xxxix., xl., xli. part i. ; vol. xlvii. part ii.—A. G. H., 47, Belsize-avenue, N.W.

"Tour of the Isle of Wight," vol. i. illustrated, 8vo. Hookham, 1790." —Address, G. Unwin, 71A, Ludgate-hill, E.C.

Index.